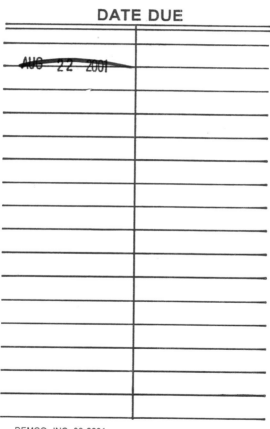

DATE DUE

AUG 22 2001

DEMCO, INC. 38-2931

On the Relevance of Metaethics
New Essays on Metaethics

On the Relevance of Metaethics

New Essays on Metaethics

EDITED BY
JOCELYNE COUTURE
&
KAI NIELSEN

BJ
1031
.062
1995

University of Calgary Press
Calgary, Alberta, Canada

ISSN 0229-7052   ISBN 0-919491-21-9

© 1995 The Canadian Journal of Philosophy
ISBN 0-919491-21-9
ISSN 0229-7051
First published in 1996

University of Calgary Press
2500 University Drive NW
Calgary, Alberta
Canada T2N 1N4

Canadian Cataloguing in Publication Data

Main entry under title:
    On the relevance of metaethics

        (Canadian Journal of Philosophy. Supplementary
volume, ISSN 0229-7051 ; 21)
        Includes bibliographical references and index.
        ISBN 1-919491-21-9

    1. Ethics. I. Couture, Jocelyne. II. Nielsen, Kai. III. Series.
BJ1031.O62 1996   170'.42   C96-910623-8

COMMITTED TO THE DEVELOPMENT OF CULTURE AND THE ARTS
Financial support provided in part by the Alberta Foundation for the Arts.

Printed and bound in Canada.
♾ This book is printed on acid-free paper.

In memory of
Jean Hampton
1954–1996

Table of Contents

Introduction: The Ages of Metaethics

JOCELYNE COUTURE
Université du Québec à Montréal
and
KAI NIELSEN
University of Calgary and Concordia University

I

To speak of ethical theory *sans phrase* is to neglect to distinguish between *normative theory* and *metatheory*. By *normative theory*, we mean the endeavor to bring some unity or system to our multifarious moral evaluations, normative commitments, practices, moral rules and principles by developing (some might even say by discovering) a coherently interrelated cluster of normative principles or procedures to represent and organize them and, as well, in the processes, to justify them. By *metatheory*, or metaethics, we mean the attempt to elucidate moral reasoning and moral discourse (essentialist philosophers would say *the nature* of moral discourse). It seeks to characterize the use of moral terms, to determine the logical and cognitive status of moral utterances, to characterize moral reasoning, to explicate the nature of disagreement in ethics, and to clarify what counts as justification in ethics. The thing is to come to a clear understanding of the nature of morality, of what it is to take the moral point of view, and of the relation between the reasons for a moral commitment and the commitment itself.

The emphasis here is on *understanding* and not on *advocacy* or *determining* (ascertaining) what is right and wrong; the task is not to get people to be good, to provide moral knowledge or, alternatively, to try to establish that nothing is right or wrong, good or bad and that there are no values or that values are only attitudes or emotions. Some not very astute philosophers thought the emotivists were trying to do the latter. (For a rather gross form of such a misunderstanding see Joad 1950.) But such moral affirmations or such iconoclastic denials are not

1

any part of metaethical theory. Rather the task is to come to understand what it is for something to be right or wrong, good or bad, justified or unjustified, reasonable or unreasonable. Perhaps, most deeply, it is the attempt to gain some understanding of the very idea of *normativity* and most particularly of moral or ethical normativity.

The term 'metaethics' came into usage with the rise of analytical philosophy, but both the concept and the practice have been with us (though often poorly understood) for almost as long as philosophy has. However, prior to the rise of analytic philosophy, it existed either as part of a larger systematic substantive moral theory, containing elements of both what we would now call normative ethics and metaethics, and much else as well. Paradigm cases of such moral theory are found in Aristotle, Kant and Sidgwick. What we now call metaethics was done there, though only as a part of a larger project. It also existed – and this was the more typical situation – either as part of an even larger comprehensive speculative scheme, as in Plato, Spinoza, Hobbes or Hegel, or as part of a speculative philosophical-theological scheme as in Augustine, Scotus, Ockham and Aquinas. But, while all these philosophers, or philosopher-theologians, occasionally made what we would now call metaethical arguments, analyses and claims, they did not do metaethics as a distinct discipline or activity with its own rationale, or simply identify it, as some analytical philosophers have, with ethical theory: taking it to be the whole of ethical theory (Frankena 1951, 44). Even Henry Sidgwick, who thought of ethical theory as a distinct subbranch of philosophy, only thought of what we now call metaethics as a proper part of a larger substantive, systematic, and critical normative enterprise. It is this enterprise, and not metaethics, that, for him, constituted ethical theory or moral philosophy. What is peculiar to our century is that there came into existence a distinctive activity that came to be called 'metaethics' and came to be taken as a distinct discipline. Some philosophers came consciously to think of themselves as doing metaethics and indeed some of them, namely most logical positivists (Moritz Schlick and Otto Neurath being notable exceptions) and some other linguistic philosophers, thought that the *only* part of ethical theory that was legitimately philosophical was metaethics. A.J. Ayer, Rudolf Carnap, Herbert Feigl, Hans Reichenbach, Arthur Pap, and Charles Stevenson, who all thought this way, believed, of course, that, as citizens and critical intellectuals, they could and should take and defend moral stances and make critical moral claims, but as *philosophers,* in attending to the domain of morality, they believed – and they were rather passionate about this – that they must restrict themselves to metaethics.

G.E. Moore did not so conceive of his philosophical work, but his most influential *practice,* vis-à-vis moral philosophy, namely the first three chapters of *Principia Ethica* (1903), though in idiom Platonic, provided an exemplar of metaethics at work and set the direction for much of Anglo-American and Scandinavian moral philosophy of our century.

We will, somewhat artificially, for there were transition periods, divide up Anglo-American and Scandinavian ethical theory into three periods: (1) The First Period was the period from the beginning of the century until around the 1930s. This was the period before metaethics became a self-conscious discipline. It was the period in which *Principia Ethica* set the tone and yielded most of the problems. (2) The Second Period, the period from the 1930s to the 1960s, was the heyday or Golden Age of metaethics or what is sometimes called, *some* would think pleonastically, analytical metaethics. We will call it, as others have as well, the *old* metaethics. (3) The Third Period is the period from the 1970s to the present – what we will call, as have others, the *new* metaethics – a metaethics arising in response to what has been dubbed The Great Expansion (Darwall et al. 1992, 121-4 and Copp 1992, 790-7).

II

During the First Period the dominant ethical theories were: (1) metaphysical ethics, (2) ethical naturalism and (3) non-naturalism (intuitionism). Metaphysical ethics had it that ethical terms are both definable in terms of, and stand for, certain distinctive metaphysical properties or entities such as God, being, or noumena. Ethical naturalism (as understood and criticized by Moore and – during that period – by many other moral philosophers as well) also had it that ethical terms are definable, but ethical naturalists, by contrast with defenders of metaphysical ethics, believed that ethical terms stand for certain empirical or natural properties (including, of course, relational properties). Non-naturalists, by contrast with both, denied that fundamental ethical terms were definable at all (Moore), or claimed that they were only interdefinable in terms of other normative terms (A.C. Ewing), and they all claimed as well, that ethical terms stood for certain non-empirical and unique nondescriptive properties – non-natural properties, as Moore called them. These non-natural realities of an allegedly *sui generis* autonomous moral realm were realities which moral agents, if they were to know them at all, had somehow to be directly aware of in some nonempirical way.

Intuitionism, as a positive doctrine, had little influence inside philosophy. The powerful and vastly influential metaethical arguments contained in *Principia Ethica* were negative arguments devoted to destroying metaphysical ethics and ethical naturalism. Moore thought both committed what he called 'the naturalistic fallacy' and thus were vulnerable to the *open-question argument* and the *non-contradiction argument*. Moore put both arguments in a misleading Platonic idiom, but later, self-consciously linguistic philosophers who adopted them, such as A.J. Ayer, Charles Stevenson, Paul Edwards, P.H. Nowell-Smith, and R.M. Hare, reformulated them in an appropriately linguistic idiom which brought out their force more clearly than Moore did himself. Moore's atheism and metaphysical realism made him in a cosmological sense a naturalist, as distinct from a supernaturalist or an idealist (Moore, 1901, 88). However, general philosophical or cosmological naturalism is one thing – as we shall see in some detail later – and ethical naturalism another. As we shall also see, W.K. Frankena was perfectly justified when, surveying the scene in ethical theory at mid-century, he remarked that "naturalism [ethical naturalism] is still strong, and intuitionism remains on the field, although not in great force. But metaphysical ethics has virtually retreated from the philosophical scene ..." (Frankena 1951, 45).

We should say something more about the senses of 'naturalism.' As Frankena, among others made clear, during the Golden Age, the sense of 'ethical naturalism,' taken over in analytical metaethics from Moore, was rather restrictive and in ways misleadingly persuasively defined. We will note three ways. First, 'naturalism' outside metaethical theory is used in a wider cosmological or worldview sense, where it denotes a general philosophical point of view standing in contrast to theism (and the various other forms of supernaturalism such as deism) and idealism (again in its various quite different forms). In this *general* sense, as we have already noted, Moore was a naturalist. His 'critique of naturalism' then applied only to ethical naturalism; that is, for him, the view that moral properties are definable in terms of empirical properties. Second, moral cognitivists who hold such a view commit, according to Moore, the naturalistic fallacy. But so do, according to Moore, moral cognitivists who hold that moral properties are definable in terms of metaphysical properties or entities. It is useful to remember here Frankena's claim that the 'naturalistic fallacy' would have been better labelled 'the definist fallacy,' for it was the definition of fundamental moral properties that Moore was really opposed to (Frankena 1939, 464-77). Thirdly, it is worth noticing that in Moore's view, the 'naturalistic fallacy' does not invalidate moral cognitivism. Moore himself was a moral cognitivist for he believed that moral properties are directly apprehensible, though not by empirical observation.

Moore's criticism of naturalism leaves untouched then (1) naturalism in the cosmological sense, (2) moral cognitivism, provided it does not allow for a non-normative definition of moral properties (naturalistic fallacy), and (3) a noncognitivism which standardly adumbrates and defends a general naturalistic philosophical point of view while articulating and defending an emotive or prescriptivist theory of ethics. W.R. Dennes, roughly a Stevensonian emotivist, defends such a view in his "Categories of Naturalism" (1944) and in his *Some Dilemmas of Naturalism* (1960). Axel Hägerström, A.J. Ayer, Richard Robinson, Charles Stevenson, and Bertrand Russell, while being naturalists in the cosmological sense, are noncognitivists in metaethics and so are, today, Allan Gibbard and Simon Blackburn.

The principal targets of Moore's criticism, as we have noted, were metaphysical ethics and ethical naturalism. Moore took Jeremy Bentham and John Stuart Mill to be paradigm-case ethical naturalists, plainly committing the naturalistic fallacy. It could, and indeed should, be argued, however, that, while they were in the general worldview sense naturalists, they were not ethical naturalists in Moore's sense, did not commit the naturalistic fallacy (if indeed it is a fallacy or some other kind of mistake) and they did not try to derive an ought from an is (Hall 1964, 101-32; and Nielsen 1977, 110-23). It was clear, in J.S. Mill's case, that, like Moore, he thought such a derivation to be quite impossible. (See the last chapter of his *System of Logic*.) What we have just noted about Bentham and Mill should also be said about the American naturalists (in the broad philosophical sense) George Santayana, John Dewey and Sidney Hook. Perhaps the only philosophers to fit Moore's specification for being an ethical naturalist are Ralph Barton Perry, C.I. Lewis, J.B. Pratt, and John R. Reid, and it is not even clear that is so for Lewis in the case of 'right' or 'obligation' as distinct from 'good' or 'valuable.'

Finally, it should also be noted that the relation conceived by Moore between cosmological naturalism and ethical non-naturalism goes the other way too. Theists (antinaturalists in the general philosophical sense) could without any inconsistency be ethical naturalists in Moore's sense, as it is perhaps correct to say of Jacques Maritain and H. Richard Niebuhr (Frankena 1964, 446) and is more plainly so of Elizabeth Anscombe, Philippa Foot, and Peter Geach.

III

In 1950 – the middle of the Golden Age of analytical metaethics – metaphysical ethics was gradually supplanted by noncognitivism (sometimes variously called nondescriptivism or nonfactualism) either in the form of an emotive theory or of a prescriptivism. The emotive theory came first, arising in the English-speaking world in the 1930s, although as early as 1911, in Sweden, Axel Hägerström in his "On the Truth of Moral Propositions" powerfully articulated an emotive metaethics which was later developed in books by Hägerström himself and by a number of other Scandinavian philosophers influenced by him (Hägerström 1964, 77-96).

We will now further and more clearly characterize what at mid-century were taken to be the three major metaethical systems: nonnaturalism (intuitionism), naturalism and noncognitivism. Frankena has provided us with a concise way of comparing them and characterizing their differences, and he has also importantly reminded us that proponents of these different metaethical theories "might quite possibly maintain the same opinions as to what is right or good in normative ethics" (Frankena 1951, 45). Frankena remarks that the following three sentences can be usefully employed to classify and compare the three metaethical theories.

(1) Ethical sentences are cognitive and true or false.

(2) Ethical terms do not name any unique or simple non-natural characteristics.

(3)   Ethical sentences are nondescriptive. (ibid., 45)

As Frankena was perfectly well aware, for later developments of Ayer's and Stevenson's views, as well as for Hägerström's initial statement, (1) and (3) would, though in nonessential ways, have to be altered to (1*) and (3*):

(1*)   Ethical sentences are cognitive and true or false in some substantial more than minimalist manner.

(3*)   Ethical sentences are *primarily* nondescriptive and only *secondarily* descriptive.

But (1) and (3) are more useful to fix thought than the more pedantic though more accurate (1*) and (3*). After all, if we adopt, as perhaps we should, a minimalist or deflationary conception of truth, the problem originally expressed by the noncognitivist denial that fundamental moral utterances could be either true or false still re-emerges as follows. Though moral utterances in declarative form plainly bear the syntactic features of assertoric discourse, still, if noncognitivism is true, moral utterances lack *truth makers*. That is, there is nothing in the world or for that matter 'out of the world' that would make moral utterances true. In that way, it is claimed, 'Hitler was vile' and 'Hitler had a black moustache' are very different. The latter has a plain truth maker. The former, however true, does not. More widely than that, even if talk of 'truth makers' smacks too much of metaphysical realism and the correspondence theory of truth, still, as Stephen Darwall, Allan Gibbard and Peter Railton put it,

> important contrasts between ethics and, say, empirical science or mathematics might remain. For there will be differences in the kinds of features of the world that figure in the (minimal) *truth conditions* of sentences in the various domains, and differences, too, in the *methods* available for establishing (minimal) truth and in the amount of *rational consensus* such methods can bring about. (Darwall et al. 1992, 129)

For fundamental moral principles, at least, noncognitivists are claiming, we have no way of establishing or ascertaining whether these principles are true or false, so that it would be reasonable to say of any of them that they are true or, for that matter, false (Altham 1986, 275-6). 'Abortion is evil' is in a syntactical form in which it would not be at all a deviation from a linguistic regularity to assert it or for that matter to deny it. If people have certain attitudes, perhaps arising from living in a certain community, they may very well say that it is true, but, if they have different attitudes, perhaps causally rooted in different beliefs of a different community, they will say, perhaps, that it is false or in some circumstances true and in other circumstances false. Perhaps there are no truth makers anywhere – belief in them being a realist myth – but certainly attitudes are real enough. Truth makers or not, there will be no rational consensus on judgments, the argument goes, concerning abortion, nor can there be, noncognitivists could claim, for there is nothing there in the world, including in our human nature, which will show 'Abortion is evil' to be true or, more radically still, even could show it to be either true or false. And similar things obtain for our other fundamental moral judgments and principles. This being so, it is less misleading to say, as emotivists do, that moral utterances are neither true nor false. Or at least so noncognitivists could plausibly claim. It involves, in our *metatheory*, a revision of how we should talk when we are engaged in theory articulation and, more generally, a revision of what we should think about truth in morals. But the revision arguably has a point.

We are not saying, or giving to understand, that we think the noncognitivists are right here. Perhaps wide reflective equilibrium or some other method will yield a method for establishing truth in moral domains or at least warrantedness (Nielsen 1994, 89-138). Moreover, if we accept that and combine it with a minimalist or deflationary account of truth, where we do without truth makers and correspondence, then we may very well be able to establish that certain moral utterances are true or that we can at least give grounds for believing them to be warranted. And this could come to include certain very fundamental moral principles. But it is also not evident that the noncognitivists are mistaken. Accepting a minimalist account of truth, which reasserts what is built into our ordinary usage, may not be sufficient to meet the challenges that noncognitivists direct at cognitivist accounts of moral discourse. *Perhaps* we cannot justifiably take such a short way with dissenters.

IV

Toward the end of the Second Period of twentieth-century metaethical theory, it was fair to say, as we look at Stevenson's work and at the work of such ethical naturalists as Philip Rice and Henry Aiken, that "noncognitivism has become more cognitivist, and cognitivists have been making concessions to noncognitivism" (Frankena 1964, 447). It is, it came to be recognized, not clear that there is such a thing as *independent* emotive meaning; that beliefs and attitudes can be as sharply distinguished as emotivists thought they could (that we can have an attitude that is not also a belief), that we can separate out the evaluative components and the descriptive components of moral terms; that there are, or even clearly can be, any disagreements in attitude that are not rooted in disagreements in belief; that talk of what is 'rational' or 'reasonable' is not just as expressive and evocative as talk of what is 'good' or 'valuable' or 'right' or, though we need a distinction between *exciting* reasons and *justifying* reasons (between goading and guiding), that what that distinction comes to when pressed, is not clear. Similar things should be said for the distinction between cognitive and noncognitive utterances or aspects of such utterances. (But see here Frankena 1958b, 146-72.) Still, the emotivists in stressing such distinctions seemed to be onto something, but, at the very least, our initial facile ways in which we drew and deployed the above distinctions faired badly under close inspection.

There are also grounds for skepticism about talk of incommensurability or *essentially* contested moral concepts, stances which in turn are not unrelated to the above puzzles. The thought is that in morality there are, when matters are pushed far enough, *ultimate* disagreements *in* attitude concerning which no reasonable grounds exist, or at least not anything even like a nearly decisive argument is possible, which would settle the matter at hand (Nielsen 1989, 196-206). It is finally, some noncognitivists thought, just a matter of being for or against something or having one attitude rather than another. Fundamental moral matters become matters of decision, subscription, or commitment and not a matter of knowing or even soundly believing that something is right or is the thing to be done. However, that this is so is not evident. That very conception, so central for many emotivists, rests, for whatever plausibility it has, not only on being able to make the bifurcating distinctions mentioned above, but also in relying implicitly on end-of-inquiry metaphors (Rorty 1984, 6-7). There is, in reality, no identifiable point where we could coherently say that we finally have arrived at an *ultimate* disagreement or, for that matter, agreement: where we agree about *all* the facts but still disagree in attitude. We have no understanding of what it would be like to have all the facts. Talk about what 'in the end' or 'in the final analysis' or 'ultimately' we would agree on is without coherent sense.

Stevenson made it evident that he was taking such disagreement to be just a logical or conceptual *possibility*. But it is unclear whether this putative possibility is even coherently conceivable. Language and thought, or so at least it appears, are idle here. We do not, that is, understand in such circumstances what we are talking about. If noncognitive analyses drive us in that direction, then noncognitive analyses are at least in some crucial respects mistaken. But, given the importance of John Dewey's work for Stevenson's own theorizing, it is not evident – some appearances to the contrary perhaps notwithstanding – that his form of noncognitivism will have that upshot (Stevenson 1963, 94-137). But if the above distinctions – cognitive/noncognitive, descriptive/evaluative, belief/attitude – rest on mistakes, at least when taken as dualisms or sharp distinctions, then disputes between non-naturalism, naturalism and noncognitivism may come to nothing. (For a fleshing out of this see our Afterword.)

Be that as it may, in the Third Period of the history of metaethics, the competition between noncognitivism and ethical naturalism is still going strong. Allan Gibbard and Simon Blackburn have given noncognitivism fresh and sophisticated reformulations as have Peter Railton, Nicholas Sturgeon, Richard Boyd and Richard Miller for ethical naturalism.

V

With the Third Period – the new metaethics – the metaethical scene becomes less restrictive, less arid. 'Analytical metaethics' is no longer a redundancy. The varieties of ethical naturalism get extensively enlarged and include varieties (*synthetic* ethical naturalism) which *may* well be immune even to sophisticated revisions of Moorean criticism.

Noncognitivism remains, but is no longer in the dominant position it came to have in the previous period, and intuitionism (non-naturalism) all but disappears from the scene. As metaphysical ethics had disappeared by the beginning of the Golden Age, so intuitionism has now gone the way of all flesh; perhaps, after all, with a certain implicit *persuasive* definition of 'progress,' there is (at least in the short run) some progress in ethical theory. But, progress or not, there is some change. It is also true that with the new metaethics the forms of ethical naturalism and noncognitivism not only proliferate, they become more complex and take to heart the at least putatively valid criticisms of each other. During the Third Period it is also true that new varieties of metaethical theories arrive on the scene (though this has its commencement during the Golden Age). We come to have (*a*) moral-point-of-view theories (Stephen Toulmin, Kurt Baier, Kai Nielsen, and W.K. Frankena), (*b*) error theories (Richard Robinson and J.L. Mackie), (*c*) quasi-realist-projectionist theories (Simon Blackburn), (*d*) practical-reasoning theories (Hobbesian in inspiration with Kurt Baier and David Gauthier or Kantian in inspiration with Thomas Nagel, Stephen Darwall, Christine Korsgaard, Alan Donagan, and Alan Gewirth), (*e*) constructivist theories (Thomas Scanlon, John Rawls, and Brian Barry), (*f*) sensibility theories (John McDowell and David Wiggins), and (*g*) contextualist-pragmatist theories (Hilary Putnam and Isaac Levi). Vis-à-vis the classic triumvirate of the Golden Age (non-naturalism, naturalism, and noncognitivism) (*a*) through (*f*) are hard to place, though quasi-realist-projectionist theories are best classified as a form of noncognitivism and sensibility theories as forms of ethical naturalism. But some error theorists (Richard Robinson) also regarded their theories as emotive theories, though J.L. Mackie thought – and went out of his way to insist on this – that he was doing the ontology of values and not doing metaethics at all (Mackie 1977, Part 1). However, under the wider dispensation of the *new* metaethics, Mackie was clearly doing metaethics, and it is possible to argue that, to the extent that his account is coherently articulated, it is, his own understanding to the contrary notwithstanding, a form of noncognitivism. What, as Mackie should have had it, and in effect had it, is so pervasively in error is not morality or morals themselves, but the rationalist meta-moral belief in a peculiar conception of moral objectivity (moral objectivism) common to intuitionism (non-naturalism), Kantian practical-reasoning theories

11

and the less articulated objectivist and objectivizing conceptions rooted in much common-sense understanding of morals, that is to say, in their implicit meta-beliefs *about* morals, particularly when they have religious roots. What is in error is the pervasive meta-moral belief that there are Objective Prescriptivities or norms mysteriously either in *re-ruyn natura* or in some mysterious *noumenal* realm. That is what 'believing in morals' comes to, but many people can be persons of moral principle and have an understanding of why they have the principles they have, including their rationale for these principles, without *so* 'believing in morals.' When we turn to moral-point-of-view theories, (*a*) we should recognize that they are not clearly metaethical and certainly not evidently *just* metaethical. Stephen Toulmin and Kurt Baier never used such conceptualizations at all, though W.K. Frankena and Kai Nielsen did. And constructivist theories (*e*) and contextualist-pragmatist theories (*g*), though they both have metaethical components, are clearly not just metaethical theories.

It is also clear that, among these new members on the new metaethics roster, some moral philosophers fit in more than one cubby-hole. Kurt Baier is both a moral-point-of-view theorist and a practical-reasoning theorist, W.K. Frankena a moral-point-of-view theorist and a sometimes reluctant noncognitivist, Kai Nielsen both a moral-point-of-view theorist and a contextualist-pragmatist, Hilary Putnam both a contextualist-pragmatist and a constructivist, Isaac Levi both a contextualist-pragmatist and a naturalist, and David Gauthier both a practical-reasoning theorist (Hobbesian clan) and a noncognitivist. Moreover, with these additions, most particularly in the cases of (*a*), (*d*), (*e*) and (*g*), the line is no longer sharply drawn between a metaethical theory and a normative ethical theory. Indeed, this is a hallmark of the Third Period of metaethics. In expanding, as it does, the conception of metaethics, the distinction gets fuzzed. Perhaps we should extend Quine's remarks about the fence being down concerning the analytic/synthetic and the necessary/contingent to metaethics/normative ethics or metaethics/substantive ethics? Moreover, it is worth reflecting on the Wittgensteinian point that perhaps all these distinctions and classifications are a waste of time and energy leading to tempests in teapots and generating more confusion than clarity. With respect to such considerations about the metaethics/normative ethics distinction, this may be in effect a reason, indeed perhaps a very good reason, to return to an older tradition of moral philosophy, where metaethics is an ancillary matter and is certainly not seen as a distinctive or self-contained activity. (See here our Afterword: Whither Ethical Theory?)

VI

We will now say something more about what makes the new metaethics *new* and what motivates it in an intellectual climate in which moral philosophers have, since the late 1960s, increasingly turned their attention to normative ethics. They have, as Holly Smith put it, "turned to developing and criticising normative systems and especially to resolving concrete moral problems – issues concerning racism, sexism, war, economic justice, medical and business practice, scientific experimentation, and so forth" (Smith 1986, 471). For good or for ill, this was the intellectual climate in and around moral philosophy as the Third Period of metaethics came into being. Holly Smith goes on to point out that much normative ethical philosophizing was "consciously conducted in the absence of any metaethical thesis about what moral judgments meant or how they could be justified" (ibid.).

With not a few philosophers there was, and still is, an ambivalence here. On the one hand, there was the felt need to get on with these normative matters without constantly, or even very intermittently, raising 'foundational' questions or meta-questions about what they are doing, questions that, as Wittgenstein stressed repeatedly, call themselves into question and generate interminably still further questions until we get in such a state that we do not know where we are or what really is at issue anymore. On the other hand, even where there was on the part of these philosophers an intense interest in and concern about pressing normative issues, there was also often (given that they were philosophers) a pressing desire to get their philosophical bearings: the old philosophical itch to get back to basics, the perhaps irrational, or maybe even incoherent, wish to finally get to 'the bottom of things.'

There was, however, in the general philosophical climate, also more theoretical matters that made the very doing of metaethics more problematical and led, where it continued to be done, to doing it somewhat differently. Moving away from the atomism and molecularism of earlier analytic philosophy, the most powerful currents of philosophy from the later 1960s up to the present (1996) have gone, more or less, holistic. As Darwall et al. put it, a conception of philosophy became dominant "in which theory, metatheory, evidence, and inferential norm, or, alternatively, content and framework were not sharply distinguished" (Darwall et al. 1992, 121-2). That, along with, and relatedly, a Quine-Putnam-Davidson rejection of any significant distinction between the analytic/synthetic, made metaethics, at least as it previously had been understood and practised, problematic (ibid.). Moreover, and additionally and distinctly, under the influence of Rawls, there was an increasing interest in large and systematic normative – plainly substantively normative – and indeed normatively political inquiry, in which the method of wide and general reflective equilibrium came to be centrally in place, as the underlying method of ethics (Rawls 1995, 141-2). This was the underlying method on which Rawlsian and related contractarians and constructivists were crucially dependent. Their contractarianism and constructivism was never free standing.

Generalizing from the above considerations, it should be noted that, as Darwall et al. put it,

> [the] narrowly language-oriented agenda of analytic metaethics was fully displaced, not so much because of a refutation of, say, noncognitivism, but because of an uneasiness about the notions of "meaning" or "analytic truth" and because reflective equilibrium arguments, which tended to set aside metaethical questions, promised to shed much greater light on substantive – and in many cases socially pressing moral questions. (Darwall et al. 1992, 123)

So it was not only renewed interest in, and post-positivist confidence about, being able as philosophers to legitimately address practical moral and normatively political questions, but, as well, deep changes in the very method, presuppositions, and self-conception of analytic philosophers, that led to the move away from metaethics and to the end of its short-lived hegemony in moral philosophy. This is the period that Darwall et al. refer to as the period of the Great Expansion.

Many philosophers saw the Great Expansion as something providing "a sense of liberation," as "moral philosophers shed the obsessions of analytic metaethics, and saw – or thought they saw – ways of exploring normative morality as a cognitive domain, without a bad philosophical conscience." But, Darwall et al. also observe, some other philosophers saw the Great Expansion as something that "partly contributed to the contemporary revival of metaethics" (ibid., 123). The method of reflective equilibrium, so central in normative inquiries, unwittingly contributed, some thought, to this revival. The method of reflective equilibrium appealed very centrally to considered judgments, many of which were "moral intuitions (not Moorean insight into the Forms but substantive moral responses that strike us as compelling)" (ibid.). Both in the adumbration of general normative ethical theories and in the examination of particular moral problems, these moral intuitions flowed abundantly. Their role in the procedure of reflective equilibrium, both in normative critique and in forging and justifying a systematic normative ethical theory or normative political theory, was analogous to that of data in the articulating and testing of scientific theory. In theory construction they were used dialectically: we shuttle back and forth between the theory-dependent principles which were articulated and an appeal to the considered judgments to be used in their rationalization and in turn to be assessed by these principles. Justification and rationalization is never a one-way street and is always a bootstrapping operation. Considered judgments functioned as *partial* checks on the adequacy of a normative theory or account. But it was this very thing that contributed to the revival of metaethics. "The method of reflective equilibrium accorded a cognitive and evidential status to moral intuitions or 'considered moral judgments,' particular and general" (ibid., 125). Some philosophers (e.g., Richard Brandt, Joseph Raz, J.L. Mackie, Simon Blackburn, Gilbert Harman) questioned whether this status was warranted and, in doing so, took us back to metaethics. They saw – or thought they saw – a host of logical, semantic, epistemic, and even metaphysical issues emerging from, and entangled in, the very use of wide reflective equilibrium. Crucial among them were questions about the "practical status of morality" (ibid., 124). So, not a few philosophers think that we must go back to basics if we are to seriously think about morality in a philosophical way.

How does the new metaethics look after so many conceptual fences are down, with holism and the near ubiquitousness of wide and general reflective equilibrium? Some of the new metaethical theorizing, rightly or wrongly, uses decision theory, game theory and rational-choice theory in thinking about questions of practical reasoning or practical justification. (In this volume, Isaac Levi's contribution is a good example of the use of decision theory as a critical tool in metaethics.)

The new metaethics is as well less analytically restrictive and takes, as something sometimes rightly entering into its domain, empirical, as say, biological, psychological, sociological and historical, considerations and theories. It also more self-consciously raises epistemological considerations and sometimes raises issues and makes claims in what is called by some philosophers the ontology of morals. Moreover, metaethics, under the new dispensation, has become more "reflective both about the limitations of the notion of meaning and about the point or prospects of philosophical inquiry itself" (ibid., 124). So the new metaethics, while remaining *second-order*, does not assume "that one can avoid normative commitments in doing metaethics" (ibid.) (though it would be useful to know just what these commitments *must* be, and skepticism concerning such claims is not unreasonable). The new metaethics does "not restrict metaethics to the analysis of moral language" but it includes in its domain, as Darwall et al., who make this claim, are quick to add, "studies of the justification and justifiability of ethical claims as well as theories of meaning and also the metaphysics and epistemology of morals and like matters" (ibid., 125-6; see also Copp 1992, 790-7). Still, the new metaethics is, after all, not so far from the old, for it remains true that the semantic interpretation of moral language continues to play a central and pivotal role in metaethical inquiry. Could it be the case that, for that very reason, the new metaethics is not immune from at least some of the old problems?

VII

We will now worry this last question a little and, in doing so, return to considerations which were central for the first two periods of metaethics. We shall ask whether in some form they are, or at least should be, still with us. To initiate the dialectic here we will characterize the central reasons why it came to be so widely thought, during those periods, that ethical naturalism must rest on a mistake. What was centrally involved here was the open-question argument. All the criticisms of it notwithstanding, not a few philosophers thought, and some still think, it makes problematical any form of ethical naturalism (Rosati 1995, 46-70). Let us see if we can sort out a bit what is involved here.

The open-question argument has frequently been taken to be the key test for the claim that there is, if not strictly a fallacy, at least a mistake, an error, that allegedly undermines *all* forms of ethical naturalism, even in its linguistically oriented revisions. But it is generally recognized now not to be the decisive argument that Moore, and many others, during the Golden Age, took it to be. The open-question argument does not *prove* that ethical naturalism must rest on a mistake. At best it shows that the naturalistic definitions of moral and other normative terms hitherto offered do not work and gives us reasons – albeit rebuttable reasons – to expect that the same fate will befall new candidates. Among other things, the open-question argument ignores that there is such a thing as the Paradox of Analysis (a paradox propounded by Moore himself). Moreover, that correct analyses may leave open questions is just the paradox of analysis, for, if they leave open questions, how can they be correct analyses? It looks as if to be correct analyses they must both leave them open and not leave them open, and thus, unless we can somehow go around that paradox, they undermine themselves. Similarly, if the establishment of the sameness of cognitive significance is the test for correctness of an analysis, it may very well be the case that we might not immediately, or even on careful reflection, recognize that the two terms have the same cognitive significance when in fact they do. Since correct analyses arguably may leave open questions, the open-question argument cannot decisively refute – prove wrong – even definitional naturalism. Moreover, the meaning or uses of words, and the concepts they express, are often not transparent, yet the open-question argument assumes they are and assumes as well that analytic truths are ready to hand and often obvious. But much of that is, to put it mildly, questionable. Moreover, definitions, both philosophical and scientific, typically do not rely on giving intentional equivalents. Indeed that very conceptual baggage can itself be put in question. But even if it is not, to assume that all good philosophical and scientific definitions must be in terms of intentional equivalences (if you will, essences) – something the open question argument assumes – is an arbitrary assumption about what good philosophical and scientific definitions, to say nothing of ordinary definitions that might find their way into a dictionary, must be. To point out – correctly – that Moore was not out to give the latter, that he was after 'real definitions,' does nothing to show that there must be, or even typically is, something wrong with such dictionary definitions. It only shows that they do not answer to Platonist purposes. But they can be perfectly all right for all of that.

Still, for all its deficiencies, the open question argument has continued to attract. Right up to the present many philosophers believe that Moore and philosophers following after him in his critique of ethical naturalism, such as Stevenson and Hare, were onto something, even when it is difficult to say exactly what (ibid.; and Darwall et al. 1992, 177-80). Moore, recall, in effect taking a metaethical turn, stressed that it was vital in doing moral philosophy to distinguish between, on the one hand, the question *'What* things are good?' and, on the other, the question 'What does the concept good mean?' Moral philosophy has repeatedly wrecked itself, Moore thought, by not keeping apart the question 'What is "goodness" – the concept?' and, the quite different question, 'What things are good?' To do a real *principia* we must begin with the question, 'What is goodness?' Otherwise, he had it, we will have failed to begin at the beginning. Previous moral philosophers, Moore contended, had not kept clearly in mind that these are distinct questions and, failing to draw that distinction, thought they had ascertained what we mean by 'good' – had discovered what goodness is – or the use of 'good,' when they had determined *what* are the fundamental goods. They thought that in ascertaining that pleasure is good, that happiness is good, that security is good, that friendship is good, that the meeting of needs is good and, even more generally, that the satisfying of interests and preferences is good, that they had discovered what goodness is: that they had come to understand what we mean by 'good.' They thought that in having ascertained these things (that pleasure is good, that happiness is good, that satisfying interests is good) they had defined 'good': had discovered the very essence of goodness. What goodness is, they mistakenly thought, Moore had it, is ascertained by finding out what things are good. This Moore, and following him Stevenson, Nowell-Smith, Hare et al., argued is a fundamental mistake; 'good' cannot be defined by reference to some natural property(s) or characteristic(s) such as answering to interests or some metaphysical property such as being willed by God or being the ground of being. And that this is so, as Stevenson and Hare put it, taking a more linguistic, less Platonic, turn than did Moore himself, could be established by attending to how we use 'good' and related terms.

It is here that the open question argument comes into play. Given any sentence of the form 'X is good' we will always recognize that it makes sense to withdraw thoughtfully and ask 'But is X good?' We – or at least most of us – believe that happiness is good, but we also realize that it makes sense to ask whether happiness is good. Moreover, someone who says that 'Happiness is good' is not saying, in saying that, that 'Happiness is happiness.' In saying 'Happiness is good,' she does not mean to be uttering a tautology. And someone who says, however mistakenly, that happiness is not good is not contradicting herself or saying something that is literally unintelligible. But it would be a contradiction and 'Happiness is good' would be a tautology, if 'happiness' and 'good' were equisignificant. But they are not, as attention to the use of 'good' reveals. That is not how the language-game is played.

Similar things apply to other clearly naturalistic definitions. For whatever X, where 'X' refers to (denotes) natural properties (characteristics) or relations, it always makes sense to ask whether X is good. The question is always open and never closed, even when we agree that X is good. It is, the argument went, only when evaluative or normative terms surreptitiously occur in the allegedly naturalistic definition that it becomes unclear whether the question is open. In, for example, 'Good is what *reflective, reasonable* people want under *ideal* conditions,' all the italicized words are evaluative and not just descriptive, so we cannot take the above as a properly naturalistic definition. Where we apply the open question test to such definitions we may be unsure, and indeed may not be able to determine, whether the question is open or closed, though note we would have to be confident it is closed to know that it was a good definition (a definition showing sameness of meaning; Nielsen 1974, 51-6). But where we have doubts about the openness of the question it is often due to the evaluative term(s) occurring in the *definiens*.

Some questions are *ersatz* self-answering questions that no one would try to ask if they understood the language in question, e.g., 'Is a father a male parent?' or 'Are emerald things green?' or 'Is goodness good?' But, for any proposed naturalistic definition, when an evaluative term is not smuggled into the definition, 'Is X good?', unlike 'Is goodness good?' is never a self-answering question but always an open question. Where X is 'what people generally approve of' we can still intelligibly ask 'Is what people generally approve of good?' or where X is 'an object of any interest' we can still intelligibly ask if what answers to any interest is good? The open-question argument, as we earlier remarked, does not *prove* that no naturalistic definition will ever be successful resulting in a closed question. But it provides a powerful method of challenge. None of the proposed definitions work – given an acceptance of Moore's traditionalist conception of definition – yielding, as they must to succeed, as does 'Are bachelors unmarried?', a closed question that someone could only ask if she did not know how to play the language-game. This is, to repeat, no proof that no new definition could succeed. But still the *prima facie* plausible candidates have been fairly well canvassed in the earlier phases of the metaethical arguments for and against ethical naturalism. And the naturalistic definitions so far proposed have never yielded clearly closed questions, where they are unambiguously naturalistic, and, even when they are not, they still are not securely closed. But their being securely closed is required – is a necessary condition – for us to be justifiably confident that any of these naturalistic definitions are correct, i.e., that such a definition really shows sameness of meaning (ibid.). 'It is a fitting object of a pro-attitude, but is it good?' or 'It is something people approve of when they have it clearly in mind and are being ethically consistent, but still is it good?' are examples of the latter. Whether these questions are open or closed is not crystal clear – they *may* rest on covert synonymies – but it is also not clear, given the occurrence of 'fitting,' 'clearly' and 'ethically consistent,' whether we have with them genuinely naturalistic definitions. Indeed, we think we have good reason to believe that they are not. But the naturalistic fallacy challenge is that, when the definition is clearly naturalistic, it never yields a self-answering closed question as it must to justify that 'good' means – is identical in meaning with – the naturalistic definition proposed.

VIII

What the naturalistic fallacy, with its utilization of the open-question argument, and the noncontradiction argument points to, is that there is some kind of gap between moral judgments and empirical characterizations of how things are. From empirical descriptions of the world, no matter how complete, we cannot deduce what is morally permissible and what is morally proscribed. Noncognitivists, in trying to account for the naturalistic fallacy, point to the emotive, expressive, evocative, or prescriptive features of moral talk. It is because of these noncognitive elements (the shadows cast by emotive meaning or force), that we cannot get the equivalencies that ethical naturalists seek. But, as John Pollock has argued, there is "an alternative explanation for the naturalistic fallacy.... What the naturalistic fallacy tells us is that there can be no truth condition analyses of moral concepts in terms of nonmoral concepts" (Pollock 1986, 508). Truth condition analysis is an analysis that insists that a concept has not been properly analyzed unless we have provided a statement of logically necessary and sufficient conditions for the exemplification of the concept in question. The naturalistic fallacy shows that this cannot be done for 'good,' 'right,' 'reasonable,' 'rational,' or any other fundamental normative notion. But – and this began to be appreciated during the Third Period in the history of metaethics – this failure of truth condition analysis is not at all peculiar to, or distinctive of, ethics or of evaluative notions generally. Rather, the situation is quite general in philosophy. Naturalistic fallacy considerations in effect gesture at or suggest the fact that philosophers ought to give up truth conditional analyses of concepts. But that was the very ideal of analysis. But the fact is that, quite generally, in domain after domain, these analyses collapsed under the pressure of counter-examples. Persistent efforts were made for some time to provide truth conditional analyses, but slowly Wittgenstein's point sank in that the idea prevalent in philosophical logic that concepts are individuated by their truth conditions was just an unworkable dogma. For most philosophically interesting concepts, as Pollock put it, "truth condition analyses are just not there to be found" (ibid., 508). That we cannot give truth conditional analyses of moral concepts shows nothing unusual about moral and other normative concepts. In this respect all concepts – or at least almost all concepts – are in the same boat.

Truth conditions always were supposed somehow to yield informative definitions of concepts (e.g., knowledge is justified true belief), but the search for such definitions – real definitions if you will – in ethics and elsewhere was a search for a will-o'-the-wisp (Robinson 1954). Concepts are not individuated by a statement of their truth conditions. Indeed, to go a little further down the Wittgensteinian road (further than Pollock will go), we should abandon talk of what concepts *essentially* are, including talk of what their *essential* roles or job descriptions are. Essentialism is a reification resting on a mistake. (With a firm recognition of this, we come to see the end of analytic philosophy, at least as traditionally conceived.)

Given these considerations, how does ethical naturalism stand? What the above considerations seem at least to do is to undermine any form of semantic or definitional ethical naturalism that would seek to define moral terms in terms of non-moral terms. Such a reductive or definitional naturalism – seeking to give intentional equivalences – seems at least to rest on a mistake. The open-question argument was important in bringing this realization.

However, matters do not end here. During the Golden Age that was just what most analytic philosophers took ethical naturalism to be. Ethical naturalism just was reductive semantical (definitional) naturalism. But the present strong contenders are not such reductive semantical naturalisms but are synthetic naturalisms which deny any *ontological* autonomy to ethics. They grant that moral terms neither mean the same as non-moral terms (including any string of them) nor can they be adequately paraphrased in non-moral terms. So much they grant to the noncognitivists or any non-naturalists that might still be around. What these ethical naturalists reject, to repeat and in doing so to amplify, is the *ontological* autonomy of non-naturalism: that moral judgments, where true, accord with a realm of *sui generis* moral facts, properties or characteristics – some occult realities, to use Jean Hampton's phrase – that are somehow independent of the world (Moore 1901, 95). There are no such facts or properties. Instead moral judgments to be true, if indeed they are true, must match with some natural facts: facts which are, directly or indirectly, empirically detectable. Moral judgments (*pace* both intuitionists and their nemesis, error theorists) are, ethical naturalists claim, in reality empirical judgments true or false in the same, or at least similar, ways that other empirical judgments are. Two terms, e.g., famously 'the morning star' and 'the evening star,' could have the same denotation even though they do not have the same meaning or the same use (the same job description). Similarly 'good' and 'answers to interests' could have the same denotation without having the same meaning or use. 'It answers to interests but is it good?' is an open, not a closed, question, but still 'good' and 'answers to interests' might have the same denotation. Semantic or definitional naturalism could be false while synthetic naturalism could be true. That the two terms ('good' and 'answers to interests') denote the same property (characteristic) could be established empirically, and, if that were so established, we would have established the truth of synthetic naturalism. That moral properties are *de facto* identical with natural properties might, the claim goes, be established by empirical research rather than by conceptual analysis. So once more we have ethical naturalism as a contender even in the face of the naturalistic fallacy (Pigden 1991, 421-31).

However, it is *perhaps* not amiss to be skeptical whether any such *de facto* identities have been established or, even more deeply, skeptical whether we have any even reasonably clear idea of how empirical research is supposed to establish them. Skepticism here does not appear to be philosophical nit-picking. Just what would it be like empirically, rather than postulationally, to establish – and of course postulations do not *establish* anything – such a *de facto* identity? What kind of research strategy do ethical naturalists have in mind? And without some idea here, isn't a postulated identity just arbitrary? None of these questions seem to us idle. But this does not gainsay the point made above that synthetic naturalism is not done in – or at least not evidently so – by naturalistic fallacy difficulties. Synthetic naturalism makes no claims about identity of meanings. (But see, for something more on the strength of naturalism, including its taking a rather different tack with a stress on asymmetric supervenience, the article by Peter Railton in this volume, as well as our discussion of it in the Afterword.)

IX

With the withering away of metaphysical ethics and intuitionism, most of the competing metaethical theories are naturalistic in *the general philosophical (cosmological) sense*, with the sometime exception of some forms of Kantian practical-reasoning theory and some forms of neo-Aristotelian ethical naturalism (Foot, Anscombe and Geach). Indeed some forms of noncognitivism (Gibbard and Blackburn), error theories, and *some* forms of ethical naturalism want to go still further and argue for, or at least assume, a sparse Galilean cosmological naturalism – a bald naturalism or physicalism – with a brute descriptive language, with a no non-excisable appeal to thick concepts. Allan Gibbard's view of the world (his cosmological naturalism) is a good example of such a pared-down physicalist picture. And, in this worldview, he wants to treat, as he puts it, "normative judgments and moral sentiments as natural phenomena" (Gibbard 1993, 34). One of his "chief aims throughout" *Wise Choices, Apt Feelings* was to do just that (ibid.). Here, in world-outlook, he is, broadly speaking, one with the other noncognitivists running from Hägerström to Ayer to Stevenson. But their treating of moral judgments as natural phenomena is very different from that of ethical naturalists. The latter want to construct a broadly scientific normative ethic where, as we have seen, moral judgments are viewed as a subspecies of empirical factual judgments: judgments that are true or false, and *establishable* as true or false, in basically the same way as any other empirical judgments are. This substantive ethical theory was to be backed up by a naturalistic metaethical theory, which, in one way or another, identified norms and values with natural facts.

Later versions claimed, as we have seen, *de facto* identities without claiming any identities in meaning (sense or use). There are indeed moral properties but they are also factual properties or, more plausibly, always properties asymmetrically supervenient on factual properties. Their very *normativity* is somehow constituted or produced by their *facticity*. Ethical naturalists are, as Peter Railton well put it, *factualists* while noncognitivists, along with that endangered species, intuitionists, are *nonfactualists* (Railton 1993, 36-51). By contrast to factualists, noncognitivists regard moral judgments as expressions and evocations of attitudes or feelings or the making of prescriptions (telling someone to make something the case). They regard moral conceptions as natural phenomena in a way analogous to (but not identical with) the way a cry, groan, or a laugh or reacting for or against something is a natural phenomenon. As they see it, moral judgments are not primarily, or perhaps sometimes even at all, conveyors of information or knowledge claims. The are rather expressive of stances for or against something. Moral sentences in the declarative mode appear on the surface to be attributing properties, but they are best understood as doing something else, namely expressing attitudes of norm acceptance. An expression of an attitude is, not, of course, a statement of fact, though the statement that an expression of attitude has been made – itself a factual statement – is a showing of how firmly, without taking an ethical naturalist outlook, moral judgments and moral sentiments can be taken to be natural phenomena. They express and tend to evoke feelings or attitudes, but that they occur is a natural phenomenon as a groan or a laugh is a natural phenomenon. They are the linguistic analogue of groans, laughs, and the like.

So the difference between noncognitivists (nonfactualists, nondescriptivists) and ethical naturalists (factualists, descriptivists) is not over whether to have a broadly scientific worldview, but, arguably, over the putative fact/value and fact/norm dualism within such a scientific worldview. Ethical naturalists traditionally have believed that it is indeed just *putative* and that there is a continuity between science and ethics, with norms and values, even fundamental ones, being a subspecies of empirical fact. (All norms are facts, but not all facts are norms.) And moral judgments are in reality empirical judgments confirmable or infirmable empirically. Moral utterances, where true, tell it like it is, and tell it like it is about the empirical (natural) world, the only kind of world there is.

Ethical naturalists of the current generation draw attention to how our language is suffused with normativity. We have thick moral concepts (e.g., courageous, erasable, diligent, bestial, crude, kind) which are both descriptive and evaluative, and there is, they claim, no analyzing them out, or paraphrasing them into, a purely descriptive (factual) component and a purely normative or evaluative component. Here they are one with Philippa Foot and Bernard Williams. Similar things obtain, they claim, for the thin, or thinner, concepts good, right, ought, fitting, rational, or reasonable. Reflecting on our language and thought, we do not find in it, ethical naturalists claim, a deep linguistic or conceptual divide or gap between the factual and the normative. We have, as the metaphor goes, empirical facts, though often with a normative tone, all the way down.

Noncognitivists (nonfactualists), though they can agree with naturalists, as Gibbard does, that our language is suffused with normativity, believe that, if we analyze it and the thought that goes with it carefully, we will be able to analyze out (isolate and identify) purely factual components and a pure normative component, thereby vindicating a fundamental fact/norm division. Gibbard, like Hare and like Blackburn, wants to keep a dualism of fact and value (fact and norm) and to treat it as fundamental to a proper understanding of morality and evaluative discourse in general. But he also remarks that he wants "to allow for lots of language that is mixed: that isn't purely normative and isn't purely factual" (Gibbard 1993, 53). It could even be the case that a language, perhaps English, "might have only mixed normative terms" (ibid.). But, if that is so (and isn't it?), shouldn't this lead Gibbard to ethical naturalism? Gibbard thinks not, for while his metalanguage (as he puts it) as a whole is English, still, he believes, we can develop a sufficient fragment of an ideal metalanguage in which "we can render meanings in a pared down, dualistic language: a language of pure facts, along with a single, pure normative element" (ibid.). The language of pure facts should be Galilean – the brute facts of a bald naturalism – and the single pure normative element is given in the term 'is rational.' Even that may not, as Gibbard speculates, under the pressure of Railton's questioning, be the *mot juste* (Railton 1993, 36-51; and Gibbard 1993, 52-8). 'Rational' may have too many connections to be expressive of a pure norm or a pure normative atom or a pure normative element. Perhaps 'is rational' is too tied to facts to so function. Perhaps it should be replaced by 'makes sense' or 'the thing to do?' But these terms in turn seem to have similar difficulties. They too seem to be tied to certain descriptions. But this does not terribly bother Gibbard, for he, in fine formalist fiddle, remarks that if English does not have such a term – an all-purpose normative term expressive of "a pure normative element" – then, he, Gibbard, will have to invent one and explain it, so as to make language live up to a fact/value distinction. But hitherto all proposed candidates have failed. And it is, moreover, problematic – to put it minimally – that we could somehow float free from our natural languages (remember Quine on how finally we have to just acquiesce in our mother tongue) and somehow or other just conceptualize 'a pure norm' or 'a pure normative element' so as to have some idea what we are talking about here. It begins to look like even *if* our last remark is somehow too strong, the search for the pure normative nugget is at best like the search for the holy grail and at worst like a search for the color of heat. Ethical naturalists will find such a strong claim of analysis as Gibbard's (as Gibbard surmises himself they will) implausible. Others will think it incoherent, and still others, who are not confident that it is incoherent, or perhaps even implausible, will think it is unmotivated, because pointless or at least unnecessary. What good is it? they will ask. We get along all right with our natural languages and with perspicuous representations of specific troubling normative notions in our language – our natural language – with only mixed, and at least seemingly inextricably mixed, normative terms (terms that are neither purely normative nor purely factual). Such terms are just all over the place. Our language is suffused with a blend of normativity and facticity. (Perhaps Dewey's talk of fact-values is not as silly as many of us took it to be?) To take our moral terms and other normative terms to be such mixed terms yields a conception that enables us to see how moral utterances are attitude-expressing, action-guiding and truth attributing all at once and quite consistently so. Moral utterances have both the dynamism and the practical-guidance quality that morality requires, and we can have some idea, as well, of when moral claims are true and, going up a level, of what it would be like for them to be true or false. We do not need, ethical naturalists will say, that old dualism which, like so many other philosophical dualisms, has baffled us more than it has enlightened us. Still, a quiet little voice may whisper to us, carrying us right back to the commencement of such discussions, 'But isn't there a distinction, which any analysis needs to capture, between describing what is the case and saying what ought to be the case, between saying what is done and saying what is *to be* done or what *must* be done?' Everything is what it is and not another thing. But if that is so – and isn't it? – isn't there a distinction – and a fundamental one – between fact/value and fact/norm and why not say it is a dualism deeply embedded in our thought and language?

Such a belief, though repeatedly challenged, has been, at least since the time of Hume and Kant and again throughout the three periods of metaethical theory, a persistent and very deeply embedded belief of many philosophers, perhaps most philosophers. And indeed the very sophisticated form of ethical naturalism defended by Peter Railton in this volume accepts a form of the is/ought gap. Whether the fact/value divide is genuine and fundamental or whether it is another confused philosophical dualism seems not to have been sorted out – *perhaps* it is not the sort of thing we can expect to sort out – or at least there is no consensus about it among informed and reflective moral philosophers. This issue (directly or indirectly) is an issue for many of the essays contained in this volume. We should see, in this respect, if things, in one way or another, get pushed along a little.

Bibliography

Altham, J.E.J. (1986). "The Legacy of Emotivism." In Graham Macdonald and Crispin Wright, eds. *Fact, Science and Morality*. Oxford: Basil Blackwell. 275-88

Brandt, Richard (1995)."Noncognitivism and Objective Criticism in Ethics." In R. Balasubramanian and Ramashanker Misra, eds., *Man, Meaning and Morality*. New Delhi: Indian Council of Philosophical Research. 111-24

Copp, David (1992)."Metaethics." In Laurence C. Becker, ed., *Encyclopedia of Ethics, vol. II*. New York: Garland 790-8

Daniels, Norman (1996). *Justice and Justification: Reflective Equilibrium in Theory and Practice*. Cambridge: Cambridge University Press

Darwall, Stephen, Allan Gibbard, Peter Railton (1992). "Toward *Fin de siècle* Ethics: Some Trends." *The Philosophical Review* **101**. 115-89

Dennes, W.R. (1944). "The Categories of Naturalism." In Yervant H. Krikorian, ed., *Naturalism and the Human Spirit*. New York: Columbia University Press. 270-94

Dennes, W.R. (1960). *Some Dilemmas of Naturalism*. New York: Columbia University Press.

Frankena, W.K. (1939). "The Naturalistic Fallacy." *Mind* **49**. 464-77

Frankena, W.K. (1951). "Moral Philosophy at Mid-Century." *Philosophical Review* **60**. 44-55

Frankena, W.K. (1957). "Ethical Naturalism Renovated." *Review of Metaphysics* **10**. 457-73

Frankena, W.K. (1958a). "Ethics." In Raymond Klibansky, ed. *Philosophy in the Mid-Century*. Firenze: La Nuova Italia Editrice. 42-77

Frankena, W.K. (1958b). "'Cognitive' and 'Noncognitive'." In Paul Henle, ed., *Language, Thought and Culture*. Ann Arbor: University of Michigan Press. 146-72

Frankena, W.K. (1963). "Recent Conceptions of Morality." In Hector-Neri Castañeda and George Nakhnikian, eds., *Morality and the Language of Conduct*. Detroit: Wayne State University Press. 1-21

Frankena, W.K. (1964). "Ethical Theory." In Roderick M. Chisholm et al., eds., *Philosophy*. Englewood Cliffs, NJ: Prentice-Hall. 347-461

Frankena, W.K. (1983). "Moral-Point-of-View Theories." In Norman E. Bowie, ed., *Ethical Theory*. Indianapolis: Hackett. 39-79

Frankena, W.K. (1995). "Stevenson's Emotive Theory of Ethics." In R. Balasubramanian and Ramashanker Misra eds., *Man, Meaning and Morality*. New Delhi: Indian Council of Philosophical Research. 125-41

Gibbard, Allan (1993). "Reply to Railton." In Enrique Villanueva, ed., *Naturalism and Normativity*. Atascadero, CA: Ridgeview. 52-9

Hägerström, Axel (1953). *Inquiries into the Nature of Law and Morals*. C.D. Broad trans. Stockholm: Almqvist and Wiksell

Hägerström, Axel (1964). *Philosophy and Religion*. trans. Robert T. Sandin. London: George Allen & Unwin

Hall, E.W. (1964). *Categorial Analysis*. Chapel Hill: University of North Carolina Press

Hallden Sören (1954). *Emotive Propositions*. Stockholm: Almqvist and Wiksell

Hare, R.M. (1985). "Ontology in Ethics." In Ted Honderich, ed., *Morality and Objectivity*. London: Routledge & Kegan Paul. 39-53

Hedenius, Ingmar (1941). *Om rätt och moral*. Stockholm: Almqvist and Wiksell

Hedenius, Ingmar (1949). "Values and Duties." *Theoria* **15**. 108-15

Hedenius, Ingmar (1959). "On Law and Morals." *The Journal of Philosophy* **56**, no. 3. 117-28

Joad, C.E.M. (1950). *Critique of Logical Positivism*. London: George Allen & Unwin

Mackie, J.L. (1946). "A Refutation of Morals." *The Australasian Journal of Psychology and Philosophy* **64**. 77-90

Mackie, J.L. (1977). *Ethics Inventing Right and Wrong*. Harmondsworth, Middlesex: Penguin

Moore, G.E. (1901). "The Value of Religion." *Ethics* **12**, no. 1. 81-98

Moore, G.E. (1903). *Principia Ethica*. Cambridge, Cambridge University Press

Nielsen, Kai (1974). "Covert and Overt Synonymity: Brandt and Moore and the 'Naturalistic Fallacy'." *Philosophical Studies* **1**. 51-6

Nielsen, Kai (1977). "Mill's Proof of Utility." In Harry R. Garvin, ed., *New Dimensions in the Humanities and Social Sciences*. Lewisburg, PA: Bucknell University Press. 110-23

Nielsen, Kai (1989). *Why be Moral?* Amherst, NY: Prometheus

Nielsen, Kai (1994). "How to Proceed in Social Philosophy: Contextualist Justice and Wide Reflective Equilibrium." *Queen's Law Journal* **20**, no. 1. 89-138

Pigden, Charles R. (1991). "Naturalism." In Peter Singer, ed., *A Companion to Ethics*. Oxford: Basil Blackwell. 421-31

Pollock, John, (1986). " A Theory of Moral Reasoning." *Ethics* **96**, no. 3. 506-23

Railton, Peter (1993). "Noncognitivism about Rationality: Benefits, Costs and an Alternative." In Enrique Villanueva, ed., *Naturalism and Normativity*. Atascadero, CA: Ridgeview. 36-51

Rawls, John (1995). "Reply to Habermas." *The Journal of Philosophy* **92**, no. 3. 132-80

Robinson, Richard (1948). "The Emotive Theory of Ethics." *Aristotelian Society Proceedings*, Supplementary **22**. 79-106

Robinson, Richard (1954). *Definition*. Oxford: Oxford University Press

Rorty. Richard (1984). "Life at the End of Inquiry." *London Review of Books* (April 1984). 6-7.

Rosati, Connie S. (1995). "Naturalism, Normativity and the Open Question Argument." *Noûs* **29**, no. 1. 46-70.

Ross, Alf (1945). "On the Logical Nature of Propositions of Value." *Theoria* **11**. 172-210.

Smith, Holly M. (1986). "Introduction: Symposium on Metaethics." *Ethics* **96**, no. 3. 471.

Stevenson, Charles (1963). *Facts and Values*. New Haven: Yale University Press.

Williams, Bernard (1985). "Ethics and the Fabric of the World." In Ted Honderich, ed., *Morality and Objectivity*. London: Routledge & Kegan Paul. 203-14.

❧ ❧ ❧ ❧ ❧

For extensive bibliographies of the first two periods of metaethics, see Wilfrid Sellars and John Hospers, eds. (1970). *Readings in Ethical Theory*, 2nd ed. New York: Appleton-Century-Crofts. 769-80; Kenneth Pahel and Marvin Schiller, eds. (1970). *Readings in Contemporary Ethical Theory*. Englewood Cliffs, NJ: Prentice-Hall. 561-72; Roderick M. Chisholm et al., (1964) *Philosophy*. Englewood Cliffs, NJ: Prentice-Hall. 456-63, Raymond Klibansky, ed. (1958). *Philosophy in the Mid-Century*. Firenze: La Nuova Italia Editrice. 73-7, and Paul Edwards, ed. (1967) *The Encyclopedia of Philosophy*, Vol. III. New York: The Macmillan Company and the Free Press. 115-17 and 132-34.

CANADIAN JOURNAL OF PHILOSOPHY
Supplementary Volume 21

On Metaethics: A Reverie

FRANCIS SPARSHOTT
University of Toronto

People engaged in teaching and research in philosophy departments are under strong and constant pressure to believe that what they are doing makes sense. Their belief may well be rooted in an initial project, formed autonomously under the guidance of teachers and fellow students; even so, it will continue to be shaped and confirmed by the requirements of peer approval and student satisfaction. The hungry sheep keep looking up. Sheer humanity requires us to show enthusiasm for what we dispense as nutrition, and a convincing display of conviction requires that we start by convincing ourselves. But in retirement all this falls apart. Often, perhaps usually, an element of belief and devotion is maintained, because the formed ego of the retiree is that of self-as-teacher or self-as-philosopher. But if, as may well be, the retiree's philosophizing was undertaken merely as gainful employment, things rapidly come to pieces. In these circumstances, a request for a paper on metaethics or any other loosely defined topic may bewilder. What, really, could be at issue here? Or so it seems. But there is something factitious in this bewilderment. To be caught up in it, the formed ego of the respondent must be determinately that of self-as-bewildered-by-past-activity or self-as-external-to-philosophy. So the response must be implicitly meta-metaphilosophical, in the sense that *something* is definitely in question from *some* point of view, even if it is in principle impossible to say exactly what.

I was thinking about metaethical questions in the 1950s, working on what would have been an Oxford BPhil thesis but turned into a book. The philosophical discourse that prevailed in my milieu was ostensibly language-oriented, cast in terms of what 'we' meant when 'we' said something or other, though (as outsiders were quick to point out, thinking they were raising a substantial objection) the underlying issue was always how certain sorts of disagreements were appropriately settled. The background issue in current metaethics was that of naturalism, that is, the extent to which questions about what was good or right to do could appropriately be settled by factual determinations; and the favorite ploy was the 'open question' thesis, to the effect that, if all the conditions agreed to be sufficient for excellence were satisfied, it would still make some sort of sense to ask whether what satisfied those conditions was really good. (Different versions of the thesis amounted to italicizing different words in that conditional.)

My own approach to this problem rested on the prephilosophical hunch (from which I have never dehunched myself) that what makes *some* sort of sense may not make enough of the right sort of sense. Ethical questions can arise only in actual or envisaged contexts of action, and a context as such is determinate and ineluctable, imposing constraints on what sorts of things can be successfully left out of account. Ethical debates are accordingly carried on in terms of the assumed values of variables that correspond to the parameters of contexts, and general accounts can be given of what those variables are and how values are assigned. The assigning of values is, indeed, free, as non-naturalists and existentialists both argued; but not all assignations are equally straightforward or explicable in a given context, and not all accounts of what the context of action is at a given time are equally viable. Granted, terms like 'viable' and 'successful' (and even 'straightforward' and 'explicable') themselves invite the 'open question' ploy; but, again, not all questions are equally open or open in the same way, and a question that is completely open risks not being a question at all.

My early excursions into metaethics could be construed as attempts to divert attention from a conceptually based logical grammar to relatively subtle strategies of argumentation. But nobody's attention was diverted. Either the philosophical world did not want to take this road, or it found no basis for fruitful discussion in my meanderings along it. In either case, it would be pointless for me now to elaborate an endeavor that has long proved abortive. But it would be equally absurd for me to enter into professional discussions based on the rejection of what I had to contribute, even if I had been keeping up with them. The following reflections, accordingly, are free-floating, little more than a daydream. They belong to metaethics as consideration of the intelligible strategies of ourselves as the kinds of agents and critics we consider ourselves to be. But they are presented not as contributions to any actual or possible debates but simply as things that one might think about, if one felt like thinking.

It has taken me a long time to reach the conclusion that in metaethics the most important thing to bear in mind is something that could be formulated somewhat as follows: what a person does at any given time is a response to whatever that person experiences as pressures at that time. A tautology, obviously; but this way of putting things should at least put us on guard against interpreting decisions in terms of maximizing interests, or gratifying desires, or observing principles, or anything of comparable specificity. An agent's plans, policies, principles, commitments, cravings, and so on are operative to the extent that they are experienced as constraining at the time of action; even if some of these theoretically function as logically architectonic or preemptive, they will really function as such only to the extent that they are in operative control at the moment. And a device, such as one enshrined in a legal system, to ensure that a policy is perpetually present to the minds of potential agents is efficacious only to the extent that the device itself has a dominant position at the moment of action. (Realizing this, the ancients argued that gods were invented by authoritarians to serve as police whose vigilance none could evade. But the ancients did not mention that the gods had neither flashlights nor handcuffs, so that there is nothing to ensure that malefactors will keep that vigilance perpetually at the forefront of their minds; nor can the preachers themselves contrive to stand at the burglar's elbow and whisper in the felonious ear.) From this point of view, principles and policies stand in no determinate functional relationship to more immediately motivating factors, responses to attractive or repellent features of a presented situation. And we have had few really compelling arguments to show why they should. For example, Kant's contention that every action conforms to a maxim that is subject to rational criticism, on pain of self-exile from the kingdom of ends, rests on a theory of agency embedded in a mechanistic world-view of dubious credentials. At the other extreme, theories of ethical maturity, according to which specific patterns of relationship between normative principles and feelingful responses correspond to sequentially ordered stages of moral maturity or autonomy, project patterns of infantile development onto the wider screen of real engagements with the world in a quite uncritical way.

Saying that action always responds to what the agent perceives at the time as pressures sounds as if it might commit us to a Deweyite account of ethical thinking as instrumental problem-solving. But I do not think it does. Dewey's model of moral intelligence is fundamentally linear: the onset and relief of pressures generate teleological structures. The model I am envisaging is non-linear: standing commitments and principles can maintain a permanent presence antecedent to any specific problem, without being continuously experienced as coercive, and a problem awaiting resolution need not be the major determinant of an agent's action. Of course, neither Dewey nor any other philosopher has thought otherwise; they have only insisted that analysis into discrete problems and compliances reveals the fundamental structure of rationality in practical thinking. What I am contending is that this is not the whole truth, that the manifold susceptibility to heterogeneous responses is at least as important as any more specific structure.

What status is to be assigned to the contention that (obviously) people are always responding to what they experience as pressure? It cannot be a matter of psychology or sociology, since it has no substantive content; it is not a matter of mere logic, since it favors one way of looking at human action over others. It is a reflection on structures of meaning, on the shapes of intelligence in the living of human lives. What can the proper deployment of reason be for an animal sustaining itself in a world on which it must be nourished and in which it may be endangered? An animal capable of reflecting on its situation, and on the implications of that capacity itself? I am arguing that, whatever it is, it must involve a readiness to respond differentially to precepts, strategies, and crises. Within a particular culture, what this means will need to be fleshed out with appropriate variables, such as 'moral law' or 'tabu' or 'yen,' specific contexts of action being experienced in ways that can be meaningfully construed as embodying values of these variables – though I see no reason why the operative set of variables need be the same for all individuals within a culture, and some important variables for an individual may not be recognizable to other individuals or even nameable by the individual in question.

Somewhere in the domain I have just sketched the center and periphery of metaethics must lie. But where? I doubt whether the question can be usefully discussed without making a detour to consider T.S. Kuhn's way of dealing with scientific revolutions.

The initial debate surrounding Kuhn's work soon turned into a rich dialectic, which in turn gave place to a complex *episteme* surrounding the procedures of science; but all we need here is the crude notion that normal science is carried on within the scope of a paradigm, a shared understanding about what constitutes an observation, a theorem, a datum, a commonplace, a skilled practitioner, a well-formed formula, and so on. Normal scientists contribute to the elaboration, completion, and correction of science as thus understood. But such paradigms are susceptible to challenge, and such challenges succeed when (for whatever reason) enough people experience the understanding yielded by the paradigm as inadequate. (What can 'inadequate' mean here? One cannot say, of course; but one would expect that normal science would be felt not to be living up to its own ideological pretensions to intellectual satisfactoriness – intelligibility, completeness, foundationality, cogency, or whatever, in the forms that the science itself projects.) A period of confusion ensues, normal science being displaced by revolutionary science, in which one or all of the elements in the old consensus are rejected in favor of new claimants; and this revolutionary science, if it succeeds in winning acceptance, hardens into a new paradigm within which a new kind of normal science is established. New and old paradigms are strictly incommensurable, in that neither accepts the standards by which the other would condemn it; but the historical displacement is irreversible, since the forces that made the revolution succeed as science must be real, though neither paradigm can contain them.

The distinction between normal and revolutionary science affects (or infects) the way we look at the familiar difference between academic philosophy and public or radical philosophy. Academic philosophy is conducted in journals and disseminated in classrooms in accordance with a paradigm of argument and rebuttal, a repertoire of established topics, problems, definitions, procedures, and positions and refutations. Public or radical philosophy attacks whatever may seem to be a pressing intellectual problem without systematic regard for what philosophy departments are up to – including the academic conventions about what radical philosophy would be. We are tempted to think of academic philosophy as 'normal' and of radical philosophy as 'revolutionary' in the Kuhnian senses. But this can be misleading. A scientific paradigm comes with an immense apparatus of findings and procedures which swamps or is swamped by its rivals in a way that is not altogether reciprocal; a scientific revolution is in the end successful or illusory, much as a political revolution finds it has to take over or replace the extant bureaucracy and somehow do all or most of what it did. But philosophy is in a rather different position. Philosophy has no warrant unless it is to be the 'pursuit of wisdom,' the constant rectification of understanding and the elimination of systematic sources of error. 'Normal' philosophy admits the possibility of 'revolutionary' philosophy not merely in principle but as its own most fundamental part; whatever a radical philosophy proposes turns out to be something the academic discipline has merely put on hold, rather than rejected. As in most professions, however, the most deeply subversive moves are accepted only if they are made by authorized wielders of the paradigm, in a suitable tone of voice.

The relevant difference between science and philosophy here is that radical philosophy is not a revolutionary transition between two normal phases, but an inevitable ongoing counterpart to an academic discipline with which it is symbiotically bound. Normal philosophy in its pure form is intolerable to anyone not vocationally committed to it, but it fills the professional journals; revolutionary philosophy, by contrast, is in its undisguised form intolerable to those vocationally engaged in normal philosophy, because it throws away all the real gains that reflection has made in a coherent evolutionary history that goes back at least to Parmenides. Interesting things, accordingly, are likely to be done somewhere on the interface between the two.

The contrast between the ways in which the antithesis of normal and revolutionary can be applied to science and to philosophy may be deceptive. I suspect that normal science, proceeding peacefully in terms of an established paradigm, is a condition that only ever obtains in very limited areas – such as, for instance, the domain of classical mechanics which Kuhn's book originally singled out. This limitation of scope is often concealed by the extraordinary convention, to which standard histories of science still subscribe, that all science depends on mechanics and the condition of mechanics is the condition of science as a whole. The convention is supported by the thesis that all phenomena must be reducible to matter in motion, and belong to science only as so reduced; but this contention has no operational warrant – one is tempted to say that it is itself part of the paradigm, but one cannot say that, because the paradigm in question is a paradigm of mechanics, and the very idea of normal science requires that it have no warrant outside its own domain.

Outside the limited areas where normal science is carried on, a fruitful chaos reigns, where there are no agreed paradigms. A privileged status is often claimed for the domains where science is well ordered – nothing else, it is said, is really science – but little sense can be made of such claims. The normality of normal science includes the autonomy of its criteria; arguments for the adequacy of the paradigm, if generated outside the domain itself, simply have the effect of undermining it. If this is really the case, the dialectic of normal and revolutionary does not apply to the totality of scientific endeavor at any given time. And it is the supposition that normality is the normal condition of science that sustains the sharp distinction between science and philosophy that was so firmly maintained a few decades ago, when the debates about naturalism in metaethics flourished.

However that may be, the 'normal' and the 'revolutionary' in philosophy are not alternative states, but symbiotic: normal philosophy incorporates an implicit subservience to the revolutionary, revolutionary philosophy can sustain a claim to attention only through operative relevance to the normal. But the distinction between them, just because the relation is dynamic, remains in principle firm. I return to this topic later. But first, it is time to say something more definite about the distinction between ethics and metaethics, and how the contrast between revolutionary and normal affects it.

It is hard to say exactly what ethics is or should be. But it is, at least, that part of philosophy that comes closest to having to do with the values of individual conduct. And within ethics we may distinguish between plain or first-order ethics, which addresses whatever problems define that branch of philosophy, and metaethics, which considers whatever problems arise from the philosophical practice of ethics itself. We may conjecture that these will mostly be of two kinds: those that arise from the identification of a subject matter and scope for first-order ethical inquiry, and those that arise from the conceptual apparatus and argumentative procedures of ethical inquiry itself. I shall be asking later whether we should add a third kind: problems concerning the status of the outcomes of ethical inquiry.

The distinction between ethics and metaethics can be made both within normal philosophy and within revolutionary philosophy. G.E. Moore's *Principia Ethica* of 1903, for instance, plainly belongs to normal ethics, affirming the reality of certain kinds of value – friendship, beauty: whatever seems most appealing in a Cambridge quadrangle on a sunny prewar afternoon – and the way they enter into the concerns of life. The affirmation is made and supported in terms that only a professional philosopher would use, deployed in arguments characteristic of the profession. But Moore's book also, and to many minds principally, engages in metaethics, evaluating arguments that rival ethicists have allegedly used and mounting a methodological critique against them. In general, the bulk of what was thought of as metaethics within the normal philosophy I was trained in discussed how value terms are to be defined, in themselves and in relation to each other. But it is obviously possible also to mount a comparable clarification and critique of that sort of metaethics itself, both in its particular manifestations and in its implicit claim to be a legitimate deployment of philosophical energies. For instance, a cloud of argumentation was soon generated within normal philosophy around Moore's masterwork, clarifying and evaluating his metaethical procedures as he had clarified and evaluated the first-order ethics of John Stuart Mill and his like. Obviously one could assign this material to a new sub-genre, metametaethics, but it has never seemed worth while to do so, all argumentation above the base level being assigned to the same genre. It is plainly a debatable question, however, what sorts of self-criticism philosophy as a professional practice should be taken to incorporate; so the precise scope and credentials of metaethics within normal philosophy remain open to question.

Within revolutionary or radical philosophy also, there is ethics. Prophetic and reformist texts of all sorts belong here. Many of them neither seek nor receive the title of philosophy; but many do. Nietzsche's *Beyond Good and Evil* and many existentialist texts, as well as many that belong to feminist and minority studies, claim and receive the name of philosophy for their reflections on the values enshrined or pursued in human relations and conduct. The ways in which these reflections are carried on implicitly call into question the supposed paradigms of normal philosophy, but do not themselves constitute a critique of them. In relation to this straightforward or first-order reflection there is room for a metaethics to examine its scope, credentials, methods, and limits. So long as normal ethics remains in place and revolutionary ethics remains revolutionary, the task (conscious or unacknowledged) of its associated metaethics will be to establish the paradigm that will constitute it a new normal philosophy – something that the first-order practice of the ethics itself would, in due course, manifest rather than define. And, as before, there is space for a third-order reflection on the proceedings and credentials of this second-order activity, as well as on the overall structure constituted by the interrelations of these various levels of philosophical activity.

According to the account I have now given, there are ethical and metaethical schemata within normal and revolutionary philosophy alike. But there are also cross-border activities. Normal ethics engages in metaethical reflection on revolutionary ethics, using normal procedures to reinterpret or censure the unorthodoxies by normal canons; and revolutionary ethics can hardly function without a metaethical castigation of some or all of the elements in the normal paradigm. In fact, this negative aspect of revolutionary thought is so much easier to carry out (being structured by the well-organized articulation of its target) than to achieve anything positive from the new standpoint that both supporters and opponents of a counterculture tend to define it by its critique rather than by its substance. In fact, we are tempted to say that revolutionary philosophy as a whole stands to normal philosophy as metaphilosophy to first-order philosophy. (The converse does not, it seems, hold; it would be worth considering whether it cannot be made out to do so, but I have nothing to offer here.) And, finally, reflection of the sort that the present paper exemplifies stands in a metaphilosophical relation to the normal and the revolutionary alike; and, to the extent that ethics is a typical component of philosophy, its content is in a sense metaethical already, and could presumably be made to appear so.

An ambiguity lurks in the very notion of metaethics, which the concluding clause of the preceding paragraph brings to the fore. Is metaethics a logic of ethics, or an ethics of ethics, or both? And if both are possible, how are they related? In my *Enquiry into Goodness*, and in the ancillary papers related to that, I was bothered by a taunt often heard from the opponents of 'ordinary language' philosophy (most conspicuously, Bertrand Russell). In explaining what 'good' means, one can only be explaining what people ('we') mean by it. But which people, and when? People say odd things, and mean odd things by what they say. But what are the criteria of oddity? While a Scandinavian school purported to elide philosophy into descriptive linguistics, some Oxford philosophers preferred to describe what they were doing as 'logical grammar.' This notion (desperately obscure, though I used it above as though I knew what I meant by it) suggested that one was explaining what people ought to mean by 'good' if arguments about the goodness of things and people were to make sense as arguments. But what counts as making sense in such arguments? Is a university common room the ideal laboratory for the stringencies of practical reason in a rough world? 'Logic, the Devil's weapon!' is what people say in our family when threatened with refutation; and we are never sure that it is altogether a joke. In the end, one is thrust back on the position outlined above. In saying what 'good' means, and otherwise indulging in metaethics, one is not describing what people do when they use a certain vocabulary, nor is one suggesting that people should use language otherwise than they do; one is saying something about intelligent behavior, about what social animals in a real world full of perils and opportunities do when they are coping with that world and with each other. Such discourse must, in the last resort, be deliberative: philosophical questions, including questions of metaethics, are about making up our minds how we had better think and act, which is a matter of what works and what doesn't work. The basic difficulty here is that people try to dispense in their philosophizing with their pervasive human understanding of what it is to maintain themselves in a world in which they sometimes succeed and sometimes fail but most often fudge along, in which some things work and some things don't and there are other things with which one can somehow make do.

This was the real lesson of Parmenides. No matter what the textbooks say, the hero of Parmenides's poem is commanded by a goddess to govern his mind by a strict logic according to which the world he lives in does not even exist, and according to which what the goddess tells the hero and his own narrative are alike unintelligible.... The boundary question, the orientating question, for metaethics must be how the embodied human mind works as it makes its way through a world among people who respond to it – not how it does behave or should behave, as if these were separate issues, but how intelligent activity *functions*. So far as I can make out, this is what cognitive science is and does – or would be and do if it were not obsessed with what can be modelled on machines.

What is the starting point of metaethics? It follows from what I have been saying that there cannot be an *absolute* starting point; that is just what is precluded by the fact that practical thinking is not only context-bound but finds itself already in mid-career by the time its language is fully formed. But is there an *accessible* starting point? It would have to be one we could reach from wherever we happen to be. Paradoxically, I provided us with one when I said that action always responds to the pressures actually experienced as impinging on the agent – paradoxically, because that principle defines itself as being accessible for thought only when the thinker is adequately motivated to think of it. But the paradox is easily resolved, like the paradoxes of free will. You can think of it when you want to, and you can want to when it occurs to you, provided you have the time; and if it doesn't occur to you the question doesn't arise, and if you haven't the time, why should you care? We will see in a little while that this is in effect the starting point that Aristotle proposed for the inquiry for which the term 'ethics' was originally coined.

Is there a general problem for metaethics? And, if so, what is it, and what are the limits to its solution? From one point of view, the problem is obviously that of the nature and proprieties of the inquiries of first-order ethics. But it is not easy to see just what that general problem would be. Is ethics the sort of thing that has a nature? Is the word 'ethics' used with enough consistency that one can identify it with an identifiable practice or project? One popular candidate for the most general problem of metaethics used to be 'Why should one be moral?' on the assumption that ethics consists of debates on questions of morality, morality being equated, roughly, with actions assumed to be incumbent or proscribed regardless of the agent's interests or motivation. But that cannot be the original question for metaethics, because we cannot begin by supposing that there is any such reason or even that there are any such actions. It will not do to start with 'What is morality?' for we have no initial reason to suppose that the term 'morality' has any determinate or legitimate application. For the same sort of reason, we cannot start by asking 'Does the term "morality" have any legitimate application?' for the term is far too culture-bound and theory-laden to figure so near to the beginning of one's investigation. And, again, we cannot even start by asking 'What is ethics all about?' or 'What should ethics be about?' because the term 'ethics' may not stand for any body of inquiry that one should try to make cohere.

The difficulty that confronted us in the preceding paragraph arises because philosophy for most of its history has been carried on within the context of a type of theology whose basic tenets are (to say the least) not philosophically grounded. This is most glaringly the case with moral philosophy. According to one traditional version of the theology in question, the universe is the free creation of a transcendent entity which first created a set of types or ideas, including that of humanity, which are more or less perfectly exemplified by individuals. The typical form of humanity functions as a norm, establishing a 'natural law' for living to which humans are obliged to conform. The human mind is not capable of discovering what this law is, but the creator has provided for a priesthood which can determine infallibly what it is and has the task of promulgating it to others, who are obliged to follow their directions.

Probably no one believes all this – for one thing, the pseudo-Platonic ontology of natural kinds cannot be fitted into what we know of the natural world – and perhaps no one ever did; but something like it has provided the set of ideas within which today's moral philosophy has developed its conceptual scheme and its problematic. The question 'Why should I be moral?', for instance, derives its force from this split between practical intelligence and law. It seems to be impossible to break free from this distorting framework. Even 'free thinkers' tend to be dominated by a hankering for it or by a struggle against it; in either case, it is assumed to be in some sense a normal part of the intellectual ambience, something the presence of which has to be taken into account. To find an interpretation of the nature and task of ethics that is not haunted by assumptions related to this sort of framework, one would have to go back to a time before philosophers took it for granted that the universe is orientated toward a transcendent creator.

Among the pre-Christian systems of ethics, only Aristotle seems to have given open attention to the question of what gives rise to the problems of ethics, and hence what those problems are, and this only in the *Nicomachean Ethics*; the *Eudemian Ethics*, preferred by many of today's professional philosophers, seems to be conceived more as a clarification of the concepts and values current in its author's milieu.

The way the *Nicomachean Ethics* is laid out suggests to me that its author sees practical philosophy as addressing a problem posed by the aspect of human agency emphasized in *On the Soul* III 10. Alone among animals, human beings have a sense of time: they conceptualize sequences of events and correlations of those sequences. They can envisage their futures. At every moment of their waking lives, like other animals, they are faced with the necessity of doing one thing rather than another. For other animals, there is no problem; they simply react to what is threatening or enticing in the situation as they perceive it. But humans are different: their possible futures fall within the scope of their practical reasoning and planning, though not of their immediate desires and aversions. They have to make choices between alternative futures. And each of us has a limited span, at the end of which we will prove to have lived a lifetime with one content and character rather than another. The questions of what sort of life to live, and what sort of life-liver to be, will have been answered in practice whether or not we choose to think about them. And we must bear in mind that anyone who asks these questions will already be caught up in complex hierarchies of organized activities, and will be living as a member of groups to which he or she has commitments. Moreover, such a being will inevitably be a member of something approximating to what Aristotle calls a 'city,' an organization of life-livers who are sufficiently autonomous for the question 'How am I to live?' to make practical sense to them.

For philosophers who make the Aristotelian starting point their own, the question for practical philosophy is simply how beings thus situated are to make choices. The original question for metaethics must be approximately whether it makes sense to say that any general answer to the problem of how to make choices is to be preferred over any other. Aristotle's answer is that it makes sense if and only if one can make true generalizations about humans (his way of putting this is to ask whether human beings as such have a function); and one certainly can do so, not only because human beings are a recognizably distinct animal species, but more importantly because humans must be such that they are capable of posing and understanding such problems as we are posing here. That is, they are essentially language-users; and it is surprising how much follows from that. The remaining tasks of metaethics are to establish what sense it makes to say that some solutions are preferable to others, and what the parameters of good solutions are. The task of first-order ethics is to determine what solutions are actually best.

A surprising amount of the *Nicomachean Ethics* is actually devoted to metaethics, though this has usually not been seen because most interpreters of the work have been sturdily committed to the task of settling just how the denizens of a created universe are to be instructed to behave. What Aristotle does is present reasons for thinking that an unavoidably problematic area confronts all humans, and explain what conditions govern its effective handling; this is the area for which he apparently coined the term 'ethics,' and it is plainly akin to, if not identical with, what we call ethics today. The relevant questions for us as latter-day metaethicists must be something like the following. Is Aristotle's approach correct and sufficient? If so, how are we to adapt this approach to our own philosophical condition, what considerations are to govern our own procedures? If his approach is not correct and sufficient, why not, and what considerations govern what we should do instead? If he misidentified the original common predicament of humans as agents in a real world, is there any other predicament that presents itself? We have to keep asking ourselves, of course, by what standards his approach is to be judged correct or incorrect, for what ends it is to be deemed sufficient or insufficient. Meanwhile, however, it is a real question whether any comparably cogent account of the necessary scope of practical reasoning has ever been devised.

In the course of developing his problematic, Aristotle confronts a question he took over from Plato, one to which recent philosophy has not given comparable emphasis. We may say that people pursue the good and avoid the bad, as if these were the only value determinants there are. But are they? Can we say generally what sorts of values enter into human life, and how are they related? Plato and Aristotle sketched several sets of relationships among such terms as the good, the beautiful, the useful, the pleasant, the right, the beloved, and so on. The topic has been generally neglected in the mainstream of English-speaking philosophy, though it was revived in a crude form some decades ago as the distinction between the right and the good. The general topic is that of axiology. First-order axiology is concerned with the diversity and dynamics of basic motivations and justifications; but there must also be a meta-axiology, a critique of the scope and methods appropriate to the first-order study, and this must be a principal part of any metaethics. It is not easy to see how we are to get a purchase on it, otherwise than through a critical history of what our elders and betters have said. However, if we start from the thesis that people act in response to whatever they actually experience as pressures, and that these pressures can include affections and ideals, plans and principles, as well as desires and aversions, we give ourselves a better chance than if we say, as some philosophers have said, that individuals and groups always act to maximize their own interests – whether we identify those interests with 'pleasure' somehow defined or with 'the good.' Suitable definition can make such theses true, even trivially true, but as a phenomenological basis for value theory they are silly. How true are they, for how much of the time, of yourself and the people you know? In my experience people mostly do what comes next, joining in common activities, getting on with their jobs, responding to requests and appeals, carrying out their projects, satisfying or dodging their commitments, betraying or living up to their ideals: doing what they do and being what they are. Aristotle's starting point was the variety and heterogeneity of such pressures and the intricacy of their interrelations. And from here we can go on, as he did, to see what generalizations are possible about the kinds of pressure and response that are involved in human lives and in human societies, and how in principle such generalizations can be derived and supported. Of course, my own presentation here is vulnerable to the objection that my catch-all term 'pressure' is no less obfuscatory than the catch-all terms 'desire,' 'pleasure,' and 'interest,' of which I am complaining; but I can't do anything about that now.

The field I have been describing is that of speculative and critical anthropology. Philosophers at one time used to dismiss this as 'armchair science,' but it is hard to see how it is to be avoided. The field is implicit in any philosophical activity, because such activity implies claims about the reliability or importance of the sort of thought it relies on; so it can hardly be illegitimate to subject it to conscious reflection. Accordingly, the next thing we have to say is that any operational idea of human nature or the human condition must correspond to a sort of metaethic, establishing conditions of relevance and warrantability for an ethic: the normative system appropriate to a being with such a nature in such a condition, just as the creationist theologies proposed. We can then say that, notionally, the sum of all such operational ideas about the nature and condition of ourselves as human beings, articulated in some persuasive order, would establish a sort of total metaethical matrix, an overall mapping of the ways in which conditions of relevance and warrantability for concrete ethics might be established. Perhaps the confident utterance of ethical pronouncements requires inner assurance about the completability in principle of such a grand architectonic.

People respond to the pressures they are aware of (even if their ideas about those pressures are groundless or mistaken). But different people are differently situated, and operational ideas of human nature or the human condition are often accused of reflecting the nature and condition of only one special set of human beings, susceptible to some sorts of pressure and ignorant of or impervious to others. Some are toads, others are butterflies. A comprehensive metaethic would order not only viable ideas of what humanity is, but the salient differences of condition and position which anchor those differences in reality: slave/ free, male/female, rich/poor, immature/mature/senile and so on. And it would have to consider what makes such a difference salient, the conditions of its relevances and irrelevances. At present, discussions of these differentiations and their relevance are ubiquitous and often persuasive, but seem mostly to be *ad hoc*. Are the relevant differences merely empirical in all cases? The question for an overall metaethics would be how we are to decide, or how discover, what principles should govern our minds here. We know well enough the sorts of things people say; what we do not know is whether any order can be introduced – or how to tell whether the sorts of purported order that have been introduced are adequate (adequate to what?).

The sorts of worry I have been ventilating in the last few paragraphs may all be dismissed, however, as the typical outcome of a familiar folly – the supposition that one can call everything into question at once. As though one could move the earth without a place to stand on, or as though one could find a place outside the earth to anchor a fulcrum on! The best one can do is what we all do, assume the stable truth of most of one's convictions and, on that basis, conduct a critique of one specific area; then, counting one's results in that area as certain, use them as part of the basis from which some other domain of belief can be subjected to a critique.

Whatever the nature and scope of metaethics, it can only exist in relation to first-order ethics, and an ethics can hardly be anything other than a set of action-guiding principles, precepts, laws, recommendations, or similarly general propositions of some sort. A question that is seldom raised, probably because it has seemed to make no sense, is: what is the function of such an ethic in the course of life? The obvious answer is that it is whatever action is to conform to, with supplementary provisions (perhaps hierarchically organized) for dealing with cases where precepts or principles conflict. But how is this answer to be reconciled with our thesis that people act in response to what they experience as constraining? By remembering that a moral principle, a resolve, a policy, can be operative only while its owner has it in mind. In the context of ethics, Aristotle set the fashion of describing this phenomenon as 'weakness of will' *(akrasia)*, with the strong implication that it is always a defect of mind and character. But how is this implication established? Action-guiding formulations can be used as constraining, as guiding, as regulating, as suggesting, or variably within limits that are to be determined. Perhaps the world goes better (from some point of view that remains to be established and evaluated) if people vary in this regard, some people being very casual about their principles, some quite rigid with regard to them all, some people veering between strictness and looseness, some people having quite various attitudes towards different principles among those they avow. That what we call our 'convictions' are not always actively convincing us is something we all know. Action-guiding principles, including principles governing *how* principles are to guide action, can operate only when they are somehow present to the minds of agents; and they need not always come to mind or, when they do, come with the same sort of force. In his discussion of 'voluntary' action Aristotle observed that one cannot *fail to notice* that murder is wrong in the same sort of way that one can fail to notice that a syringe is loaded with Interferon rather than Inferon. I am sure that is true; but it does not follow that some special disaster has to overtake the mind before an avowed principle can fail to be fully present and dominant. We tend to regret such absences, or pretend to do so. But perhaps this is the way things should be, perhaps the presence of functioning ethics in the world is tolerable only if ethical systems and principles are observed in hit-or-miss kinds of ways. More generally: perhaps the human world carries on, not in spite of the prevalent inefficiency, ignorance, and general mess, but just because it is the sort of mess it is, the sort of environment in which alone humanity can function.

Laws, rules and regulations, moral laws, principles, maxims, pre-ferred strategies, procedures – all such things together make up a loosely structured cognitive environment, within which (as within the physi-cal environment) choices are made and actions performed. Institutions are devised and directed as if they were meant for perfect compliance, but they are actually designed and operated with imperfect compli-ance in mind: strict deadlines, for instance, are imposed, and plans are based on them, but in the knowledge that some people are going to ignore the deadline. And, of course, it is not always clear what is meant by saying that an institution *exists*. The institution itself, with the for-mulation of its procedures, is always as fitful and uneven a presence as the compliances. An emperor (Frederick II, *stupor mundi*, if memory serves) is said to have responded to some complaint of his son with the words: *An nescis, fili mi, quantilla sapientia regitur orbis terrarum?* – 'Do you not know, my son, with how little wisdom the world is governed?' This is usually taken to be inculcating a resigned acceptance of governmental (and, in general, human) imperfection; but it could equally have been a non-judgmental recognition of the way the world inevitably operates.

In the last few paragraphs, I have been rattling the bars of our cage. I have been brooding on the overall assignment of metaethics as the functional analysis of reason in personal and social practice. But what, in the light of this assignment, are we to make of the debates about 'naturalism' that preoccupied so many of us in the early years of the century? The naturalist fallacy was the supposition that some value-free description of a state of affairs closed all question of its goodness. Well, of course, nobody could really suppose that; the terms in which the question was posed precluded it. But, as I remarked above, it was less clear that all purported value-free descriptions were equal, and in what sense questions of goodness were left 'open' by assertions that could be recognized as descriptions of *actions* and *situations*. Attempts, like those of my *Enquiry into Goodness*, to construct a dialectic more appropriate to practical thinking, failed by implying a social context of rational discussion of which the status in social reality was never clari-fied – a failure I eventually acknowledged in a discussion of the word 'good' appended to my *Theory of the Arts* in 1982.

What happened to the debates about naturalism was that they had considerable success in clarifying certain issues in explicit ways. After the clarification had reached a certain point it became pointless to continue – one really has to decide how many places of decimals one is going to admit into one's calculations. The starting point of the controversy is still intelligible; the sensible thing to do with it is to go back and read as much of what was then written as one has time and stomach for; one can still learn from it, just as one can learn from medieval controversies about nominalism and realism, but there is no point in pretending that one can realistically make the relevant standpoints one's own.

In conclusion, then. The overall task of metaethics must be to determine the general status of all *this* sort of discourse. All *what* sort? One cannot say. And what is to govern its status? Again one cannot say. It is useless to talk about reflective equilibrium, since equilibrium requires a fulcrum and a determinate direction identifiable as up and down. Like agents whom Aristotle postulated in his original posing of the problem for ethics, philosophers considering the scope and parameters of metaethics find themselves already engaged in partly structured and partly amorphous controversies, in which their starting points and strategies are already partially formed, and able to relate somehow to other philosophers analogously situated. The field in which they may be said to operate is constituted by the moves they find they can make and recognize, and the differential capacities of themselves and others to respond to such moves. Different philosophers, normal and revolutionary alike, fudge along in loose relation to each other; and various non-philosophers join in the conversations as occasion arises. But the word 'conversation' is misleading here if it suggests anything like a cocktail party within which chattering groups form and reform, engaging in phatic communion. Philosophy remains a meaningful enterprise only while areas of normal philosophy remain recognizably normal, dialectically and historically related to each other. True, there are two sorts of histories: normal histories, and revolutionary histories. But even revisionist histories are not easy to set up, and revolutionary history is more often proclaimed than practised. Retired philosophers, removed from the constraints of pedagogy and current controversy, may feel the domain of metaethics, like the wider domains of philosophy and academia themselves, coming to pieces in their hands. But as soon as one re-enters the domain far enough to understand anything in it the familiar constraints operate in the same old ways.

As for the immediate future of metaethics, which is what we would really like to know – that is just what we cannot tell. In philosophy, any formulation of what the future holds would itself be its own realization, hence a manifestation of the present and not a prediction at all. And to predict the continuation of the present into the future would itself be to continue it. All one can predict in philosophy is which among present preoccupations and problems will attract teachers, researchers, students, editors, funding agencies, and so forth. There is a sense in which the future of these concentrations of energy and subvention is the future of philosophy. But there is a sense in which it is not.

CANADIAN JOURNAL OF PHILOSOPHY
Supplementary Volume 21

Foundationalism for Moral Theory

RICHARD B. BRANDT
University of Michigan

It seems to be generally agreed that a foundationalist view of any area of justified beliefs is the affirmation that there are some (basic) beliefs which are to some degree credible for a person independently of reflection on logical relations to any others of his beliefs, and that any other beliefs of his are justified because of appropriate logical relations to these basic beliefs – thus contrary to the coherentist thesis that beliefs can only be justified by appeal to their relation to other beliefs of a person, independently of whether these other beliefs are themselves independently credible. Thus, for the area of moral beliefs, foundationalism is the view that there is at least a subset of a person's moral beliefs which are either justified independently of logical relations to any other beliefs, or are justified by their logical relations to some other beliefs, either independently credible moral beliefs, or independently credible non-moral ones.

I am here restricting 'ethical' beliefs to *moral* beliefs, as distinct from beliefs that something is a good thing or intrinsically good or good for a person.

It is well known that many philosophers do not subscribe to any foundationalist view of ethics/morals, or as a basis for supporting acceptance of any beliefs, including those of science.

If we look away from ethical or moral beliefs to the beliefs of a scientist, say in the area of physics, what a foundationalist will hold is that there are some of his beliefs which are immediately justified because they are simply reports of the scientist's observations or how he is being appeared to, such as, 'It appears to me as if the needle of the instrument is pointing to the number 2.1.' There can be differences of opinion about how strongly justified such reports can be, or must be. Some philosophers have held that they can be matters of certainty, but most foundationalists appear willing to settle for less – that the reports are 'independently credible' to a certain degree. But these basic beliefs are thought to justify the whole of the science, in that the superstructure is adopted as the best explanation of the basic data/beliefs.

How close a parallel to this can there be for moral beliefs?

The parallel would amount to an identity if one were a 'naturalist' about the *meaning* of moral predicates, that is, if one held that the actual meaning of a moral predicate like 'is morally required' or 'morally wrong' is the same as a predicate that can be appraised by the methods of science such as 'will contribute maximally to the happiness of sentient creatures,'[1] or if 'is morally wrong' is the same predicate as 'would be disapproved of by any person who was factually omniscient, impartial, devoid of emotions toward particular persons, but otherwise a normal person.'[2] But, partly as a result of arguments put forward by G.E. Moore in 1903, this naturalist identity-of-meaning view has been generally given up. So how any moral beliefs can be justified immediately, and which ones may be, has become far from clear.

One possibility is to claim that some moral beliefs are just self-evidently true. After all, there are some synthetic propositions which are so. Thus we can infer that anything which is a cube in shape has twelve edges, although 'having twelve edges' is not a logical entailment of 'being a cube,' or that if something is red in color it will color-resemble anything orange in color more than it will resemble anything yellow. What is the difference between moral statements and the ones I have just listed as ones the truth of which we can ascertain just by thinking? This could be hard to say, but there is one obvious difference; this is that there is no disagreement among educated people about the statements listed as ones we can appraise just by taking thought. But edu-

---

1 Jeremy Bentham, *An Introduction to the Principles of Morals and Legislation* (Oxford: Clarendon Press 1876) 3-4

2 Roderick Firth, "Ethical Absolutism and the Ideal Observer," *Philosophy and Phenomenological Research* **12** (1952)

cated people do differ sharply about moral statements: some think that if you have made a promise there is some obligation to keep it – 'A promise is a promise' – whereas others have thought there is an obligation to keep a promise only if breach of it would be harmful to the promisee in some way. Much more do people differ from one another on the morality of abortion and capital punishment.

But what might we in general mean by saying some person's *factual* belief is 'justified'?[3] I suggest we might mean that there are some beliefs about *observations*, present or past (assuming some reason can be given for relying on memory reports of past observations), such that the formulation of a theory which is the best *explanation* of them, free from factual error and conceptual confusion, will (for the circumstances) imply the observation beliefs. Such a situation will recommend the theory and be convincing to every thoughtful, rational, and factually generally informed person. (The superstructure in empirical science may obviously have this status, and so be justified.)

Can moral beliefs be justified in this sense?

Obviously the first thing we must do, to go about answering this question, is to explain what it is to have a 'moral belief.' For this, we need to identify the state of mind a person is expressing when he affirms that some action is 'morally wrong' or 'morally good,' etc. The main traditional view about this has been *cognitivist*: that moral statements affirm that something has the property of being right or wrong, a property it has which is conceptually independent of anyone's thoughts or attitudes about the matter, and that a true moral judgment is one that affirms a proposition corresponding to such a real state of affairs. This view would be defensible either if naturalism were a cor-

---

3 In Mark Timmons's helpful "Foundationalism and the Structure of Ethical Justification," *Ethics* **97** (1987) 596ff., there seems not to be an account of the meaning of 'justified' beyond enjoying a 'warrant increasing' property. He properly notes that a foundationalism is not committed to a nonnaturalist conception of ethical terms. He later, however (p. 606), speaks of a "foundationalist conception of being justified [as] an account of how one could be justified in believing certain ethical propositions without the justification's deriving from other ethical beliefs." An account of this sort is precisely what I am offering.

rect view about the meaning of moral statements, or if the truth of moral statements could be appraised just by taking thought – both of which views I have suggested are indefensible.

There is, however, another main, but noncognitivist, explanation of 'moral beliefs': a *motivational* one. This view, held roughly by David Hume and J.S. Mill, and widely held today, is that the phrase '*A* is morally wrong' normally *expresses a syndrome* in the mind of the speaker: roughly that he has a non-self-interested aversion to doing things like *A* in the same circumstances (so an aversion to *acts* of *a given type*), that if he infringes one of these he will feel guilt or remorse (or shame), that if he knows someone else has done so he will feel indignation, coolness, or something of the sort toward that person. This explanation needs to be amplified just a bit since, as stated, it sounds a bit as if moral language were mostly a device for condemning persons who *harm* others. But this need not be so: Rashdall thought that incest is disgusting, and Kant thought that masturbation is degrading, and these appraisals were surely unfavorable expressions of their moralities, irrespective of the fact that no harm is claimed to have been done. Again, a person's morality can also be expressed by statements that something was 'morally good,' expressing admiration or gratitude for the agent, in the speaker. So we should not limit a person's 'morality' to attitudes expressed in judgments of condemnation, but recognize, among other things, the opposite attitudes, expressed in judgments in praise. Thus moral statements may express any one of the *whole set of dispositions to favor or disfavor persons(including self) on account of behavior (or attitudes)*. Obviously a person's moral norms, in this sense, are different from his regard for legal obligations or for etiquette, or custom, or prudence.

Can anything be said in appraisal of moral beliefs in this sense?

Well, at least some psychologists, some years back, Karl Duncker[4] and Solomon Asch,[5] affirmed that people's moral beliefs do not differ from one another, so long as we keep fixed the 'meaning' of an act for

---

4 "Ethical Relativity?" *Mind* 1939

5 *Social Psychology* (Englewood Cliffs, NJ: Prentice-Hall. 1952) chs. 11-14

a person. For instance, Duncker affirmed that while charging interest was prohibited in the Middle Ages but is taken for granted today, in the Middle Ages loans were mostly used for personal consumption, whereas today they are mostly used for investment. (One might wonder about credit card purchases!) The thesis is important, for, if it is correct, all *moral disputes* can be resolved by science and conceptual clarity, by ascertaining what is the correct description of some projected action. If that were granted, it would be one step toward showing some sort of objectivity in moral beliefs.

Very much the Duncker-Asch view is defended by some contemporary philosophers, e.g., David Wiggins.[6] Thus Wiggins says we can expect convergence in most moral judgments by "people of a certain culture who have what it takes to understand a certain sort of judgment." Then he says:

> What matters is only that the judgments should represent an answer to a question asked with respect to a given place and time, that that question should have a sense fixed by reference to the historical context and circumstances of that place and time, and that the answer should be better than all competing answers to that question, so understood.

So he seems to think there need not be disagreement among persons who intimately understand a situation being judged about. As for objections from the psychological theory of the learning of moral attitudes, he says these overlook the fact that moral tutoring is itself "a response to something that is simply there (there to be found by anyone, or by anyone who is sufficiently attuned to what bears upon the matter)" and goes on to doubt "whether one can imagine a psychological theorist's dispensing entirely with value properties not just in the case of non-standard reactions but in every case."[7]

It is not easy to be certain whether these theses affirming uniformity are true. But they are difficult to believe. Consider the treatment of animals. In some parts of South America, according to a verbal report

---

6 David Wiggins, *Needs Values, Truth* (Oxford: Blackwell 1992) 162

7 *Ibid.*, 158, 159

from the anthropologist Ralph Linton, a chicken is (was) plucked before it is killed, on the theory this makes for a more succulent dish. Hopi children are notorious for their (permitted by parents) maltreatment of small animals. We need not go so far afield: hunters, trappers, and fishermen among ourselves are not known to be careful to avoid causing pain to those they kill. Most of us will disapprove of all these things. (There seem to be obvious disagreements among members of civilized societies about abortion, euthanasia, and tax policies!)

Moreover, the Duncker/Asch/Wiggins theses are difficult to reconcile with what we know about changes in social moralities, say, when two cultures are in contact – changes which may well take place independently of changes in the view of the actions being appraised. How about the influence of missionaries? Their influence may arise not from their providing a new picture of the behavior being appraised morally, but simply because their appraisals are thought to represent a more civilized way of thinking. The same occurs if some prestigious figure, e.g., a chief, is baptized and accepts Christian values. H.G. Barnett showed that this process is accelerated if some individuals in the recipient group are frustrated and motivated to identify with the dominant group.[8] E.Z. Vogt made a study of the values of Navaho veterans. He found that any tendency to be receptive to white values was influenced by extensive connections with older and more conservative relatives, especially the father, the extent of contact with the white world and its friendliness toward Indians, and the utility of traditional beliefs in resolving psychological problems, e.g., the belief in witchcraft.[9] All these influences seem to be independent of changes in the conception of the acts being appraised.

Is all this consistent with the Duncker-Asch thesis? No: at least largely not: the facts mostly exemplify changes in moral norms, apparently

---

8 "Personal Conflicts and Culture Change," *Social Forces* **20**, 160-71. See also A.M. Padilla, *Acculturation: Theories, Models and some New Findings* (Boulder, CO: Westview Press 1980).

9 "Navaho Veterans: a Study of Changing Values," *Papers of the Peabody Museum* **41** (1951) no. 1

without any (or at least much) change in the conception of the behavior. So the optimistic Duncker-Asch thesis should be abandoned.

Some contemporary moral philosophers, however, think that we can know many moral statements to be true by the kind of argument used to support scientific statements. Nicholas Sturgeon, for instance, thinks that the *wrongness* of children pouring gasoline onto a cat and setting it afire is established essentially in the same way as we establish the existence of electrons. For, he thinks, the assumption of wrongness is essential to the causal explanation of observers of such an act taking it to be wrong, despite the fact that there is an alternative explanation – that the response of the observers was a result of their observations plus their moral attitudes, either native or imbued by parents. (The latter explanation manifestly fits psychological knowledge better.) Sturgeon, however, is not satisfied with this. He says that

> if a particular assumption [here of the wrongness of the act] is completely irrelevant to the explanation of a certain fact [the belief that it is wrong], then the fact [belief of wrongness] would have obtained and we could have explained it as well, even if the assumption had been false.[10]

Thus, if children are burning a cat, if the (assumed) wrongness of this is causally irrelevant to observers' belief that what the children are doing is wrong, then the fact that children are burning the cat, plus the empathy and/or moral attitudes of the observers, cannot explain the beliefs; for that, we have to take into account the act's actual wrongness. Why so? We know enough about the psychology of moral disapproval to see that observation of the treatment of the cat is sufficient to produce the disapproval in most observers. Moreover, it is logically possible that for some reason the treatment of the cat was not wrong – perhaps it was all part of an important experiment, or perhaps the children were so stupid as to be beyond moral criticism. Whether or not this is so is irrelevant to production of the belief. We should not rely on Sturgeon's argument.

---

10   Nicholas Sturgeon, "Moral Explanations," in G. Sayre-McCord, *Essays in Moral Realism* (Cornell University Press, 1988) 245

Some other contemporary writers hold that moral statements can be evaluated for truth very much like scientific statements, in that there is a basis for moral judgments comparable to *observation* in science, in the former our 'spontaneous beliefs' (= moral intuitions) just as in science there is a basis in sensory stimulation.[11] And it is true that there are 'spontaneous moral beliefs.' If we observe a bank official making a sexist denigrating remark to an underling, or observe boys maltreating a cat, there is a rush of angry feeling, culminating in an unfavorable moral judgment. But one must ask exactly how such 'spontaneous moral beliefs' can support an objective moral truth. In science, the observation may be explained by a theory which predicts the observations that have been made, in the circumstances. In the case of moral judgments there could be and is an *explanatory* theory – a psychological theory which might predict the 'observations,' but which in no sense would imply which attitudes are correct.

The most widely held view about how we may proceed from such experiences to *support* a systematic set of moral principles is that we proceed by appeal to 'reflective equilibrium.' We start with these experiences and express the reactions to each in the language of moral judgment ('It is surely *prima facie* wrong to ...'). We then collect such judgments we have made along with ones we might affirm as a reaction to the posing of hypothetical cases. We then attempt to formulate a *system* of principles, *as far as possible* including the whole set of initial judgments, but developed into a coherent set that may exclude some of these, but also include some principles we may have taken from those prevalent in our society, or which we may have learned from parents. This set of principles might turn out to be somewhat abstract – say a loose set of independent principles like the *'prima facie* obligations' advocated by W.D. Ross, or perhaps those found in some form of utilitarianism. It is thought that a set of moral principles arrived at in this way is thereby justified. This way of supporting, or underwriting, moral principles has been convincing to many philosophers. But should it be?

---

11 W.G. Lycan, "Moral Facts and Moral Knowledge," *Southern Journal of Philosophy* **24**, supplement, 86ff.

I suggest, however, that the use of 'reflective equilibrium' to arrive at sound moral principles is at least to be sharply contrasted with the reasoning that goes on in the natural sciences in the formulation of explanatory theories. In science, the argument is provided by an explanatory theory which entails that the observations that are made are ones that are logically bound to be made in the circumstances. In the case of moral judgments an *explanatory* theory would be a psychological theory which predicts the moral attitudes but which in no sense would imply which attitudes are *correct*. Still, the method of reflective equilibrium has been convincing to many philosophers, for all its difference from the type of reasoning that occurs in the natural sciences.

But one is led to wonder if there is no alternative support we can give for normative generalizations, which are equally as serious as reasoning in the natural sciences – one which will recommend them to all thoughtful, rational, and factually informed persons?

One possibility is to show persons that, if they were fully informed, the would *want* a certain sort of moral system to be taught and prevail *in the whole society* in which they expect to live.[12] Such a showing would *recommend* that sort of moral system to rational persons. For, if it is shown that persons, free of misconceptions and fully informed, would *want* a certain kind of moral system for their society, that will surely be a recommendation to them.

But how shall we show people that a certain moral system is the one they would want to be taught and to prevail in their society? Well, we may be able to show that all/most people in fact do have certain desires, and as a result the expectable effects of such a moral system will render it attractive to them, in view of these desires. But which desires?

---

12 Timmons, op. cit., 607ff., suggests that critics of foundationalism have denied that "relevant background theories sufficient for constraining a choice among competing moral systems, can be developed independently of moral considerations." This view he attributes, among others, to Norman Daniels, in his "Moral Theory and the Plasticity of Persons," *Monist* **62** (1979) 265-87, at 273. The points to be presented below are precisely intended as grounds for rejecting the Daniels view.

There is one desire (which, however, we perhaps cannot say is present in everyone as part of human nature) which is especially important: that of empathic/sympathetic altruism, emphasis on which goes back to David Hume and Francis Hutcheson. The conception has recently been developed by the psychologist Martin Hoffman, in a series of articles, primarily on the basis of observation of young children.[13] He uses 'empathy' to refer to an affective reaction, particularly distress, *appropriate* to the situation of another, not just mimicking the emotion the target expresses, facially or otherwise. Why there should be such a disposition is a question. Probably the theory of evolution is the best explanation, since it can explain why a gene stream with this phenotypical expression would be selected, since in early society such a widespread disposition would contribute to the survival of the society. But there is another possibility.[14] This is that small babies cry when in pain, and then by conditioning the sound of a cry (by any other child) comes to be aversive. (Note how adults feel sad when they hear/ see someone cry.) By more conditioning, a representation of the unhappy internal states of another may also become aversive. Whichever the right explanation turns out to be, young children do regularly show sympathetic responses to the ills of others. If this is the fact, then we may expect that a person's preference for a social moral system would be affected by his aversion to others being in distress. Of course, we must recall that not everyone necessarily has such a disposition, much less has it to the same degree. But to the extent it is there we may expect persons to have attitudes favoring a moral system the protection of which extend to animals and future generations. But this need not necessarily be a recommendation of such attitudes in us, if we are without them.

---

13 See his "Development of Prosocial Motivation: Empathy and Guilt," in N. Eisenberg, ed., *The Development of Prosocial Behavior* (New York: Academic Press 1982) 281-313; "Is Altruism Part of Human Nature," *Journal of Personality and Social Psychology* **40** (1981) 121-37; "Empathy and Justice in Society," *Social Science Research* 3 (1989) 283-311

14 See R.B. Brandt, "The Psychology of Benevolence and its Implications for Philosophy," *Journal of Philosophy* **78** (1976) 429-53

According to Martin Hoffman, the most successful form of moral teaching is by 'induction' – a parent showing a child that a certain kind of behavior is likely to be helpful/harmful to others: for example, telling lies, breaking promises, discrimination on the basis of race or sex. So the 'rules' of a child's morality could well be requirements on behavior which result from connecting his sympathetic altruism to various types of action.

Of course, empathy/sympathy does not explain all widespread moral views: the objection to incest, the ideal of chastity, the objection to suicide, the ideal of loving God and remembering the Sabbath day, to keep it holy. So not all moral beliefs can be explained in this way.

Aside from appeals to empathy/sympathy, how can we recommend a social moral system to a person? One thing we can do is draw a parallel with criminal and tort laws. A thoughtful person will presumably want these laws because of the protection they give against forms of injury, taking of property, and so on. People do not want to be assaulted, raped, kidnapped, killed, to have major ambitions frustrated, or to undergo even threats of these. The law protects against these things – and so may a certain kind of morality. So, if people understand this, we can count on their wanting a social moral system which provides these protections.

But will *everyone* want *out of self-interest* a social morality which provides protection against poverty and all the things, like defective education, that tend to go wrong it? This will depend on one's circumstances: wealth, connections, etc. Much more is this a problem in relation to groups a long way off. Must we feel a *self-interested* obligation to help the women of India? It is not clear that the protective morality that everyone will want out of self-interest will reach to these things. It is at this point that a person's empathy/sympathy will play a major role: a moral code one might not want out of self-interest one may well want in view of one's sympathetic altruism. And, if Hoffman is right that this trait is nearly universal, we can count on being able to recommend a humanitarian morality to nearly everyone. But Hoffman may not be right in being so optimistic about this.

These facts about human nature may be viewed as the 'foundation' of a morality, since they will lead human beings to want a certain sort of morality for their society, which fact in its turn will recommend that system to them.

But what kind of morality can be supported by such a foundation? Evidently some kind of humanitarian morality, extended to animals.

So, very possibly, *some* form of utilitarianism, if we define a utilitarian morality as one the main features of which are designed to enhance the good, or well-being, of sentient creatures. (This theory, however, may not lend support to all of the moral commitments of some people, such as the ideal of chastity, or of regular attendance at Christian religious meetings.) But, to be more specific, what kind of utilitarianism would this be? In the first place, it will contain a number of specific requirements or prohibitions, rather like W.D. Ross's list of *prima facie* duties, but much more numerous, rather like commonsense morality. The code cannot consist of just a rule so unspecific as just, always, to do what will likely be most socially beneficial; such a vague commandment would open an invitation to rationalization, and not provide other people with specific expectations about what moral people will do, thereby making rational planning difficult. So, if people generally subscribed only to this principle, business agreements might be quite unstable. Rather, an acceptable form of utilitarianism will contain more specific rules, such as prohibition of dishonest dealing and keeping contracts – since the teaching and prevalence of such motivations would promote well-being in the long run, what the suggested rational moral persons will want. It is true that some prohibitions (like 'Don't lie,' 'Don't injure anyone') may give conflicting directives, and when they do, we may ask what, according to the theory, moral persons are to do. Doubtless ideally the rules should be taught with a specific degree of weight, so that in conflict it would be clear which is strongest. But such fine tuning is probably too much to expect in a motivational moral code. When there is such conflict, it seems moral reflection must go rather like the law, which refers such decisions to judgments of appellate courts, these then deciding which interpretation would be the most socially beneficial precedent, and one that leaves the law an organic whole. So, according to the proposed theory, the individual must *think*: decide which obligation is stronger on the same basis I suggested he can use to justify a moral system as a whole – long-range social benefit, all costs and benefits taken into account, in view of desire for protection and empathy/sympathy. This necessity may be worrisome, since it opens the door to rationalization and defective predictability of what people will do. But we need not worry too much: as Berkeley pointed out long ago, in his (ground-breaking) defense of a kind of 'rule-utilitarianism,' the *basic moral principles* "to right reason evidently appear to have a necessary connection with the Universal well-being."[15] His view was that, at least in the case of the major prohibitions to be taught, it is manifest that their teaching and prevalence will be roughly beneficial to the relevant society, at least as compared with no such teaching – that the society will be much better off if people have interiorized the recommended motivations as compared with having no such standards or different ones, despite some costs of teaching. Only the minor points, such as allowable exceptions in special circumstances, or the relative weight of principles where there is conflict, must be matters of agent-judgment and of some uncertainty. Fortunately, the moral rules which will optimally govern the main business of society will, we may think along with Berkeley, not be controversial, so that, normally, one person can reliably predict what another will do in a certain situation, provided this other person is a moral person. The main rules of morality – not those requiring agent-judgment – will be publicly known, shared by a whole society (or at least a sub-group like physicians). So a main pragmatic criticism (that it makes prediction of behavior difficult) raised against the simple act-utilitarian theory – viz., the theory that a person is obligated always just to do what on his evidence will probably maximize the general well-being – is to a degree applicable to the present *'conscience-utilitarian'* theory, but only to a minor extent. I see no reason why this amount of possible disagreement should be a pragmatic obstacle to the acceptance of the general proposal.

Such a conscience-utilitarian morality will surely permit or even enjoin behavior otherwise prohibited by its rules for normal cases, when omission of such behavior would be disastrously harmful.[16] Presumably an agent will normally abide by the standard optimal rules em-

---

15 George Berkeley, *Passive Obedience* (1712), reprinted in M.W. Calkins, ed., *Berkeley* (New York: Charles Scribners' Sons, 1929) 436

16 J.S. Mill wrote, about a page from the end of chapter 5 of *Utilitarianism*: "Particular cases may occur in which some other social duty is so important as to overrule any one of the general maxims of justice. Thus, to serve a life it may be not only allowable, but a duty, to steal or take by force the necessary food or medicine, or to kidnap and compel to officiate the only qualified medical practitioner."

bedded in his own conscience in many or most cases, and surely not be always looking around for some harm which might justify ignoring these built-in rules of conscience; it is only when the prospect of a loss (or gain) from breach happens to become salient in his consciousness that the general theory will recommend that he reflect on whether the gain/loss in benefit justifies a breach of a normal rule.[17]

But in what sense, then, may we say that something is the 'foundation' of a utilitarian normative view of this sort being 'justified'? Well, I suggested that for a factual belief to be 'justified' is for there to be some reflection or observation, free from factual error or conceptual confusion, to a theory which is the *best explanation* of the basic beliefs and which will *recommend* that belief, as convincing, to every thoughtful and factually informed person. Is there any belief/observation which will so recommend the suggested form of utilitarian morality?

The answer to this, I have suggested, is that all (or nearly all) people do have an empathic/sympathetic altruism about the suffering (or well-being) of other persons, and that they do universally (or nearly so) want the kind of personal protection a utilitarian-type morality (as described) would provide. These facts about them, and their awareness of them, *will suffice to produce approval, for their society, of the described type of utilitarian morality*, and in that sense to 'recommend' it. So these facts about persons, and their awareness of them, may be said to be the 'foundation' of this sort of utilitarian morality. Their approval of a utilitarian morality for their society cannot be said to be a theory which *explains* these wants, and so is unlike the kind of justification that can be given for factual beliefs. The approval of a utilitarian morality for their society is rather the *result* of people's empathetic altruism and of their desire for protection. So far there is a disparity between the kind of 'justification' that can be given for factual beliefs, and the kind of recommendation possible for moral commitments.

---

17 This way of putting matters is due to a personal communication from Sanford Levy.

Might one not equally well say that it is our sensed disposition not to injure other people in any way, or our feeling of guilt/remorse if we do, and our indignation at others we think have done so, that is a kind of 'intuitive' support for such a moral code? These facts are, indeed, our evidence for thinking that we do have a certain kind of morality. But they are not the *foundation* of that morality. They do not explain *why* we have that kind of morality. For this we need to go back a bit, and pay attention to the facts about us – or human nature generally – that are the moving reasons why we have that kind of morality.

This sort of proposal is not a coherentism about morality, since the facts cited are not themselves more *moral* beliefs. They are non-moral facts about us, awareness of which serves to recommend, and hence justify, our moral beliefs. In that sense they are properly said to be the 'foundation' of a morality – and in particular of the specific kind of utilitarian morality proposed.

CANADIAN JOURNAL OF PHILOSOPHY
Supplementary Volume 21

Off on the Wrong Foot

R.M. HARE
Oxford University

1   Professor Foot's Hart Lecture, now published (1995), is largely devoted to an attack on people she calls 'subjectivists' and 'non-cognitivists', among whom she includes myself, although she is so good as to allow me, in a footnote, to reject the *names*. She seems to imply thereby that this is a mere matter of nomenclature or terminology. But in truth her use of these terms makes one suspect that she has not fully understood either the issues or what I have said about them.

It may therefore be useful to explain yet again why I reject these descriptions. I have done so already in a paper to a conference in Moscow which she heard, and to which she kindly refers (Hare 1993a). These explanations would not be important if she were the only person to be confused about this matter; but the confusions are so widespread, even among professional philosophers who should know better, and are so often taught to succeeding generations of students, that it is worth while to make yet another attempt to clear them up – though the confusions are so insidious that I have not much hope that they will ever be eradicated.

2   I will start with the easier term of the two. 'Non-cognitivism' means by etymology the view that moral judgments cannot be known (sc. to be true). It is taken that this is because such judgments cannot *be* true or false. They do not have truth-conditions. Beginner students are often taught that the distinguishing mark of a 'non-cognitivist' is to say this. I have tried to give a clear account of my view on the truth-conditions of moral judgments, which they certainly have, in Hare 1991: 458.

Those who thought that meaning is tied to truth-conditions sometimes said that moral judgments are meaningless; but though the early Ayer (1936) seemed to imply this, even he later (1949) came to see that truth-conditions are only one way of determining meaning, and that moral judgments can have meaning in other ways.

In this later view he was deeply influenced by Stevenson, whose distinction between descriptive and what he called 'emotive' (he should have said 'evaluative' or 'prescriptive') meaning was perhaps the single most important contribution in this century to the understanding of moral language (1945: 62). Foot, though she alludes to this distinction, has not fully grasped it, and that is the main source of her misunderstandings.

Mackie, Blackburn and Gibbard, whom she also mentions, make use of this distinction in other terms; the first, Mackie, thought that moral judgments have truth-conditions but that they are never fulfilled, and the other two that the main element in the meaning of moral judgments does not tie it to truth-conditions. This is not to say that truth-conditions do not come in in other ways. My own view is similar; I expressed it in terms of a distinction between the meaning (in the central sense) of moral words (the evaluative or prescriptive meaning) and the criteria for their application, which I called (following Stevenson) the descriptive meaning. Foot puts the distinction, which she rejects, in terms of one between the grounds of moral judgment and the judgment itself: the mistake which she claims to detect in subjectivism "is the mistake of so construing what is 'special' about moral judgment that the grounds of a moral judgment do not reach all the way to it" (1995: 3).

To explain the distinction more fully: the descriptive meaning is simply the truth-conditions of statements containing moral words, i.e., the criteria for their application. Anybody who acknowledges that they have such truth-conditions obviously cannot be accused of thinking that moral statements are not true or false. So if there are noncognitivists, I am not one of them. Those who think that I am should quote chapter and verse.

However, descriptivist philosophers, as I shall call them, have an over-simple view about the meaning of moral statements: they think that their descriptive meaning is all the meaning that they have. They therefore think that there is a choice between saying that their meaning resides entirely in the truth-conditions, and saying that they have no meaning at all. Faced, as they think, with this choice, it is natural to opt for the more respectable view, namely that their meaning is tied exclusively to truth-conditions (though some rebels like the early Ayer opted for the opposite view that they are 'literally meaningless').

Professor Foot and I came on the scene when the 'emotivists', as they were called, were in fashion. She has changed her views from time to time, though always defending some kind of descriptivism; I can claim to have consistently defended the distinction between meaning and criteria, or between evaluative and descriptive meaning. This enabled me to explain in a more convincing way what was wrong with the emotivists. Their error was not that they (quite rightly) broke with descriptivism, but rather that they had too narrow a view of the alternative possibilities of meaningful utterance, and in particular of the possibilities of *rational* utterance of moral statements. The descriptivists could have learnt from Wittgenstein that there are *different* language games. Some of the latter's disciples still have not learnt this, when they harp on *Investigations* 242 in support of their descriptivism, though it is as clear as can be that Wittgenstein was not a descriptivist in ethics (Hare 1996a).

The point about the truth-conditions of moral statements is not that they do not exist, but that they are relative to cultures (Hare 1993a). All forms of descriptivism are therefore destined to collapse into relativism. To seek to make moral judgments objective by making them descriptive is futile from the start. Objectivity in moral statements, as Kant saw, is attainable only by attention to the *prescriptive* element in the meaning of moral statements, which can be invariant even between cultures with quite different moral opinions (ibid.).

3   I shall be returning shortly to the distinction between evaluative and descriptive meaning and the reasons why Foot thinks she can ignore it. But first I have to explain why 'subjectivism' is a misleading word for my views. The confusions about this word are even more difficult to eradicate, though I have tried more than once (Hare 1976, 1981a[1] 12.1, 216). I must start by noting an ambiguity in Foot's paper.

---

1 Hereinafter referred to as '*MT*'.

In 1995: 3 she uses the expression 'conditions of use'. This could mean 'truth-conditions', i.e., 'conditions whose breach makes a statement false'. Or it could mean 'conditions for the use of a sentence to express the speaker's meaning'. I have complained before about such ambiguities (Hare 1963, in answer to Foot 1961). They are designed to obliterate the distinction between the descriptive and the evaluative or prescriptive meaning of moral words, simply by ignoring the latter.

They thus make it hard to see the difference between 'old-fashioned subjectivism' and non-descriptivism. Descriptivists, forced, as they think, to choose between two kinds of descriptivism to attribute to their opponents, naturally opt for the subjective kind. Although 'old-fashioned subjectivism' has recently received a sophisticated restatement by David Lewis (1989), I was convinced by Ayer (1936) that it would not do, and it has never been my view.

'Old-fashioned subjectivism' is a form of descriptivism. According to this view, the truth-conditions of a moral judgment are that a speaker be motivated in a certain way. It holds, in its simplest form, that if I say, (e.g.) 'You ought to tell her the truth', when I do not approve of telling her the truth, my statement is false.

My own view, like those of Blackburn and Gibbard, is a form of non-descriptivism. It holds that, whatever may be said about the truth-conditions of moral judgments, they do *not* consist in the speaker's having certain motivations. Speaking for myself, the truth-conditions of moral judgments are the grounds on which they are made, and these vary with the mores of those who make them. There is a wide consensus about these between cultures (which is why it is so easy for unthinking philosophers to be descriptivists). But the consensus breaks down just where moral thinking becomes difficult and important.

4   Let us first take some examples which do *not* serve to settle the issue between those who maintain and those who reject the distinction between meaning and criteria. I pass over quickly Foot's favourite examples about "the wrongness of running round trees right handed, or looking at hedgehogs in the light of the moon" (1995: 2). This makes it look as if she still does not distinguish between the view that it would be bizarre (in the absence of special circumstances) to think that such actions are wrong, and the view that it is hard to understand what is being said. What is bizarre is that anybody should actually hold such a view. How could one call a view bizarre before one had understood

what the view was? What is bizarre about it is that there seem to be no conceivable grounds for it. The *meaning* of what is being said is clear. So these examples show, if they show anything, the necessity of distinguishing between meaning and criteria. But perhaps they do not show even that. They certainly do *not* show that these are not moral judgments at all. A crazy moral judgment is still a moral judgment.

Turning to more serious examples, it will not do, either, to produce examples about which everybody agrees, because there are different ways of accounting for the agreement. Descriptivists will say that the agreement stems either from a common moral conviction, which they take as a datum, that a certain action (say that of torturing children for fun) would be wrong (intuitionism), or that the wrongness of certain actions is implicit in the very meaning of the word 'wrong' (naturalism). Their non-descriptivist opponents will hold that the reason for the agreement is that people nearly all have the attitude that such actions are wrong. They no doubt have reasons for this attitude, and what these are may be stated differently in different theories, or even by different individuals. I have my own explanation of the reasons (*MT* pt. 2). But at any rate such examples do not decide the issue between the descriptivists and their opponents.

What will decide it are examples about which people *disagree*; and these are not hard to find. Sometimes it seems that descriptivists simply have not looked for them, being too obsessed with examples where people *agree*, and which they think (wrongly) they can rely on to support their case. People are deeply divided about the wrongness of abortion and euthanasia, for example. Descriptivists (including Foot) have written about these questions; but to shed much light on them requires a deeper understanding of the logic of moral reasoning such as I have tried to achieve, following Kant (Hare 1975a, 1975b, 1989c). The same is true of the issues raised by pacifists (Hare 1985).

But examples of moral disagreement are so easy to find that I will venture a new one. A little time ago, a young American was sentenced in Singapore to receive six strokes of the cane (later reduced to four) for vandalism. Some Americans were horrified; others thought that he got what he deserved. It was clear enough what he had done, and what was to be done to him in retribution. Having been caned on the bare behind at my prep-school (with more strokes, though not, admittedly, by an expert in karate) I find it easy to imagine what he went through.

The disagreement was not about the facts, but about the attitude to be taken to them. The view that the dispute was *really* about the facts is most implausible and suggests that axes are being ground.

Of course arguments about what attitude to take to such punishments will have to go deeply into moral and political philosophy; but at least the facts of the case are clear. What remain are the reasons for the attitudes, and about these there can be argument (I have said a lot about this in other places, e.g., Hare 1989b, esp. ch. 15). But what descriptivists need to show is that, once it is established that he was caned, and for what, there can be no disagreement in people's attitude to these facts. But this is hard to swallow. Foot may answer that facts about human nature and 'Aristotelian necessities' also need to be taken into account; but I find this unconvincing (see next section).

5   I now turn to what Foot has to say positively about how, in spite of being purely descriptive, moral judgments can still be 'action guiding'. She explains this in terms of what she calls "practical rationality" (1995: 3). I am not sure that I have fully understood this expression; but her argument seems to go something like this. She rightly retracts the view that there is only one kind of rationality, namely prudence, or giving *oneself* the maximum probability of desire-fulfilment. I myself put a similar point in another way, by saying that rationality is "a property of thought directed to the answering of questions" and that different questions "demand different properties in thought directed to answering them, if it is to be rational" (*MT* 12.4, 216). We may infer from what Foot says about practical rationality that the questions are practical ones; but there are many kinds of practical questions, some of which are listed on the same page of *MT*. Only some of these are moral questions.

Moral questions, in my view as in Kant's, are one kind (there are others) of universal prescriptive questions. In asking what I ought to do, I am asking what I can rationally prescribe for all cases exactly similar in their universal properties to my own, no matter who occupies what roles in them. 'Rationally' here means "after full consideration of logic and the non-moral facts" (*MT* 12.3, 214, cf. Brandt 1979: 10). Foot's view is not all that different. She relates practical rationality to "reason recognition and reason following" (1995: 6). So far I can agree. The same point can be put in terms either of following good principles or displaying virtues (Hare 1994). The question is, 'What count as good reasons, or good principles, or virtues?' I have my way of answering this question. But what is Foot's? On this she is not at all clear. It is not enough to say that *there are* virtues or good principles; one needs to say how to specify them.

Foot's way of doing this is reminiscent of Geach's, to which I replied long ago. He derived moral principles from the *ratio* of a man, or from his specific good (Geach 1957, cf. Hare 1957). Similarly, Foot thinks that particular species have specific goods. She gives examples: "it is necessary for plants to have water, for birds to build nests, for wolves to hunt in packs, and for lionesses to teach their cubs to kill" (1995: 8). Such "Aristotelian necessities", as she calls them (following Anscombe 1981), "depend on what the particular species of plants and animals need". But humans sometimes also hunt in packs and teach their children to kill, and under natural conditions they need to. How does Foot propose to derive *moral* judgments from these 'Aristotelian necessities'?

My own solution to this problem, like Kant's, draws on the feature of universalizability that moral judgments have, of which Foot has spoken slightingly in the past (1954). The reason why we should refrain from ethnic cleansing, for example, is that we cannot rationally prescribe it universally for when we are in the victims' positions. If some ethologists are right, such prohibitions on massacre are genetically implanted (Singer 1981, Hare 1981b). But notoriously they do not commonly extend beyond the tribe. It may be that, to use Singer's expression, the circle of morality can be expanded to include all humans and even sentient animals. But Foot does not tell us how. It is supposed to be a necessity for the species; but tell that to the Serbs and Croats!

Whether universalizability is a logical requirement for moral judgments, as Kant seems to have thought, or whether, as Blackburn has told me that he thinks, it is simply that people are on the whole open to appeals to human (or Humian) sympathy, is an important question upon which Foot sheds little light. She hardly introduces universalizability at all; but it is surely, whether in the Kantian or the Humian form, crucial to moral reasoning.

6   Hume and Kant, and also Mill, are prescriptivists (see Hare 1996b and especially Mill, *System of Logic*, last chapter). So is Aristotle, though his prescriptivism, like Plato's, is so heavily overlaid by descriptivist elements that descriptivists have not noticed it – they did not want to! Nevertheless, *phronêsis*, the faculty which produces practical precepts,

is called by him *'epitâktikê'*, which *means* 'prescriptive', and the first premisses of his practical syllogisms are all prescriptive, otherwise the syllogisms, which typically conclude in an action, would be invalid (see Hare 1992a, 1996b). Prescriptivism is not something new.

I will end by dealing with some of the people who, it is alleged, can have moral thoughts without any (or at least any moral) motivations. I have described some of these elsewhere, so I can be brief. If they exist, they demand an explanation (different explanations for different kinds of alleged counter-examples to prescriptivism). They include the acratic or weak-willed person (there are many kinds even of these), the amoralist (several kinds of these too), the nihilist, the satanist, and others.

I list the more important types of acratic in Hare 1992a, together with a brief exposition of Aristotle's account of them, which, though it needs careful interpretation and supplementation, is basically correct. It is a thoroughly prescriptivist account. I deal with one kind of amoralist in *MT*, chs. 10 and 11, and with another, alleged by David Brink as an objection to prescriptivism, in Hare 1996a. The nihilist (the person who on principle rejects morality and all moral judgments) and the satanist (the person who, it is claimed, does wrong just because it is wrong), I deal with in Hare 1992b, ch. 6.

Into which of these categories, if any, does Foot's 'shameless' person fall? Shamelessness "can coexist with the use of moral language" (1995: 11), and so can most of the conditions I have listed. For example the amoralist described in Hare *MT*: 10.7, 184 can use moral language to make judgments of moral indifference, and the nihilist can use it in *rejecting* moral judgments. The satanist makes judgments opposite to the approved ones ('Evil, be thou my good'). Shamelessness also "is not the same as insincerity" (ibid.); but nor are any of the above conditions except one rather unimportant kind of acrasia, namely hypocrisy.

Foot quotes the summary of my position in *MT* 1.6: 21:

> We say something prescriptive if and only if, for some act *A*, some situation *S*, and some person *P*, if *P* were to assent (orally) to what we say, and not, in *S*, do *A*, he logically must be assenting insincerely.

She seems to assume that that is all I have to say about the matter, and to ignore all the qualifications and explanations that have to go along with it. Admittedly, I said in the Preface to my first book,

> Almost every paragraph in this book, as in other works of philosophy, requires some qualification; but to supply it on every occasion would be to make my main contentions difficult to grasp. I have therefore tried to adopt throughout as definite a standpoint as possible, in the belief that it is more important that there should be discussion of the points herein raised, than that I should survive it unscathed. (Hare 1952: v)

However, I have supplied since then, over many years, the necessary qualifications (I have cited only the most recent); so it is only fair to draw them to Foot's attention.

We can perhaps see what she is getting at by looking at her examples (1995: 11 ff.). The 'city lout' who goes out hunting and defends it by saying 'If I choose to spend my day out in the countryside doing whatever I feel like, then that's what I'll do' could be any of the people I have listed (most probably an amoralist on the particular question of hunting; see *MT* 10.7: 185).

The Brooklyn politician who claims to be 'standing up day after day, week after week, for what is wrong' could be a satanist, but is more probably someone who finds morality inconvenient and therefore does not treat it as a guide to his actions. This is readily explained in my theory by saying that what he has thrown over is conventional morality (amply allowed for even in Hare 1952). This explanation is greatly assisted by a two-level account of moral thinking such as I have more recently adopted: judgments at the intuitive level are easily combined with action in breach of them, especially for Brooklyn politicians.

Alec D'Urberville is not sufficiently specified by Foot, though he is in Hardy's novel. He said 'I have lived bad, and I shall die bad', meaning what he said, according to Foot, but 'without the slightest intention to reform'. He also could be a satanist, but is more probably rejecting conventional morality. The best thing to say about all these characters is that, as non-philosophers, they have pardonably not thought enough about these distinctions within the class of those who in some sense or other act contrary to morality and do not intend to reform. Philosophers like Foot, however, should attend to them. I agree with her that Thrasymachus, Callicles, Nietzsche and Gide (all of whom are different) are different also from Foot's examples. But it would be superficial to suppose that there are not many different kinds of person who act contrary to the moral judgments that they make.

It would be unfair to expect Foot in a single lecture to consider all the defenses that those whom she calls 'subjectivists' can put up, and indeed have put up. It would be unfair even to ask her to read them all. I have not read all her works, though I have read most of them. The most one can ask is that she should show some understanding of the positions she is attacking.

References*

Anscombe, G.E.M. (1981). *Collected Philosophical Papers* 3. Oxford: Blackwell

Ayer, A.J. (1936). *Language, Truth and Logic.* Gollancz

Ayer, A.J. (1949). "On the Analysis of Moral Judgements", *Horizon* **20**. Repr. in his *Philosophical Essays*. London: Macmillan, 1954

Brandt, R.B. (1979). *A Theory of the Good and the Right*, Oxford University Press

Foot, P.R. (1954). "When is Principle a Moral Principle?", *Ar. Soc.* supp. 28

Foot, P.R. (1961). "Goodness and Choice", *Ar. Soc.* supp. 35

Foot, P.R. (1995). "Does Moral Subjectivism Rest on a Mistake?", *Oxford J. of Legal St.* **15**

Geach, P.T. (1957). "Good and Evil", *Analysis* **17**

Hare, R.M. (1952). *The Language of Morals.* Oxford University Press

Hare, R.M. (1957). "Geach: Good and Evil", *Analysis* **17**. Repr. in Hare 1972

Hare, R.M. (1963). "Descriptivism", *Proc. of Br. Acad.* **49**. Repr. in Hare 1972

Hare, R.M. (1972). *Essays on the Moral Concepts.* London: Macmillan

Hare, R.M. (1975a). "Abortion and the Golden Rule", *Ph. and Pub. Aff.* **4**. Repr. in Hare 1993b

Hare, R.M. (1975b). "Euthanasia: a Christian View", *Philosophic Exchange* **2**. Repr. in 1992b

Hare, R.M. (1976). "Some Confusions about Subjectivity". In Bricke, J., ed., *Freedom and Morality*, Lindley Lectures, U. of Kansas. Repr. in Hare 1989

Hare, R.M. (1981a). *Moral Thinking.* Oxford University Press

---

* Dates after 1995 are conjectural.

Hare, R.M. (1981b). Review of P. Singer, *The Expanding Circle. New Republic*, 7 Feb.

Hare, R.M. (1985). "Philosophy and Practice: Some Issues about War and Peace". In Griffiths, A.P., ed., *Philosophy and Practice*. R. Inst. of Phil. Lectures. Cambridge University Press. Repr. in Hare 1989b

Hare, R.M. (1989a). *Essays in Ethical Theory*. Oxford University Press

Hare, R.M. (1989b). *Essays on Political Morality*. Oxford University Press

Hare, R.M. (1989c). "A Kantian Approach to Abortion", *Social Theory and Practice* **15**. Repr. in 1993b

Hare, R.M. (1991). "Universal Prescriptivism". In Singer, P., *Companion to Ethics*. Oxford: Blackwell

Hare, R.M. (1992a). "Weakness of Will". In Becker, L., ed., *Encyclopedia of Ethics*. Garland

Hare, R.M. (1992b). *Essays on Religion and Education*. Oxford University Press

Hare, R.M. (1993a). "Objective Prescriptions". In Villanueva, E., ed., *Naturalism and Normativity. Philosophical Issues* 4. Ridgeview, CA: Atascadero. Also in Griffiths, A.P. ed., *Ethics* (R. Inst. of Phil. Lectures). Cambridge: Cambridge University Press 1993

Hare, R.M. (1993b). *Essays on Bioethics*. Oxford University Press

Hare, R.M. (1994). *Methods of Bioethics: Some Defective Proposals, Monash Bioethics Review*, **13**. Repr. in Sumner, L.W., and J. Boyle, eds., *Philosophical Perspectives on Bioethics*. Toronto: University of Toronto Press

Hare, R.M. (1996a) "Internalism and Externalism in Ethics", In *Proc. of 18th International Wittgenstein Congress*, Kirchberg, 1994

Hare, R.M. (1996b). "Prescriptivism". In Craig, E., ed., *Encyclopedia of Philosophy*. London: Routledge.

Lewis, D. (1989). "Dispositional Theories of Value". *Ar. Soc.* supp. 63

Singer, P. (1981). *The Expanding Circle*. Oxford University Press

Stevenson, C.L. (1945). *Ethics and Language*. New Haven: Yale University Press

Wittgenstein, L. (1953). *Philosophical Investigations*. Oxford: Blackwell

CANADIAN JOURNAL OF PHILOSOPHY
Supplementary Volume 21

Made in the Shade: Moral Compatibilism and the Aims of Moral Theory

PETER RAILTON
University of Michigan

> The general facts about human needs and abilities are perhaps clear enough and I shall assume that commonsense knowledge suffices for our purposes here.
>
> *John Rawls*[1]

I

Theorizing is a distinctive activity. Within almost any discipline, for example, one finds a recognized distinction between theorists and non-theorists, theoretical work and non-theoretical work. To be sure, the distinction is often a matter of degree. Typically, theorists are identified by their commitment to developing an understanding of their subject matter that possesses certain characteristic features – they aim for generality, comprehensiveness, coherence, well-foundedness, and explanatoriness. They aim to formulate and justify systematic representational systems.

Theorizing is not to be confused with *reflection*, which can be more or less lacking in theoretical ambition. Nor is theorizing to be confused with *criticism*, which can be piecemeal. Theorizing is a form of reflection, and it can be critical, but theories can be vindicatory, even apologetic. One reason often invoked on behalf of the need for theorizing is that the search for generality, coherence, or explanatoriness affords a

---

1 *A Theory of Justice* (Cambridge: Harvard University Press 1971) 425.

critical perspective. In particular, it can help counteract certain kinds of parochialism and provide an alternative to excessive deference to common sense. But common sense itself often is theoretical – stereotypes, for example, embody a good deal of implicit theory. Sometimes genuinely reflective criticism of common sense would do better to resist all-too-eager generalizing tendencies and call instead for greater attention to concrete experience: 'Think concretely about French people you actually know well – is Gilles, or Ariane, or Anne-Marie really like that?' And theorizing has its own ways of being parochial, such as insisting upon the reduction of complex reality to a few privileged categories, forcing the novel onto the procrustean bed of the familiar, or imposing abstract schemes where they don't belong.

Indeed, self-conscious theorizing can be inappropriate or bootless for various reasons. It can be premature – we might have too little evidence to go by or too little background theory to work with, or lots of background theory and too little new evidence. It can be an interference – learning to bicycle will go more smoothly if one does not attempt to articulate to oneself the physics and physiology of what one is doing. It can mislead – too much attention to the theoretical virtues can make one insensitive to phenomena right before one's eyes. It can be pointless – we might have no real need for theory in certain areas, or a subject matter might lack the features that would permit one to formulate interesting generalizations about it.

It should, then, always be a live question whether a given form of self-conscious theorizing is appropriate in a given domain at a given time. Some philosophers believe that theorizing is largely a misbegotten enterprise in moral thought. According to this view, the nature of morality is such that the familiar aims of theorizing are out of place in moral thinking.

Certainly this much can be granted right away: many acts owe their specific value or efficacy to the state of mind with which they are performed, and theorizing can in various circumstances inhibit, distance, distract, or mislead the agent. The unexamined life may not be worth living. But the over-examined life is no bargain, either.[2]

---

2 This quip is attributed to Sidney Morgenbesser.

What is controversial, however, is a much broader claim. Consider the following position:

> Theorizing is *in general* an obstacle to moral understanding, since morality belongs to a domain of practical, not theoretical, understanding. Moral judgments and concepts, if they answer to anything at all, must answer to the condition of agents with aims and interests, agents facing choices about how to live and seeking conditions of mutual cooperation and respect. These are hardly the usual desiderata of theoretical reason. Theorizing has, moreover, a history of promoting gratuitous skepticism about morality. The mere fact that moral thought would be problematic if assessed relative to certain norms of theoretical inquiry could hardly show that moral practice is not well grounded.

Now perhaps one can be forgiven for thinking that this sort of critique of moral theorizing itself sounds suspiciously like a piece of moral theorizing. The critique involves an attempt to formulate coherent, comprehensive generalizations about the nature of morality and the implications thereof. Can we therefore dismiss this genre of criticism as self-defeating, as we watch it kicking away at the very ladder atop which it stands?

That might be too hasty. Let us instead ask whether we might understand such criticism in a less paradoxical way. To do so, we will need to distinguish three different kinds of criticism:[3]

(1) *Deliberative criticisms* concern the appropriate role of theorizing as an activity in a good life – theorizing, one might claim, should occupy only a limited place in a worthwhile or morally decent life;

(2) *Regimentation criticisms* concern the effort to bring to substantive moral judgment certain norms or patterns of thought appropriate to other domains of judgment – norms of comprehensiveness, simplicity, economy, etc. might make perfectly good sense in the theoretical sciences, but be anathema to good moral reasoning;

(3) *Integrative criticisms* concern the demand that the methods and categories of moral thought be held to epistemological or metaphysical standards drawn from outside morality – moral

---

3 These categories are introduced with the hope that they will facilitate exposition. They are not meant to be exhaustive or mutually exclusive.

concepts might not pass various tests we deem appropriate for scientific theorizing, for example, but this could be of no relevance to the credibility of moral assessment.

Moreover, it is important for us to distinguish at the same time at least two different sorts of 'moral theory':

(a) *Normative moral theories*, which purport to systematize substantive moral evaluation by giving a fairly general, coherent set of principles to guide moral evaluation and conduct. The principles need not be monistic in character or few in number. Nor need these principles be set forth as the preferred basis for actual moral deliberation – they might furnish, for example, a theory of objective moral rightness.[4]

(b) *Funding theories for morality*, which purport to give a fairly general, coherent account of what sort of thing morality is, what it presupposes or entails, how it stands in relation to the rest of human activity and inquiry, and what it would need to be in good order. A funding theory can be offered for any domain of human discourse and practice. It attempts to provide an integrated set of answers to questions about the meaning, epistemology, origin, function, and metaphysics of that discourse and practice. Funding theories can be vindicatory – they can show morality to be 'well funded' – or decertifying. Funding theories are not necessarily *foundationalist* theories. By analogy, the 'full faith and credit' of a responsible government or the mutual trust of a community of traders can underwrite a paper currency as well as gold bars. A funding theory for morality could, for example, show it to be a social construction in good working order.[5]

---

4 Quite a variety of normative moral theories seem possible, including pluralistic theories of *prima facie* duties, virtue theories, and so on. What seems to me most distinctive about normative moral *theories*, as opposed to mere collections of normative moral judgments, is not the degree of simplification or the insistence upon something like a decision procedure, but rather the effort to achieve coherence and articulate some sort of structure.

5 It seems to me that the notion of a funding theory is close to T.M. Scanlon's notion of a 'philosophical theory,' as found in his "Contractualism and Utilitari-

These distinctions are rough and incomplete, but they might help us to state more clearly the issues here at stake.

Deliberative criticisms can certainly be made with respect to both normative and funding theorizing. Such theorizing could have a greater or lesser role in a good life, though it is hard to see how one might say in advance what size this role should have. I propose largely to set aside deliberative criticisms in what follows.

Regimentation and integrative criticisms, however, seem to bear rather differently on normative *vs.* funding theories.

Strongly unifying normative theories like utilitarianism have been the favored target of regimentation criticisms. Why should we expect substantive moral thought, which has such diverse historical roots, to be amenable to a powerful systematization in terms of a few basic principles? This is a good question, which may have a good answer. But it is not my ambition to discuss either question or answer here.

Rather, I propose to focus on integrative criticisms, the chief target of which has been, appropriately enough, funding theories.

---

anism," in A. Sen and B. Williams, eds., *Utilitarianism and Beyond* (Cambridge: Cambridge University Press 1982) 106f.

Bernard Williams, in an influential discussion of ethical theory, divides things up differently. On his account: "An ethical theory is a theoretical account of what ethical thought and practice are, which account either implies a general test of the correctness of basic ethical beliefs and principles or else implies that there cannot be such a test." Up to the comma, I would say, Williams could be describing the general aim of a funding theory. After the comma, however, Williams adds a quite special condition, which implies that a funding theory that allowed for a plurality of 'tests of correctness' would *not* (for Williams) constitute an 'ethical theory.' See his *Ethics and the Limits of Philosophy* (Cambridge: Harvard University Press, 1985) 72.

'Funding theory' is a more catholic category than 'metaethics,' at least as the latter term has been understood in recent years. For it need not present its central theses in the form of theories of the *meaning* of moral terms; nor need it carry the assumption that the theories developed will always be analytic, arrived at a priori, or that the theories will be devoid of substantive moral content ('neutral'). If we could remove these associations from the term – for indeed they are no more than associations – then 'metaethics' would serve admirably in place of the cumbersome 'funding theory for morality.'

Finally, a funding theory need not be realist in ambition. Antirealists and irrealists are often at pains to show that their accounts show moral thought and practice to be in good order.

Regimentation criticisms are less relevant to funding theories, which typically do not purport to be *moral* theories at all. Rather, funding theories usually draw heavily upon the philosophy of language and mind, the theory of action, metaphysics and epistemology, the philosophy of social and natural science, and so on, as well as upon substantive theories in psychology, anthropology, history, biology, and other disciplines. Some funding theories indeed are presented as 'morally neutral,' though a funding theory might also reject this label and the dichotomies it appears to assume. Funding theories are, however, quite vulnerable to integrative criticisms since such theories may well be seen as embodying inappropriate presuppositions about the criteria to be brought to bear on the question of what it would require for morality to be in good order.

As we have already noted, the very formulation of integrative criticisms tends to involve the critic in propounding an alternative funding theory. This species of criticism of moral theory therefore is most charitably seen as directed not at the question 'Should we have funding theories?' but rather 'What sorts of funding theories are really appropriate for morality?' Certain funding theories involve claims or criteria that could be seen as compromising the independence or integrity of moral thought. To borrow a phrase from a philosopher who has long been concerned about the imposition of inappropriate notions of 'well-fundedness' upon morality, we might say that some overly integrative approaches to funding theory fail to respect the *autonomy* of moral thought.[6] In effect, these approaches demand that moral norms and categories be made to answer to the norms and categories of nonmoral thought – or face rejection or replacement.

Perhaps the chief active integrative threat to the (purported) autonomy of moral thought is *naturalism*. But it was not always so. Historically, the greatest threat to the autonomy of moral thought came for many centuries from *supernaturalism*. Platonic idealists, rationalist

---

6 See Thomas Nagel, "Ethics as an Autonomous Theoretical Subject," in Gunther Stent, ed., *Morality as a Biological Phenomenon* (Berkeley: University of California Press 1978). I do not claim to be explicating Nagel's view, but I hope that he would find he has some sympathies with the 'autonomist' position represented herein.

metaphysicians, and theists each held in their distinctive way that a special sort of inquiry independent of the vagaries of moral experience could yield knowledge of truths that dictated the substance of morality. Indeed, such non-moral inquiry was held to be capable in principle of correcting ordinary moral thought. No piece of ordinary moral experience or reasoning could hold its ground against the Eternal Forms, Natural Law, or Divine Plan.

Times change, and in dominant intellectual circles we hear much less of the Forms, Laws of Reason, or God. Ethics has emerged, albeit late, from the shadows of idealism, rationalism, and theology. Yet even as ethics began to come out into its own, another shadow fell across it. Like so much else in our culture, ethics found itself in the shade of the Scientific World View. Meyerson wrote, "L'ontologie fait corps avec la science elle-même et ne peut en être séparée." There is no place, it was claimed, for theories of *what exists* that stand on grounds or deploy methods autonomous from the course of empirical theorizing and experimentation. In an increasingly naturalistic intellectual climate, can we avoid saying the same thing concerning theories of *what ought to be* – that 'L'éthique fait corps avec la science elle-même'?

The ethical autonomist wants to resist the hegemony of science and to revindicate distinctively moral forms of experience and reasoning. On a view of this kind, imposing upon ethics – or upon the domain of practical reason in general – notions of theory construction and norms of theory choice derived from the domain of science would be as unwarranted, in its own way, as imposing moral norms upon scientific theory choice. Consider a principal investigator who drew his research group together to say 'Yes, I realize that the epidemiological evidence and clinical results support the hypothesis of a substantial genetic contribution to this disease, but we must reject any such conclusion as morally unacceptable.' We would say that this individual, however humane his aspiration, had stopped doing science. Moreover, we would withhold from him more than the label 'scientist.' In contemporary intellectual life scientific conclusions are attributed a certain epistemic authority – a standing or role in our deliberations about what to think and what to do. Were we to become convinced that a well-known researcher had begun deciding among competing hypotheses on moral or political rather than evidential grounds, we would no longer accord his conclusions that epistemic authority.

Similarly, the argument runs, if we reverse the situation. Suppose someone were to impose upon moral reasoning a norm drawn from theory choice in the empirical sciences. For example, consider the norm that purported moral properties must be either (1) strictly reducible to properties figuring in our best going scientific theories, or (2) capable of earning a place in their own right in such theories in virtue of contributing to the best scientific explanation of experience. How much moral authority would we accord this person if he reasoned as follows:

> I realize that I have failed to do what I sincerely promised you I would do. As a result, I have indeed caused you pain and disappointment. But you cannot complain that I have violated any moral obligation. For I have recently studied the matter in depth and can say with assurance that the category "*x* is a duty to keep one's promises" does not figure in the best explanatory theories of human behavior.

The case for the autonomy of moral thought is striking. Is it in the end compelling?

II

We might begin by asking what naturalism is. Unsurprisingly, there is no single answer. One can, however, distinguish at least two predominant forms of contemporary naturalism, which are often found together and which are both relevant to our concerns here.

The first form is *methodological*. Roughly, it involves a commitment to employing the norms and methods of inquiry characteristic of the developed empirical sciences. Such a commitment might be local or global – one might adopt a methodologically naturalistic stance with regard to a given domain of inquiry, or inquiry in general. It is a matter of controversy, of course, just what the methods of empirical science are, or for that matter just what the empirical sciences themselves are. For example, does empirical science in general employ an abductive ('inference to the best explanation') method? Does mathematical reasoning, given its extensive role in empirical science, have appropriate naturalistic standing in its own right? And so on. Some bold methodological naturalists about *ethics* have asserted that moral reasoning is already a serious part of empirical reasoning about history and society. Others have argued that we cannot take *sui generis* 'moral explanations' for granted, and that a naturalistic approach must scrutinize moral thought without presupposing it.

The second form of naturalism is *substantive*. Here naturalism is a doctrine about the appropriate interpretation of language, or the nature of properties, entities, or concepts. Once again, this doctrine can be either local or global. One might be a substantive naturalist about epistemic properties, mathematical entities, mental concepts, and so on, without global ambitions. Or one might claim that *all* actually instantiated properties are natural properties (even if one does not claim that all concepts are natural concepts). And so on. Once again, there is controversy. When is a property a natural one? Or a concept? Most attempts to answer involve gesturing at going empirical theories or causal/explanatory paradigms. Substantive naturalism might be developed and defended along methodologically naturalistic lines, or it might not. A philosopher could argue on analytic a priori grounds that the meaning of moral terms is naturalistic, e.g., that this meaning essentially involves a notion of 'proper function' belonging to a (supposedly) biological theory of human nature. And methodological naturalism need not lead to substantive naturalism – the best explanatory theory of moral discourse might require interpreting moral language as nonfactual.

The autonomy of morality might be seen as threatened by either methodological or substantive naturalism, and defense of the autonomy of morality thus has itself taken on both substantive and methodological aspects. G.E. Moore, defending morality against the integrative threat of Spencer's evolutionism, attempted to give a demonstration that moral concepts are non-natural and irreducible.[7] C.L. Stevenson, defending morality against the integrative threat of Dewey's all-purpose invocation of science, argued that moral questions were in part distinguished by the fact that they cannot themselves be resolved by scientific methods.[8]

---

7 See G.E. Moore, *Principia Ethica* (Cambridge: Cambridge University Press 1903).

8 Stevenson went on to give a substantive explanation of this claim about the limits of scientific method: the non-cognitive character of moral judgments. See C.L. Stevenson, "The Emotive Meaning of Ethical Terms," *Mind* **46** (1937) 14-31, esp. 16-17.

The autonomist's integrative criticism might thus be put as follows:

> What's wrong with naturalistic approaches to ethics is not they seek to develop and assess a funding theory for morality. Anyone who would take morality seriously in a philosophical context owes us an account of what sort of thing morality is, how it is connected with other human endeavors, what moral judgments mean or how they function linguistically, how such judgments are made or justified, and so on. This account should enable us to pose questions about whether moral discourse and practice are in good order. Naturalists typically go wrong on the next step, when they adopt a scientistic conception of what a funding theory must be or do.

The autonomist's criticism of naturalistic approaches to morality must be distinguished from many other criticisms of 'moral theory.' For example, a frequently voiced criticism of moral theory is that it is acontextual, insensitive to the social, cultural, or historical contexts within which moral norms exist. Yet naturalistic funding theories often are seen as committing the opposite error – they too often are *all* context, focusing on social, psychological, or even biological origins, replacing evaluation with explanation, never really reaching the core of moral reasoning. Critics argue that nothing they have seen by way of naturalistic explanation of morality constitutes for them a greater source of moral insight, confidence, or reasonableness than ethical discourse itself.

This effective irrelevance to the real questions and challenges of moral practice can be traced, critics believe, to the naturalist's false picture of moral thought and its potential objectivity. In this picture, moral thought is an attempt – like empirical science and mathematics or, in earlier centuries, theology or rationalist metaphysics – to represent a reality that underlies experience, a reality of which experience is at best an appearance and practice at best a reflection. But morality should be seen, critics argue, as practical rather than representational. Its notion of objectivity is the notion of what it is reasonable for agents to agree to, or to accept as normative in deliberation about action. This is not an idea of representational accuracy or empirical adequacy.

Critics often argue that moral practice is already in working order and does not need further epistemic or metaphysical underpinning. This is not, however, tantamount to denying the critical aspects of ethical thought or insisting that all moral experience be taken at face value.

Indeed, ordinary moral experience is full of contestation and questioning. But true criticism in ethics, in the eyes of these critics, takes place within a living moral practice. Within such a practice one can formulate questions about what reasons we have for acting, or for encouraging certain traits of character, or for defending or changing our institutions, and so on. These are irreducibly normative questions, searching for moral reasons, and responsive to distinctively moral – not scientific – norms of justification.

III

Let us therefore try working from within. That is, let us ask what an autonomous approach to the question of funding morality might look like. We might begin by asking what sort of picture we should have of the nature and grounds of moral judgment. We already have part of the answer. It would *not* be a form of rationalist intuition, or divine revelation, or scientific psychology. Its proper domain is the realm of moral practice and experience.

Moral experience might be viewed as akin to perceptual experience. In many familiar cases we do say, quite credibly, that we 'see' or 'feel' what is right or wrong. Coming upon a gang of boys lighting a cat afire, Harman argued, one can see that this is wrong.[9] However, we would be well advised not to make excessive demands upon the perceptual analogy. Too much of moral thought and practice seems not to fit the picture of a species of judgment guided by a distinctive phenomenology.

For example, suppose we come across a gang of men in khaki dress, shooting repeatedly and effectively from a moving jeep into a large herd of deer. The deer are terrified and dart about in panic. Wounded deer stumble and groan. Fawns, unable to find their mothers, stand frozen with fear. And still the guns blaze away. Is this wrong? Surely the phenomenology of our experience is of a quality comparable to our experience of the immolated cat. But perhaps what we are wit-

---

9 Gilbert Harman, *The Nature of Morality* (New York: Oxford University Press 1977) ch. 1.

nessing is a desperate effort on the part of a group of park rangers to reduce a deer population that otherwise faces certain starvation in the coming weeks of winter. Among the deer we see are many infected with a disease that will surely spread through the weakened herd as winter sets in, and federal budget cuts have made unaffordable any more humane form of killing. Are the rangers acting wrongly? More importantly for our purposes, does *perception* guide our search for an answer among the multiplicity of factors we believe we must consider?

Contrast a housepainter seeking to balance a range of factors in touching up the paint on the old courthouse. He must worry about color, about perceived surface reflectance and texture, about the changing light as the angle of the sun, or the cloud cover, varies, and so on. His all-things-considered judgment arises from careful attention to what he sees when combining paint and pigments to retouch the wall. And he knows – and we know – when he's gotten it right by 'seeing how it looks.' This is perceptually guided judgment *par excellence*. Here seeing *is* believing. But is there any comparable, distinctive phenomenology which guides our all-things-considered deliberation about whether the park rangers' horrifying act is indeed morally best? Is there a distinctive phenomenology that would serve to induce moral agreement amongst us?

If moral judgment does not follow in the train of a distinctive phenomenology, what does guide it? A suggestion that seems truer to moral practice is the process of 'reflective equilibrium.' We think about the particular case at hand, about similar kinds of cases, about general principles that would either fit or exclude the particular cases, about how people we admire would conduct themselves, about antecedents and precedents, and so on. Our verdicts about particular cases emerge from this evolving equilibrium, as we seek a balance that tends to minimize tensions and maximize coherence within our moral world. Although some principles are much more central than others, and some verdicts much more resistant to revision, very little seems to be entirely imperturbable within that moral world. We remain aware that considerations not thought of might lead us to revise our opinions.[10]

---

10 The classic discussion of reflective equilibrium is to be found in John Rawls, *A Theory of Justice*, esp. secs. 9 and 87.

This method of carrying on moral deliberation has become known as *narrow* reflective equilibrium because it operates within the sphere of morality. Following this method, individually or collectively, is a matter of equilibrating particular judgments of acts and actors with the principles that constitute our moral commitments. It thus appears to be fully respectful of the autonomy of moral reasoning.

Let us, however, look a bit closer at the sorts of principles that would figure in the evolution of narrow reflective equilibria. Some would be substantive moral principles such as 'Avoid harm to innocents' and 'Don't punish merely for retribution.' But some of the principles would be (what might be called) meta-principles: 'Treat like cases alike,' or '"Ought" implies "can".' Meta-principles, either implicit or explicit, play a central role in shaping ordinary moral deliberation. We rely upon 'Treat like cases alike' when we test our initial judgment of a case by casting our mind over relevantly similar cases and ask how we would judge them. We rely upon '"Ought" implies "can"' when we ask whether someone was in a state or circumstance that would excuse his apparent misconduct.

Indeed, these two meta-principles – whose proper formulation and interpretation are by no means simple matters – have been seen by some philosophers as *partially constitutive* of moral reasoning. We cannot respect the autonomy of moral thought without respecting them as well. Nevertheless, these principles work from *within* moral reasoning to enlarge its scope, its evidence, and its methods beyond the distinctively moral. What began as narrow reflective equilibrium becomes, by its own logic, *broad* reflective equilibrium.[11]

To be sure, questions about whether two cases are alike, for example, are hardly devoid of normative content. The similarity at issue is not exact similarity – no two cases are exactly similar – but morally

---

11 For an influential early discussion of the distinction between narrow and broad (what he calls 'wide') reflective equilibrium, see Norman Daniels, "Wide Reflective Equilibrium and Theory Acceptance in Ethics," *Journal of Philosophy* **76** (1979) 256-82.

relevant similarity. Likewise, what an agent can do is not, in this context, a mere question of physical capability at the moment. Rather, it depends upon what an agent might non-negligently have done in the past and might reasonably be expected to do in the future. Still, despite their normative content, these questions cannot be answered without venturing well beyond a narrow reflective equilibrium confined to the normative sphere.

Perhaps no defender of the autonomy of morals ever wanted to say that empirical reasoning beyond the bounds of moral norms is strictly irrelevant to moral thought. The autonomist might, however, insist that if naturalism is to be an interesting thesis it must involve something more than peripheral non-moral 'inputs' to moral thought and take us to the heart of moral reasoning itself.

IV

One way or another, it seems, any naturalist who wishes to defend the idea that ethical inquiry is continuous with empirical, theoretical inquiry in general will have to confront the seemingly absurd idea that moral reasoning or categories are appropriately constrained by the sorts of causal/explanatory norms characteristic of contemporary science. This is not to say that the naturalist must view these as the *only* relevant norms, sufficient unto themselves for conducting moral inquiry. Many with naturalistic leanings would argue, for example, that social-scientific inquiry is governed by an interpretive norm such as the 'principle of charity' while the physical sciences are not – we need not seek 'rationalizing' explanations of the behavior of electrons. Yet as the history of this very example shows, the question whether these other norms can even be *reconciled* with causal/explanatory norms – or demand instead the adoption of essentially distinct 'perspectives' – is no simple one.

To revert to an earlier example, it seems obviously beside the point in the moral case to invoke issues about the explanatory value of the notion of obligation in assessing what we ought to do. Moral norms do not seem to be causally relevant in their own right, nor do those features of agents or social relations that we do take to be explanatorily relevant – e.g., aggression, inclusive fitness, *ressentiment*, etc. – thereby earn any positive moral standing.[12]

But perhaps all this is not so obvious. Let us consider another example.

For a considerable time, it has been said, Anglo-American ethics has focused almost exclusively on duty. A number of moral philosophers have challenged this emphasis, and concluded that it is high time virtue be accorded a more significant place in moral thought and practice. Partly as a result, 'virtue ethics' is undergoing a considerable revival in both academic and popular moral thought.[13]

The case for virtue has been put forward primarily on grounds that would appear to belong to autonomous moral theorizing. For example, character has been seen as an important dimension of moral understanding and action, reflecting the constitutive role of motivation and perception in shaping conduct we find admirable. But note that if virtues are to play such a role they must be more than explanatorily inert ideals. For to possess a virtue is *inter alia* to possess a relatively stable, indwelling trait of character that shapes perception in systematic ways and that leads a person to act in a similar, distinctive manner across a variety of contexts. Thus, a courageous person would display vigor and coolness in response to a range of different kinds and contexts of risk, not only in situations which are so familiar as to be routine, but also in novel or especially demanding conditions. Likewise, an honest person would eschew deception or theft in a very wide range of circumstances, and especially those in which context imposes certain pressures and temptations. Virtues thus are thought to provide a basis for predictability, for attachment and loyalty, and for sociability and mutual trust. Moreover, it is generally thought that virtues can be acquired or at least reinforced by appropriate kinds of moral education and the

---

12 This point is made by David Copp, "Explanation and Justification in Ethics," *Ethics* **100** (1990) 237-58.

13 On the academic side, see the special issue, "Ethical Theory: Character and Virtue," of *Midwest Studies in Philosophy* **13** (1988) and also Michael Slote, *From Morality to Virtue* (Oxford: Oxford University Press 1992).

experience of living in the right sorts of moral community. When present, virtues are held to be motivationally effective in more than a dutiful sense: a virtuous person has an inner strength leading to stability and resilience in conduct, and finds a kind of satisfaction in good or right action that the merely dutiful typically does not.

It is noteworthy that virtue ethics are being advocated partly in the name of giving greater importance to the 'moral psychology' of the agent than duty-based ethics afforded. Of course, moral psychology need not be 'merely psychological' – talk of virtue is not usually supposed to be reducible to purely psychological terms. But the virtues would not be able to do their job if they did not possess or engage an interconnected set of causal powers. These powers would help explain why the virtuous act, or see things, as they do.

In consequence, virtue theory – however attractive it might be evaluatively – is empirically vulnerable. Recent work in cognitive psychology concerning traits of character has challenged the folk idea that individuals possess relatively stable, indwelling traits that yield constancy in behavior across a wide variety of contexts.[14] Except for a few dimensions of 'personality,' circumstance and context seem to be more predictive of behavior than imputed character – cross-situational correlations are often on the order of only .1 or .2, not impressively greater than chance. Although virtually all results in psychology are deservedly controversial, what is important for present purposes is that there is a lively empirical debate on this question whose outcome is far from certain.

How might commonsense moral reasoning contend with these new theories of personality? Their claims do not obviously equilibrate with our moral experience, for to many of us it seems evident that people possess a rich array of character traits which explain a great deal about their conduct. There is, however, an alternative explanation of this moral experience that also enjoys substantial empirical support and there-

---

14 See the discussion of the classic experiments of Newcombe on extroversion and Hartshorne and May on honesty, as well as the more recent controversy over Mischel's claims about cross-situational consistency, found in L. Ross and R. Nisbett, *The Person and the Situation* (Philadelphia: Temple University Press 1991) ch. 4.

fore should enter our broad reflective equilibrium. Considerable evidence has been assembled in recent decades to suggest that trait-attributing beliefs of this kind are often the result of reliance on certain implicit folk theories and cognitive strategies that render us ready in general – for people, animals, substances, etc. – to impute stable, ind-welling traits on the basis of very little evidence, and that also render us very resistant to disconfirming evidence when it arrives. We quickly form an impression of the 'nature' of a person, an animal, a substance, an institution, a nationality, a 'race,' etc., based upon very few remarks or observations. And once we have formed such notions, we tend to follow a highly conservative cognitive strategy in which positive in-stances are treated as confirmatory and negative evidence is explained away or even unnoticed as such. Stereotypes, for example, can cross long evidential deserts without losing any of their force. If they then stumble across a case that fits (or that can be seen as fitting), they find themselves strikingly confirmed.[15] Moreover, our encounters with many individuals take place within highly structured, fairly stable environ-ments – classrooms, workplaces, regular meetings, self-selected activi-ties, etc. This may induce constancies in what we perceive of their behavior, constancies we tend to attribute to the 'personality' of the individual as such, without much by way of controlling experiences on our part.

In short, inferential strategies, implicit theories, and environmental constancies offer a non-vindicatory explanation of why it seems to us so evident a feature of experience that people possess definite traits of char-acter. We need not accept this explanation in part or in full to see the force of the example: a central moral notion, virtue, has sufficient causal/ex-planatory content that broad reflective equilibrium with going empirical theories might require *systematic* revision of our sense of its relevance or importance – however attractive we might initially find this notion.

---

15 For discussion of the 'representativeness heuristic,' the 'fundamental attribution error,' and the asymmetries between positive and negative evidence, see R. Nisbett and L. Ross, *Human Inference: Strategies and Shortcomings of Social Judgment* (Englewood Cliffs: Prentice-Hall 1980).

In an earlier example, it seemed silly when someone attempted to deny the existence of a moral obligation to keep a promise because the property 'being a duty' would not figure in a good explanatory psychological theory. Yet in the present context it seems quite appropriate to challenge the tenability of virtue ethics on causal-explanatory grounds. It is crucial to virtue theory that the virtuous individual's action can be explained by appeal to her virtues, character traits that purportedly produce constancies of behavior across a wide range of contexts. This is not a privileged or idiosyncratic 'moral' sense of explanation. Rather, it is one of the most familiar everyday schemata used to explain action.

Doubtless, there is a further element to add to our reflective equilibrium: one would be ill-advised to assign too much weight to the latest psychological theory. Such theories are usually the subject of intense dispute even within psychology, and last decade's received wisdom is often this decade's favorite example of how otherwise intelligent people can be led astray by a one-sided approach or a tendentious interpretation of experimental evidence.

Moreover, one might respond, virtue is highly singular as a moral notion precisely because of its causal/explanatory content. From this perspective, it is no accident that those defending the possibility of informative 'moral explanations' have often appealed to examples involving virtues and vices.[16] But what of other central moral categories? What explanatory ambition is embodied in talk of *duty* or *obligation*, say?

Here we have come by an indirect route upon a long-standing debate. The classical notion of duty was founded upon the possibility of a special sort of *rational motivation* independent of appetite, desire, or inclination. In its most impressive forms, the classical notion of duty was allied to a conception of moral freedom that entailed a complete autonomy of the will of the agent relative to the causal order. So concerned was Kant, for example, to secure such autonomy for the will, and so aware was he of the anomalousness of any such idea with regard to the causal universe as described by natural science, that he

---

16 See for example Nicholas Sturgeon's well-known discussion of Hitler and of Passed Midshipman Woodworth in his "Moral Explanations," in David Copp and David Zimmerman, eds., *Morality, Reason, and Truth* (Totowa, NJ: Rowman and Allanheld 1985).

devised an ambitious scheme involving both noumenal and phenomenal worlds. The seriousness with which Kant took the enterprise of reconciling the causal and the moral is visible not only in his writings on morality, but in his philosophy of history as well.

It is important to emphasize that Kant defended his view of action from duty precisely in order to capture (what he took to be) commonsense moral notions and to show what things would have to be like in order for these notions to be borne out. Moreover, one can represent Kant's strategy as a form of broad reflective equilibrium in which certain intuitive judgments concerning morality and agency have been given very great weight owing to the conviction they carry for us. Noumenal agency is postulated as a way of accommodating these intuitive judgments without repudiating scientific thought about human behavior and the empirical world. The result, however, is not the juxtaposition of a non-explanatory, 'subjective' moralizing scheme alongside an explanatory, 'objective' scientific one. On the contrary, part of the genius of Kant's philosophical imagination is that he sought thoroughly to rearrange the terms of this dichotomy. It is the noumenal world that embodies things as they are in themselves, and the phenomenal world – the world of scientific inquiry, among other things – that embodies things as they are for us. Scientific explanation, which can be seen as an epistemic enterprise structured around notions such as causation, has its place in the phenomenal world. But the noumenal world is not for that reason explanatorily irrelevant to human conduct. When we act in accord with duty and against inclination, this may resist a *causal* understanding, but it is not therefore without explanatory grounding. The grounding is to be found in the autonomy of the noumenal agent.[17]

---

17 Not all explanations are causal. Rationalists in general need to avail themselves of a notion of explanation in which a non-causal, underlying rational order can explain the realm of (causal) appearances. (Compare here Leibniz's notion of 'well-founded phenomena.') But rationalism aside, even in contemporary natural science, many explanations are not evidently causal in nature – e.g., explanation by reduction, by reference to the structure of space-time, by 'least energy' principles, and so on. Recent formulations of the doctrine of 'inference to the best explanation,' it should also be noted, do not assume that all explanations are causal. Mathematical explanations, for example, need not be. See G. Harman, "The Inference to the Best Explanation," *The Philosophical Review* **74** (1965) 88-95.

Kant in effect gives a funding theory for the morality of duty. His way of reconciling the notion of action from duty with a naturalistic psychology strikes most of us, however, as an expensive one. It requires the pure postulation of an entire (and admittedly opaque) order of reality. Modern Kantians by and large have not found the notion of noumenal agency congenial. Instead, they accept the idea that we have to make do with one world. This is no doubt a sensible response, but it does disturb the reflective equilibrium Kant constructs. Whether equilibrium can be restored depends upon whether the modern Kantian wishes to retain the notion of duty as action independent of inclination, and whether, if so, he or she is able to provide an alternative account of agency that both renders it intelligible and exhibits its compatibility with empirical psychology.

Thus the modern Kantian, just as much as the modern Humean, must shoulder a *compatibilist* burden. Kantian agency may be in part a normative notion, as some have claimed, but it also is an essentially explanatory one – for we must be able to distinguish between keeping a promise from duty and keeping a promise from inclination or inadvertence (even while intending to do one's duty). If this sort of explanatory difference is not itself causal, then it must nonetheless be such as to be realizable by a being who is (among other things) a causal being situated in a causal world.

Return to the fellow who denies he has violated his duty in breaking his word. If it were impossible to give a credible account of how action from duty could be accomplished by empirical human beings, then the situation that before seemed absurd has come to pass. He may well be doing something worthy of moral condemnation, but not on account of failing to act from duty. Here, of course, we encounter a set of concerns familiar from the controversy over 'hard determinism' *vs.* compatibilism. Those of us who reject incompatibilism about duty do so, I suspect, chiefly because we believe that there are worthwhile conceptions of duty that do not require a model of action fundamentally incompatible with seeing ourselves as part of the natural universe. However involved certain historical notions of duty might be with conceptions of agency as transcending or potentially contravening empirical causation, our workaday notion of duty can survive without such aspirations. But certainly the alternative position that it cannot do so, and that there thus is a fundamental problem for understanding ourselves as moral agents which no compatibilist account has successfully addressed, is not unintelligible. This suggests two points of special interest in the current discussion.

First, it suggests that the interlacing of central moral categories – not only virtue, but duty as well – with the explanation of action is sufficiently tight that we cannot view the introduction of explanatory norms of reasoning into moral thought or the request to relate moral categories to our going causal/explanatory framework as a mere intrusion.

Second, it suggests a general scheme for thinking about how moral thought might stand in relation to the naturalistic point of view. Crudely put, we face these possibilities: (1) protecting moral thought against the possibility of radical revision by simply rejecting the naturalistic point of view and the scientific account of the world that goes with it – moral conviction is conviction enough, on this view, and if empirical theory threatens to undermine it, then we must see this as counting against the credibility of empirical theory rather than against the tenability of morality; (2) working toward a funding theory of morality that would enable us to see the compatibility of our moral categories and assumptions with going empirical theory; and (3) rejecting various moral categories and assumptions owing to their incompatibility with a naturalistic point of view. The first position has few adherents in contemporary philosophy, but is not unknown in popular culture – witness the creationism debate. The third has become a recognized philosophical position under the name given it by J.L. Mackie, 'error theory.' The second is most familiar philosophically in the context of the free-will debate, but the term 'compatibilism' deserves wider use, quite apart from questions about a supposedly deterministic causal order.

It is important to emphasize that the relevance of a naturalistic perspective to the applicability of moral categories or norms does not turn on the question of the *reduction* of moral thought. Even so stalwart a non-naturalist as Moore realized that the *supervenience* of moral properties upon natural properties brought an inevitable commitment to seeing the morality as such that the natural world could support it. Moral assessment, virtually everyone concedes, supervenes upon the natural world in the following sense: two situations can differ in their moral qualities just in case they also differ in some natural qualities.[18] For some, this is a metaphysical claim: the distribution of natural properties fixes the distribution of moral properties. For others, the principle of supervenience is non-metaphysical and carries no presupposition of the existence of moral properties. Instead, it is viewed as a normative constraint on moral judgment: if one judges two situations to be morally distinct, one is committed to judging them to be different as well in their (non-indexical) natural properties. Somewhat more strongly, one is committed to explaining or justifying this moral difference in terms of (non-indexical) natural differences.

Metaphysical or normative as the supervenience of the moral might be, a question to ask is 'Why should there be this constraint?' It is often said that one would not understand the nature of moral judgment if one did not recognize supervenience. The idea that two situations cannot differ *solely* in their moral character, distinguishes moral from (say) supernatural or magical qualities or judgments. Moral features cannot simply be added to the other, non-moral features of a situation. Instead, they somehow depend upon them. But how might we explain this?

The moral noncognitivist offers an explanation: there are no moral properties, so *a fortiori* no self-subsistent moral properties. To understand morality is to understand that moral judgment expresses a human *response* of a distinctive sort to the world, not the discovery of a special, additional set of worldly features. This explanation is, however, incomplete, for it does not yet account for the peculiar discipline that normative supervenience imposes on our responses. Some of our responses to the world vary *ad lib* (e.g., in matters of likes and dislikes), and we do not take this to be ground for second-guessing them. ('But you liked it last time ... ! Oh well, there's no accounting for taste.') Moral responses are not allowed this freedom. Rather, they are held accountable to the facts – specifically, to a certain kind of consistency patterned upon sameness of fact. One avenue of explanation would be to observe that morality is social, serving to mediate social relations,

---

18 There are, of course, many versions of supervenience. It is widely held that the supervenience of the moral upon the natural is (what has been called) *strong* supervenience.

encourage cooperation and collective action, etc. It therefore must be attached to what can be agreed upon across differences in the normative stance of individuals, groups, or ideologies. This would yield something like supervenience.

It does not, however, lead us to a *natural* basis for supervenience. That is, so long as the subjacent basis can serve the role of mediating conflict, it seems irrelevant what this basis might be. Why not simply the most uncontroversial phenomena in the social world? What makes the natural causal order salient in moral dispute – despite persistent controversy over its nature – is what G.E. Moore observed when he first brought supervenience explicitly to the attention of the philosophical world:

> It is true, indeed, that I should never have thought of suggesting that goodness was "non-natural," unless I had supposed that it was "derivative" in the sense that, whenever a thing is good (in the sense in question) its goodness (in Mr. Broad's words) "depends on the presence of certain non-ethical characteristics" possessed by the thing in question: I have always supposed that it did so "depend," in the sense that, if a thing is good (in my sense), then that it is so *follows* from the fact that it possesses certain natural intrinsic properties, which are such that from the fact that it is good it does *not* follow conversely that it has those properties.[19]

The thought then is this: even if judgments of moral value do not function semantically simply to *report* some natural state of affairs, they nonetheless have an intimate relation to such states of affairs – moral qualities are *constituted by* or *grounded in* natural qualities. They do not merely correlate or harmonize with them. If moral judgment is ever in place, it is in place because the world (apart from moral opinion) is such as to make it so. But then questions about the way the world is, questions about what explains what, questions about what constitutes what – in short, questions raised by the development of empirical inquiry – can reach to the heart of morality.

---

19 G.E. Moore, "A Reply to My Critics," in P.A. Schilpp, ed., *The Philosophy of G.E. Moore*, vol. 2 (La Salle, IL: Open Court 1942) 588.

This talk of constitution, echoing Moore's account of the relation of the moral to the non-moral, is in fact stronger than supervenience alone. Supervenience can be reciprocal. For example, if fixing the world's A properties would settle its B properties, it is also possible that fixing the world's B properties would settle the A's. 'A iff B' could be a necessary truth. But the relation of the moral to the non-moral is not reciprocal, as Moore saw. The non-moral must *constitute* or *produce* the moral. This demand is quite strong indeed. For example, it is stronger than the demand for compatibility in the case of free will and determinism – there seems to be nothing incoherent about a dualist form of compatibilism. It is stronger even than a demand for *asymmetric supervenience*, which need not involve the idea of the subjacent base constituting or producing suggested by Moore. It is, however, *at least* asymmetric supervenience, which might be seen as an expression of this stronger, constitutive relationship.

In light of the strength of this demand, there is nothing sinister about the way in which morality emerged from the shadow of religion only to find itself in the shadow of science. As an asymmetrically supervenient discourse, it cannot really claim its own place in the sun. The demand that we explain compatibility by coming to an understanding of what morality asks of the world and attempting to determine whether the world can give it – this demand is no imposition of over-eager naturalists upon an autonomous moral realm. The invitation to explain comes from a core truism of the moral realm – the dependence of the moral upon the natural.

Once again, none of this entails a naturalistic reduction. Morality can win a place in the shade of our dominant non-moral theory if a form of compatibility that would allow us to understand constitution or asymmetric supervenience could be secured.

V

A not-very-distant perspective on the evolution of human thought would reveal that, although folk theories of physics, biology, psychology, and so on, once held sway, scientific alternatives have arisen which revise or even overturn a good deal of common sense. Many of us take these non-folk alternatives to be more credible. Is there reason to expect a similar progression to take place in ethics? Hume argued otherwise.

> We shall only observe ... that though an appeal to general opinion may justly, in the speculative sciences of metaphysics, natural philosophy, or astronomy, be deemed unfair and inconclusive, yet in all questions with regard to morals, as well as criticism, there is really no other standard by which any controversy can ever be decided. And nothing is a clearer proof that a theory of this kind is erroneous than to find that it leads to paradoxes repugnant to the common sentiments of mankind and to the practice and opinion of all nations and ages.[20]

This would appear to weigh heavily against the prospect, discussed above, of a systematic critique of the notions of virtue or duty on grounds drawn from theoretical science.

But this conservative position runs a substantial risk of self-defeat. To attempt to exclude radical revisionism of fundamental principles of moral thought would itself require radical revision of certain fundamental principles of moral thought, namely, those principles of '"ought" implies "can",' 'treat like cases alike,' and asymmetric supervenience discussed above, and which led to the compatibilist project. It would no doubt be less paradoxical – to pick up on Hume's own word – to interpret Hume more charitably as defending caution against revisionist enthusiasm when what is at issue are practices and institutions which have been hammered out over centuries of human experience, negotiation, and contestation. Too often we but poorly understand the consequences of change.

With that cautionary note sounded, however, it is noteworthy that the target of Hume's criticism was Locke's enthusiasm for government based upon consent. Since Hume wrote, this Lockean enthusiasm – however imperfectly expressed in classic social contract theory and imperfectly practised in real civil societies – has itself become a "com-

---

20 David Hume, "Of the Original Contract," *Essays Moral, Political, and Literary.* The passage quoted here can be found on p. 60 of the selected volume of Hume's *Political Essays*, C.W. Hendel, ed. (Indianapolis: Bobbs-Merrill 1953).

mon sentiment of mankind." Changes in common moral sentiments are not vanishingly rare – think only of such central questions as slavery, the subordination of women, the legitimacy of democracy, and the rights of children. Nor are such changes to be explained only by exogenous social change. A crucial role has been played in the evolution of moral opinion (as well as in social evolution itself) by changing theories of the non-moral world.

Nonetheless, a kind of autonomy of moral thought survives our discussion of the need for compatibility. Innovations in empirical theory, for example, do not dictate innovations in ethics in the way that innovations in physics are typically thought to dictate innovations in chemistry. There is a logical gap between any alleged fact and any conclusion expressed in moral terms. For example, the asymmetric supervenience of the moral does not guarantee that fixing the natural properties of the actual world a priori guarantees the presence of any moral properties, even if we set moral expressivism aside. For supervenience is compatible with moral skepticism – the possibility that our moral thought is massively in error. At least this much of the 'is'/'ought' gap survives: 'Ought to x' implies 'Can do x,' perhaps, so 'Not[Can do x]' implies 'Not[Ought to x].' But 'Not[Ought to x]' does not imply 'Ought not to x.' For 'Not[Ought to x]' sustains an error-theoretic reading: there are no real *oughts*, not even *ought nots*.

The gap between 'is' and 'ought' calls for normative reflection. Is any particular account of the causal structure of the world sufficient to rule out the possibility of funding moral assessment? This is the sort of claim hard determinists have made. But whether they – or any other incompatibilists – are right is no simple, local matter. It depends upon how far we might go in reflective equilibrium; and that, in turn, will depend upon our morals as well as our metaphysics.

VI

A few remarks by way of conclusion:

(1) Is ethics methodologically autonomous? The 'is'/'ought' gap secures the logical autonomy of ethics, but reflective equilibrium

knows of connections that are more-than-logical. And we have seen how one is naturally led from narrow reflective equilibrium to broad. Part of broad reflective equilibrium will be avoiding intolerable strains with the substantive and methodological elements of empirical science. This is not to say that, for example, discovering an explanatory role for a property confirms it as a moral notion, but rather, that when moral notions take on explanatory obligations – as do such central notions as virtue, duty, and agency – the explanatory roles thereby attributed must be compatible with whatever else we know about how the world operates. Moral thought is not supplanted, but it must be responsive to empirical methods and results. Showing compatibility is a way of promoting the autonomy of moral reasoning, for it would show that we are not running afoul of our own convictions about the relation of the moral to the natural. Showing compatibility – even showing asymmetric supervenience or constitution – is not tantamount to reduction. But even reduction need not be feared as such. Many forms of reduction are vindicatory rather than eliminative: if moral properties can, for example, be identified with (possibly complex or functional) natural properties, this could secure their place and assure their supervenience. They would indeed have it made in the shade.

(2) Moral compatibilism (at a minimum) is common ground. Reflective moral thought, if it is to avoid falling into systematic error or being saddled with 'necessary illusions' or unintelligible but necessary postulates, must be underwritten by a compatibilist account of moral notions. It is common ground because it emerges from truisms of moral thought, independent of philosophical positions such as naturalism.

(3) Thus we are led, without taking either naturalism or the need for a funding theory as our starting point, to the conclusion that there is a central role in our ordinary thinking about ethics for the question: Is ethics such, and is the natural world such, as to underwrite our moral thought and practice? So there is at least that much continuity with the cases of folk psychology and physics. And, as in those cases, we see some aspects of commonsense thought underwritten, some revised, and some explained away. Not only does 'ought' imply 'can' for action – it does so for belief as well. *Can* we

believe this ethics business? If our moral confidence is to survive reflective equilibrium – and, once again, the call for reflective equilibration comes from within the sphere of moral reasons itself – we must be able to understand and believe in what we are doing.[21]

·

---

21 A number of people have tried to improve my thinking about moral theory and its appropriateness. I am especially grateful to Paul Boghossian, Stephen Darwall, Ronald Dworkin, Allan Gibbard, Thomas Nagel, and Samuel Scheffler.

Naturalism and Moral Reasons

JEAN HAMPTON
University of Arizona

Why are traditional 'objectivist' theories of morality, such as those put forward by Aristotle, or Kant, or even Bentham, commonly thought not to pass 'scientific muster' insofar as they are not 'naturalist'? My interest in this question is based on my being a moral objectivist, but answering this question is one that moral skeptics should be as interested in as I. The view that the commitments of science preclude us from accepting such theories is the basis of the moral skeptic's position. Yet showing what is wrong with a moral objectivist position is surprisingly difficult. It involves reflecting on what 'scientific muster' is supposed to be, and on why a theory is commonly thought to be disreputable unless it passes it. It also involves locating the 'queer' element in objectivist moral theory that makes it scientifically disreputable. Yet, as I hope to show in this article, there is no commonly accepted statement of what makes a theory scientifically acceptable or unacceptable, and (perhaps even more surprisingly) no rigorous account of what the queer component of objectivist moral theory is that makes any such theory scientifically unacceptable. Moral skeptics have been working from insufficiently defined intuitions and ideas – both about science and about morality.

I. Naturalism

To examine what makes a theory either scientifically acceptable or scientifically disreputable, we should begin with the concept of the 'natural,' because contemporary moral skeptics invariably invoke this concept to explain what science is committed to, and what objectivist moral theories flout.[1] We can locate two ways in which the concept of the natural informs theorizing in contemporary philosophy.[2] *Methodological naturalism* is the view that philosophy, and indeed, any other intellectual discipline, must pursue knowledge via empirical methods exemplified by the sciences, and not by a priori or nonempirical methods. Quine is the preeminent example of a methodological naturalist; it has been a position attractive to those theorists

> impressed by the fact that claims about the world which have, historically, been deemed by philosophers to be a priori true – the principle of sufficient reason, the Euclidean structure of space, the restriction of mechanical interaction to local contact, the nonexistence of vacua, and so on – have, with distressing regularity, been revised or abandoned in the face of scientific theories.[3]

Nonetheless, it is a view that many find difficult to square with the apparently nonempirical methods employed by mathematicians, even in the fact of arguments from some philosophers that logic and mathematics are empirical enterprises after all.[4] *Substantive naturalism*, in contrast, is the view that a given domain of inquiry can only yield true or false judgments if those judgments are identical with, reducible to, or supervenient upon, factual statements of the sort that are normally allowed by our best scientific theories.[5] Hence, those who are substan-

---

1 Gilbert Harman, "Is There a Single True Morality?" in David Copp and David Zimmerman, eds., *Morality, Reason and Truth* (Totowa, NJ: Roman and Allanheld, 1985) 29

2 Peter Railton, "Naturalism and Prescriptivity," *Social Philosophy and Policy* 7, no. 1, 155-7

3 Ibid., 156

4 See, for example, John Stuart Mill, *System of Logic*, especially book 3. Mill's position met with powerful counter-arguments from Gottlob Frege, *The Foundations of Arithmetic*. (See the edition translated by J.L. Austin [Oxford: Blackwell, 1974], esp. 12-14.)

5 The phrase 'allowed by' here is ambiguous: naturalists could make it precise in a number of ways. At one extreme, they could argue that it means merely 'con-

tive naturalists can believe about any particular theory either (1) that the judgments of the theory supervene upon or are reducible to such factual statements, or (2) that such a reduction or supervenience relation is not possible, so that the theory does not yield true or false judgments.[6] Note that substantive naturalism is *not* the same as the view (which Railton calls 'scientism'[7]) that holds all knowledge, and all meaningful language, comes (only) from science. Such a dismissal of the importance and worth of nonscientific activities and ways of knowing about the world, especially in art or literature, is in no way fundamental to the substantive naturalist, who is only committed to holding that true or false judgments must be in terms that are 'allowed' by our best scientific theories – although how we should understand 'allowed' here requires spelling out.

In general, most of the moral skeptics tend to be substantive naturalists (although many of them also embrace methodological naturalism); hence it is this form of naturalism that will primarily concern us. As we shall see, however, substantive naturalism is not fundamentally an ontological thesis (although it can involve ontological commitments), but a metaphysical one, deeply connected to a view about what counts as a satisfactory explanation of any event in the world.

Using the preceding definition of substantive naturalism, let us propose that any theory is acceptable from a scientific point of view, if it is a substantively naturalist position. Can objectivist moral theories qualify as substantively naturalist?

---

sistent with,' which would yield a very broad conception of the natural; at the other extreme, they could argue that it means 'explicable in terms of,' which would yield a very narrow conception of the natural.

6 I am following Harman in wishing to include moral nihilism among the possible naturalist positions in ethics. See Harman, "Is There a Single True Morality?" loc. cit. Contrast Nicholas Sturgeon's use of the term, which would recognize only those positions that believe reduction or analysis of moral terms into scientifically acceptable statements count as naturalist theories. See Sturgeon, "Moral Explanations," in Geoffrey Sayre-McCord, ed., *Essays on Moral Realism* (Ithaca: Cornell University Press 1988) 229-55.

7 Railton, op. cit., 159

II. Mackie's arguments

J.L. Mackie is a substantive naturalist who contends that much of the moral language of the Aristotelian, Kantian, rights-based, and utilitarian traditions is violative of substantive naturalism, and thus irreconcilable with science, for two reasons. He argues, first, that such language refers to objects or properties that are metaphysically 'queer' by virtue of being inherently prescriptive. Since the best scientific theories we have – in physics, chemistry, biology – neither recognize nor require for explanation any such object or property, Mackie concludes that we are not licensed to believe that they exist. On Mackie's view, science requires us to understand the world both as 'attitudinatively and motivationally neutral,'[8] and as 'justificationally neutral' from a moral point of view. Second, Mackie complains that if such objects or properties existed, they would have to be discovered by an intuitive capacity unlike any recognized sensory capacity, almost magical in its ability to detect entities with objective 'pull.'[9] Since science recognizes no such special sense in human beings, not only does Mackie conclude that such a sense doesn't exist, but also that the objects or properties it would detect don't exist.

But how can Mackie be so sure that moral properties and objects are precluded from scientific acceptance? What exactly is this inherent 'authoritative prescriptivity'[10] that makes the objects or properties supposedly possessing it too queer to be believed? And what exactly does Mackie believe are the characteristics of those objects or properties that are 'natural' or 'real'? Mackie's arguments are clearly motivated by a substantive assumption about what kind of object or property can be natural, such that it is capable of being recognized by science. And yet he never clarifies what this substantive assumption is. Hence, although we readers are sure to have some intuitive sense of what is scientifically

---

8 See John McDowell, "Values and Secondary Qualities," in G. Sayre-McCord, ed., *Essays on Moral Realism* (Ithaca: Cornell University Press 1988) 166-80.

9 John Mackie, *Ethics: Inventing Right and Wrong* (Harmondsworth, Middlesex: Penguin, 1977) 38-42

10 Ibid., 39

problematic about moral prescriptivity, since Mackie explicitly defines neither it nor the conception of 'natural' with which he is working, he never conclusively demonstrates that moral prescriptivity is unnatural.

Mackie tries to suggest the problem he doesn't make explicit by using the term 'value' to describe the component within ethics that is supposed to be irreconcilable with science. It is a term that immediately calls to mind the fact/value distinction, and the traditional claim, made by many, that science does (and should) trade only in facts, and not in values. But a good look at science reveals that valuation is not something that is, or need be, excluded from our best scientific explanations, especially in fields such as biology.[11] It is perfectly acceptable, for example, to say that the snub-nosed guitarfish has adapted well to its ocean environment. Most biologists would regard the phrase 'adapted well' in this process as heuristic shorthand, entirely reducible to scientifically acceptable ideas. Indeed, we can rephrase the sentence to show this, as follows:

> The species named "snub-nosed guitar fish" has genetically responded to its environment in the ocean (from date x to date y), given changes in that environment during that period, such that its numbers were more likely to remain steady or increase during that period.

And there is nothing scientifically unacceptable in this sentence, demonstrating that the phrase 'adapted well' is merely a stand-in for the concept of inclusive fitness, and is thus useful metaphorical shorthand for a fundamental scientific concept. The conclusion seems to be that evaluative terms are acceptable to the naturalist, even when they occur in scientific investigations, if and only if they can be *reduced* to descriptive language permitted or recognized by, and/or used in, the sciences.

A more daring biologist might also suggest that we can interpret the evaluative words in this sentence as more than mere metaphorical

---

11 See, for example, Mohan Matthen and Edwin Levy, "Teleology, Error and the Human Immune System," *Journal of Philosophy* **81**, no. 7 (1984) 351-72. See also Wesley Salmon on teleological explanation in "Four Decades of Scientific Explanation," in Philip Kitcher and Wesley Salmon, eds., *Scientific Explanation* (Minneapolis: University of Minnesota Press 1989) 26-32.

shorthand. For example, Dennett, following Darwin, argues that such ways of talking also show how biologists appeal to the concept of a 'rational design.'[12] On his view, modern biology is supposed to have shown us that we can appeal to the concept of design without anthropomorphizing nature or postulating a divine designer. But Dennett has an interestingly generous view of when, and how, we are justified in imputing intentions to an entity. If an entity is a type of complex system such that it is predictively valuable to impute intentions to it, then Dennett believes we are warranted in doing so. Intentionality is therefore a concept whose legitimacy is a function of its instrumentality for scientists. This position seems to imply that if it turns out we gain predictive power as scientists by thinking about species as 'designed for the end of survival,' we are warranted in imputing intentionality to some unseen natural force which has, as an intention, that end. So it seems that Dennett's position allows us to believe that, just as you and I are intentional agents, so too is 'Mother Nature'! (Or alternatively, just as the behavior of a particular *homo sapiens* can be better predicted by imputing intention to it, so too might the natural events on the earth be better predicted by imputing intention to it.)

The reader can decide the extent to which he or she is sympathetic to Dennett's views. Those who dislike the Dennettian view of intentionality, can avoid it, and salvage the legitimacy of evaluative language in biology and other sciences, by insisting that intentionality talk (invoking words such as 'design') is literally false in these areas of inquiry, and should be reinterpreted as useful metaphorical shorthand for nonevaluative, nonintentional concepts.

But Mackie would presumably maintain that he objects only to those forms of evaluation, of which ethical evaluation is an instance, which admit of no scientifically acceptable reduction. It is a hallmark of the fact/value distinction as it is made by theorists such as Mackie (who have been influenced by R.M. Hare) that an ethical evaluation will generally

---

12 See Daniel Dennett, "Why the Law of Effect Will Not Go Away," in *Brainstorms: Philosophical Essays on Mind and Psychology* (Montgomery, VT: Bradford 1978) 73.

be thought to have two components: a descriptive component, and a prescriptive component, that is in some way linked to the description. It is the prescriptive component that is supposed to be problematic from a scientific point of view. Because the biological evaluation above can be reduced to entirely descriptive notions, it would seem to be scientifically acceptable insofar as it does not contain this problematic prescriptive element.

Alas, this reply merely restates the problem. Mackie never tells us what this prescriptivity is, and hence we can still complain that he has not conclusively established that it is unnatural or unscientific. Moreover there is another problem with this reply. Consider that it is not always clear one can make a sharp distinction between the descriptive and prescriptive components of a moral evaluation. The claim that one can is at least superficially plausible with respect to evaluations that rely on what Williams has called 'thin' ethical concepts, such as *good*, *bad*, *right*, and *wrong*. If these conceptions are used to apply to some component of the world (subject to a pure description), the naturalist would question what object or property these terms are meant to signify. But we also use terms in which the valuation and the description seem thoroughly entangled,[13] such as *cowardly*, *mean-minded*, *manipulative*, or *cheerful*; Williams calls these "thick" ethical concepts.[14] A number of theorists (e.g., McDowell) have denied that one can isolate a descriptive component of any of these terms, or provide synonyms for the 'purely' descriptive component that is devoid of any evaluative content.[15] And on a more Wittgensteinian note, some of these theorists

---

13 Putnam uses the phrase "entanglement of fact and value" in a number of places. See for instance his "The Absolute Conception of the World" in *Renewing Philosophy* (Cambridge, MA: Harvard University Press 1992).

14 See B. Williams, *Ethics and the Limits of Philosophy* (Cambridge: Cambridge University Press 1985), e.g., chs. 7 and 8.

15 See John McDowell, "Are Moral Imperatives Hypothetical?" *Proceedings of the Aristotelian Society* **52** (1978) suppl. vol.; and "Virtue and Reason," *Monist* **62** (1979). And see Williams, *Ethics and the Limits of Philosophy*, esp. 141-2; Hilary Putnam, "The Absolute Conception of the World," op. cit., and Iris Murdoch, *The Sovereignty of Good* (New York: Schocken 1975).

have charged that it is impossible to understand what these terms mean, unless one grasps them as evaluations.[16] For reasons that I will not go into here, I am dubious about whether this position is correct. However, if it is, then the ethical is thoroughly entangled with the factual. And doesn't this show that value is as much a part of our world as anything scientific, and hence allowed by science, albeit perhaps not studied by science or used in any scientific theory? Indeed, since such evaluations are fundamental to our functioning in our social worlds, and used by us all the time in our dealings with other human beings, it would seem they are as central to our conception of the world in which we live as any scientific description. So why should they be regarded as problematic?

One can also reply to Mackie's queerness argument by noting the way it is overly indebted to G.E. Moore's open-question argument, which purports to show that moral goodness must be understood as a 'nonnatural' property. This argument plays into Mackie's hands. For if, as Moore wants us to conclude on the basis of that argument, moral goodness is supposed to be some kind of nonnatural property 'out there' in the world, why should any naturalist believe it is real, or believe that human beings can have access to such a strange property? However, there are many moral objectivists who don't understand goodness (or rightness) in Moore's way. For example, Kantians who accept that there is a kind of moral proof procedure, analogous to, say, proof procedures in mathematics (which Kant himself calls the 'Moral Law'), utterly reject that idea that moral objectivity must be grounded in the

---

16 See Williams, *Ethics and the Limits of Philosophy*, 141-2, "An insightful observer can indeed come to understand and anticipate the use of the concept without actually sharing the values of the people who use it.... But in imaginatively anticipating the use of the concept, the observer also has to grasp imaginatively its evaluative point. He cannot stand quite outside the evaluative interests of the community he is observing, and pick up the concept simply as a device for dividing up in a rather strange way certain neutral features of the world" (141-2). Williams cites a number of discussions that trace the Wittgensteinian aspects of this claim. See 217-8, n.7.

existence of moral objects and properties that are 'out there' albeit different in kind from any other sort of property or object recognized as natural. Mackie's queerness argument seems motivated by the assumption that the only way one can argue for moral objectivity is to be a moral Platonist of a Moorean stripe, but that is no more true than to claim that the only way to argue for mathematical objectivity is to be a mathematical Platonist who posits the existence of numbers as 'nonnatural' objects.

Mackie also tries to undercut the idea of moral objectivity by pointing to the disagreements both within and across cultures about what counts as moral and immoral behavior. Once again, however, this sort of argument fails to persuade the opposition. There has been, and continues to be, disagreement among scientists about what counts as a satisfactory scientific theory, and disagreements between scientists and nonscientists about what kind of theory of the world is true (think of the controversy between evolutionary biologists and creationists), and yet the fact of that disagreement, in the eyes of scientific realists, does not show that there is no true theory of the world, nor that science cannot approximate it. Moreover, Mackie can't claim uncontroversially that our disagreements about moral matters is such that we do not expect to resolve them; in fact the opposite seems true. People argue hard and passionately for their moral views, intent on persuading their opponents. They call them 'wrong,' or even 'evil.' They do not simply air their disagreements as if they were unresolvable, in the way that they might air their unresolvable disagreements over, for example, the best flavor of ice cream, or the best printer font. So if the fact of disagreement doesn't signal the unreality of the objects being disagreed about, and if the nature of our moral disagreement seems to presuppose that all parties accept that there is a fact of the matter about who is right, why should we believe Mackie that moral disagreements undercut the idea that morality is objective? He can only persuade us if he specifies what it is about moral disagreement that makes it (permanently) unresolvable.

III. Harman's Arguments

There is another well-known argument questioning the substantive naturalism of morality, put forward by Gilbert Harman.[17] Suppose, says Harman, we come upon some boys inflicting great pain on an animal just for the fun of it, and we say we believe the boys' action is wrong. But the putative wrongness of the boys' action does not itself play any role in the reason why the boys hurt the animal. The scientist in a laboratory sees a vapor trail, and explains it by positing a proton; the observation is evidence for his theory because the theory posits the proton, which explains the vapor trail, which explains your observation.[18] But in the case of the boys hurting the animal, your observation that their action is wrong does not explain their action. Even if the boys claim they hurt the animal 'in order to do something wrong,' we still need not explain their action by appealing to the putative wrongness of what they did, but only by appealing to their belief (most likely shaped by their society) that what they did was wrong. "The actual rightness or wrongness of their action seems to have nothing to do with why they did it."[19]

In general, Harman maintains that we can explain our moral (or immoral) beliefs or behavior by positing a societally shaped sensibility, or set of beliefs about what is right and wrong, and then saying that our moral judgment or our moral (or immoral) actions simply originate from that societally shaped moral sensibility or set of beliefs.[20] If he is right, the truth or falsity of moral judgments is completely irrelevant to why we make and act on such judgments. Harman concludes that whereas in science our observations of the physical world are best explained by positing the existence of physical facts, our moral obser-

---

17 See Harman's *The Nature of Morality* (New York: Oxford 1977), especially chapter 1, and his "Moral Explanations of Natural Facts – Can Moral Claims be Tested Against Morality?" *The Southern Journal of Philosophy* **24** (1986) supplement.

18 See Harman, *The Nature of Morality*, 6.

19 Ibid., 9.

20 Ibid., 4.

vations are *not* best explained by appeal to purported 'moral facts' but merely to beliefs whose generation within us is largely a function of our psychology and the society in which we live. Harman also argues that it is impossible to argue for moral facts by assimilating them to mathematical facts. The latter are also facts that we cannot perceive directly, but Harman maintains that these facts are real, on the grounds that when they explain the observations that support a physical theory, scientists typically appeal to mathematical principles. And, according to Harman, 'since an observation is evidence for what best explains it,'[21] and 'since mathematics often figures in the explanations of scientific observations, there is indirect observational evidence for mathematics.'[22]

Harman's arguments assume that science gives us two principles upon which to argue for the existence of any facts:

1. A fact obtains if it figures in the best explanation of a putative observation of that fact.

2. A fact obtains if it figures in a physical theory that provides the best explanation of certain observations.

Since moral facts play no role in the content of scientific theories, it would seem that we cannot appeal to principle 2 in order to defend them. But is he correct to say that moral facts do not figure in the best explanation of observations of moral phenomena, such that principle 1 cannot be used to establish them?

It all depends on what one means by 'best' explanation, and Harman doesn't explicitly tell us what he means by 'best.' Consider Jane, who sees the boys hurting the animal, and interferes in order to stop them because, she says, 'What they're doing is morally wrong and for that reason I have to stop them.' Harman can offer (what I will call) a 'psychological' explanation of Jane's action, but a moral objectivist will explain what Jane did in terms of the fact that she was (correctly) responsive to an objective moral obligation. Harman will think his

---

21 Ibid., 10.

22 Ibid.

explanation is better. But why? Some (such as Sturgeon[23]) have argued that, *contra* Harman, we often appeal to moral facts (which we take to supervene on natural facts) in our explanations, even if they don't tend to appear in scientific explanations, as when we say that Hitler's actions are explained by his moral depravity (and when we say that we believe he was morally depraved because he *was* morally depraved).[24] So why doesn't (1), in conjunction with our actual explanatory practices, permit us to posit the existence of moral facts?

Harman's argument is incomplete, and thus ultimately unpersuasive, unless he can provide an answer to these questions. One answer he suggests, but never gives explicitly, is that even if we are prone to appealing to moral objects or properties in our everyday moral practices, in fact science does not and should not do so, because there is something about these objects or properties that disqualifies them from scientific recognition. This appears to be the point he is making when he says that there is no independent scientific way of verifying the existence of moral facts: it is, he maintains, "obscure how the rightness or wrongness of an action can manifest itself in a world in a way that can affect the sense organs of people."[25]

This remark is not particularly perspicuous, but it sounds to me as if Harman, with these remarks, means to be relying on something like Mackie's 'queerness' idea to complete his argument against the existence of moral facts. That would mean he is relying on the idea that such facts are too different from the sort of facts that science recognizes to allow us to believe such facts exist, especially when we have a competing explanation for our moral judgments that is completely consistent

---

23 Sturgeon, "Moral Explanations"

24 Ibid. Discussed by Harman in "Moral Explanations of Natural Facts – Can Moral Claims Be Tested Against Morality?" 61-64. And see Sturgeon's 'Harman on Moral Explanations of Natural Facts,' commenting on this Harman article, in *The Southern Journal of Philosophy* **24** (1986) supplement.

25 See Harman, "Moral Explanations," 66. And see his *The Nature of Morality*, 8: "there does not seem to be any way in which the actual rightness or wrongness of a given situation can have any effect on your perceptual apparatus."

with the physicalist assumptions of science. But we have already explored the queerness argument in our discussion of Mackie's views, and found that it has not, at least thus far, been successfully developed.

Might Harman argue that scientific explanations are more parsimonious than moral explanations? Perhaps he means to say that all we need to explain Jane's action from a scientific point of view is an account of what she sees and an account of how she categorizes what she sees in her mind, concluding with a certain kind of negative projection on to the events she witnesses, whereas an explanation from a moral objectivist point of view must include the additional appeal to moral facts that affect Jane in some (mysterious) way. So on Ockhamite grounds, isn't the scientific explanation superior?

Not necessarily; certainly Harman hasn't shown that it is. The only reason that the moral account might seem less simple than the scientific account is that Harman has not given us the full outline of what the scientific account would have to include to be genuinely explanatory. In particular, he has not told us how the property of wrongness got into Jane's head, and how she came to learn to apply it to events such as malicious cat burnings. The moral objectivist has the beginnings of an answer to this question, which of course Harman doesn't like: that is, Jane somehow had access to objective moral facts (e.g., via something like a Kantian moral law) from which she learned that cat-burning was wrong. But the naturalist must also answer that question, not only by appealing to the influence on Jane of such things as cultural norms, sentiments and emotions, habituation and conditioning, but also by giving an account of how and why these norms arose, or why these sentiments came to be engaged in a certain way in Jane, or why she was conditioned to behave as she did (along with the identity of the conditioning agent). Is this second kind of explanation 'simpler' than the first? Who knows? That question is hard to answer in the abstract, without concrete instances of the two kinds of theory in front of one. But more importantly, the explanations are so different, it seems to be beside the point whether one is 'simpler' than the other. Certainly someone such as Harman who is committed to naturalist explanations will vastly prefer the scientific one, but the question is: Why? Again, we are driven back to the idea that Harman must be implicitly assuming that there is something queer about the moral objectivist explanation, but it is a queerness that he does not articulate.

Mackie and Harman have plenty of company in this view that moral facts are, in some way, occult. In a lecture, Frank Ramsey once said:

> Most of us would agree that the objectivity of good was a thing we had settled and dismissed with the existence of God. Theology and Absolute Ethics are two famous subjects which we have realized have no real objects.[26]

So 'us right-thinking people' are supposed to have concluded that both God and Good are fantasies, postulating objects that are, from a scientific point of view, simply unbelievable. But alas, we still do not know precisely *what* it is about moral objects and properties that makes them too queer to be believed. Nor is such an account useful only as a support for the moral skeptics' position; anyone who wants to be in a position to dismiss such things as demonology and astrology must be able to say what it is about these theories that makes them unscientific. So how do we go about doing so?

IV. Other Theories of the Natural

Given that moral skeptics have had trouble putting their finger on exactly what it is about moral objectivist theories that precludes them from being 'naturalist,' it is not surprising that theorists calling themselves moral realists have insisted that there is nothing scientifically questionable, from either a metaphysical or an epistemological point of view, about moral evaluation.[27] Such theorists defend the idea that there are moral facts by claiming that morality is, as an enterprise, allowed by, and (in many ways) no different than, science. These theorists have two groups of opponents: those, such as Mackie, Harman and Ramsey,

---

26 See Frank Plumton Ramsey, "There is Nothing to Discuss" Epilogue in R.B. Braithwaite, ed. *Foundations of Mathematics* (New York: Harcourt-Brace 1931) 291-2; this passage and other parts of this work are quoted by Hilary Putnam in "Beyond the Fact/Value Dichotomy" in *Realism with a Human Face* (Cambridge, MA: Harvard University Press 1990) 135-6.

27 See Brink, 210; and Sturgeon.

who are skeptical on naturalist grounds that there can be moral facts and moral knowledge and those who think ethics is queer, but argue that the same queerness is (covertly) present in science. These two classes of opponents of moral realism are interesting bedfellows on this matter; although they disagree with each other about whether or not there are moral facts, they join hands in opposing the moral realists in their insistence that there is a genuine problem fitting ethics into the scientific world view. Yet these bedfellows find it remarkably difficult to pin down precisely what this problem is.

Part of the reason I believe they have had such difficulty is that they are working with a notion of 'natural' that is not precisely defined. In fact there are two ways in which this term can be cashed out, the first of which is insufficient to justify their rejection of moral objects and properties, and the second of which has never been developed satisfactorily to justify that rejection.

The first definition of 'natural' is that which is allowed and/or studied by science; I will call it the 'science-based' definition.[28] This definition makes the current theories of science the ultimate arbiters of what counts as natural: on this view, science is not defined in terms of the natural, but rather the reverse.

The second meaning of the term 'natural' is substantive; on this view, the term 'natural' denotes a kind of object or property which is the opposite of nonnatural.[29] This distinction is supposed to be one that we grasp intuitively. What is natural, in this sense, is conceptually prior to our understanding of science, and (at least in part) determinative of

---

28 For example, this definition is suggested by David Brink, *Moral Realism and the Foundations of Ethics* (Cambridge: Cambridge University Press 1989) 22.

29 Nominalists may use this term, meaning the opposite of abstract. But nominalism and the physicalist ideas that underlie contemporary naturalism are not the same. Believers in universals can consistently deny or affirm that all properties or objects that exist are 'natural'; and nominalists may equally deny or affirm that all properties or objects that exist are 'natural.' See Tim Crane and D.H. Mellor, "There is No Question of Physicalism," *Mind* 99 (April 1990) 185. For a discussion of nominalism, see Hartry Field, *Science Without Numbers*, chapter 1. And see W.V. Quine, *Word and Object* (Cambridge, MA: MIT Press 1960) ch. 7.

the subject matter of science.[30] I will call this the 'substantive' definition. (Note that those who endorse the science-based definition might be implicitly doing so because they accept the second sense; that is, they may regard science as the arbiter of the natural because science is committed to recognizing and studying what is natural, defined substantively.)

It must be the second, substantive sense of 'natural' that is driving the queerness arguments of theorists such as Mackie, Harman and Ramsey, because the first sense is too weak to support such arguments. The most one could do, using the first sense, is to argue that, right now, we cannot say moral objects or properties exist, since right now, science does not recognize them. Now I am not at all sure that this is true: exactly how do the commitments of present-day science to things such as quarks or DNA preclude commitments to rights and obligations? But even if it were, this position does not allow one to say that we could *never* acknowledge that these objects and properties exist, since it would seem possible that science could evolve in a way that would require it to recognize their existence.[31] All that we would be licensed to conclude is that moral objects or properties seem queer from the *present* scientific point of view, but might one day be scientifically acceptable after all. But theorists such as Mackie want to say that moral objects or properties are, by their nature, disqualified from existing, so that no credible science – either now or in the future – could ever recognize them. Hence theorists such as Mackie must be working from a substantive

---

30 See G.E. Moore, *Principia Ethica* (Cambridge: Cambridge University Press 1903) chapters 1, 2, 4; and David Brink, op. cit., 22. And consider the following remark by Quine with respect to the word 'real': "It was a lexicographer, Dr. Johnson, who demonstrated the reality of a stone by kicking it; and to begin with, at least, we have little better to go on than Johnsonian usage" (*Word and Object*, 3).

31 It may be that some of those who adopt the first definition are implicitly doing so because they have a substantive conception of what counts as natural, and insofar as they assume that scientific theories will always describe what is natural in this sense, they take it that these theories are a reliable guide to what actually exists.

conception of what is natural. If we could pin down what that conception is, we would be able to determine the extent to which moral objects and properties fail to qualify as real given that conception, as well as the extent to which science is really committed to that conception.

But articulating that conception is no easy task! Part of the difficulty of doing so is that physics itself undermined in this century a popular and seemingly sensible conception of the natural that animated the thinking of many scientists and philosophers through the nineteenth century. Consider that, starting in the seventeenth century, naturalists called themselves 'materialists,' insofar as they thought of the world as made up of 'solid, inert, impenetrable and conserved' matter that interacts deterministically and through contact.[32] But twentieth-century physics has posited entities, and interactions between these entities, that do not fit the materialist characterization of the real. So what does the naturalist do? In the words of Crane and Mellor:

> Faced with these discoveries, materialism's modern descendants have – understandably – lost their metaphysical nerve. No longer trying to limit the matter of physics a priori, they now take a more subservient attitude: the empirical world, they claim, contains just what a true complete physical science would say it contains.[33]

But why should we believe that the subject matter of physics will never involve the recognition of things (e.g., norms, mental representations) that have standardly been dismissed as nonphysical heretofore – especially since this has been exactly what has happened since the last century?

There is another problem with relying on physics to define what the natural can be. It is understandable why physics would be the arbiter of the real if we have a well-founded conception of what counts as real, and physics is understood to be designed to uncover and clarify the

---

32 Tim Crane and D.H. Mellor, "There is No Question of Physicalism," *Mind*, **99** (April 1990) 186. See in reply Philip Pettit, "A Definition of Physicalism," *Analysis* **53** (October 1993) 213-23.

33 Crane and Mellor, "Physicalism," 186

nature of real objects or properties so defined; but without that conception, what makes us think that the subject matter of physics, whatever it turns out to be at any given time, is licensed to define what is real? The metaphysical authority of physics is puzzling if the natural is defined in terms of it, rather than vice versa. *If* it is true that the world is made up of all and only the sorts of entities that physics studies, then what physics tells us about the world should be authoritative for our beliefs. But if we don't have any way of knowing, or even characterizing, what is real independent of any particular theory, then for any of our favorite theories (take your pick) we have no particular reason to believe that (only) this theory depicts the real or the natural. Who says it does? Why should we believe what the physicists say is real (particularly when they keep changing their minds) and not, say, the pope or the dalai lama? How do the former constitute a 'real' authority about the world in the way that the latter does not?

There are various explanations one could offer of that authority. For example, some readers might claim that the success of science, a success that has, among other things, enabled us to go to the moon, gives us reason to treat it as an authority about the world. Indeed, I believe that this account may well be useful in explaining why we take physics seriously, but not, say, numerology. But this account is insufficient to lend scientific explanations the authority to prevail over objectivist moral explanations, for two reasons. First, throughout history there have been many theories, of all sorts – religious, political and metaphysical – that have enabled people in various cultures to do things. But we do not think that this instrumental value is sufficient, by itself, to make them accurate descriptive accounts of the world. So why does the fact that our present-day theories have allowed us to make rockets, mobile phones, and camcorders show that they are reliable indicators of what reality contains? Second, such an argument claims to show more than it does. How has science been successful? We can't say it has been successful in giving us the only true description of the world, because that is precisely what is at issue. Of course it has played a role in enabling us to go to the moon, and develop all those rockets, phones and camcorders, but such achievements are also (perhaps even mostly) a function of improvements in the capacity of human beings to cooperate socially, economically and politically, since all these achievements have presupposed the operation of a liberal democratic society and a reasonably free market economy. So why aren't such achievements an argument for the truth of certain moral, political, social, or economic theories (for example the moral thesis that 'human flourishing requires treating individuals as free and equal') just as much as physical ones?

Another explanation one might offer of the authority of science has to do with the fact that scientific theories, in particular, physical theories about microparticles, understood as the fundamental constituents of the world, seem to have been highly successful as predictive theories of the world. Hence, if predictive power is held to be an important goal of a theory (and, arguably, an indicator of the degree to which it is true), scientific theories would seem to meet that goal best, and accordingly be authoritative with respect to our beliefs. But even if it is true that scientific theories are predictively successful, they are predictively successful with respect to certain aspects of the world (e.g., microparticles, chemical events, biological species). And why should their predictive success with respect to these things have any bearing on the reality of moral objects or properties? Only if one thought that *all* there is in the world is what science studies, would one believe (by virtue of the fact that moral objects and properties are not the subject matter of any scientific theory) that predictively successful scientific theories 'show us' that they do not exist. And what justifies one in believing that all that exists is what science (at any given time) posits? This ontological faith is undefended, and difficult to know how to defend.

Indeed, is there even a particular ontology to which a defender of science is committed? There seems to be "a bewildering variety of alternative rational reconstructions" of theories in science with very different ontologies.[34] For example, at the level of commonsense objects such as stones, we can say they are mereological sums of space-time parts, or mereological sums of field points (where these two positions are not consistent), or we can say that they are composed of different time slices of particles in different possible worlds that cannot be identical with the mereological sum of time slices of particles; and at the

---

34 Putnam, "Objectivity and the Science/Ethics Distinction," in *Realism with a Human Face* (Cambridge, MA: Harvard University Press, 1990) 170

level of physics, we can take space-time points to be individuals or mere limits.[35]

Perhaps the person who most brilliantly ridicules the idea that there is some obviously correct naturalist ontology to which all scientifically inclined people are committed is W.V. Quine, himself a committed naturalist. In the article "On What There Is"[36] Quine spends a great deal of time developing a semantics of existence claims. But having done that, he notes that he has not touched the issue of what there *actually* is:

> Now how are we to adjudicate among rival ontologies? Certainly the answer is not provided by the semantical formula "To be is to be the value of a variable"; this formula serves rather, conversely, in testing the conformity of a given remark or doctrine to a prior ontological standard. We look to bound variables in connection with ontology not in order to know what there is, but in order to know what a given remark or doctrine, ours or someone else's, *says* there is; and this much is quite properly a problem involving language. But what there is is another question.[37]

Quine goes on to say that, in order to find out about reality, we need to rely on an ontological *standard*. A standard is a normative entity; an ontological standard tells us what sort of entities we ought to believe or disbelieve. Now that's odd – how can this naturalist use a normative object to define a naturalist ontology, if normative objects are problematic? But isn't asking which theory is 'best' inevitably going to involve appealing to a standard? If Quine is right that ontological disputes, like any theory dispute in science, are adjudicated by appeal to certain norms thought to be appropriate in theory construction, then isn't it true that norms are 'figuring' in science after all, not in the content of the scientific theories, but in their construction?[38] And doesn't that mean

---

35 Putnam, "Objectivity and the Science/Ethics Distinction," 170-1

36 Quine, *From A Logical Point of View*, 2nd ed. (Cambridge, MA: Harvard University Press 1980) 1-19

37 Quine, "On What There Is," 15-6

38 Hilary Putnam has often remarked on the oddity of Quine's reliance on a standard in the course of arguing that there are facts but not values. For example, see Putnam, "Beyond the Fact/Value Dichotomy."

they should be acknowledged as the sort of thing that is real, according to Harman's second principle?

Never appearing to notice this oddity, Quine tells us his ontological standard – it is simplicity:

> Our acceptance of an ontology is, I think, similar in principle to our acceptance of a scientific theory, say a system of physics: we adopt, at least insofar as we are reasonable, the simplest conceptual scheme into which the disordered fragments of raw experience can be fitted and arranged.[39]

But the standard of simplicity, in Quine's view, doesn't pick out one unique ontology. Two that Quine regards as equally simple are the physicalist conception, which regards as real physical objects (to which our sensory apparatus responds) and the phenomenalistic conception, in which the values of bound variables are individual subjective events of sensation or reflection. What is striking about the phenomenalistic conception, especially with respect to Harman's argument against morality, is that it treats physical objects as 'myths.' Just as classes or attributes are dismissed as mythical Platonist objects by the physicalist, so too are physical objects themselves treated as mythical Platonist objects by the phenomenalist. Quine concludes "The quality of myth ... is relative; relative, in this case, to the epistemological point of view."[40] But if one person's myth is another person's reality, and there are only normative standards we can use to adjudicate their dispute – standards that may be themselves disputed and that may not decisively pick out one view as best – how can any naturalist claim that there is a compelling reason to believe that (only) explanations that use a particular naturalist ontology (but which one?) are true? And how can he rule out the objectivity of moral norms by claiming that norms aren't real if he can only defend his own ontological theory by appeal to norms?

In a much later work Quine develops an argument that essentially ridicules anyone who would attempt to define a naturalist ontology.

---

39 Quine, "On What There Is," 16

40 Ibid., 19

The argument goes as follows: If the ultimate constituents of the universe are space-time regions, as contemporary physics can be interpreted to say, we can represent these as classes of quadruples of numbers according to an arbitrarily adopted system of coordinates. But the numbers in these quadruples can be modelled using set theory, and if these sets can themselves be constructed from the null set, then the null set is the ultimate constituent of the universe.[41] The argument portrays what Quine takes to be the foolishness of ontological speculation about the ultimate components of the world.[42] But if such ontological speculation is foolish, how can we show that moral objects or properties are disqualified as real? Without such an argument, theorists such as Ramsey, Mackie and Harman (and indeed, Quine himself) would seem to be guilty of unjustified prejudice against these objects and properties.

However, Quine has a suggestion for the naturalist: even if ontological speculation is foolish, he says that "structure is what matters to a theory, and not the choice of its objects."[43] So perhaps we can define the natural with reference to the physical sciences by defining the (authoritative) structure that is the hallmark of the physical sciences. But what is this compelling structure, and how does it rule out moral objects and properties? Does 'structure' refer to a certain kind of causal explanation in science, that is not possible in objectivist moral theories? Perhaps; but it is an idea that is extremely hard to develop satisfactorily.[44] On the face of it, an appeal to causes ought to be troubling to the naturalist in virtue of Hume's attack on the idea. Didn't Hume give us good reason to worry that the idea of cause and effect is merely projected on to the world by the workings of the human mind? And if this is so, shouldn't a scientific portrayal

---

41 See Quine's "Things and Their Place in Theories" in *Theories and Things* (Cambridge, MA: Harvard University Press 1981) 17-18.

42 Ibid., 20

43 Ibid., 20

44 See Wesley Salmon, op. cit. For my own purposes I try developing it in chapters 2 and 3 of Hampton, *A Theory of Reasons* (Cambridge: Cambridge University Press, forthcoming).

of the world be purged of such mind-dependent notions? This Humean attack has prompted many philosophers to try distancing science from the notion of cause (including Russell, who considers the notion anthropomorphic).[45] Moreover, replacing an appeal to causation with an appeal to the idea of 'laws of science' is, at least arguably, even worse from a naturalist point of view, insofar as natural laws, were they to exist, would seem to presuppose some kind of mysterious necessity in the world. And if that necessity is real, why not also recognize the reality of moral norms?

One might think that the positivists had a way of characterizing the 'structure' of scientific theories in a way that rules out morality understood objectively: According to the positivists, scientific statements are meaningful because they are publicly verifiable; and since ethical statements are not so verifiable, they are meaningless. Moreover, they are unverifiable *in principle*, along with sentences in metaphysics, religion and poetry.[46] But aside from a few enthusiasts for positivism left in economics, positivism has largely been abandoned. Positivism requires that *single* propositions be verifiable, but many propositions in science cannot meet this demand. And if we say (as Harman suggests) that unverifiable propositions are nonetheless 'indirectly' meaningful if they are part of a larger theory possessing observation sentences that are publicly verifiable, then we can no longer exclude the moral and metaphysical 'nonsense' that, as positivists, we had originally opposed, since our larger theory might possess all sorts of values. As Vivian Walsh explains:

> To borrow and adapt Quine's vivid image, if a theory may be black with fact and white with convention, it might well (as far as logical empiricism can tell) be red with values. Since for [the positivists] confirmation or falsification had to be a property of a theory *as a whole*, they had no way of unravelling this whole cloth.[47]

---

45 See Bertrand Russell, "On the Notion of Cause" in *Mysticism and Logic* (Garden City, NY: Doubleday 1957).

46 See Putnam, "Objectivity and the Science/Ethics Distinction," 163.

47 Vivian Walsh, "Philosophy and Economics" in J. Eatwell, M. Milgate, and P. Newman, eds. *The New Palgrave: A Dictionary of Economics*, vol. 3 (London: Macmillan, and New York: Stockton 1987) quoted by Putnam, "Objectivity and the Science/Ethics Distinction," 164.

That is, it would seem this whole cloth could now include 'oughts' and 'shoulds,' standards and principles – just the material the moral objectivist needs. So once the positivist abandoned the idea that *each* sentence in a theory must be verifiable (an abandonment that science forces upon him), he lost his way of disqualifying the meaningfulness of moral sentences.

Putnam notes with exasperation the persistence of the fact/value distinction in the face of the collapse of positivism.[48] I suspect that persistence is due to the deep-seated grip on philosophers' minds of a certain conception of what counts as 'natural' to which they believe science is committed. Positivism fails to articulate that conception. But the conception still survives, albeit in an inchoate form, and continues to influence philosophers under its sway, despite the fact that there now exists no articulation or explication of it.

V. Williams's View

One philosopher under its sway is Bernard Williams, who distinguishes between 'absolute' truths and 'perspectival' truths. The former are what science gives us, the latter are what most human enterprises give us. Our everyday conceptions of objects, our ideas of color, and our moral values are based on our interests – either as a species, or, as is usually the case in morality, as members of a particular community, and they are *projected* by us onto the world. Thus, they yield only perspectival truths, that is, truths given our interests and natures. But they do not yield absolute truths, that is, they do not tell us about the world to the maximum degree independent of perspective.[49] To understand this, admits Williams, is destabilizing to us; for once we realize that our ethical 'truths' are perspectival and parochial, we recognize the 'truth

---

48 See Putnam, "Objectivity and the Science/Ethics Distinction," 165.

49 See Bernard Williams, *Ethics and the Limits of Philosophy*, 138-40; discussed by Putnam, in "The Absolute Conception of the World" and "Objectivity and the Science/Ethics Distinction."

in relativism' that moral praise or condemnation of ways of life in social groups distant from ours loses all point.

But Williams's views amount only to another way of *stating* the naturalist's position, not a way of *justifying* it. Any moral realist will simply deny that moral values are projections, and demand to know why the recognition of these moral values as (in some way) existent independent of us is scientifically precluded. Of course, Williams *believes* that science precludes us from recognizing them, and he paints a picture of the world that is acceptable to a naturalist who rejects the possibility of 'absolute' moral knowledge. But as opponents such as Putnam point out, Williams gives no decisive argument that separates 'the absolute' from 'the perspectival' and that locates scientific concepts (e.g., those in physics) only in the former category. Nor does he show decisively that moral concepts *must* be understood perspectivally, as projections generated by the interests of human beings living in societies. Why aren't moral properties and objects part of the absolute perspective? What precludes us from accepting them along with the other properties and objects that are recognized by the various sciences? Williams's discussion is clearly animated by a deep-seated assumption that moral properties and objects are 'unnatural,' but that notion is neither explicated nor defended. Accordingly, Williams gives those skeptical of such a picture no reason to embrace it.[50]

It is interesting, nonetheless, that Williams takes his discussion to be compelling. Putnam complains in virtue of Williams's remark in *Ethics and the Limits of Philosophy* that his viewpoint in the book constitutes the 'contemporary' point of view, that Williams's book is "not a serious argument for ethical 'non-objectivism,' but rather the expression

---

50 Putnam argues against Williams by attacking the metaphysical realism inherent in the view. But the quarrel between metaphysical realists and (what Putnam calls) 'internal' realists (or idealists, broadly understood) is irrelevant to the debate about the relationship between science and ethics. One can be an internal realist, or an idealist, and still deny that there are ethical truths (imagine a Kantian who disavows the Second Critique), or one can be an internal realist and accept such truths. Defending a certain metaphysics does not *by itself* save the idea that there can be ethical truths if there is something about the world – understood either in a realist, or an idealist way – that disqualifies ethical statements from being true or false.

of a mood."[51] The word 'mood' suggests that the views being expressed are groundless – amounting only to a kind of emotional patina that attends contemporary intellectual life. Yet Williams's 'mood' is the same one that philosophical naturalists such as Ramsey, Mackie and Harman are in, and the 'mood' that prevails among an enormous number of physical and social scientists generally. If so many have it, it would seem there must be a reason for them to have it – indeed, an attractive (perhaps even irresistible) reason. But it is this reason that still escapes us.

Might that reason simply be that it constitutes a way of thinking about the world that strikes many as liberating? Williams argues that those who accept that "values are not in the world," i.e., that "a properly untendentious description of the world would not mention any values, that our values are in some sense imposed or projected on to our surroundings" may meet this belief with despair; but they can also view it "as a liberation, and a radical form of freedom may be found in the fact that we cannot be forced by the world to accept one set of values rather than another."[52] But clearly, the fact that it may be (for some) a pleasing thought that values are not in the world does not constitute an argument for the idea. Regardless of whether this way of thinking about reality is pleasing or not, is it true?

VI. Conclusion

So we return to our original question: what is it about moral objects or properties that precludes their scientific recognition? The fact that this question has not been satisfactorily answered reflects the extent to which naturalists hostile to morality have thought they occupied the philosophical high ground. But this discussion should show that they do not. It is remarkable that objectivist moral philosophers have been so thoroughly on the defensive for so many years about morality's stand-

---

51 Putnam, "The Absolute Conception of the World," 107

52 Williams, *Ethics and the Limits of Philosophy*, 128

ing and credentials as a realm of human knowledge when there exists no successful and widely accepted argument establishing that there is anything about such theories that makes them scientifically problematic.

To those readers who are persuaded that they *do* know what it is about objectivist moral theories that makes them scientifically unacceptable, I say: Fine, tell us what it is. Perhaps naturalists have been right all along to dismiss these theories as unacceptable. But if so, we need a rigorous account of the problem these theories are supposed to have. Up to now, all of us, no matter which side of the debate we've been on, have been working from hunches. Until we resolve whether that account is possible, I suggest that no one is in a position to claim the high ground.[53]

---

53 This article is, in a way, an introduction to my own attempt to articulate what, from a scientific point of view, is 'wrong' with objectivist moral theories. See Hampton, *A Theory of Reasons* (Cambridge: Cambridge University Press, forthcoming). Now I am a moral objectivist, and moral skeptics may be dubious about the attempts of an objectivist to explain what is unnatural about objectivist moral theory. However, my aim in this book is to agree with them that objectivist moral theories contain occult, nonnatural elements, but I go on to show that the same occult, nonnatural elements occur, and must occur, in scientific theories. My thanks go to Richard Healey, James Bogen, Ernan McMullin, and the graduate students in my seminars at the University of Arizona for discussion of the ideas in this article. I am also very grateful to the Pew Charitable Trusts, for their grant support (through their Evangelical Scholars Program) during much of the time this article was written.

CANADIAN JOURNAL OF PHILOSOPHY
Supplementary Volume 21

Perception as Input
and as Reason for Action

ISAAC LEVI
Columbia University

1

John McDowell (1979) suggests that virtuous agents have a perceptual sensitivity allowing them to determine reliably what to do in any specific context of deliberation. Moreover, the reliable perception yields an accurate depiction not only of the facts of the situation but of the morally right act to do. Finally, the reliably kind behavior of a kind person

> is not the outcome of a blind, non-rational habit or instinct, like the courageous behaviour – so called only by courtesy – of a lioness defending her cubs. Rather, that the situation requires a certain sort of behaviour is ... his reason for behaving in that way, on each of the relevant occasions (331). Perception delivers a reason for action.

I have two difficulties with this view:

(*a*) Value commitments such as goals, desires, moral principles, etc. constrain the way agents who endorse such commitments evaluate options in a given context of deliberation. According to McDowell, the perceptual sensitivity of virtuous agents furnishes information concerning the 'right' way of evaluating options in the given context if there is a right way (348, n.5). The deliberating agent, however, cannot coherently assign truth values to ways of evaluating options. That is to say, they cannot coherently be believed to be true or be believed to be false. Suspension of judgment respecting their truth values cannot be sensibly endorsed. An agent cannot have varying degrees of certainty or credal probability judgment respecting their truth. It is then difficult to understand the sense of reliability according to which a virtuous agent has a reliable perceptual sensitivity.

(*b*) Even if the worry registered under (*a*) could be overcome, what is true in science and everyday life should apply to the case of virtuous agents. Perceptual processes sometimes terminate in the acquisition of new beliefs or information that may then serve as part of the evidence or reasons recommending one option over another in deliberation. But the new beliefs are not themselves acquired by inference from other premises injected by the perceptual process even though the new beliefs are formed in response to the sensory stimulation initiating the process. In such cases, the beliefs are not acquired for a reason that warrants acquiring them. Similarly actions may be taken in response to sensory stimulation without the perceptual process producing a reason for the action. Indeed, perception would play a less useful role in deliberation and inquiry than it actually does if it afforded reasons for action and belief.

Failure to appreciate this last point reflects, I think, a confusion between the idea of using data as input and using data as evidence. I shall start by explaining the way I understand the notions of reliability and the distinction between using data as input and using it as evidence in settings where virtue is not the focal issue although deciding what to do sometimes is.

2

Jack informs Jill that the box he is holding contains 100 balls. He also tells her that either 99 of them are black and one white (H_b) or 99 are white and one black (H_w). Jack offers Jill the choice between two envelopes. The black envelope provides her with a $1,000 if ($H_b$) is true and nothing otherwise. The white envelope provides her with a $1,000 if H_w) is true and nothing otherwise. Jill has nothing to lose by taking one of the envelopes given that she is interested in money. How should she choose between the envelopes?

An influential point of view insists that Jill, as a rational agent, is committed, whether she recognizes it or not, to some judgment as to how probable it is that H_b and H_w respectively are true in numerical terms. Jill may not be in a position to identify precisely what her commitments regarding the number x – that is the value of $p(H_b)$ – and the corresponding value $1-x$ – for $p(H_w)$ – should be. In our example, she does not need to be. As long as she can say that one of the two hypotheses about the contents of the urn is more probable than the other, a decision between the two envelopes can be reached. Of course, if Jill thinks x and $1-x$ are 0.5, she should be indifferent in her choice. In order to break the impasse if that is desirable, she might ask Jack for an opportunity to inspect the outcome of random sampling from the urn. Suppose Jack relents and affords her an opportunity to observe the outcome of a single random draw.

After making the observation, Jill has acquired new information, new full beliefs. Suppose that the new information is that e_b – the ball selected is black. According to the prescriptions of so-called Bayesian rationality, Jill should now have a probabilistic degree of belief (credal probability) of 0.99 that H_b is true and should clearly take the black envelope. A similar story could be told if the new information is that e_w – that ball selected is white. Here the recommendation is to choose the white envelope.

In this case, the 'new information' is *used as evidence or as a premise* in a deliberation whose conclusion is a decision to act on one of the options. The new evidence e_b is part of the reason warranting the degree of belief 0.99 that H_b is true. I shall postpone for a short while discussion of the role perceptual processes play in acquiring the belief that e_b. All that is being claimed is that in the case being discussed, the perceptual process somehow leads to the acquisition of a new belief that can serve as a reason for action.

3

There is another case to consider. Jill not only cannot tell what her numerically definite credal state before sampling is, but she has not and does not think she should have such a state of credal probability judgment. Critics of 'Bayesian' decision theory used to say that in such cases, Jill has no credal state. I think it advantageous to represent Jill as being in a state of indeterminate credal probability judgment. She is quite clear that no numerically definite value of x from 0 to 1 is to be ruled out as being permissible for use in computing expected utility or value.

That is to say, all values of x between 0 and 1 count as permissible for this purpose. Prior to sampling, both choosing the black envelope and choosing the white envelope are best according to some permissible credal probability judgments. So both options are *admissible* for choice even though they are not equipreferred but are rather noncomparable or 'incommensurable' in their value.[1]

If Jill were to accept Jack's offer to look at a randomly selected ball first and use the information obtained as evidence as before, the credal probability judgment made after observation will remain unaltered. Let x be any permissible value of Jill's 'prior credal state' and y the permissible value derived from x via Bayes theorem in Jill's 'posterior credal state' on the basis of evidence e_b. For the value $x = 0.1$, $y = 0.5$. For values of x from 0 to 0.1, y ranges from 0 to 0.5 and for values of x greater than 0.1, y ranges from 0.5 to 1. In the credal state relative to the information after finding out that e_b is true the full range of values from 0 to 1 remain permissible to use in computing expected utility. Picking the black envelope and picking the white envelope remain admissible. And looking at large numbers of draws will not help either. Whether the 'datum' is e_b or e_w, using the datum as evidence is of no value in forming a decision. Believing that e_b is not a reason for picking the black envelope or for picking the white envelope. The same holds for believing that e_w.

In any context of deliberation where the prior credal state is fairly indeterminate, using data as evidence will be quite useless for the purpose of deriving a posterior credal state on the basis of which decisions are to be taken. Indeterminacy of this kind is, in my judgment, quite common. I do not mean to deny the importance of using data as evidence but we should not overrate its importance.

There is a way of using the data represented by e_b and e_w that avoids treating the data as useless. Suppose that after Jack offers to let Jill look at the results of a random selection of a ball from the urn but before she makes an observation, Jill formulates a program for stipulating what

---

1 Indeterminate probability judgment as a form of suspense is discussed in Levi, 1974, 1980a and 1986 along with an account of how rational agents should choose in the face of such indeterminacy.

she will do upon observing a black or a white ball. One plan might be to pick the black envelope regardless of what is observed. Another might be to pick the white envelope. A third might be to pick the envelope with color matching the color of the ball selected. And finally the envelope picked may carry the color different from the color of the ball selected. In choosing to implement any one of these plans, Jill deprives herself of the option of choosing between the black and white envelope on the basis of the information available to her after the observation is made. Once the plan is chosen, making observations and responding to them according to plan is part of the activity of implementing that choice. Deliberation and observation may have furnished a reason for choosing the plan but not for selecting an envelope.

Before coming to full belief that e_b or e_w is true, Jill can calculate the expected values of each of the four plans. The first plan carries the value or utility of \$1,000 if H_b is true and the value of \$0 otherwise if H_w is true. For each permissible value x of the probability of the first hypothesis and $1 - x$ for the second, there is an expected value calculation that gives some permissible expected value in the given range. The same is true for the second plan where white and black are permuted.

The third plans yields a more determinate expected value. If H_b is true, the expected value is (0.99)(value(\$1000)). The same is true if H_w is true. So no matter what permissible value x is used for the 'prior' probability for H_b, the expected value is the same. In the third case, the expected value before finding out the color of ball drawn is (0.01)(value(\$1000)).

It seems clear that relative to Jill's viewpoint before finding out the color of the ball drawn, the third plan is better than the fourth. Considerations of expected value do not warrant a judgment as to the relative merits of the first, second, and third plans. They are all admissible for choice as far as considerations of expected value are concerned; but these considerations do not warrant rating any one of these options as better than, worse than, or equivaluable to, any other.

On the other hand, since expected value cannot render a verdict, Jill might appeal to some other consideration or value to arbitrate between the options that are admissible with respect to expected utility. As long as the injunction against choosing an option that fails to be best according to any ranking with respect to expected utility is observed, there can be no objection to this. On this basis, the third plan may be recommended over the first and second plans. In following the third plan one can guarantee getting an expected benefit of (0.99)(value($1000)). The minimum guaranteed expected benefit for the first and second plans is an expected benefit of 0.01(value($1000)).

Notice that the argument just offered purports to show why it might be a good idea to follow the third plan. The reasons for favoring this recommendation invoke the information at Jill's disposal *prior* to finding out whether the ball sampled is black (e_b) or white (e_w). No use has been made in the argument of the outcome of sampling. Indeed, adopting the third plan is not choosing an envelope but is rather adopting a program for receiving an envelope as the outcome of a process where no further deliberation towards a decision takes place. In following the plan, Jill is not to use the information about the color of the ball she obtains through observation as additional premises or reasons for the action she chooses. The deliverances of perception are input, not additional evidence. If they were used as evidence, Jill would have to employ them in a recalculation of the expected value of her plan and it is easy to show that the expected value of continuing with the plan or reneging on it would lead to the predicament that both options are admissible. The idea is that Jill should implement the third plan or be committed to doing so prior to obtaining the information about the result of the random draw from the urn for use as evidence.

The implementation of a program for routine decision making such as that required by the third plan calls for Jill to observe the ball drawn and in response take the black envelope if the ball drawn is observed to be black and take the white envelope otherwise.

It may be objected that this implementation demands that Jill come to full belief that the color of the ball drawn is, say, black and then decide what to do. Jill's acquiring such belief is entirely unnecessary. Jill could have instructed a black-white sensitive automaton or a human stooge to carry out the plan for her. Her decision is reflected in the instructions she gives to the stooge.

Consider the automaton. When confronted with the randomly selected ball, the automaton registers a color (e.g., by means of a pointer that goes up or down for black and white). The automaton does not come to believe that e_b. It responds to the external input by a motion of the pointer that in turn sets in motion the printout of the inscription 'accept the black envelope' that Jack then uses to decide whether Jill has won or lost the bet.

We (including Jill) may interpret the automaton's pointer response as a 'reporting that e_b' without attributing to the automaton any belief or, indeed, any propositional attitude at all.

The stooge who substitutes for the automaton may (but need not always) upon observation come to believe that e_b. But the coming to believe that e_b is either also a reporting that e_b or is preceded by a reporting that e_b. It does not matter which it is. The instructions at least implicitly command the stooge to 'obey the orders' specified for reporting that e_b in response to observation regardless of whether he comes to believe that e_b or not.

In both the case of the stooge and the automaton, believing that e_b is not a reason for taking the black envelope. The same is true of the reporting that e_b. The report is a response to the external input that is used as input in a further development of the program terminating in the 'printout' of the instruction to Jack to give Jill the black envelope.

Jill can be her own stooge. She may, indeed, do it automatically and out of habit without reflection much like the automaton without coming to believe that e_b but merely registering or reporting that e_b. Even though Jill is deliberately implementing the plan (or following the rule), the intentionality derives from having chosen through deliberation to implement the plan. Such deliberation furnishes reasons for implementing the plan in the specific context; but it does not furnish reasons for selecting the black envelope. Implementation may be deliberate without the presence of any deliberation at all in the process of implementation.

On the other hand, Jill might very well self-consciously seek to implement the program. Indeed, in statistical experiments of a complicated design, the results of the experiment may require elaborate procedures of reporting and computation. But the information or beliefs thus obtained and used in implementation are beliefs *concerning what is reported or registered*. It is one thing for Jill to acquire the belief that she reports that e_b. It is quite another for her to acquire the belief that e_b or belief that she has such a belief. In cases where the implementation of a program for routine decision making involves elaborate data processing and computation, the agent may utilize beliefs as to the reports that are made as part of the process. Such information may be used as reasons for following the instructions of the program concerning one contingency (where the ball drawn is reported to be black) and not another (where the ball drawn is reported to be white). It does not matter whether Jill also comes to believe that e_b is true; for in implementing the program the information that the ball drawn is black plays no role. Jill is *not* using the belief that e_b as evidence or as a reason for choosing the black envelope. As we have seen, if e_b is used as evidence, it cannot be a reason for choosing the black envelope rather than the white. All Jill is concerned with is implementing the instructions as she has already given herself. *For this purpose*, her belief that e_b has no role to play. Her reporting that e_b does play a role; but it is not the role of a reason for choosing the black envelope. The report is just output of the external stimulus that itself serves as input to subsequent steps in implementation of the program. The 'data' (the reporting) are not converted into information used to justify further steps as would be the case if Jill had numerically determinate priors, came to believe that e_b, and used that belief as part of the evidence on the basis of which she reached a decision as to which envelope to take.

I am not suggesting that in the case where the prior credal probabilities for H_b and H_w are indeterminate, Jill would be incoherent in using the acquired belief that e_b as evidence in deciding on an envelope. That is to say, Jill would not have been incoherent if she had not chosen a plan before making the observation but had instead waited until after making observations and coming to believe that e_b before deciding what to do. I do claim, however, that as long as the prior credal state is sufficiently indeterminate, the new evidence does not provide any better basis for choosing between the black and white envelopes than existed prior to observation. This means that in such cases making observations cannot provide a reason for choosing the black envelope anyhow. All this maneuver can do is yield the judgment that there is no reason to choose the black envelope over the white.

The upshot is that whether Jill uses the data as input or as evidence, the data cannot be a reason for the action taken when the prior credal state is sufficiently indeterminate.

For Jill to undertake to implement the plan to use the data as input is for Jill to deprive herself deliberately of the opportunity to renege. Of course, only if Jill can take as certain that she is able to rule out the availability of such opportunity can she choose rationally to implement the plan. Otherwise choice lapses into wishful thinking.

The kind of routine decision making I have been describing by means of Jill's predicament is what I think Jerzy Neyman and Egon S. Pearson thought statistical reasoning ought to be addressing in their pioneer work in the 1930s. Its basic elements had already been elaborated by Charles Peirce in the 1870s and 1880s.[2]

Unfortunately in his case, Peirce called the following of a routine a species of inductive *inference*. The move is unfortunate not because we have been speaking of decision making here. I think (*pace* B. Williams, 1973, ch. 9) that inductive inference is a species of decision making where the conclusion is a decision to commit oneself to full belief in some claim. But inference is not only inference to a conclusion to be believed. It is inference from premises that are believed already. Inductive inference in the sense discussed by Peirce cannot be inference from information about observations already believed. Observations are treated as inputs and not as premises.

I am not concerned here with a verbal and pedantic point about the meaning of 'premise,' 'evidence,' 'inference,' or 'reason.' There is a very substantive issue involved here that I have sought to illustrate by showing how using data as input can be advantageous on some occasions where using it as evidence is not. It is the distinction that is important here – not the words. My distinction between using data as input and using it as evidence is intended to capture the substantive point. In my opinion, Peirce understood the distinction well enough and made an unfortunate terminological decision. His understanding is revealed in the kind of rationale he gave for his account of induction.

---

2 See Hacking, 1980 and Levi, 1980b for a discussion of Peirce's anticipation of the Neyman-Pearson approach. For a philosophically oriented discussion of the Neyman-Pearson theory, see Seidenfeld, 1979. The use of the distinction between using data as input and as evidence to elaborate the core idea behind the Neyman-Pearson approach is found in Levi, 1980a. References to the works of Peirce, Neyman and Pearson can be found in these discussions.

4

Sometimes routine decision making involves the use of routines to determine what to believe and not how to act. The two most common types of this species of routine decision making (I have called it 'routine expansion' in Levi, 1980a and 1991, ch. 3) are the acquisition of new belief via the testimony of the senses and the testimony of other agents. In relying on the testimony of the senses, the agent responds to external stimulation of the sensory apparatus by making reports that initiate the formation of new beliefs. The programs for routine expansion in such cases are not typically chosen in deliberation but are acquired through nature and nurture. And they are ordinarily implemented with little self-consciousness or reflection.

There are cases where observation becomes more deliberate and more closely resembles implementation of a Neyman-Pearson rule for 'inductive behavior.' This is true in experimental scientific work where protocols are often brought under severe critical control. And even in ordinary life such deliberateness may intrude.

I discovered in my early 30's I was mildly color blind and became more cautious in translating my reports of colors of cloth into acquired beliefs. But this greater caution was reflected in an alteration in the way I routinely expanded into beliefs about the colors of cloth. In reporting the color to be dark grey (rather than dark blue, dark green, dark brown), I no longer came to believe that it was dark grey but came to suspend judgment between the hypotheses that it was dark blue, dark green or dark brown (while ruling out that it was red, orange, etc.) I did not infer this from the report. The report was not a premise but was a registering in response to sensory stimulation.

Before acclimating to my new routine, I continued to believe that I made the report that the cloth was dark grey (i.e., that it looked dark grey) upon making the report. However, this belief was not used as evidence for hypotheses about the color even though I may have used it as evidence to determine 'how to go on' in implementing the new program.

New information obtained by routine expansion is obtained 'directly' – not by inference from premises. But either tacit or explicit convictions lurk in the background assumptions of the agent utilizing the program for routine expansion. In the case of Jill, the background assumptions concerned the assumptions made about the urn and its contents as well as the method of drawing balls from the urn. This emerges in the overall judgment that the use of the program is 'reliable' – i.e., has a low probability of importing false beliefs. When we trust our senses, as when we trust the testimony of others, we assume that the programs for routine expansion grounded on such trust are reliable in something like the sense just indicated even when we cannot spell out the details of such programs or the explanation of their reliability.

Routine expansion (whether by appeal to the senses, the testimony of others or confidence interval estimation) is needed when acquiring information by inference from premises already available cannot answer the questions under investigation. New 'external' sources of information are sought. Programs for routine expansion process the information from such external sources.

But information from such sources cannot be said to carry epistemological privilege of any sort. Routine expansion can lead agents not only into error but into inconsistency. An agent may believe that the Golden Gate Bridge is painted silver, trust his color perception and take a look at the bridge, and observe it to be painted a reddish color, only to find himself in conflict between the testimony of his senses and his initial convictions. In this case, it will not take too much effort for the agent to modify his initial convictions. In other cases, it will. I have received an e-mail message from a friend convincing me that he will be in California on Monday. On Monday, I look and see him in my office in New York. In my surprise, I may look again. I do not trust my initial impression and call into question both the testimony of the senses and parts of my background information. When Michelson obtained a null result incompatible with background theory, both the results of experimentation and the background theory were called into question. There is nothing empirically privileged here about the testimony of the senses any more than there is about the testimony of witnesses. We rely on both because we need external sources of information. To make the testimony of senses (or of authorities) foundational is going too far in the direction of making a virtue out of necessity.

That routine expansion is conflict injecting is an important respect in which routine expansion differs from inferential expansion. No legitimate expansion by inference should lead to contradiction. Routines judged reliable by the inquiring or deliberating agents can.

The capacity to inject conflict also allows for a response to a familiar objection to approaches such as the one I am advocating. A person is entitled to reconsider the good sense of continuing to implement a program for routine decision making upon which he is embarked – so the objection begins. This would appear to nullify the benefits of using data as input; for as soon as routine expansion is implemented, one should be entitled to reconsider implementation relative to the new information.

Jephthah the Gileadite made a vow to God to sacrifice the first living thing that should greet him upon his returning home victorious over the Ammonites (Judg. 11:30-1). He was committed to a program for routine decision making where data would be used as input – not as evidence.

I leave it to others to comment on the wisdom of Jephthah's having chosen to adopt this program in the first place. But once Jephthah met his daughter coming to greet him, a conflict was injected into his point of view; for in addition to implementing the routine for deciding what to sacrifice, Jephthah added via routine expansion the claim that his daughter was the first living thing to greet him. Moreover, we may suppose that Jephthah was already committed at the time he made his vow to moral injunctions against human sacrifice in general and sacrifice of his daughter in particular. Thus, Jephthah recognized that he had undertaken two commitments: to sacrifice the first living thing he greeted and eschew sacrifice of his daughter. He also came to believe that he could not, given the facts, jointly satisfy the two commitments in the particular case. In the face of such conflict, it would have been appropriate for Jephthah to move to a position of doubt about the applicability of his two commitments to the particular case and seek to resolve the doubt. This would have required reneging on implementing the program for routine decision making upon which Jephthah had embarked pending deliberation as to whether he should take it up again or abandon it. Jephthah had a good ('internal') reason for taking time out for deliberation. Jephthah did take time out but not for such deliberation. His daughter was given a two-month reprieve to mourn her virginity.

Thus, agents should sometimes halt implementation of programs for routine decision making *when conflicts arise that furnish good reason to reconsider the matter*. And sometimes the outcome of such reconsideration may be a decision to renege. Such good reasons arise when the decision maker comes to recognize that the program cannot be implemented simultaneously with some other undertaking to which he is committed. But in the absence of good reasons, the obligation to fulfil the commitment stands.

Even from his own point of view, Jephthah had good reason for reneging. On the other hand, Jill's coming to believe that e_b is not a good reason for reconsidering the program for routine expansion Jill had already decided to implement. Inconsistency neither in beliefs nor in value commitments is introduced by the new belief. Jill is already committed to taking the black envelope with no good reason to renege or call even a temporary halt to the proceedings.

This is supposed to be an essay on metaethics. But I have been speaking of epistemological issues. What is the connection?

5

Jill devised a plan for routine decision making. Virtuous agents in general do not devise such plans but acquire through training and acculturation into a given moral perspective sensitivities to differences in various situations that give reliable indication of the appropriate way to behave (according perhaps to devotees of that moral perspective).

One might envisage a predicament like the following suggested by McDowell (333): The virtuous agent faces a predicament where being kind to person X violates the rights of person Y. No option is available that meets the demands of sensitivity to X's feelings while satisfying Y's claims for justice. Insofar as the demands of kindness and the claims of justice apply to the situation, there is a genuine conflict. I have argued elsewhere (Levi, 1986 chs. 1 and 2) that insofar as such conflict is inconsistency, the agent should move to a state of suspense that no longer insists that both recommendations apply but regards both as permissible. What has led many writers to argue that there is no conflict is a tendency to confuse suspension of judgment between rival ways of evaluating options in a given context of deliberation with a case of conflict in values (resulting, perhaps, through inadvertence) in the sense of commitment to inconsistent values.

Although McDowell is not entirely clear on this point, it seems that the virtuous person may face a situation where he does not know in advance what to do, recognizes at least the permissibility of evaluating the situation according to the requirements of kindness, and also the permissibility of evaluating the same situation according to the demands of justice. McDowell claims, as I read him, that in recognizing this much, the virtuous agent already acknowledges a sensitivity to facts about the case. But McDowell wants to claim more. If there is a truth of the matter as to which way of evaluating the options is the right one, the reliably virtuous agent will detect it and this detection will be a good reason for acting accordingly.

In some respects, this kind of predicament does resemble Jill's situation. Jill needed to display a kind of perceptual sensitivity in deciding what to do – a sensitivity directed at assessing the hypotheses about the contents of the urn. Picking the right envelope in some sense involves making a correct judgment as to the contents of the urn.

Let me now restate my two objections to McDowell's view.

First, if an agent is in doubt between two ways of evaluating options, there is *no* coherent way of claiming that one is true and the other false. As a consequence, it is far from clear that good sense can be made of the notion of reliability.

Second, suppose, for the sake of the argument, that the first objection can be met. If perception involves using data as input rather than as evidence in either action or coming to believe, the data cannot be used as premises or as evidence. Perhaps, the perception may serve as part of causal explanation for action; but it cannot serve as a reason serving as a premise justifying or rationalizing the action. If the data are used as evidence, on the other hand, they will often fail to serve as the desired reasons for action.

6

The second objection grants (for the sake of the argument) to McDowell that the perceptual sensitivities displayed by virtuous agents are just as cognitive as the corresponding sensitivities displayed by chicken sexers. The reasons why the deliverances of such sensitivities cannot be reasons for action are precisely the same as those discussed in the toy statistical example about Jill. The virtuous agent is in suspense as to whether the dictates of kindness or equity are legislative in the situation. Before utilizing his perceptual skill, he takes for granted that the utilization of the skill will deliver reliably. If kindness is mandated, it will deliver a verdict in favor of kindness with high probability. If righteousness is dictated, it will declare for justice. Either way, it will deliver a correct verdict with high probability. In the situation, the agent is not committed to any determinate prior probability that kindness or justice is favored. If the virtuous agent declares for justice in virtue of his perception of the situation, he cannot then infer that justice is favored. Given the declaration for justice is used as evidence, it is a 'nuisance' because it undermines the high confidence that the agent's perceptual sensitivity is highly reliable that was warranted prior to obtaining this evidence in the sense that the high confidence now becomes an indeterminate grade of confidence.

Suppose, however, that the agent adopts a program for routine action, specifying a program whose output is the judgment that justice is favored if the report that it is favored is the input, and is the judgment that kindness is favored if the report that kindness is favored is the input. On the information available to the virtuous agent prior to making the report, implementing the program is robustly reliable. If this program is implemented, the perceptual judgment is a report used as an input and not converted into belief used as a premise in any argument (not even a practical syllogism) whose output is a decision. In this sense, it is not a reason for the decision.

Notice that in routine decision making, the report used as input may be regarded as a link in a causal nexus. But it is not a reason warranting the decision made.

Notice further that the objection to treating the perception as evidence or a reason is that used as a reason it will be useless as a basis for reaching a decision.

7

Let us now turn to the first objection. It asserts that rival ways of evaluating options as better or worse (morally, economically, or whatever), right or wrong are not true or false, and, hence, it becomes unclear what the reliability of perceptual judgments made by virtuous agents is supposed to be. The problem is akin to the difficulty in explicating

the notion of reliable forecasters where such forecasters specify probabilities of sunny skies, rain, snow, etc. There are various proposals for
reliable probability judgment on offer. Most of them have to do with
some version of the notion of being 'well calibrated' that changes the
subject from that of characterizing the 'reliability' of probabilistic judgments to something else.

My argument rests on the assumption that, when claims are truth
valued, agents can fully believe that they are true or that they are false,
and can suspend judgment with respect to their truth; and when in
suspense, the agent can make judgments of credal probability as to the
truth of the alternatives that may be numerically determinate or extremely
indeterminate. When truth value is lacking, suspense with respect to truth
is incoherent. Suspension of judgment, if it is coherent at all, is to be understood in a different way. This requirement does not demand appeal to
some standard of truth 'external' to the agent's point of view in judging
truth and falsity – an appeal that McDowell rightly dismisses.

To deny that ways of evaluating options are truth valued so that
suspension of judgment between permissible ways of evaluation is not
assimilable into suspension of judgment between two possibly true
hypotheses is not a feature peculiar to value judgments. Judgments of
degrees of belief or credal probability also lack truth values as Frank
Ramsey pointed out a long time ago.[3] And there is an excellent
'internalist' reason why this should be so. If X could be in doubt as to
whether to believe h to degree 0.9 or 0.1 and there is a truth of the
matter according to X, X should be able to make some sort of credal
probability judgment concerning which hypothesis is true. Let x be the
credal probability X assigns to the hypothesis that the right credal probability is 0.9 and let $1-x$ be the corresponding credal probability for the
hypothesis that the right credal probability is 0.1. Then the dictates of
the calculus of probability require that X's subjective or credal probability that h be $0.9x + 0.1(1-x)$. If x is 1 (or 0), X is not in suspense
between the alleged rival truth value bearing alternatives but is convinced that 0.9 (or 0.1) is the right probability judgment. If x is positive

---

3 F.P. Ramsey, "Truth and Probability" of 1926; reprinted in Ramsey, 1990, ch.4.

but less than 1, the credal probability that h should be distinct from 0.9 and 0.1 – counter to the assumption of suspension of judgment between those two. If the agent assigns credal probabilities to credal probabilities coherently, he must be opinionated abut them. This result might be accepted by one who insisted that credal probability judgments are not only truth valued but necessarily true if true and necessarily false if false. If this is as unpalatable as I suppose it to be, we should not assign credal probabilities to judgments of credal probability at all. But to claim that credal probability judgments carry truth values while forbidding credal probability judgments of credal probability judgments runs foul of a minimal demand on propositional attitudes. If they are true or false, it must be at least coherent to assign credal probabilities to the prospects of their being true or false.

This argument extends L.J. Savage's argument (1954, 58) against the coherence of subjective probabilities of subjective probabilities to an argument in favor of Ramsey's claim that credal probability judgments lack truth values. It is *not* an objection against assigning subjective probabilities to hypotheses about objective or factual or statistical probabilities such as H_b and H_w considered earlier in this essay. Moreover, it is not an argument based on truth as judged or understood outside the agent's perspective. I have been arguing against rational agents coherently from their own points of view according credal probabilities to credal probabilities.

There is an entirely parallel argument applying to an agent's valuations of options in a context of deliberation. Suppose A is the kind but unjust act and B the unkind but just act. Ranking A over B speaks for kindness and ranking B over A speaks for justice. If suspension of judgment between this ranking is suspension of judgment with respect to truth, credal probabilities should be assignable to them. If the credal probability is heavily in favor of A over B, this ranking will be recommended. There is no suspense counter to our supposition. If the credal probability favors the ranking B over A, this ranking will be recommended. Again no suspense. Finally, if the probabilities are nearly equal, A and B will be ranked equally. Not only is there no suspense but neither of the first two rankings allegedly in suspense is endorsed.

We may conclude that suspension of judgment with respect to truth is not available and that ways of evaluating options are neither true nor false. If that is so, how can the virtuous agent by reliably sensitive in the sense of selecting the right ranking if there is one except vacuously?

8

McDowell sees the virtuous agent as "wholeheartedly engaged" in a Wittgensteinian form of life that he at least partially shares with other members of some community (McDowell, 1979, 340-1). Given the agent's commitment to evaluating options in conformity with the evaluations endorsed by the form of life, the agent's task is to ascertain what these evaluations are. The virtuous agent's perceptual sensitivity can then be seen as a reliable recognition of the view sustained by the form of life as long as the form of life sustains a view regarding the specific issue under consideration.

Let the virtuous man as a creature of Wittgensteinian moral fashion come to doubt some aspect of the community way of life. This doubt need not arise because of a "vertigo" induced by adopting an "external standpoint outside our immersions in our familiar way of life" (341). The conflict between being kind and being just may be an entirely novel predicament for which the agent's way of life has not made even tacit provision. The community and the agent committed to the form of life took it for granted that such a conflict could not arise and made no provision for 'how to go on' in case it does arise. Reliable perception could lead to beliefs incompatible with this conviction and, as a consequence, to doubts as to whether kindness or justice should be applied in the unprecedented case. The agent who is virtuous in the sense of being well attuned to the niceties of the way of life in which he participates and of acting in conformity with them will lack reliable perceptions of community views as to how to proceed because there are no community standards to go on.

McDowell does not appear to countenance the possibility that the form of life fails to provide for unprecedented hard cases. He seems to think of the tension between kindness and justice, for example, as a question of determining whether the specific context under consideration falls within the scope of the injunction to be kind or the injunction to be just. According to McDowell, an agent immersed in the form of life will have the capacity to respond correctly when the case confronts him. He will understand the concepts of kindness and justice and apply them correctly. This understanding will enable him to perceive whether considerations of kindness or justice are 'salient' in the particular situation (344). Hard cases are akin to situations where someone has not followed a proof or cannot make a computation correctly. When people fail in such activities, we seek to instill in them the skills that will make them more effective participants in our forms of life. The failure is due to deficiencies in the individuals – not in the form of life.

This view is unacceptable. There would be no need for perception of saliences in the specific hard case were it not for the fact that the hard case is a predicament where the agent is in doubt as to what to do. That is to say, his 'conception of how to live' does not provide him with guidance as to what to do *by his own lights*! The agent need not be totally skeptical of the dictates of the form of life. He is not taking a stand external to his conception of how to live or, indeed, to the form of life in which he is 'immersed.' He merely thinks that the understanding furnished by immersion in the form of life fails to give an answer in the hard case he now confronts. The deliverances of the form of life may be sound but they are not complete.

McDowell seems to be blaming the agent by equating the agent's doubt with a form of conceptual confusion. The deliverances of the form of life are complete. It is up to the agent to comprehend them. A reliably virtuous agent does comprehend. Just as the slave boy's perceptual processes in the *Meno* remind the boy of geometrical truths he already knew, the virtuous agent's perceptual processes are an element in his acquiring comprehension.

Recognizing a conflict in the values to which one is initially committed is not a species of conceptual confusion. To the contrary, even from within the form of life, it may be a conceptual confusion to think that it is confusion. In hard cases, a clearheaded agent will regard the presence of conflict as an excellent reason for coming to doubt the claims of the competing value commitments on our allegiance. Even if we were totally immersed in a form of life beforehand and continue to be immersed in it, we come to recognize that the form of life offers incomplete guidance. For reasons mentioned in the previous section, we cannot coherently suspend judgment with respect to the truth of rival ways of evaluating options. And for reasons just considered, we cannot be in suspense as to what the prescriptions of our form of life are if there are no such recommendations. No program for utilizing perceptual processes to obtain a verdict can be said, therefore, to be a reliable indicator of what these prescriptions are or what the true way of evaluating options is.

But even if McDowell had succeeded in making out a case for thinking that perceptual judgments reliably detect the presence of true or conceptually approved ways of valuing options in specific contexts of choice, at most he would have showed that we could offer reasons for adopting reliable routines for action. No reasons for specific actions resulting from such routine decision making would be forthcoming.

Using data as input should not be confused with using data as evidence. Avoiding the mistake calls for vigilance not only in examining perceptual processes implicated in virtuous behavior but applies in empirical work in science and elsewhere. When data are used as input rather than as evidence, as I believe they are in perception leading causally to belief, perception fails to provide reasons warranting action just as it fails to provide reasons warranting belief.

References

Hacking, I. (1980) "The Theory of Probable Inference: Neyman, Peirce and Braithwaite." In D.H. Mellor, ed. *Science Belief and Behaviour*, Essays in honour of R.B. Braithwaite. Cambridge: Cambridge University Press

Levi, I. (1974) "On Indeterminate Probabilities," *Journal of Philosophy* **71** 391-418

Levi, I. (1980a) *The Enterprise of Knowledge.* Cambridge, MA: MIT Press

Levi, I. (1980b) "Induction as Self Correcting According to Peirce," In D.H. Mellor, ed. *Science, Belief and Behaviour*, Essays in honour of R.B. Braithwaite. Cambridge: Cambridge University Press

Levi, I. (1986) *Hard Choices.* Cambridge: Cambridge University Press

Levi, I. (1991) *The Fixation of Belief and its Undoing.* Cambridge University Press

McDowell, J. (1979) "Virtue and Reason." *The Monist* **62** 331-50

Seidenfeld, T. (1979) *Philosophical Problems of Statistical Inference.* Dordrecht: Reisdel

Williams, B. (1973) *Problems of the Self.* Cambridge: Cambridge University Press

CANADIAN JOURNAL OF PHILOSOPHY
Supplementary Volume 21

Evil and Explanation

NICHOLAS L. STURGEON
Cornell University

In the first part of this paper I want to consider the relation between two familiar philosophical views that have not to my knowledge been considered in any depth together, even by philosophers who are well known for defending each separately. These views have a certain natural affinity, in that each has been attractive to philosophers of a generally naturalistic bent. Thus, since I intend to argue that there is a difficulty in reconciling them, I will be pointing out a difficulty, not, I think, in philosophical naturalism, but nevertheless in one package often accepted by naturalists. One of the views is that the problem of evil is, at the very least, a serious theoretical difficulty for theism. The other is nihilism about value, the thesis that there are no real values in the world and that statements ascribing values to things are never true. I hope it is obvious why there is at least a *prima facie* difficulty in combining these views: how can someone who thinks that nothing is really good or evil also think that we find in the world more evil than we would expect if theism were correct? It may also seem obvious, with a moment's thought, how one might try to make the inconsistency disappear. But I shall argue that there remains, in the end, a very serious problem in reconciling these positions.

In the second part of my paper, I shall use my conclusions from the first part to illustrate and refine a claim I have defended elsewhere about the interpretation of moral and other evaluative explanations. Roughly, the connection is this. Opponents of realism about value have now mostly stopped saying that we never offer evaluative explanations.[1] Some seem inclined to the view that such explanations are a mistake.[2] A few others, however, noticing how central they are to our discourse, have instead begun looking for ways we might understand evaluative explanations so as to accept them without committing ourselves to value realism. I want to use the confrontation between theists and their opponents to test one of the few 'quasi-realist' suggestions in this vein that has actually been put forward. It comes as that term suggests from Simon Blackburn. It is a proposal with the advantages of clarity, simplicity, and, I think, a certain intuitive appeal; and it differs from an alternative proposal Blackburn also likes in drawing only on fairly uncontroversial assumptions in metaethics.[3] Theism is relevant to its assessment because theists

---

1 As Gilbert Harman did in *The Nature of Morality* (New York: Oxford University Press 1977) 22.

2 This presumably has to be Mackie's position. It also appears to be Allan Gibbard's view in ch. 6 of *Wise Choices, Apt Feelings* (Cambridge, MA: Harvard University Press 1990), although Gibbard has indicated in conversation that his considered view would now be more complex.

3 Simon Blackburn, "Just Causes," *Philosophical Studies* **61** (1991) 11-15, reprinted in his *Essays in Quasi-Realism* (New York: Oxford University Press 1993). Blackburn actually mentions three proposals, but notes that the first fails for many cases. I focus on the second (12-13).

   Blackburn's third proposal, which he also endorses, "*allows* that there exists a moral feature, injustice, and even allows that it can itself be causally relevant" (13, emphasis in original). There is no doubt that this position can accommodate moral explanations. But, as Blackburn immediately notes, "it will not be obvious that this position is available to the projectivist" (13) – that is, to a moral irrealist. He is right. Technical difficulties aside, there is the problem that he has argued, just three pages earlier, that it is an advantage of his irrealist position over a moral realist one, precisely that it *does not* postulate a moral property, such as injustice, as part of the explanation of agents' diversely based thoughts on this topic (9-11); so it is quite puzzling that he should then cheerfully countenance introduction of that same property to explain, say, revolutionary discontent, when what is being explained will of course include thoughts of that kind. Thus, my reason for putting this proposal to one side is that it is highly doubtful – at the least, very controversial – whether it is really a proposal that an ethical irrealist can consistently make.

offer an evaluative explanation for the existence and character of the world, and their naturalistic opponents press the problem of evil as an objection to that explanation. This of course does not commit the opponents, directly, to *accepting* any evaluative explanations. They do have to understand the theist's explanation in such a way that their own argument is an objection to it, however. And I shall argue that this precludes their applying Blackburn's proposal to the understanding of that explanation.

There is thus a common pattern to the argument of the two sections of my paper. It would considerably overstate my claim to say that I am going to argue in both sections that, if you want to see the problem of evil as a serious problem for theism, you need to be a realist about value. What I certainly shall argue in two different ways, however, is that, if you want to see the problem of evil as a powerful objection to theism, there are prominent irrealist views in ethics that you need to avoid.

I

I should begin by saying something about the doctrines whose relation I want to investigate. Unadorned nihilism about values is of course a rather simple and extreme position. What a lot of naturalistically minded philosophers actually say, when they feel their naturalism pushing them towards a soft line on ethics, is more complex. There is typically the part that sounds like nihilism, but then there is also the part where considerable ingenuity is expended in saving the discourse, so that we are allowed to say after all, perhaps in a different logical tone of voice, that kindness is better than cruelty, analytic philosophy better than deconstruction, and so on.

Still, I have three reasons for focusing first on the unadorned doctrine. One is just that it seems a reasonable strategy to begin by examining the trouble simple doctrines create, in order to see better which qualifications to them would actually help. A second, independent reason is that I don't think the efforts to save the discourse work very well anyway. So my own view is that although the philosophers I have mentioned don't want to endorse unqualified value nihilism, they are in fact stuck with something closer to it than they would like. I have defended this estimate elsewhere about various noncognitivist, relativist and subjectivist proposals;[4] and since I shall extend that argument in my discussion of Blackburn's proposal for preserving evaluative explanations, we shall in fact have looked at one more complex nihilist proposal anyway before I am through.

And then, third, there is the fact that when I cast about for examples of writers well known both for defending, from a naturalistic perspective, some kind of soft position on values, and also for pressing the problem of evil against theism, I really find only two choices, David Hume and John Mackie. And it is obvious which of these is the more manageable to discuss. Hume's remarks on value are complex, difficult to interpret and probably not entirely consistent. Mackie's thesis, at least in the well-known first chapter of his book on ethics, is by contrast clear and simple. He really holds that the world contains no evil, and not even any rottenness.[5] And he also argues, just as emphatically (though in a different place), that the problem of evil is a serious, even fatal difficulty for orthodox theism.[6] The question of how he thinks he can combine these two views would surely be interesting even if the combination were quite idiosyncratic. However, as I have indicated, I think that this combination, or something very like it, is in fact rather common; so I shall frequently refer to Mackie's views to illustrate the difficulty I am talking about.

I shall also simply appropriate Mackie's presentation of the problem of evil, taking it as my central example for purposes of discussion. As should be clear, I am not really concerned here with whether this objection to theism succeeds; my interest is in the question of what

---

4 In "What Difference Does It Make Whether Moral Realism is True?" *The Southern Journal of Philosophy* **24** (1986) supplement, 115-41; in "Contents and Causes," *Philosophical Studies* **61** (1991) 19-37, esp. 27-30; in "Moral Disagreement and Moral Relativism," *Social Philosophy and Policy* **11** (1994) 80-115; and in a critical study of Gibbard's *Wise Choices, Apt Feelings* in *Noûs* **29** (1995) 402-24.

5 J.L. Mackie, *Ethics: Inventing Right and Wrong* (Harmondsworth, Middlesex: Penguin, 1977) 15

6 J.L. Mackie, *The Miracle of Theism* (Oxford: Clarendon Press, 1982) ch. 9. See also his "Omnipotence and Evil," *Mind* **64** (1955).

someone who *thinks* it succeeds, or thinks even that it poses a serious challenge to theism, must think about metaethical issues. Still, Mackie's presentation is both standard and sophisticated enough to belong in any discussion of whether the objection does succeed; and that helps give it the advantage, for my purposes, that anyone who sees theism as threatened by the problem of evil is very likely to accept much of what Mackie says as explaining why. His presentation is also useful because, although he never explicitly addresses the difficulty I am inquiring about, his exposition seems shaped in places by what looks like the obvious reply. And, indeed, it may initially seem obvious, not just that this reply is the one he should give but that it is satisfactory. I shall argue that it is not obviously satisfactory and, especially, that it cannot appear satisfactory to Mackie. We need to begin, however, by seeing what the proposed solution is, and how it shows up in Mackie's discussion.[7]

The problem, recall, is how someone who denies that the world contains any evil can also hold that it contains more evil than a theist should

---

7 It might seem that there is another way Mackie could avoid the objection, by altering slightly his argument against theism. There is doubt about how he can say that the world contains evil, but of course none about how he can say that it contains no value at all, since that is the view he explicitly defends in ch. 1 of *Ethics: Inventing Right and Wrong*. Theists get into difficulties about evil, however, partly because they hold that the world, being the handiwork of a perfect God, is good. So Mackie seems in position just to object that they are mistaken, because nothing in or about the world is *either* good or bad. We might call this the 'problem of no value' rather than the problem of evil.

Although this suggestion provides no help in understanding what Mackie is doing in pressing (as he clearly does) the problem of evil, it does indicate how an ethical nihilist might object to theism, on the basis of a view about value, without turning to the more famous problem at all. However, Mackie's apparent reasons for *not* arguing in this way are interesting. He surely agrees that his value nihilism conflicts with theism in the manner indicated, but appears to think that this argument would nevertheless get the order of evidence wrong. For he says more than once (*Ethics: Inventing Right and Wrong*, 48; *The Miracle of Theism*, 114-18) that if (though, probably, only if) there is a God, the world might contain objective values. His argument for value nihilism is thus based on his philosophical naturalism, understood already to include atheism; and the value nihilism is thus not available as a premise from which to argue for the atheism.

expect. The solution that may seem obvious is that the nihilist about value might press the second of these claims only dialectically, as a purely *ad hominem* objection to theism. This idea certainly appears in Mackie's discussion, though in two different forms, the first simpler, the second somewhat more complex. What he says first is that his objection only concerns logical consistency.[8] Theism, in its orthodox forms, *says* that there are evils in the world; Mackie does not have to supply this premise, nor need he believe it. In its first formulation, then, his objection is just that this central theistic doctrine, when combined with standard views about the divine attributes, leads to a contradiction.

As Mackie's discussion proceeds, however, it quickly becomes apparent that this initial formulation can only have been intended as a first approximation. Two things show this. One is his explicit concession that the theist has, after all, enough maneuvering room to avoid outright inconsistency; the other, close on its heels, and of even more interest for our purposes, consists in his suddenly endorsing a number of obviously evaluative claims, seemingly in his own voice. To illustrate both points, I need to explain some terminology Mackie introduces. Call any good that logically requires the existence of some evil, a second-order good: examples might be sympathy with suffering or triumph over adversity. And call any evil that fits in this organic way into a greater second-order good, an absorbed evil. Then the theist can avoid any threatening inconsistency, Mackie admits, by maintaining that although there are evils, they are all absorbed evils.[9] But, he immediately objects, this thesis just isn't true.

> On the one hand there are surplus first-order evils, suffering and the like which are not actually used in any good organic whole, and on the other there are second-order evils: these will not be incorporated in second-order goods but will contrast with them: malevolence, cruelty, callousness, cowardice [and others].[10]

---

8 *The Miracle of Theism*, 150-1

9 *Ibid.*, 153-54. His concession also depends on the understanding that omnipotence does not include the power to do the logically impossible (150, 154).

10 *Ibid.*, 155

Here we have Mackie suddenly sounding more vulnerable to the objection we are exploring. How does he know which organic wholes are the good ones? What is a nihilist about value doing calling malevolence, cruelty, callousness and cowardice evils?

But there is still a possible answer, and it is one that he appears more than once to endorse. "It is for the theist," he says at one point, "not for me, to say what counts as good."[11] So he might maintain that he is here taking his evaluative standards entirely from his opponents, and is not in that respect speaking in his own voice. Theists not only concede that there are evils, after all, but have views about what kinds of things they include: and on their list, typically, are malevolence, cruelty, callousness, cowardice and the rest. Theists also have ideas about which organic wholes would be good. So Mackie might claim that what he is doing, here and in some other similar-sounding passages, is merely using the theist's evaluative standards to report, in a summary way, nonevaluative *facts* that the theist would prefer to ignore; but, he could say, in using the theist's standards in this way he is not endorsing them. His argument would thus be that, taking the nonevaluative

---

11   *Ibid.*, 173. The quoted words are actually prefaced by, "But, as I have said before." The reference appears to be to this earlier passage: "But it is not for me to make assumptions about this either way. Since I am charging the theist with holding incompatible beliefs, it is *his* conceptions of good, evil and so on that are in play here" (165). See also his reference (159) to "real, deplorable, unabsorbed evils, such as theists themselves constantly condemn."

The remark from p. 165 contains an oddity, in that it comes well after his general admission, amply illustrated, that he is *not* simply accusing the theist of holding incompatible beliefs. If this is not just carelessness, the explanation may be that this characterization is meant not to apply to his entire argument in this chapter, but only to a dilemma he is pressing in that passage, in which he does argue that certain of the theist's beliefs are inconsistent, and that an inconsistency remains whatever the theist says about a certain issue of value. The quotation from p. 173 also occurs in what appears to be the statement of a similar dilemma.

So, I note, it is possible that Mackie does *not* mean, in any of these passages, that all of his evaluative standards are borrowed from his opponent. However, he is certainly barred from supplying these standards himself; and he offers no other suggestions about where he might get them.

empirical facts as *he* sees them, and standards of value as his *opponent* sees them, theism fails. This argument would not be entirely *ad hominem* on nonevaluative issues such as how much suffering there is or whether there is always someone to sympathize with it; but it *would* remain *ad hominem* on such evaluative issues as whether suffering is an evil or whether sympathy with suffering of a certain description is ever a greater good than the suffering is an evil. So it would also remain an argument that a nihilist about values can consistently make.

Now, I certainly don't deny that one can press the problem of evil some distance, against the right opponent, in one or the other of these ways: perhaps by finding inconsistencies in the theist's position, more likely by pressing nonevaluative claims of one's own, to be combined with evaluative standards the theist already accepts. What I shall argue, however, is that these procedures clearly fall far short of doing for Mackie, or for most other proponents of the problem of evil, what the proponents actually think their arguments accomplish against theism. Unless the value nihilist can do better than this, he cannot see the problem of evil as a serious problem for theism.

I can illustrate the difficulty with two passages from Mackie. The first is a remarkable short discussion in which he hopes to dismiss what he calls an attempt "to sidestep the problem." This is an approach that

> may be summed up in the phrase, "God's goodness is not ours." In other words, when the theist says that God is wholly good he does not mean that God has anything like the purposes and tendencies that would count as good in a human being.

Against this position Mackie quotes with approval a strongly worded objection by John Stuart Mill (who is in turn expressing agreement with his father, James Mill). Here, beginning with his paraphrase of Mill, is Mackie's entire argument against this attempt at a theodicy.

> In effect, God is being *called* good, while at the same time he is being *described* as bad, that is, as having purposes and acting upon motives which in all ordinary circumstances we would recognize as bad; he is depicted as behaving in some respects like a malevolent demon, in others like a petulant tyrant, and in others again like a mischievous and thoughtless child. Now certainly if such motives as these are ascribed to God, there will be no difficulty in reconciling his omnipotence with the occurrence of what would ordinarily be called evils. But to

argue in this way is merely to defend a shadow, while abandoning the substance, of the traditional claim that God is good.[12]

Many will no doubt be inclined to agree with Mackie and the Mills
that this describes too cheap a defense of theism. But Mackie's argument here does not fall into either of the safe patterns we have identified. He does not call the position he is criticizing inconsistent. Nor
does he suggest that it can be rebutted by accepting the proponents'
standards of evaluation while pointing to empirical evidence they have
overlooked. On the contrary, he explicitly concedes that *if* we accept
the proponents' somewhat alarming standards for divine moral perfection, the problem of evil disappears. His complaint is instead about
the standards. Here we might have hoped for a less roundabout statement of just what is wrong with the standards. But I do not see what
Mackie can mean, in saying that these thinkers call God good but *describe*
him as bad, unless he holds, first, that their standards are mistaken, indeed obviously mistaken; and, second, that by more nearly correct standards a deity such as they praise would count as bad, not good. But a
value nihilist cannot in consistency say that these standards are any more
mistaken than the Mills', or that any alternative standards are correct.[13]

The other passage to which I draw attention is one in which it is at
least equally clear that Mackie is engaged in evaluation. As I have noted,

---

12 *The Miracle of Theism*, 156. Emphasis in original.

13 There may appear to be an alternative suggestion at the conclusion of the paragraph. Perhaps the evaluative standards are simply *different* enough from those
traditionally invoked to force us to see an ambiguity in the evaluative terminology, even though neither set of standards is correct. Can the Mackie of *Ethics:
Inventing Right and Wrong* really say, however, that two speakers calling God
good, both with the appropriate recommendatory force but with different standards, do not agree in their evaluation of God? I do not see how to understand
this view except as implying that the standards set at least rough truth-conditions for statements by speakers who accept them, so that in calling bad a God
such as these speakers praise, speakers with more traditional standards speak
truly. That, of course, is what I have noted that Mackie appears to say earlier in
the passage. So, if I am right, this isn't after all a different suggestion, and it isn't
one a value nihilist can accept.

it is at least in principle possible that in all the places where he appears to be doing this he is merely borrowing his opponents' standards; but in this passage the plausibility of this reading is minimal. He is considering the suggestion that sin, when followed by repentance and redemption, is what I called above an absorbed evil. He explicitly notes the considerable Biblical authority behind this view: "Joy shall be in heaven over one sinner that repenteth, more than over ninety and nine just persons, which need no repentance."[14] He mentions the parables of the prodigal son, who produces more joy by his return than the son who never strayed, and of the frugal housewife pleased to have found a coin supposed lost, by implication more pleased than she would have been never to have lost several coins of equal value. But he dismisses this familiar Christian doctrine as a "strange view"; he rejects as muddled any reasoning that goes from what he concedes are understandable human reactions to any thesis about overall preferability; and he concludes that "It would be hard ... to endorse the sober evaluation that sin plus repentance is, as an organic whole, better than sinlessness."[15] Whatever he may be doing in this passage, Mackie is certainly not just arguing *from* values his Christian opponents endorse. He can of course take from them the view that sin is an evil; but in holding, against the familiar understanding of these well-known New Testament passages, that it remains even when repented and forgiven an unabsorbed evil, he does not appear to be appealing to further Christian views on value. He is instead playing, not here village atheist but, in the popular sense of the term, village ethical rationalist; he really doesn't see, on reflection, how the doctrine makes sense.[16]

---

14 Luke 15:7, quoted by Mackie, *The Miracle of Theism*, 159. The two parables are also from Luke 15. The view Mackie defends here would no doubt appeal to the prodigal's brother (Luke 15:25-32).

15 *The Miracle of Theism*, 159

16 Of course, any Christian might be influenced by these same thoughts, and so come to share Mackie's evaluative standards even here. More generally, Mackie will almost never be arguing from evaluations shared by no one else. But when he describes his argument as *ad hominem*, he takes his opponent to be "the theist" (ibid., 159, 165, 173), and this generic target seems to be disappearing rapidly from his sights. So, here, is "the Christian."

Someone might at this point concede that Mackie seems in these passages to slip into arguing from evaluative premises not shared by the opponents he is addressing. But she might wonder how central these arguments are to Mackie's case, and more generally how typical this sort of difficulty will be for naturalistic philosophers pressing the problem of evil. The thesis that God's goodness 'is not ours' (and is whatever escaping the problem of evil turns out to require it to be) seems very extreme; and not every version of the problem of evil will attack the evident meaning of Gospel parables head-on. I could easily provide more examples from Mackie's discussion, however. In addressing the free-will defense, for example, he takes several strong stands about the value, or lack of it, of various imagined forms of free will, with no indication of how he might be arguing by his opponents' standards; and it is hard to see how any credible version of the problem of evil could avoid this topic.[17] The two Mills addressed the thesis that God's goodness is different, moreover, because they took it to have wide currency among theists, and Mackie does not discuss it as if it were merely a historical curiosity. And even with that thesis to one side, I believe that, in the respect that matters to my discussion, these examples from Mackie's argument are quite typical of what happens when atheists confront theists over the issue of theodicy. To describe the matter from one side, it does often seem to atheists that theists, in these debates, bend their standards of evaluation unreasonably to save the deity and the deity's works from adverse judgment – that, at least in theodicy, and in the choice of standards for divine goodness, Christian charity begins at home. And while the imputation of unreasonableness may be mistaken, I believe that the perception of frequent and firm if sometimes subtle evaluative disagreement is not. Nor should this be surprising. People's values at all levels of generality are affected by their nonevaluative beliefs about what the world is like. Theists

---

17 Ibid., 165-66, 168-72. He argues, about one form of freedom, that it might reasonably be valued *by* the agent who possesses it, but would nevertheless not have value from a divine point of view. The argument is intriguing, but I do not see how he could imagine establishing all this just from the values of his average fellow atheist, let alone those of a representative theist.

and atheists differ profoundly in these beliefs. So, while it may turn out that theists hold enough of the values Mackie and other philosophical naturalists hope they do, in order to allow them to be tripped up dialectically by the problem of evil, there would certainly be no mystery if it turned out that they do not.

Our conclusion to this point, then, seems to be that the value nihilist, restricted to arguing by her opponents' standards in pressing the problem of evil, cannot say nearly as much against the theist as Mackie actually does say, or as almost every proponent of the objection hopes to say. But there is one more possibility to consider. For it might be suggested that I have so far been understanding the notion of the 'opponents' standards' too narrowly, more narrowly than is charitable in understanding Mackie. (Though, I should emphasize, Mackie nowhere explicitly suggests anything like the possibility I am now raising.) I have been taking the relevant evaluative standards to be what we might call *express* standards: what the opponent would sincerely say about the issue or would think about it, perhaps after minimal discussion or questioning. The vagueness of this latter qualification, however, suggests a range of possible alternative understandings that might yield more promising results. It is easy to suspect, for example, that proponents of the 'God's goodness is different' thesis might have to modify their position if they were required to reflect systematically and dispassionately on its connections with their other views, including methodological scruples they honor in other areas against saving favored explanations by purely *ad hoc* maneuvers. And perhaps Christians would find it necessary, after suitable reflection, to agree that it would be better for there to be sinless lives than lives in which sin is a prelude to repentance and forgiveness. So we might define someone's *implicit* standards as the ones he would come to accept expressly if he were to subject his views to an appropriate, perhaps quite idealized, process of reflection and rational adjustment. And then we might explore whether it would help to allow the value nihilist to argue by her opponents' implicit evaluative standards rather than the express ones. Perhaps Mackie could even claim that that is what he is doing in the examples I have cited.

This is a sketch, hardly a concrete proposal, since I have gestured only vaguely at what might count as appropriate rational reflection.

Even with the suggestion put this abstractly, however, I can say why the proposal, although it might appear promising to me, cannot appear promising to Mackie and is quite unlikely to look that way to other value nihilists. The reason is that optimism about this proposal amounts to optimism about the rational resolvability of deep evaluative disagreements. Here after all is Mackie, speaking as far as we have been able to settle in his own voice (even if he shouldn't be), and taking stands that look reasonable by his standards but look unreasonable to many theists, on issues such as the evaluation of the deity, the value of a sinless life as against that of a sinner redeemed, the value of libertarian free will. What he would have to believe in order to regard the proposal I have just sketched as successful, therefore, is that every theist, after appropriate rational reflection, would come to agree with these evaluations (as well as with any others he relies on). In one way, admittedly, this isn't as optimistic as thinking that all rational inquirers would agree under appropriate circumstances, but it's still striking optimism. In two other respects, however, optimism about this proposal would actually seem to require *greater* optimism than merely thinking the issues abstractly resolvable. One concerns who wins: for Mackie would have to think, not just that *some* standards would be agreed on, but that his own, or others sufficiently similar to his, would be. And the other concerns what to count as appropriate circumstances. For the general question about resolvability is typically understood to concern whether parties who had access to all relevant non-evaluative information could come to agree rationally about values. It would seem question-begging in this dialectical setting, however, in which Mackie and the theist are debating about values in order to argue about the existence of God, to understand the theist's implicit evaluative standards to be the ones she would reach if, in her reflection, she already knew that atheism was correct – even if atheism *is* correct. If so, then in order to see the theist's implicit evaluative standards as matching his own, Mackie would have to expect rational reflection to lead her into agreement with him even if she had no access to one very large piece of information that might certainly help to nudge her in his direction.

What makes this point relevant, of course, is that rational resolvability is an issue on which value nihilists tend to be committed. A pessimistic estimate on this issue is typically one of the central supports for their view, as it explicitly is in Mackie's case.[18] I won't claim that this *must* be so. Perhaps we can just imagine an alternative Mackie, still led to nihilism about values by what he calls his "argument from queerness,"[19] but noting with surprise that people who discuss evaluative issues are always able to reach rational agreement.[20] I believe that this imagined position would be quite unstable.[21] I shall defer to the possibility it represents, however, by carefully saying only that it is most unlikely that a value nihilist could adopt an optimistic position about the rational resolvability of deep evaluative disagreements. And, if that is right, it is just about as unlikely that a nihilist pressing the problem of evil could expect any benefit from arguing, dialectically, from the theist's implicit standards of value rather than from his ex-

---

18 *Ethics: Inventing Right and Wrong*, 36-8

19 Ibid., 38-42

20 If we look beyond unadorned value nihilism to views that attempt to preserve a role for evaluative discourse, R.M. Hare's recent position may be another example: no value judgments are true, and evaluative terms represent nothing real, but, when the discourse obeys the appropriate noncognitive rules, moral disagreements, at least, are resolvable because utilitarianism is demonstrable. (R.M. Hare, *Moral Thinking: Its Levels, Method and Point* [Oxford: Clarendon Press 1981].) The demonstration offered is unpersuasive, but the position at least illustrates the bare possibility of thinking a form of nihilism defensible without relying on any claims about the irresolvabililty of evaluative disagreements.

21 It would be unstable because the resolvability of the disputes would invite explanation, and the obvious explanation to consider would be that the evaluative terminology refers to features that the discussants are in position to find out about. I agree with Mackie, however, that that wouldn't completely settle the question of whether there are real values; we would need in addition to think that the features referred to were really values. (For comparison, we might think that the terms of some polytheistic religion actually refer to natural forces; that would not commit us to thinking that those forces were gods.) On the other hand, I think that Mackie's story about how strange real values would have to be is quite easily countered, and that plausible naturalistic accounts of value are available. Hence my compromise: I concede the possibility of a position that was nihilist though not supported by pessimism about rational resolvability, but I think it extremely unlikely that such a view could be made plausible.

press standards. Of course, this change in understanding would make some difference, because people's implicit standards undoubtedly differ from their express ones. But, if optimism about rational resolvability is unjustified, this difference may as easily be a hindrance as a help to the nihilist pressing the problem of evil. Perhaps the theist who has reflected will find himself even more convinced, rather than less, of the moral perfection of a jealous, vengeful, capricious God, or of the superior value of sin forgiven, or of the good of libertarian free will.

The conclusion I draw, therefore, is that my initial suspicion was correct. A consistent nihilist about values is most unlikely to be able to see the problem of evil as a serious difficulty for theism, and Mackie certainly cannot do so. He thus faces a choice; and so, almost certainly, does any other philosopher attracted to both these views. There are of course two main options. One, which I commend to a reader's attention, is to acknowledge that, as Mackie convincingly shows (in one book), the problem of evil is a serious difficulty for theism; and to note that there are familiar, perhaps even persuasive replies to all the familiar naturalistic arguments, including Mackie's (in the other book) for value nihilism. The other option, which will no doubt remain attractive to some, is to stick with the nihilism while conceding that theism does not, after all, face a serious problem about evil.

II

At this point, however, someone still attracted by the arguments for nihilism, but unhappy about letting the theist off the hook, might recall that I have quite deliberately confined my attention so far to what I called unadorned nihilism about values. How would things look, he might wonder, if we instead added one of those schemes for saving the discourse? Isn't there some way we could agree with the nihilist when we do sober metaphysics and epistemology, yet still join Mackie and the two Mills in saying, by way of objection to the theist's explanation, that a malevolent, petulant and mischievous God would be bad, not good?

I am skeptical about this possibility. It would be foolish to pretend to settle so large an issue here, but I shall illustrate my doubts by using the points I have made to examine in detail the proposal I mentioned in my introduction concerning the interpretation of evaluative explanations. I attribute the suggestion, as I have indicated, to Simon Blackburn, since he has defended it. He was not the first to discuss it, however; I had earlier mentioned it as a natural, undoubtedly initially attractive view for an irrealist or nihilist about values to try out. I did that in order to criticize it briefly, as I have also done in a bit more detail elsewhere.[22] I return to it here because the example we have been considering provides such a good opportunity to illustrate why the proposal is disappointing. Before we can begin to assess it, however, I need to explain several background points about the general debate to which it is a contribution.

Blackburn offers his proposal in the service of a general program for interpreting evaluative language that he calls 'projectivist' or 'expressivist' and that I would call 'noncognitivist.' As he usually presents it, and as I shall understand it, this program is a form of value nihilism, but it is one mitigated by the hope of preserving much of our evaluative discourse by describing an appropriate role for it in the expression of attitudes – at any rate, of something primarily affective or conative rather than cognitive. His proposal about evaluative explanations is thus made against the background of two assumptions. One assumption is that noncognitivism can successfully explain an expressive point for *some* of our evaluative discourse, even if value nihilism is correct, although it is controversial how far this success extends. The second is that one of the controversial areas concerns evaluative explanations: that is, that it needs to be shown, as of course this proposal is intended to do, that noncognitivism can bring the explanatory role of evaluative language within its orbit. Blackburn thus sees his proposal as an attempt to extend an already partly successful program. This is worth noting in advance because it might be missed. The proposal, as we shall see, can certainly be explained without this background, but some of its apparent usefulness to the value nihilist would then be hidden, as would some difficulties it encounters.

---

22 Nicholas Sturgeon "What Difference Does It Make Whether Moral Realism is True?" 123. Since Blackburn's "Just Causes" is a reply to this article, I assume that he is unimpressed by the criticism. I offer more criticism in "Contents and Causes," 27-30, a continuation of the discussion with Blackburn.

I do not challenge these assumptions, especially when the first is stated this vaguely, and when it does not imply that noncognitivism will provide the best interpretation on balance even in areas where it meets the least objection. The second is of course no problem for me, since I am one of the people who doubts that the extension can be made. This picture of the problem Blackburn and I are addressing is an easy one to share, I think, if one looks at examples. Suppose someone calls a government's long-term treatment of a certain population unjust. We have a general sense of what a noncognitivist will say about this. The assessor is expressing dismay or indignation or, more likely, some negative attitude requiring far more nuanced characterization; and we can see how it is at least arguable that she might be able to express this attitude without seeing herself as attributing any property, injustice, to the situation. But now imagine that she adds that the injustice, while merely demoralizing some of the population, is contributing to revolutionary sentiment in other quarters. It seems far less clear how any value nihilist, including the noncognitivist, is to construe this remark. No doubt our assessor still has whatever negative attitude she already had to what she labels as unjust, but she now seems to be attributing causal power to something – on the face of it, to injustice. What is a noncognitivist to say?

As the example indicates, one reason evaluative explanations have attracted attention in metaethical debate is that people who cite a feature as explanatory seem to have to regard it as real. This appearance can be challenged, as for example by fictionalist accounts of scientific explanation; but, in fact, it is not challenged in any wholesale way by Blackburn or by many other participants in this debate who are nevertheless skeptical about the reality of values. They are prepared in general to take what we regard as explanatory as one guide to what we suppose to exist. Thus, if we imagine the explanation expanded to say that the revolutionary discontent is due not merely to injustice but to poverty, they take our assessor to regard poverty as real. What about injustice? They might of course say that she regards this as real, too, but is mistaken. This sort of explanatory use of evaluative notions is so central and common, however, that if they take this line generally they will have to accuse us of a lot of mistakes. And it is an interesting feature of this debate that it is generally acknowledged, even by unadorned nihilists like Mackie who bite the bullet,[23] to be a count against a theory that it should convict us of pervasive error in this way. Hence the general attraction to the value nihilist, even apart from the arguments about theism we have looked at, of a project like Blackburn's: of finding a way to construe evaluative explanations as committed to less than they seem, and in particular as not committed to the reality of the values they appear to invoke.

Theism has not figured much in the arguments of either side in this discussion. I suspect that it is a certain feature of the dialectical situation that largely explains why. Orthodox theism offers a great big evaluative explanation, so you might have expected it to attract attention. Theists see the entire physical world and its inhabitants as dependent for their existence and character on a completely perfect being. But theists are boring in this context because they typically also believe in the reality of the values they invoke. Thus, they do not need value realists to point out to them the unnoticed apparent implications of what they are saying; they have noticed and already agree. Nor are they in the market for quasi-realist devices that would allow them to preserve their explanations while shedding the burden of their unwanted belief that supreme goodness is really an attribute of God. Atheists by contrast are more interesting because some of them, at least, have doubts about whether values are real. So they need realists to catch them when they offer evaluative explanations and point out to them what they are committing themselves to; and then, no doubt, they may welcome quasi-realists to save them from the clutches of the realists. Any evaluative explanations they offer, however, will of course not be theistic ones: those they reject. So, whether we look at theists or atheists, theistic explanations do not seem useful examples for either side to use in changing anyone's mind about these metaethical issues.

This sounds plausible, but it overlooks something. Theistic explanations can provide an important test in the debate over evaluative explanations and value realism even if atheists are the more interest-

---

23 *Ethics: Inventing Right and Wrong*, 35

ing crowd to address with arguments, because *rejecting* an evaluative explanation on the basis of evidence can commit one to realism every bit as much as accepting one can. This can happen in two ways, one emphasized in the first section of my paper, the other my primary topic in this section but easily illustrated by that same earlier discussion. (*a*) First, we were unable to find any way in which proponents of the problem of evil could make their case against the theist's evaluative explanation without seeming to abandon value nihilism. Either they take a number of evaluative stands of their own against the theist, as Mackie does, or they endorse an optimism about the rational resolvability of evaluative disagreements that is almost certainly unavailable to a nihilist, and certainly not to Mackie.

Of course, to take these stands is, so far, only to have abandoned unadorned nihilism. This is a problem for Mackie, and so a significant result, but perhaps it is less of one for a nihilist willing to turn to noncognitivism to save the discourse.[24] (*b*) However, my second point,

---

24 This seems an appropriate point to address an objection that may occur to those who have read past the first chapter of *Ethics: Inventing Right and Wrong*: an objection, not to the truth of my conclusion in the first section of this paper, but to its interest. For, the objector might contend, anyone who has read all of that book already knows that Mackie is inconsistent, and does not need to look at his version of the problem of evil to learn this. For after declaring in chapter 1 that all first-order moral judgments are false, Mackie proceeds in the later chapters to debate a great many first-order moral issues. As Gilbert Harman says, "It is almost as if he had first demonstrated that God does not exist and had then gone on to consider whether He is wise and loving" ("Is There a Single True Morality?" in David Copp and David Zimmerman, eds., *Morality, Reason and Truth* [Totowa, NJ: Rowman and Allenheld, 1985] 30). So what is the great interest in learning that there is a similar inconsistency between chapter 1 and the evaluative theorizing in his presentation of the problem of evil?

There are two answers. (*a*) First, there is a tempting resolution to the latter inconsistency that has no plausibility at all when applied to the former: namely, that Mackie is arguing solely in an *ad hominem* fashion, by his opponent's evaluative standards. So it is interesting to see that, as I have shown in the first part of this paper, that solution fails. (*b*) Second, as Harman notes, another possibility is that in the latter part of the ethics book, Mackie has adopted "some sort of noncognitivist account of the judgments that are to replace the old moral judg-

atheists pressing the problem of evil are committed not just to value judgments but to other views about their debate with the theist. They take themselves – Mackie certainly does – to be disagreeing with the theist's evaluative explanation, and to be pressing objections relevant to it. So, we will need to see whether a noncognitivist account of evaluative explanations can ratify these estimates of univocality and relevance. If it cannot, then anyone who shares the atheist's commitments in this debate with the theist must reject not only unadorned nihilism but also noncognitivism. That may not leave realism as the only option, but it does pare down the alternatives. This is why the interest of any proposal like Blackburn's, designed to accommodate evaluative explanations, will include interest in its implications about objections to them.

We need then to look at Blackburn's proposal. It is in a way quite a natural one; it, or something close to it, seems to me to have been presupposed in other discussions in which it is not explicitly stated, and I have encountered it a number of times in conversation. One reason it can be hard to tell what a discussion assumes, however, is that this proposal is easily confused with another, superficially similar (and which I also believe to be mistaken), but which is irrelevant to the issue we are concerned with here. A good way to introduce Blackburn's proposal is thus to distinguish it from this alternative.

What makes these two proposals susceptible to confusion is their possession of two significant similarities. First, both take advantage (*a*) of the commonly acknowledged view that evaluative properties, if there are any, supervene and are dependent upon the nonevaluative features of things – and (*b*) of the fact that this *is* commonly acknowledged, not just believed by philosophers but somehow presupposed in ordinary

---

ments" (idem.). So here is a possible solution to the apparent inconsistency within the ethics book: that Mackie is distinguishing two different readings of evaluative judgments, a strict one, reflecting what they now standardly mean, on which they are all false, and a 'fall-back' noncognitivist understanding with which we might *replace* the standard one. Could this also be a solution to the apparent inconsistency between chapter 1 of *Ethics: Inventing Right and Wrong*, and what he says in pressing the problem of evil? *That* will depend partly on whether a noncognitivist can construe Mackie as objecting to the same explanation that his theistic opponent is offering: my principal topic in this section of my paper.

thought and discussion. Second, both use this acknowledged view to argue that, although there is a way in which evaluative explanations can be correct, all that they should be understood as saying, and all that is true when they are true, is that certain indicated nonevaluative features explain something. In short, both say that these explanations are really nonevaluative explanations.[25] The two doctrines are nevertheless quite distinct in a way that should please philosophers, for the difference depends on where you place an existential quantifier.[26] According to Blackburn's proposal, what is true is this. When someone offers an evaluative explanation, there is some possibly quite complex nonevaluative feature which *he takes* the values he mentions to supervene and depend upon; and what his explanation should be understood to say is that that nonevaluative feature explains whatever is said to be explained. The other proposal says instead that when someone offers an evaluative explanation, what he believes, and what we should understand as the content of the explanation, is this: that there is some nonevaluative feature, possibly quite complex, on which the indicated value supervenes and depends, and that that nonevaluative feature explains whatever is said to be explained. For reasons that will become clearer as we proceed, call the first of these, which is defended by Blackburn, the 'Speaker's Standards proposal,' and the second the 'Real Supervenience proposal.'

The reason that the Real Supervenience proposal doesn't help with the main issue we are considering is that, although it eliminates from evaluative explanations any claim that evaluative features cause or explain anything, it doesn't eliminate the claim that these features exist

---

25 Another similarity, no doubt less important, is that philosophers like me, sympathetic to realism about values, tend to reject both proposals, sometimes for similar-sounding reasons. (An exception appears to be Robert Audi, who accepts realism about values but also accepts what I call below the 'Real Supervenience proposal' about evaluative explanations. See his "Ethical Naturalism and the Explanatory Power of Moral Concepts," in Steven J. Wagner and Richard Warner, eds., *Naturalism: A Critical Appraisal* [Notre Dame: University of Notre Dame Press 1993] 95-115.)

26 Blackburn, "Just Causes," 12-13; Sturgeon, "Contents and Causes," 28, 36 (n. 17)

(or, at a minimum, that there are evaluative truths). You tell me that injustice is causing revolutionary sentiment; according to the Real Supervenience proposal, what you are really telling me is that some nonevaluative feature is doing this. But *which* nonevaluative feature? Well, according to you, whichever one the injustice really supervenes upon (hence my choice of name). You may have one idea about which nonevaluative feature this is and I another, but that makes no difference to the content of your explanation and to the conditions under which it would be correct. If we are both mistaken in our views of injustice, but injustice really supervenes upon a nonevaluative feature neither of us had thought of, and that feature is causing the discontent, then on this construal what you are telling me is true. On the other hand, and crucially, if as value nihilists claim there is no such thing as injustice, so that it doesn't really supervene on anything, then your explanation comes out mistaken.

That is why the Real Supervenience proposal is of no use to a value nihilist looking for a way to preserve evaluative explanations: this way of preserving them abandons the nihilism. So if we are to use either of these two approaches it will have to be the Speaker's Standards version, as Blackburn does. This proposal, unlike the Real Supervenience proposal, does eliminate from evaluative explanations any commitment to evaluative truths or properties. It works this way. If you tell me that injustice is causing social discontent, I need to know, as I put it before, what possibly complex nonevaluative feature you take injustice to supervene on: or, less grandly, what your nonevaluative standards are for the application of this concept or term (hence my name for the proposal). I then understand you to be offering an explanation that appeals only to that nonevaluative feature, the one picked out by your standards. Thus, if you are John Rawls, I take you to be offering one explanation, and if you are Robert Nozick, another. If, like most people who haven't yet written their book on justice, you have rather vague standards on this question, then you have offered a vague explanation. In no case, however, have you offered an explanation that I can assess only by forming views about justice or injustice myself. I need give no thought to such evaluative issues in assessing the explanation; and neither need you.

There is, to be sure, one complication. For although neither you nor I need take a stand on any evaluative issue to assess your explanation, once we have it in hand, it is clear in this scenario that you, the proponent of the explanation, must *have* views on such issues, if your words are to state any explanation at all. We can perhaps dismiss my realist-sounding shorthand imputing to you a picture of one property, injustice, supervening on others, for you might not think in terms of properties. But you must have *standards* for applying the corresponding concept or term, for they are what is supposed to determine what explanation you are offering.[27] So, although this proposal describes a way for the value nihilist to assess and perhaps even accept evaluative explanations proposed by others, it doesn't by itself explain how any value nihilist could offer such an explanation, or how there could be a place for this form of evaluative discourse in a community of value nihilists. However, the proposal doesn't have to do either of these things by itself to be useful for our purposes. There are two reasons: (*a*) First, the example I have focused on, and the one against which I shall test this proposal, is a debate in which theists offer an evaluative explanation and atheists object to it; and even if the atheists are value nihilists, the theists aren't. So this proposal tells the atheists how to understand the theist's explanation, even if they would never offer an evaluative explanation themselves. (*b*) Second, as I explained above, this is in any case not a free-standing proposal. It is a suggestion for extending noncognitivism from areas where it is already assumed to have some plausibility to another where its applicability is in question. And any area of our evaluative discourse for which noncognitivism provides even a possible interpretation will be one that already involves the application of evaluative terms by standards – even if the noncognitivism is so simple as to see this as little different from saying 'Boo' and 'Hurrah' by standards.

---

27 Might we also have eliminated this realist-sounding talk of one property supervening on others, in our statement of the Real Supervenience proposal? Yes, but only by replacing it with an equally realist-sounding reference, not to the speaker's standards, but to the *correct* standards. For if you tell me that injustice is causing discontent, you are, on that proposal, attributing this effect to whatever nonevaluative feature fits the correct standards for injustice.

This reminder that the proposal is a noncognitivist one, and supposed to fit into a larger noncognitivist program, is thus useful, as I promised, in helping to see its point. But it is also helpful in seeing why the proposal is more vulnerable than one might have thought to the sort of criticism I shall now raise against it. My objection is basically quite simple. It is that if we accept this formula for understanding evaluative explanations, we cannot see Mackie, in his presentation of the problem of evil, as actually *disagreeing* with the explanation any of his theistic opponents is putting forward. This is most obvious in the extreme case, of those theists whose idea of a good God is one who is malevolent, petulant and mischievous. For on this proposal the explanation we are to understand them as advancing, when they say that the world owes its character to a good God, is that it owes its character to a God like *that*. But Mackie doesn't bother to challenge that explanation: he brushes it aside as an attempt to "sidestep the problem" by changing the subject. The problem is apparent if not so patent in less extreme cases, too. Other theists understand by a good God one who would value a life in which sin is followed by redemption over a wholly sinless one, and who would value a world in which agents have libertarian freedom to do evil over one in which they lack this freedom.[28]

---

28 Here is a question that the proposal, as so far formulated, doesn't explicitly address: what are we to do when there is evaluative terminology not just in the explanans but also in the explanandum of an explanation? What are we to make of someone's saying that the reason certain children are thriving is that they have been raised with decency and humanity (taking it that 'thriving' may be an evaluative expression here), or of a theist's saying that God's goodness explains the goodness we notice in much of creation? I have here dealt with the latter example without needing a general answer to this question, by assuming that the theist's idea of a good God will include that God prefers what is better on all issues – so that the theist's standards on other questions automatically become incorporated in her idea of what a good God would be like. This won't work for the general case, however. I assume that the general answer has to be that we interpret by the speaker's standards throughout. (If we don't, then we get a very odd ambiguity when the speaker adds that the children's thriving explains something nonevaluative, say the relative comfort with which they deal with both their peers and adults. For *here* we are already committed to interpreting 'thriving' by the speaker's standards.)

Their explanation, when they say that the world owes its character to a good God, is thus to be understood as saying no more than that it owes its character to a God of that sort. But, again, this is not an explanation that Mackie challenges in discussing the problem of evil. We of course know about this latter explanation, as about the one appealing to the malevolent, petulant, mischievous deity, that he does in fact reject it. But we don't know this from anything he says in discussing the problem of evil, where all that he argues, on evaluative grounds, is that these explanations would be no help to the defense of the theist's explanation even if they were correct. However, I claim, it is obvious that in this discussion Mackie is, as he supposes, attacking the explanation the theist puts forward, the explanation that says that the world owes its character to God's goodness. So this proposal for interpreting the theist's explanation is mistaken.

More abstractly, we can put the problem this way. *Which* explanation anyone would be offering, according to this proposal, in saying that the world owes its existence and character to a good God, depends on her standards for calling God good. This means, among other things, that different theists undoubtedly count as offering different explanations, not just the same explanation differently defended. But the explanation Mackie is attacking appears to be none of these. To a good first approximation, in fact, what he is attacking is instead the explanation that, according to this proposal, *he* would be putting forward if *he* were to say that the world owes its existence and character to the goodness of a perfect God.[29] This should not seem surprising: in asking whether this explanation might be correct, he naturally uses his own standards for goodness. Since he is officially a value nihilist, and

---

29 This strikes me as still only an approximation, because Mackie's implicit assumption here seems to me even more realist than this. He seems to be understanding the explanation he is attacking to be determined neither by his opponent's standards nor by his own, but instead by the correct standards, whatever they are. His own standards are then relevant only because he trusts them as correct. (However, it is beyond my scope in this paper to *show* that Mackie is assuming so much; at a minimum, that would require ruling out other irrealist construals of his remarks that I do not consider here.)

of the unadorned variety, perhaps he shouldn't have any such standards, but we have seen that he certainly does.

And then the situation is this. The explanation Mackie is attacking, and the one this proposal has any of his opponents defending, would be the same *if* their standards for judging God's goodness were the same. We would certainly have this happy result, for example, if Mackie were simply borrowing the theist's evaluative standards, to use against him *ad hominem* (and in that case we'd have a happy story for Mackie, about how he came up with any such standards at all). But we have seen that he and his opponents don't share the same *express* standards. Might they nevertheless have the same *implicit* standards, defined, remember, as the standards they would accept after appropriate rational reflection? And, if they did, couldn't we solve this problem by taking the standards that fix the content of the evaluative explanation to be the speaker's implicit rather than his express standards? The answer is complex, but should be clear from what I said about a similar question above. To anyone with the value realist's typical optimism about the rational resolvability of evaluative disagreements, this last, more sophisticated noncognitivist proposal will appear to fare not too badly. At least, it will give what seem the right answers about the issues of univocality I have just been pressing. Value nihilists, on the other hand, are almost certainly committed to a more pessimistic view about rational resolvability; and that will require pessimism in turn about the prospects of this amended proposal's giving intuitively satisfying answers about who Mackie is disagreeing with and about what. And noncognitivists, on whose behalf this proposal is made, are value nihilists.

When I said that it would be useful to remember that this proposal is a noncognitivist one, I had in mind not just this dialectical point but also a more general one about possible responses to this criticism. So, for example, one tempting reply might focus on the weight the criticism accords to claims about univocality. Our intuitions on such matters, it might say, are notoriously variable, context-sensitive and, in a word, soft: not a strong basis, therefore, for attacking an otherwise attractive theory. I suspect that this reply states – though, perhaps, overstates – a useful caution. But, however it might look from mine or any other perspective, this defense is anyway not one easily available to the noncognitivist. The reason for this is that there is a standard argument for noncognitivism, so central to the major works in the tradition to deserve being called the 'Noncognitivist

Master Argument' against ethical naturalism, that rests every bit as heavily on intuitions about univocality.[30] The basic idea is that if evaluative terms just referred to natural properties of some sort, that reference would have to depend on the standards speakers use in applying the terms: in the jargon, on the terms' descriptive or cognitive meaning. However, it is said, we recognize as univocal some disagreements between speakers with such different standards that they could not possibly be referring to the same natural property. The solution offered is to preserve our intuition of univocality by construing the evaluative disagreement as a disagreement in attitude, as noncognitivism proposes, rather than as any sort of disagreement in belief.[31]

---

30 Thus Charles Stevenson's remark: "My methodological conclusions center less on my conception of meaning than on my conception of agreement and disagreement" ('Meaning: Descriptive and Emotive,' in *Facts and Values* [New Haven: Yale University Press 1963] 170). The argument is quite explicit in R.M. Hare, *The Language of Morals* (Oxford: Clarendon Press 1952) 49; in his *Moral Thinking* (Oxford: Clarendon Press, 1981) 69; and in Simon Blackburn, *Spreading the Word* (Oxford: Clarendon Press, 1984) 168. The argument does not take quite this form in Gibbard's *Wise Choices, Apt Feelings*, but Gibbard does conclude that noncognitivist views locate a "common element in dispute" (9) that all naturalistic accounts miss.

Blackburn's most recent position in "Just Causes" is a bit more complex but is no exception to this pattern. I now see that I was mistaken, in "Contents and Causes," to say (25-7) that his position there is no longer noncognitivist (in his terms, projectivist) and that he is barred from relying on this argument. His position is an attenuated form of noncognitivism, but it remains noncognitivist. What seems likely to me is that it is *so* attenuated that he will not be able to deploy this standard argument with any plausibility, because it will be so hard for him to find cases where his theory gives a different answer about univocality, even less a more plausible answer, than does a sophisticated cognitivist theory. However, his estimate of the resources of cognitivist theories is lower than mine, so he undoubtedly sees the matter differently.

31 Since this argument is descended from Moore's open question argument, it is perhaps not surprising that it is not equally an attack on a nonnaturalist account of value. Classical intuitionists are typically understood from this perspective to solve the problem of univocality by postulating a property, simple and accessible through intuition, that both speakers can refer to despite their difference in standards; the usual noncognitivist objection to this solution is to the extravagant metaphysics and epistemology it requires.

A similar remark applies to another possible line of response. The proposal, as I presented it, is rather simple, and one might wonder if it could be made to fit our intuitions about univocality better if it were modified in obvious ways. I have already pointed out that one alteration, moving from the speaker's express standards to her implicit ones, almost certainly cannot be seen by a noncognitivist as helping, even if it would do so in fact. That is because of the noncognitivist's almost certainly being committed to pessimism about the resolvability of evaluative disagreements. But a similar comment applies to that and any other alteration because of the noncognitivist's need for the other argument I just mentioned, the Noncognitivist Master Argument. There are certainly other changes one might suggest. As it stands, the proposal is absurdly individualist, for example, counting two theists with only slightly different ideas of divine goodness as saying different things when they both ascribe the character of the world to God's perfection. We could change that by noting familiar ways in which reference is social: speakers typically mean to co-refer, and defer to some extent for standards to one another and to recognized authorities. Having brought other people back in, we might try to follow Hilary Putnam's advice to put the world back in the semantic story as well:[32] an interesting project to contemplate in this example, just because, whether theism or atheism is correct, one side or the other must include a lot of people whose picture of what is controlling their evaluative thought and talk is far wide of the facts. I do not need to explore any of these possibilities, however, because a general comment will suffice. These are all proposals for enriching our account of what noncognitivists call the cognitive meaning of evaluative terms, when those terms are used in explanations, to try to make that account fit our judgments of univocality better. There is no apparent reason, moreover, to think that if this project succeeded for evaluative terms when used in explanations, it wouldn't succeed for evaluative language generally. Any noncognitivist who relies on the Noncognitivist Master Argument,

---

32 Hilary Putnam, "The Meaning of 'Meaning'," *Philosophical Papers* (Cambridge: Cambridge University Press 1975) II, 271.

however, is committed to the view that such proposals *cannot* succeed generally, for that argument requires that cognitive meaning be idiosyncratic is some way that conflicts with plausible intuitions about univocality. As a fan of naturalism and of realism about values I would be quite happy for this commitment to turn out to be false. But I do not see how a noncognitivist could be.

We have come far enough from where we began in criticism of this proposal that it may be helpful to recall why I initially called the proposal, the Speaker's Standard proposal, a noncognitivist one. There is the fact that it has been put forward by Blackburn as part of a noncognitivist program. And then there is the point that, if it is to help a value nihilist preserve the explanatory use of evaluative terms, it has to be parasitic on some account already in place of how the nihilist can apply evaluative terms by standards: and, for a value nihilist, noncognitivism is an obvious choice for this role. In addition there is the possibility – although I have not argued for this, and it would take work to establish – that it is the most plausible suggestion one could make on behalf of a noncognitivist who wished to preserve this area of evaluative discourse. Certainly, as I mentioned, the only other proposal Blackburn recommends would rest on far more controversial premises. But, with all that said, what I have been pointing out is that there is also a way in which this is a very odd proposal to hear from a noncognitivist. For what it proposes is to interpret evaluative terminology, in a certain context, entirely through these terms' cognitive meaning; and a central noncognitivist argument commits its adherents to thinking that any such procedure is bound to yield implausible, counterintuitive results. That is why, if the proposal *could* be developed in directions that made its applications more plausible, that would almost surely be more of a disadvantage than an advantage to the noncognitivist program as a whole.

There is thus a certain similarity between the arguments of the first part of my paper and the second, in respects that it may help to enumerate. (1) In each case I have taken as an example certain views expressed or obviously held by John Mackie in his presentation of the problem of evil: first (*a*) the evaluative stands he takes in his argument, then (*b*) his view that in presenting these he is objecting to, and disagreeing with, the theist's evaluative explanation. (2) In each case I asked whether these views of Mackie's could be accommodated by a strategy introduced to defend a certain form of value irrealism or nihilism. (*a*) In my first section, the nihilism in question is the unadorned variety Mackie actually defends, his 'error theory,' and the specific strategy for accommodating his remarks is to see him as arguing by his opponents' standards. (*b*) In the second section the nihilism is a mitigated variety that hopes to preserve evaluative discourse, noncognitivism, and the specific strategy for accommodating his debate with the theist is the proposal we have looked at for interpreting evaluative explanations, the Speaker's Standards proposal. (3) And, finally, in each case the answer has turned out to be no – whether the specific strategy works or not. Thus, (*a*) Mackie's evaluative stands certainly conflict with his unadorned value nihilism if he is making them in his own voice. But if we can instead see him as arguing by his opponents' standards, that is equally a threat to nihilism, because that could be so only if evaluative disagreements are rationally resolvable in a way his defense of nihilism denies. Similarly, (*b*) Mackie's intuitions that he is engaged in a genuine disagreement with the theist certainly conflict with noncognitivism if the latter view has no way to accommodate debate about evaluative explanations at all. If the Speaker's Standards proposal can be shaped so that it *does* accommodate these intuitions, on the other hand, that is also at least equally a threat to the noncognitivism, because this success would undermine a standard, central argument for noncognitivism. (4) In both cases the feature of Mackie's situation that creates this odd result is the same: that he is engaged in a serious evaluative disagreement, in which the parties are applying different standards. And in both cases, what would be needed to fit these views of Mackie's with the form of nihilism in question would be a better specific strategy of accommodation. In the case of his own unadorned value nihilism, I cannot imagine what such a strategy might be; I do not believe that there is one. In the case of noncognitivism and evaluative explanations, there may well be other suggestions worth discussing: the challenge to noncognitivists will be to develop them and make them plausible.

I have not claimed that Mackie's argument against theism presupposes realism about values. But that argument does presuppose things that matter to the debate about realism: the falsity, almost certainly, of his own extreme value nihilism, and the inadequacy of a natural proposal to accommodate evaluative explanations within noncognitivism.

I have mentioned the widely shared view that the presuppositions of our evaluative discourse carry at least some weight in metaethical debate. I haven't said a word about why they do; but I assume that, if they do, they count for more when they can be located even in the writings of an able thinker explicitly unsympathetic to them. That is one reason for my having focused so heavily on Mackie. I also noted at the outset, however, that Mackie's problems are interesting partly because they may not be just his. There are, I believe, many philosophers inclined to see the problem of evil as a serious difficulty for theism, but also sympathetic to a soft line about values: if not exactly to Mackie's unadorned nihilism, then, perhaps, to some form of noncognitivism. If the conclusions I have defended here are correct, all of these thinkers face more difficulty than has commonly been recognized in reconciling these views with one another.[33]

---

33 An earlier version of this paper was presented to the Philosophy Department at the University of Michigan. I am grateful for numerous helpful comments on that occasion. I have also benefited from conversation with David Alm, Todd Blanke and Eric Hiddleston.

CANADIAN JOURNAL OF PHILOSOPHY
Supplementary Volume 21

Moral Obligation and Moral Motivation*

DAVID COPP
University of California, Davis

'Internalism' in ethics is a cluster of views according to which there is an 'internal' connection between moral obligations and either motivations or reasons to act morally; 'externalism' says that such connections are contingent. So described, the dispute between internalism and externalism may seem a technical debate of minor interest. However, the issues that motivate it include deep problems about moral truth, realism, normativity, and objectivity. Indeed, I think that some philosophers view externalism as undermining the 'dignity' of morality. They might say that if morality needs an 'external sanction' – if the belief that one has an obligation is not sufficient motive or reason to do the right thing – then morality is debased in status. Even an arbitrary system of etiquette could attract an external sanction under appropriate conditions.

Although I believe that the more interesting internalist theses are false, there are important truths that internalism is attempting to capture. The most important of these is the fact that moral judgments are intrinsically 'normative' or 'choice-guiding,' that they are, very roughly, relevant to action or choice because of their content. Internalism tries to explain the

---

* I am grateful to Philip Clark, Earl Conee, Jeffrey C. King, and Michael Smith for their helpful comments. An earlier version of this paper was presented to the 1995 Philosophy Colloquium at the University of North Carolina, Greensboro. I am grateful to all of those who contributed to the discussion on that occasion.

normativity of moral judgment in terms of motivations or reasons, and I believe that this is its mistake. But internalism is correct that normativity is 'internal' to moral judgment. Externalist theories have denied this intrinsic normativity, or they have not done well at explaining it.

My goal in this paper is to introduce an account of moral judgment and moral conviction that is strictly speaking externalist even though it accommodates the internalists' insight about the normativity of moral judgment. I want to explain how the account does this, and also to explain how it accommodates other important and plausible intuitions that motivate internalism. I have presented this account in a recent book, but my discussion of internalism in the book was distributed over several chapters.[1] I want to bring the key points together in this paper. Moreover, I want to show in more detail how my account can respond to certain internalist objections, paying special attention to some new arguments by Michael Smith.[2] I begin with a few preliminary issues.

1. The Debate Between Internalism and Externalism

The term 'internalism' is used to name doctrines about motivation as well as doctrines about reasons. In general, an internalist doctrine claims there is a necessary connection between the state of having a moral obligation, or the state of believing or recognizing one has a moral obligation, and the state of being motivated – or the state of having reason – to fulfill that obligation. Each internalist thesis corresponds to a version of 'externalism,' which is simply its denial. Externalism as such would deny all internalist doctrines.

I will begin with internalist doctrines about motivation. Using terminology introduced by David Brink, we can distinguish among

---

1 David Copp, *Morality, Normativity, and Society* (New York: Oxford University Press 1995)

2 Michael Smith, *The Moral Problem* (Oxford: Blackwell 1994)

'agent internalism,' 'belief internalism,' and 'hybrid internalism.'[3] Agent internalism is the doctrine that it is a necessary truth that if a person has a moral obligation to do something, then the person has some motivation to do it (or she would have some motivation under relevant conditions). Belief internalism holds that it is a person's belief that she has a moral obligation which entails that she is relevantly motivated. Hybrid internalism holds that it is a person's belief, when the belief is true, which guarantees that she is relevantly motivated.[4]

Internalism can allow for cases in which the person with the obligation – or with the belief or the true belief that she has an obligation – is not actually or 'occurrently' motivated. This explains the qualification in the above formulations: The person in question has some motivation to do the relevant thing, or *would have* some motivation *under relevant conditions*. Different internalists would specify the relevant conditions in different ways,[5] but it is obviously important for an internalist to avoid trivializing her position. It is trivial that a person with a moral obligation necessarily would acquire the relevant moti-

---

3 David O. Brink, *Moral Realism and the Foundations of Ethics* (Cambridge: Cambridge University Press 1989) 40. Brink speaks of "appraiser internalism," which appears to be the same as the view I call "belief internalism." W.K. Frankena recognized the distinctions in his classic essay, "Obligation and Motivation in Recent Moral Philosophy," in Kenneth E. Goodpaster, ed., *Perspectives on Morality: Essays of William K. Frankena* (Notre Dame, IN: Notre Dame University Press 1976) 60. The doctrines Frankena labels (1), (7), and (8) are, respectively, agent, belief, and hybrid forms of internalism.

4 That is, according to belief internalism, it is a necessary truth that if a person believes she has a moral obligation to do something, then she has some motivation to do it (or would have some motivation under relevant conditions). According to hybrid internalism, it is a necessary truth that if a person believes truly that she has a moral obligation to do something, then she has some motivation to do it (or would have some motivation under relevant conditions).

5 For example, Michael Smith defends a version of belief internalism according to which, if a person is not actually motivated to do what she believes would be right, then she is "practically irrational." That is, her motivations are subject to a "distorting influence" of some form of "practical unreason," such as weakness of will. Smith, *The Moral Problem*, 61.

vation under *some* circumstances, but we should count a position as internalist only if it makes a non-trivial claim about the connection between obligation and motivation. This means that the distinction between internalism and externalism is blurred at the edges, because of vagueness in the notion of the trivial, but the literature fortunately contains clear cases of both internalism and externalism.

As I said, 'internalism' is sometimes used to name a thesis about a necessary connection between obligation and *reasons*. We can distinguish versions of reasons-internalism that correspond to the versions of motivation-internalism; there is an agent version as well as a belief version and a hybrid version.

There are complications regarding the notion of a reason. If someone has a moral obligation to do something, it is trivial that he has a *moral* reason to do it. But reasons-internalism would normally be taken to imply, I think, that a moral obligation, or a belief that one has an obligation, guarantees a reason-without-qualification – a 'Reason' that would motivate anyone to act as it requires, if he were rational.[6] Some philosophers combine reasons-internalism with an internalist doctrine about the connection between *reasons* and *motivation*, a doctrine to the effect that motivation is 'internal' to the state of having a reason or of believing or believing truly that one has a reason.[7] I will largely ignore such doctrines and limit attention to internalist doctrines about obligation. Also, until later, I will focus on the belief version of motivation-internalism.

According to this doctrine, there is a *necessary* connection between a person's belief that he has an obligation and his being appropriately motivated. Consider, however, a putative counter-example, the case of Alice: Alice was raised to believe that the divine command theory is correct. That is, as Alice herself might say, she was raised to believe that our moral obligations are determined by the commands of God.

---

6 Such a view seems to be held by Smith, as we will see. Smith, *The Moral Problem*, 62. In this connection, Smith cites Christine Korsgaard, "Skepticism about Practical Reason," *Journal of Philosophy* **83** (1986) 5-25.

7 Such a view is defended by Bernard Williams in "Internal and External Reasons," in his *Moral Luck* (Cambridge: Cambridge University Press 1981).

She was also raised to believe that God is a vengeful ruler and that He wills us to take an eye for an eye. On the principle of an eye for an eye, Alice believes that capital punishment is obligatory in cases of murder, and she believes she has an obligation to support capital punishment. But she is deeply compassionate, and she is quite out of sympathy with what she takes to be God's vengefulness. Because of her compassion she is not motivated in the least to support capital punishment. She is in fact active in opposing it, even though she believes she is morally forbidden to do so.

Externalists would be inclined to accept Alice's state of mind as both psychologically and logically possible, but a belief-internalist would have to reject the example. To be sure, any plausible version of belief internalism is a qualified doctrine to the effect that a believed moral obligation entails motivation *under relevant conditions*. But presumably we could fill in our description of the case so that Alice is clearly in what the internalist would count as relevant conditions. If we did this, then the internalist would have to claim either that Alice does not genuinely *believe* that she is morally obligated to support capital punishment, or that if she believes this, she is in fact *motivated* to some degree to support it. For example, Michael Smith would argue that Alice cannot actually believe she has a *moral* obligation to oppose capital punishment, that she does not make a *moral* judgment when she says she is 'morally obligated' to oppose capital punishment.[8] His argument depends on the 'practicality requirement,' which I will discuss later on. In general, the internalist must insist that the concept or nature of moral obligation rules out the logical possibility of Alice's having the psychology attributed to her in the example.[9]

---

8 Smith, *The Moral Problem*, 66-71. Smith is replying to an argument by David Brink.

9 Disagreements of this kind between externalists and internalists led W.D. Falk to conclude in effect that externalists and internalists have different concepts of moral obligation. But if this were so, then externalists and internalists would not really be disagreeing; they would be making claims about different kinds of obligation. I think on the contrary that they have a genuine disagreement. See W.D. Falk, "'Ought' and Motivation," *Proceedings of the Aristotelian Society* N.S. **48** (1947-48) 137, 124-5.

An internalist would typically hold that her doctrine is entailed by a proper analysis of the concept of moral obligation.[10] But because this concept is itself the subject of controversy, an internalist cannot defend her doctrine simply by deriving it from a proposed analysis of the concept. Some internalists do offer explicit independent arguments for their doctrines, as we will see, but the arguments do not appear to be the source of their belief in internalism, for they are not typically inclined to abandon internalism when an argument is found to be unsound. Moreover, to defend belief internalism in the face of Alice's case, the internalist needs to argue that Alice cannot have the concept of moral obligation, or that her words do not express the moral judgment they seem to express. Accordingly, belief-internalism needs to be backed up by an account of what is involved in having a concept, as well as by an account of the semantics of moral judgment.

In fact, I believe, the disagreement between internalists and externalists is driven by differences about large metaethical issues rather than by a difference restricted to an analytic question about the shared concept of moral obligation. W.K. Frankena said, "Each [internalist and externalist] theory has strengths and weaknesses, and deciding between them involves determining their relative total values as accounts of morality. But such a determination ... calls for a very broad inquiry ... about the nature and function of morality, of moral discourse, and of moral theory...."[11] We must realize that "neither kind of moral philosophy can be decisively refuted by the other, and ... we must give up the quest for certainty in the sense of no longer hoping for such refutations."[12] On Frankena's account, the issues raised by the debate between internalism and externalism ramify throughout metaethical

---

10 Smith says that "our concept of rightness" supports a "conceptual connection between moral judgment and the will" and a "conceptual connection between ... the moral facts ... and our reasons for action." Smith, *The Moral Problem*, 61, 65, 37-8. Brink views the versions of internalism as doctrines about the concept of moral obligation. Brink, *Moral Realism and the Foundations of Ethics*, 40.

11 Frankena, "Obligation and Motivation in Recent Moral Philosophy," 73

12 Ibid., 69

theory. A position in the debate cannot adequately be defended without defending a metaethical theory that addresses issues about moral truth, realism, normativity, and objectivity, among others.

To see this, consider the idea that claims of moral obligation are normative. Some internalists have held that the most plausible explanation of this would construe moral judgment, insofar as it is normative, as an expression of an attitude rather than an expression of belief in a proposition. Now, since the view that moral claims express propositions is usually called 'cognitivism' or 'descriptivism,' these internalists are *noncognitivists*.[13] They are arguing that noncognitivism is supported by the normativity of moral judgment. The debate between internalism and externalism is linked in this way to debates about moral truth and moral realism, since moral realism and the idea that there are moral truths presuppose cognitivism.[14]

Now consider the idea that claims of moral obligation are 'categorical' in at least this sense: A conceptually competent person who sincerely made a moral claim to the effect that he is obligated to do something would not (appropriately) retract his claim merely on realizing that he lacks any motivation to do it. If this is correct, then no simple form of belief internalism can be true, for, on a simple form of belief internalism, a person would not actually believe he has an obligation if he were not motivated appropriately. That is, if a person realizes he is not motivated in a certain way, what he realizes entails that he lacks the belief that he is obligated to act in that way, and, because of this, it would be appropriate for him to cease to express the belief. The debate between internalism and externalism is linked in this way to the idea that claims of obligation are categorical. Belief internalists must hedge their claims about the connection between obligation and motivation or else explain away the appearance that claims of obligation are categorical.

---

13 R.M. Hare and Allan Gibbard are internalists who reject (or appear to reject) cognitivism. See R.M. Hare, *The Language of Morals* (Oxford: Oxford University Press 1952); Allan Gibbard, *Wise Choices, Apt Feelings: A Theory of Normative Judgment* (Cambridge, MA: Harvard University Press 1990).

14 I have not worried about formulating internalism to be compatible with noncognitivism because I am going to be assuming a cognitivist view.

If we accept internalism and cognitivism and also think that claims of moral obligation are categorical in the sense I explained, we are on the way to accepting the premises of J.L. Mackie's 'argument from queerness,' which Mackie thought established that no moral proposition is true.[15] So it can seem that only an externalist position can vindicate moral judgment as cognitive, categorical, and sometimes correct.

Given the issues at stake, it seems clear that the debate about internalism will not be settled on the basis of finely honed arguments that might be viewed as prior to, or as setting constraints on, the larger debate about the nature of morality. Frankena said the debate "cannot be resolved, as so many seem to think, by ... small-scale logical or semi-logical arguments...."[16] It also will not be resolved by putative counterexamples. Rather, we must consider the issue on a "macroscopic rather than a microscopic plane."[17] This is what I propose to do in this paper, admittedly in a sketchy way. I will propose an externalist theory of moral judgment and moral conviction and then attempt to show how the theory can handle certain internalist objections.

2. The Standard-Based Theory of Normative Judgment[18]

I do not aim to provide either a decisive argument for externalism or a decisive argument against internalism. Rather, in this and the next section, I will offer a partial account of the content of propositions about moral obligation as well as an account of moral conviction. I want to show that these accounts, although externalist, nevertheless preserve many of the intuitions that motivate internalism. If I am correct, my

---

15 J.L. Mackie, *Ethics: Inventing Right and Wrong* (Harmondsworth, Middlesex: Penguin 1977) 38-42

16 Frankena, "Obligation and Motivation in Recent Moral Philosophy," 69

17 Ibid., 49

18 In the following two sections, I present ideas that are developed more fully in my *Morality, Normativity, and Society* (New York: Oxford University Press 1995).

argument undermines internalism to the extent that its appeal is due to the thought that only an internalist theory can preserve the intuitions.

I will simplify matters in several ways. First, I will restrict attention to claims in which an agent is said to have a moral obligation. Frankena calls such claims, "judgments of moral obligation."[19] I will ignore the many other kinds of moral claims. Second, I will ignore any differences there might be among judgments about moral obligations, judgments about moral duties, and judgments to the effect that an agent ought morally to do something. I will refer to all of these as 'judgments of moral obligation.'

I will also assume that *cognitivism* or *descriptivism* is true, that moral claims express propositions. When we make a moral claim, we utter a declarative sentence and thereby assert something; it is reasonable to assume that what we assert is either true or false, that we express a proposition just as we do in non-moral cases.[20] I need to assume that cognitivism is correct so that I can proceed efficiently to the issues I wish to address.

I propose the following as a partial account of the content or truth conditions of the propositions expressed by judgments of moral obligation:

> A proposition to the effect that an agent has a moral obligation to do something entails (nontrivially) that there is a justified moral standard that calls for the agent to do that thing.

A number of ideas need to be explained.

To begin, let me emphasize that I am proposing only a necessary condition for the truth of a proposition of moral obligation. It may seem that this will pose a problem for my argument, but the other conditions that are necessary for the truth of such propositions are irrelevant

---

19 Frankena, "Obligation and Motivation in Recent Moral Philosophy," 71

20 See Nathan Salmon and Scott Soames, "Introduction," in Nathan Salmon and Scott Soames, eds., *Propositions and Attitudes* (New York: Oxford University Press 1988) 1.

to what I will be attempting to show. Compare, for example, the proposition that Jimmy Carter's attempt to rescue the hostages was morally obligatory and the proposition that Richard Nixon's recognition of China discharged a moral duty. These are obviously distinct propositions with different truth conditions. Yet the difference between them is not relevant to anything I will be arguing.

Let me now explain the substance of my proposal, beginning with the notion of a standard. Rules, norms, and imperatives are examples of standards. Allan Gibbard's notion of a norm appears to be the same as my notion of a standard. Gibbard says that a norm is "a possible rule or prescription, expressible by an imperative."[21] This formulation would be adequate to explain what I mean by a standard. To say that a standard 'calls for' an action is to say that the standard is *conformed to* just in case the action is performed. For example, the imperative 'Shut the door,' calls for the door to be shut.

We need the notion of a standard in semantic theory in order to give an account of what is expressed by imperatival sentences – although we obviously do not need to call what is expressed a 'standard.' Frege said, "We should not wish to deny sense to a command, but this sense is not such that the question of truth could arise for it. Therefore I shall not call the sense of a command a thought."[22]

Frege appears to be claiming that although imperatival sentences express something, or have 'sense,' they do not express propositions, for, he says, the question of truth does not arise with respect to whatever it is that is expressed by an imperatival sentence. In my terminology, such sentences express 'standards.' Just as propositions are expressed by typical declarative sentences, standards are expressed by typical imperatival sentences.

In order for a standard to qualify as justified, it is not necessary that anyone have presented any argument about it, or have proven any-

---

21 Gibbard, *Wise Choices, Apt Feelings: A Theory of Normative Judgment*, 46

22 Gottlob Frege, "Thoughts," trans. P. Geach and R.H. Stoothoff, in Nathan Salmon and Scott Soames, eds., *Propositions and Attitudes* (New York: Oxford University Press 1988) 37

thing about it. For a standard to be justified is for it to possess a *status*, the status of being morally 'binding.' The idea is that unless a standard has this status, corresponding propositions of obligation are not true.

The status at issue is not possessed by standards that are arbitrary, contrived or unwarranted; we do not believe that corresponding moral propositions are true. For example, we do not think that the standards accepted by Nietzsche that call for us to strive to become overmen have the status they would need in order for it to be true that we are obligated to strive to become overmen. We do not believe that we have any obligation to strive to become overmen. On the other hand, we believe that we have an obligation to oppose slavery, and we can formulate a relevant standard calling on us to oppose slavery. We would agree that this standard is justified or morally binding.

In my recent book, I provide a substantive theory of the status possessed by justified standards.[23] Here I need to be less ambitious. Fortunately, many different accounts of the justification of moral standards are familiar from the literature; they are not usually described as theories of the justification of moral standards, but they can usefully be viewed as such in the framework I am proposing.

It is possible of course to take our understanding of the status of *being justified* to be derivative from our understanding of moral truth. We might insist that if a proposition of moral obligation is true, then there is a related justified moral standard, and we might say no more about what the status of being justified consists in. We would have to give some account of the conditions under which a proposition of moral obligation would be true. But, again, we could finesse this issue by simply asserting that such a proposition is true just in case the relevant action has the property of being morally obligatory. We could leave it at that, although to do so would not be philosophically illuminating.

More useful for my purposes are theories in the Kantian, Aristotelian, or rational choice theoretic schools, including contemporary Hobbesian accounts, to the extent that such theories can be viewed as providing accounts of the conditions under which a moral standard

---

23 See my *Morality, Normativity, and Society*.

would be justified. A Kantian might say that a moral standard is justified just in case a person acting on it could "at the same time will that it should become a universal law."[24] Or, a Kantian might say, a moral standard is justified just in case any fully rational agent with only purely rational incentives would intend to comply with it.[25] An Aristotelian might say that a moral standard is justified just in case any person living a life that would be fulfilling for a human would, by that very fact, have intentions that would lead him to conform with the standard.[26] A contemporary Hobbesian, such as David Gauthier, might say that a moral standard is justified just in case an agent maximizing the satisfaction of his preferences would be rational to dispose himself to comply with it.[27]

For my own part, I would defend a theory according to which a moral standard is justified in relation to a society just in case, if the society were to choose a moral code for currency in it, the society would be rationally required to select a moral code that contains or implies the standard. Obviously I cannot defend this approach here.

These are extremely abbreviated and crude versions of the theories in question, but the details do not matter for present purposes. Each of these theories gives a different account of the status possessed by a moral standard that is morally binding. But if we can understand the nature of the debate among these theories, and understand it as relevant to the issue of which moral propositions are true, and on what basis they are true, then the notion of the justification of a moral standard should not be mysterious.

Any theory of the conditions under which moral standards are justified would raise deep philosophical questions about the nature of morality. But my proposed necessary condition for the truth of a judg-

---

24 Immanuel Kant, *Grounding for the Metaphysics of Morals*, James W. Ellington, trans. (Indianapolis: Hackett 1981) Ak 421

25 Ibid., Ak 449

26 This is at least vaguely Aristotelian, I hope.

27 David Gauthier, *Morals by Agreement* (Oxford: Oxford University Press 1986). See chap. 6.

ment of obligation is neutral among these different theories. I think that once it is clear what my proposal is, it should not seem controversial – except to those who doubt the cognitivism I am assuming here.

Now, I claim, the fact that a proposition of moral obligation entails (nontrivially) that some relevant standard is justified is what explains its normativity as well as the normativity of the sentences we use to express it. A normative proposition is intrinsically relevant to action or choice. The fact that a proposition of moral obligation entails that some relevant standard is justified is what explains the connection between a proposition of obligation and action. For it means that if a person has a moral obligation to do something, then there is a standard that *calls for* the person to do the thing, and that standard is *justified*. Call this the 'standard-based' account of normativity.[28]

One very powerful intuition shared by internalists is that propositions of moral obligation are intrinsically normative. Mackie says that moral properties are "intrinsically action-guiding." He says that a wrong action would have "not-to-be-doneness somehow built into it."[29] Jonathan Dancy argues that "morality is essentially practical, so that it would be odd for someone to say 'This action is wrong but I don't see that as at all relevant to my choice.'"[30]

The intuition that normativity is internal to propositions of moral obligation is supported by the standard-based account. For the account implies that a moral proposition is normative in virtue of its content,

---

28 It is actually a schema for an account since it needs to be completed by a theory of justification for moral standards. I provide a full account in *Morality, Normativity, and Society*.

29 Mackie, *Ethics: Inventing Right and Wrong*, 32, 40, respectively.

30 Jonathan Dancy, *Moral Reasons* (Oxford: Blackwell 1993) 4. Dancy adds that "moral considerations are ones whose practical relevance cannot be escaped by saying 'I don't care about that sort of thing.'" But if moral claims are categorical in the sense I explained before, then something stronger is true, namely, the 'practical relevance' of a proposition of moral obligation cannot be escaped by saying "I am not at all motivated by that sort of thing." This undermines internalism rather than supporting it.

in virtue of the fact that it entails (nontrivially) that a relevant moral standard is justified. Moreover, if we extended the account in a natural way, it would say that moral properties are intrinsically normative. Leaving aside irrelevant details, an action has the property of being obligatory if and only if it is called for by a justified moral standard, a standard according to which it is to-be-done. The wrongness of an action is 'relevant' to choice because it entails that the action is precluded by a justified moral standard. A natural extension of the account would entail, in addition, that if a person has a moral obligation to do something, she has a *moral reason* to do it. For, I would argue, a person has a moral reason to do something just in case a justified moral standard calls for her to do it.

All of this is fully compatible with externalism. As for motivation, the account leaves open the possibility that a person may be morally obligated to do something and yet fail to be motivated to any degree to do it. It also leaves open the possibility that a person may believe she is morally obligated to do something and yet fail to be motivated to any degree to do it. To have such a belief is simply to accept a proposition which entails that a justified standard calls for some action, and nothing about the believer's motivations is entailed by her accepting such a proposition. Turning now to internalism about reasons, a person may have a moral obligation, and therefore have a *moral* reason to act accordingly, without having a reason-without-qualification, a Reason that would motivate any rational agent. And she may not have a reason of 'self-interest,' or, to use a terminology I prefer, a 'self-grounded reason,' a reason grounded in her own nature. Finally, the account leaves it open that a person who *believes* she has a moral obligation may not have a Reason, or a self-grounded reason, to act accordingly.

Properly speaking, to be sure, the standard-based account is neutral between internalism and externalism. When combined with some theories of justification, it does not imply any internalist doctrine. Yet when combined with certain other theories of justification, it does imply internalist doctrines; in fact, any internalist doctrine is presumably entailed by some theory of justification when it is combined with the standard-based account. David Gauthier, for example, aims to show that "all the duties" of morality "are also truly endorsed in each individual's reason."[31] His account of morality entails a version of reasons-internalism, and it is compatible with my standard-based approach. Nevertheless, in using the standard-based account to explain the normativity of moral judgment, I did not use any internalist ideas. The explanation was externalist; it presupposed nothing about motivations or Reasons.

I have not spelled out my theory of the justification of moral standards, and I have given only a necessary condition of the truth of claims of obligation. It might therefore be objected that for all I have said, internalism may enter the explanation of normativity through my theory of justification, or through some hidden necessary condition for the truth of a claim of moral obligation.[32] Of course I cannot prove that this is not so. However, one could see by inspection that my society-centered account of the justification of moral standards is externalist; it does not entail any internalist doctrine – except for doctrines that are not seriously in dispute, such as the doctrine that anyone with a moral obligation has a corresponding moral reason.

My central claim is that the normativity of a proposition of moral obligation is explained by the fact that it entails nontrivially, and in virtue of its content, that some relevant moral standard is justified. As I said, a standard to the effect that something is to be done *calls for* an action, which gives sense to the idea that such a standard 'directs' the choice of action.[33] In summary, the standard-based account explains that moral propositions are intrinsically normative, that they are apt to direct choice in virtue of their content. It is a version of cognitivism. And, combined with an appropriate theory of justification, it implies that moral claims are categorical in the sense I explained before.

---

31 Gauthier, *Morals by Agreement*, 1

32 Both Earl Conee and Michael Smith urged this objection.

33 Of course, some standards are concerned with things other than actions, such as states of character or the structure of institutions.

3. Moral Belief and Conviction

The noncognitivist theories of Allan Gibbard and R.M. Hare are similar to the standard-based theory in that they also use the idea of a standard.[34] But Gibbard and Hare see the normativity of moral judgment as arising from *assent* to a standard rather than from the way that standards enter the semantics of moral claims. Gibbard says the acceptance of 'norms' involves an element of endorsement, and he says this is "the special element that makes normative thought and language normative."[35] Hare says that sincerely assenting to a command addressed to oneself involves doing or resolving to do what one has been told to do.[36] Theories of this kind say that the normativity of judgments of moral obligation is explained by the fact that a person making such a judgment expresses her endorsement of a standard.

We often take people's behavior as evidence of their moral beliefs. Noncognitivists such as Gibbard and Hare explain this by viewing moral 'belief' as essentially a matter of endorsing a norm rather than a matter of accepting a proposition. For to endorse a norm is presumably at least in part a matter of being disposed to act appropriately. Of course, I reject noncognitivism and internalism. But it does seem plausible that a person who believes sincerely that she has a moral obligation would normally be motivated to act accordingly.

The standard-based theory can accept this despite insisting, as against noncognitivism, that moral belief is literally *belief*. The standard-based view distinguishes between the *proposition* a person expresses in making a claim of moral obligation and the 'corresponding' *standard*, the standard the justification of which is entailed by that proposition.

---

34 Gibbard, *Wise Choices, Apt Feelings*. Hare, *The Language of Morals*. Gibbard calls standards 'norms,' and Hare calls them 'imperatives.' Hare uses the term 'standards' in a different way, to speak of the moral imperatives that have currency in a society or that are subscribed to by a person (Hare, *The Language of Morals*, 7).

35 Gibbard, *Wise Choices, Apt Feelings: A Theory of Normative Judgment*, 33

36 Hare, *The Language of Morals*, 19-20

Of course, it makes no sense to suppose someone believes a standard, but a person who sincerely makes a moral claim does normally *subscribe* to the relevant standard. In typical cases, then, where a person making a claim of moral obligation is sincere, she both believes the proposition she expresses and subscribes to the corresponding standard. In such cases, I will say, her claim expresses a 'moral conviction,' a combination of belief and subscription to the corresponding standard.

The idea of 'subscription' to a standard is similar to Gibbard's idea of norm acceptance and to Hare's idea of assent to a command. The important point for present purposes is that a person who 'subscribes' to a standard to which she can conform intends to conform to it, or makes it a policy to conform to it. More specifically, a person 'subscribes morally' to a standard only if

(1) she intends to conform to it herself, or makes it a policy to conform, assuming it is a standard to which she can conform, and

(2) she intends to support conformity to it, or makes it a policy to support conformity.

The remaining details that would be required in a full account do not matter for present purposes.

I am saying, then, that in typical cases where a person is sincere in making a claim of moral obligation, she has a 'moral conviction,' which implies that she subscribes to the corresponding standard. She is therefore motivated to conform to the standard, for she intends to conform. A person with the conviction that she has a moral obligation to do something is, therefore, motivated to some degree to do it.

Given the way in which we acquire moral attitudes and beliefs, and given the psychological dissonance that would be experienced by a person who did not subscribe to standards that correspond to her moral beliefs – that she is committed to viewing as justified – it is to be expected that people typically subscribe to such standards. Moral beliefs typically are full convictions. Parents who teach children about morality presumably do aim to create appropriate beliefs, for we reason about moral issues, and the moral propositions we believe are the vehicles for our reasoning. Yet it is at least equally important in teaching about morality to bring it about that children subscribe to appropriate standards, the standards corresponding to the beliefs we want them to have.

We want people to live their lives in accord with certain standards, and to have certain policies governing their behavior, which is to say that we want them to subscribe to the relevant standards. We want them to believe that these standards are justified or warranted, which is to say that we want them to have corresponding moral beliefs. And ideally we want them to subscribe to the standards because they believe them to be justified. So it is to be expected that moral education and the social mechanisms that support and reinforce moral education would aim to instill moral belief as well as subscription to corresponding standards.

There is, nevertheless, a real possibility of a person believing that he has a moral obligation without subscribing to the corresponding standard, or vice versa. The best examples of this, I think, are cases in which a person has a metaethical belief that is in tension with his underlying moral attitudes.

Consider again the case of Alice. Alice was raised to believe the divine command theory and to view God as a vengeful ruler who wills us to support capital punishment. Alice still believes all of this, but she is a kind and compassionate person. Her compassion leads her to fail to support capital punishment, and she does not in fact intend to support it or make it a policy to support it. She therefore does not subscribe to a standard calling on her to support capital punishment even though she believes this behavior is morally obligatory.

The case of Huckleberry Finn may illustrate the same possibility. Huck believes he is obligated to turn Jim over to the authorities because Jim is an escaped slave, but Huck does not turn him in. Of course, his failure to turn Jim in is not sufficient to show he lacks a policy of turning in escaped slaves, for we sometimes do fail to conform to our own personal policies, but we can certainly imagine that Huck does not have a policy of turning in slaves, or the intention to turn them in. Hence, there is an elaboration of Huck's case in which, although he believes he is obligated to turn escaped slaves over to the authorities, he does not subscribe to the corresponding standard.

Finally, consider the case of Bill. Bill is a naive nihilist who is convinced that no moral standard is justified and therefore that no (basic, simple) moral proposition is true. Yet he was raised with moral values and he still has those values. He subscribes to a variety of standards including, for example, a prohibition of capital punishment. He would admit he is morally opposed to capital punishment, yet he would deny that capital punishment is wrong or that he is morally obligated to oppose it, and he would deny that he *believes* these things. Now one can be self-deceptive about what one believes, but I stipulate in this case that Bill is correct. He does not believe capital punishment is wrong. He is committed by his nihilism to believing it is false that capital punishment is wrong, so it would be inconsistent for him to believe that capital punishment is wrong. He certainly is not committed to this inconsistency simply in virtue of his moral opposition to capital punishment – in virtue of his subscription to a standard that prohibits capital punishment.

Mackie remarks that "first and second order views ... are completely independent.... A man could hold strong moral views ... while believing that they were simply attitudes and policies with regard to conduct that he and other people held."[37] It is not obvious how best to interpret this remark. In my terminology, Mackie may be pointing out the possibility of having moral beliefs while believing (falsely) that there is 'simply' the fact that we subscribe to certain standards. Alternatively, he may be pointing out the possibility of subscribing to moral standards while at the same time believing (again falsely) that there are no moral truths and no moral beliefs, strictly speaking, and that there is 'simply' the fact that we happen to subscribe to certain standards. It seems to me that it is a virtue of my account that it enables us to see these possible positions as at least coherent.

The examples of Alice, Huck, and Bill support my idea that moral convictions are not simply beliefs. Of course, I have made this true by stipulating that 'moral conviction' consists of belief plus subscription, but I believe that this stipulation is not artificial. There is the complex state of believing a moral proposition and subscribing to the corresponding standard, and it is this state that we typically are interested in when we attempt to determine the nature of a person's moral convictions. For it is this state, not the more simple state of believing a moral proposition, that entails motivation. A person with the conviction that he has a moral obligation to do something is motivated to some degree to do it. A person who merely believes this may not be

---

37 Mackie, *Ethics: Inventing Right and Wrong*, 16

motivated to do it. For, as the examples suggest, although moral belief is normally accompanied by subscription to the corresponding standard, it need not be.

Externalist positions usually suppose that our motivation for meeting our obligations is a desire to act morally, and they construe this desire as external to moral belief. I agree, of course, that moral *belief* does not itself guarantee any motivation to meet our believed obligations. But moral *conviction* is the more complex state that combines belief with subscription, and moral conviction does guarantee motivation to meet the obligations of which we are 'convinced.' We therefore can be internalists about moral convictions even if we are externalists about moral beliefs, and we do not need to accept the crude moral psychology of standard forms of externalism. Perhaps people do have the desire to act morally, but moral motivation in typical cases is explained by the subscription to a standard that is constitutive of moral conviction.

4. Internalist Objections

Following Frankena, I recommended that we take a 'macroscopic' perspective on the debate between internalism and externalism. Ideally, we would evaluate my proposal as a whole, comparing its overall advantages and disadvantages with those of its competitors. I cannot hope to do this in an essay, of course. Nevertheless, one may object to my proposal on account of its externalism without comparing it to fully developed internalist competitors. To do this fruitfully, one would need to argue directly for an internalist doctrine. Many internalists rely more on appeals to intuition than on developed arguments, but Michael Smith presents arguments for two internalist doctrines, each of which is incompatible with my view.

Smith's defense of the two doctrines is part of a larger argument intended to show that judgments of moral obligation are propositions about what we would want if we were fully rational.[38] I am going to restrict attention, however, to his arguments for the two internalist doctrines.

---

38   Smith, *The Moral Problem*, 184

The first is the doctrine he calls "rationalism": "If it is [morally obligatory] for agents to [do *A*] in circumstances *C*, then there is a reason for those agents to [do *A*] in *C*."[39] Recalling the distinctions we made before, we can see that rationalism is an agent version of reasons-internalism; it claims there are reasons for an agent to do what she has a moral obligation to do.

Smith calls his second doctrine the "practicality requirement": "If an agent judges that it is [morally obligatory] for her to [do *A*] in circumstances *C*, then either she is motivated to [do *A*] in *C* or she is practically irrational."[40] The practicality requirement is a belief version of motivation-internalism. It is a doctrine about the motivations an agent will have if she believes that she has a moral obligation – provided that she is not afflicted by any form of 'practical' irrationality, such as weakness of will or depression.[41]

I shall begin with the practicality requirement, for it is the key to Smith's internalism. It is a premise in his main argument for rationalism,[42] and it is a premise he uses in replying to certain objections to internalism.[43] It is also a premise in the argument he

---

39 Ibid., 62. Smith formulates both doctrines as claims about moral rightness rather than as claims about moral obligation. But I have been including judgments of right action under the rubric, 'judgments of moral obligation.' Nothing of substance will be lost if I express his doctrines as claims about moral obligation.

40 Ibid., 61. See 62.

41 Ibid., 61, 120

42 Ibid., 86. At 87-90, Smith offers a second argument for rationalism that appears not to depend on the practicality requirement. I discuss it below. Smith also thinks that rationalism entails the practicality requirement (62).

43 Smith replies to Brink's argument that internalism cannot take the challenge of the 'amoralist' seriously enough. See Brink, *Moral Realism and the Foundations of Ethics*, 45-50, 57-62. Smith argues that the amoralist does not really make moral judgments, but his argument relies on the practicality requirement. Smith, *The Moral Problem*, 68-71. Smith also replies to Foot's argument that moral requirements are analogous to the requirements of etiquette, and, like the latter, they are not requirements of reason. Smith argues against the analogy, but his argument relies on the practicality requirement. Smith, *The Moral Problem*, 80-4

would use to show that Alice cannot genuinely believe she has a moral obligation.

Smith's argument for the practicality requirement begins with what he calls the "striking fact" that "a *change in motivation* follows reliably in the wake of a *change in moral judgment*, at least in the good and strong-willed person."[44] Suppose you manage to convince Carol that her most fundamental values are wrong, and, as a result, she comes to have quite different moral beliefs from those she had before. She comes to believe that she has an obligation to oppose capital punishment where, before, she believed she had an obligation to support capital punishment. If she is a "good and strong-willed person," Smith says, she will now be motivated to oppose capital punishment even though, before, she was motivated to support capital punishment. This example illustrates a connection between change of moral belief and change of motivation that Smith believes is quite reliable. He argues that the reliability of this connection must be explained in one of two ways. First, it might be explained in terms of the "content of moral judgment" by citing the practicality requirement. Or second, it might be explained in terms of "the motivational dispositions possessed by the good and strong-willed person." Smith argues that any explanation of the second kind would badly misconstrue the nature of the good person. Hence, the practicality requirement gives the only viable explanation of the reliable connection. We must accept the practicality requirement or else reject the reliable connection.

How exactly does the practicality requirement explain the reliable connection? The requirement postulates a connection between moral belief and motivation in a *rational* person, but Smith's reliable connection is between moral belief and motivation in a *good* and *strong-willed* person. Smith must therefore be assuming that no good and strong-willed person could suffer from any form of practical irrationality. Since weakness of will is his chief example of practical irrationality, I assume that he intends the term 'strong-willed person' to pick out exactly the people who lack any form of practical irrationality. On this assumption, it follows immediately from the practicality requirement that a

---

44 Ibid., 71. In this and the following paragraphs, I summarize and reconstruct Smith's argument in *The Moral Problem*, 71-6.

strong-willed person who newly comes to believe that he has a certain obligation also comes to have a corresponding new motivation (unless, of course, he coincidentally had the relevant motivation all along). On my assumption, therefore, the practicality requirement at least begins to explain Smith's reliable connection.[45]

Externalists who deny the practicality requirement obviously must explain the connection in some other way. As we saw, Smith argues that they must explain it in terms of something in the nature of the good and strong-willed person. In particular, he argues, they must explain it on the supposition that a good person invariably desires to do whatever she is obligated to do. The problem, Smith believes, is that this desire is vicious, so a *good* person does *not* have the desire.

As Smith sees things, the good person cares directly for such things as honesty, justice, and the well-being of her friends. To be sure, anything she takes to be morally obligatory is such that she desires to-do-it, but this is not to say that she has the desire to-do-anything-that-is-morally-obligatory. Smith calls this the *"de dicto* desire." If the good person's desire to be honest were explained by the *de dicto* desire, it would not be a direct desire to be honest; it would be a derived desire explained by this *de dicto* desire together with her belief that she is obligated to be honest. The desire to-do-whatever-one-is-obligated-to-do is "a fetish or moral vice," Smith thinks.[46] Since the externalist explanation of the reliable connection depends on the idea that the good and strong-willed person is characterized by this desire, it must be rejected.

I will argue that Smith's key claims about the *de dicto* desire are incorrect. The desire is not vicious; a good person *could* be motivated by it. Moreover, the reliable connection does not exist in people who are merely good without being strong-willed. Because of this, the externalist can appeal to the *de dicto* desire to explain the reliable connection in

---

45 If my assumption is incorrect, and being 'strong-willed' is compatible with some forms of practical irrationality, then the practicality requirement does not explain the reliable connection. A strong-willed and good person might fail to experience a change of motivation consequent on a change of moral belief, for he might be depressed or be suffering from some other form of 'irrationality.'

46 Ibid., 75

people who are both good *and* strong-willed while denying that the *de dicto* desire is essential to being a good person. Finally, there are externalist explanations of the reliable connection that do not make reference to the *de dicto* desire.

Let me begin with the last point. Externalists can explain Smith's reliable connection in terms of the nature of the strong-willed person. For Smith, a weak-willed person is one who at least sometimes fails to desire to do what he believes to be morally obligatory.[47] Presumably, then, the *strong-willed* person does *not* fail to desire to do what he believes to be obligatory. Therefore, when a *good and strong-willed* person undergoes a change in his beliefs about his obligations, he undergoes a corresponding change in his motivations (unless, of course, he coincidentally had the relevant motivations all along). This explanation of the reliability of Smith's connection can be accepted by an externalist. It does not require the externalist to think that what Smith calls "weakness of will" is irrational, or a kind of weakness, properly so-called. It relies merely on the idea that strength of will excludes (what Smith calls) weakness of will.

The second point is related. It is that there is not a reliable connection between change of moral belief and change of motivation in people who are good but not strong-willed. Suppose a demagogue convinces Carol that she is in fact obligated to support capital punishment. A while ago, you persuaded her that she ought to oppose it, and you managed to link her fundamentally compassionate nature to her opposition to capital punishment. This link is cemented so firmly, let us suppose, that the demagogue is unable to overcome Carol's revulsion to the death penalty. He successfully convinces her that she is obligated to support it, but she continues to oppose it. Now Carol may well be a good person, it seems to me, despite the fact that she is 'weak-willed'; her belief about capital punishment has changed without an accompanying change in motivation, yet (I assume) her fundamental

---

47 Otherwise, weakness of will would not be a form of practical irrationality that could 'break the connection' between the judgment that one has an obligation and motivation to act accordingly. Ibid., 120

motivations or values are appropriate. Indeed, her goodness seems to depend on her not having the desire to-do-whatever-she-is-obligated-to-do, for if she had this desire, her wavering beliefs about her obligations would bring about wavering motivations. The example shows that a good person may experience a change of moral belief without undergoing a corresponding change of motivation. This means that Smith's reliable connection is not found in good persons without restriction. It is found only in good persons who are strong-willed. To explain this, an externalist must therefore make use of the idea that strength of will excludes weakness of will.

Smith might deny that Carol is a good person, for he claims that "it is constitutive of being a morally good person that you have direct concern for what you think is right."[48] That is, if Carol is a good person, then, for anything she believes she is morally obligated to do, she has a direct concern to do it. But the example is meant to challenge this idea. If I am correct, Carol is a good person in the example even though she both believes that she is obligated to support the death penalty and is not concerned to support it. The way I see things, goodness is fundamentally a matter of one's motivations rather than of one's beliefs or the connection between one's beliefs and one's motivations. A good person subscribes to appropriate moral standards. Smith might reply that Carol is not good in the relevant sense, for she is not *principled*.[49] This is not clear, however, for if she subscribes to a moral standard that prohibits capital punishment, then it is not merely her feelings that move her to oppose capital punishment, it is her attitude to a principle. If so, I think we would intuitively count her as principled. In any event, Smith's argument is unpersuasive if we take him to be talking about the 'principled' person rather than the 'good' person. As we saw, he argues that the good person cares directly for such things as honesty, justice, and the well-being of her friends. Whatever we think of these claims about the good person, they are certainly less plausible if read as claims about the 'principled' person. A principled person acts on rules or

---

48 Note that "this is read *de re* and not *de dicto*." Ibid., 76

49 Smith suggested this reply in correspondence.

principles, I would suppose, rather than from certain direct concerns. I will therefore continue to investigate the idea of the good person.

Let me now turn to Smith's claim that the *de dicto* desire is "a fetish or moral vice."[50] If he is correct, then *no* (entirely) good person has this desire, not even a good person who is also strong-willed. The key point in his reasoning is the claim that it is characteristic of a good person that she has a set of direct concerns. This may well be correct, but it does not follow that no good person can have the *de dicto* desire. To see this, consider the case of Dena. Dena lacks the *de dicto* desire. She has a range of direct concerns for such things as justice, honesty, and the well-being of her friends, and, for anything she thinks she is morally obligated to do, she is motivated to do it. She is a good person. But now suppose that Dena *acquires* the *de dicto* desire. Smith must now say she is no longer a good person, but he is surely wrong about this. Nor is Dena less good than she used to be. She still cares directly for the things she used to care for. The only change is that she has come to have the desire to-do-whatever-she-is-obligated-to-do. There is no reason to think that this desire is vicious in her, for she still cares for all the right things in all the right ways and only cares additionally for doing-the-obligatory-thing.

Smith's worry is presumably about what would happen to Dena if she were to acquire a new belief about what she is obligated to do. He must think that it would be in some way vicious for her to derive her desire to do the new thing from her newly acquired belief together with the *de dicto* desire. Suppose then that this is how Dena acquires a desire to do a new thing. Is this vicious? Dena initially cares only in a derivative way about the new thing. Yet this is not enough to show that she is a less good person than she used to be, for she still cares directly about (almost) everything that she used to care about, and if she continues to care about the new thing, she may well come to care about it directly and not merely because she believes it is obligatory. Nor does it seem that Dena would have been a better person if she had been able immediately to acquire a direct and non-derivative desire to

---

50   Ibid., 75

do the new thing. I suppose she *might* have been a better person in that case, but it seems to me that this is a contingent matter.

For all I have said, Smith may be correct that a person whose moral motivations were *entirely* derivative from the *de dicto* desire would not be a good person. This, however, is no objection to the externalist's attempt to use the *de dicto* desire to explain Smith's reliable connection. For even if some good persons lack the *de dicto* desire, as is illustrated by the example of Carol, and even if any good person must have *some* direct concerns, it may well be that any *good and strong-willed* person would have the *de dicto* desire in addition to her direct concerns.

I conclude, therefore, that Smith's attempt to support the practicality requirement fails. An externalist can explain the reliability of the connection between change of moral belief and change of motivation in a good and strong-willed person on the basis that such people are reliably motivated to do whatever they believe to be obligatory. Such people are, after all, strong-willed.

The combination of my standard-based theory with my account of moral conviction has a number of advantages over standard externalist accounts that invoke the *de dicto* desire to explain moral motivation. First, my account can provide a more plausible account of the psychology of the good person than the account that relies on the *de dicto* desire. We *may* have the desire-to-do-whatever-is-obligatory, but we also normally subscribe to a 'second-order' standard, a standard that calls on us to subscribe to moral standards that correspond to the moral propositions we accept. As a matter of subscribing to this standard, we have an intention or a policy that, with respect to the things we believe would be right, we form the intention or make it a policy to do those things. That is, we subscribe to a standard calling on us to convert moral beliefs into moral convictions.

Second, subscription to this second-order standard can help provide an externalist explanation of Smith's reliable connection. For it explains why, normally, a good person who comes to have a new moral belief comes to subscribe to the corresponding moral standard. And the fact that he comes to subscribe to this standard explains how he comes to be motivated to do what he believes to be obligatory.

Given that my account makes room for a distinction between moral belief and moral conviction, it suggests the possibility that Smith has misdescribed our intuition about the reliable connection. Perhaps our intuition is in fact best understood as an intuition to the effect that a change of moral *conviction* results in a change of motivation rather than as an intuition about change of moral belief, strictly so-called. It is no mystery that a new conviction that one has a moral obligation entails a new motivation to act appropriately, for a moral conviction combines a moral belief with subscription to a corresponding moral standard, and subscription to a standard entails appropriate motivation.

Finally, my account can explain why the practicality requirement might seem plausible. For if an agent has the moral *conviction* that it is obligatory for him to do *A* in circumstances *C*, he is motivated to do *A* in *C*. Something very much like the practicality requirement is therefore true according to the account I provided earlier in this paper. But it is not true that an agent who *believes* he is morally obligated to do something is necessarily motivated to do it unless he is practically irrational. Recall the case of Alice. Alice believes she is morally obligated to support capital punishment on the basis of God's commands but she is compassionate in a way that means she is not motivated to support capital punishment. Her lack of this motivation is due to her compassion, not to any irrationality that I can see.[51]

Let me now turn to Smith's rationalism, his doctrine that if it is morally obligatory for agents to do *A* in circumstances *C*, then there is a reason for them to do *A* in *C*. It is trivial, of course, that if an agent has a moral obligation to do something, she has a *moral* reason to do it. I explained before that this is implied by the standard-based theory. But according to rationalism an agent's having a moral obligation to do something entails that there is a *Reason* for her to do it, a reason such that anyone "would be motivated to act in that way if she were rational." A person is "practically irrational if she is not motivated to act accordingly."[52] Earlier, for simplicity, I referred to Reasons as 'reasons-

---

51 Smith would view Alice as weak-willed, and he regards weakness of will as a form of irrationality (61). But if a person who fails to be motivated to do what he thinks is obligatory is held to be irrational on that basis alone, then the practicality requirement is tautological. I submit that despite the fact that Alice is what Smith would call 'weak-willed,' she may be rational in every respect.

52 Ibid., 62. Here Smith cites Korsgaard, "Skepticism about Practical Reason."

without-qualification.' Smith claims it is a conceptual truth that the existence of a moral obligation implies the existence of a reason-without-qualification. This is not a trivial claim.

By way of analogy, consider etiquette. Etiquette requires setting the table with the fork on the left side of a place setting. It follows that there is a reason of etiquette to set the table in this way. But this does not mean that there is a Reason to set the table in this way – a reason such that anyone would be motivated to set the table in this way if he were rational. There is a substantive question whether we are rationally required to act as we are required by etiquette to act, and most would think that the answer to the question is negative. Similarly, there is at least a tradition in philosophy of thinking that there is a substantive question whether we are rationally required to act as we are morally obligated to act. Rationalism gives an answer to this question that needs independent defense.

Smith's argument for rationalism begins with the premise that we 'expect' rational agents to do what they are morally required to do.[53] That is, he says, we believe that rational agents *will* do what they are morally required to do.[54] "Being rational, as such, must therefore suffice to ground our [belief] that rational agents will do what they are morally required to do." But if this belief is well-grounded for all rational agents solely on the ground that they are rational, there must be *Reasons* for rational agents to do what they are morally obligated to do. Hence, he concludes, it must be the case that if it is morally obligatory for agents to do something, then there is a Reason for them to do it.[55]

Smith does not explain what he means by 'rational agent,' but it follows from the definition of a 'Reason' that, necessarily, if there is a Reason to do something, a rational agent is motivated to do it. To simplify the discussion, I will assume that any Reason is a Reason 'all things considered,' and that any rational agent *does* whatever there is a Reason

---

53 Ibid., 85-6. In the following, I summarize and reconstruct Smith's argument.

54 Ibid., 89, 85-6

55 Ibid., 85

to do. It will be useful to distinguish between agents who are invariably moved by Reasons, and agents who may sometimes fail to be moved by Reasons yet have the *capacity* to be moved by them. I will write that the former are *Rational* while the latter are merely *c-rational*.

The key premise in Smith's argument is the proposition that we reasonably believe 'rational agents' *will* do what they are morally required to do. Of course, we realize that agents who are merely *c-rational* can fail to act morally even if there are Reasons to act morally. Smith's premise must therefore be that we are reasonable to believe that *Rational* agents will act morally. Smith offers two arguments to support this premise. His main argument relies on the practicality requirement, so it can be ignored here.[56] His second argument is concerned with the appropriateness of attitudes of approval and disapproval.[57]

This second argument depends on the doctrine that our moral disapproval of people's wrongful behavior presupposes the 'legitimacy of our expectation' that they will act rightly; that is, Smith says he means, our moral disapproval presupposes the justifiability of the belief that agents *will* do what they are morally required to do.[58] But moral disapproval would be appropriate in any case where a Rational agent did not do what she is morally required to do,[59] and this presupposes the justifiability of the belief that any Rational agent will do what she is morally required to do. That is, "Being rational suffices to ground the expectation that people will do what they are morally required to do."[60]

---

56 For this argument, see Smith, *The Moral Problem*, 86-7.

57 Ibid., 87-91

58 Ibid., 89. As Smith notes, "to say we expect someone to do something can mean either that we believe that they *will*, or that we believe that they *should*." Smith says that he intends the former interpretation throughout. (Ibid., 85-6. Smith emphasized this in personal correspondence as well.) The former is the relevant interpretation, for the proposition he is trying to support is that we believe rational agents *will* do what they are morally required to do.

59 Ibid., 89. See 85.

60 Ibid., 90

Assuming that the preconditions of moral disapproval are satisfied, then, we can reasonably believe Rational people will do what they are obligated to do simply because they are Rational.[61]

But Smith is surely wrong to think that the legitimacy of disapproval presupposes the reasonableness of believing that people will act rightly. To be sure, it is not entirely clear what Smith means. However, first, the legitimacy of disapproving of a person, or of his action, does not presuppose that we reasonably believed, or would have been reasonable to believe, that the agent *himself* would act rightly. Even if we know quite well that someone will do something wrong, this does not mean it will be inappropriate for us to disapprove. Suppose there is someone we know to be an inveterate liar who will lie if he has anything to gain. This does not make it inappropriate for us to disapprove of him and of his lying. There need be nothing morally questionable in disapproving of the behavior of amoralists or of people who for some other reason do not acknowledge their obligations. Nor, second, does the legitimacy of disapproving of a person or his action presuppose that we believe that *people in general* will act rightly. Suppose the bad people kill all but one of the good people, so that from then on people in general do not act rightly. This would not make it inappropriate for the one remaining good person to disapprove of the bad people.

One might propose that it is legitimate to disapprove of people only if they have the ability to *know* what they are morally obligated to do. Since it would be legitimate to disapprove of Rational agents if they acted wrongly, and the only thing they are guaranteed to have in common is their Rationality, it must be possible for them to know what they are morally obligated to do solely by the exercise of their common reason. It must therefore be the case that moral knowledge is a priori. Unfortunately, even if we accept this reasoning for the sake of argument, it does not help Smith's argument, for it does not show that moral knowledge is knowledge of Reasons. It does not show that there is a Reason to do whatever is morally obligatory.

---

61 Ibid., 90

It might be objected that if there are not Reasons to do what we are obligated to do – if moral reasons are not Reasons – then a Rational agent *could* not do what she is obligated to do. This result may seem in conflict with the maxim that 'ought' implies 'can.' But the inference is mistaken; even if moral reasons are not Reasons, it does not follow that a Rational agent cannot do what she is obligated to do. To see this, suppose that Earl is Rational. It is a necessary truth that as long as Earl is Rational, he acts on Reasons. But it does not follow that Earl cannot act rightly unless there is a Reason for him to act rightly. For one thing, it is not a necessary truth that Earl is Rational. He can act rightly even if there are no Reasons to act rightly because he can cease to be Rational. Therefore, the idea that moral reasons are not Reasons does not entail that Rational agents lack any moral obligations.

In short, I do not see how to generate a successful argument for rationalism from Smith's remarks.

The standard-based theory supports a doctrine that is superficially very similar to rationalism, for, as I said before, it implies that if an agent has a moral obligation to do something, he has a *moral* reason to do it. It follows that if there is a moral obligation to do something, there is a reason (of some kind) to do it. But rationalism is the stronger thesis that if an agent has a moral obligation to do something, then there is a Reason or a 'reason-without-qualification' for him to do it. The existence of a reason-without-qualification to fulfill our moral obligations does not follow from the existence of a reason *of some kind* to fulfill our moral obligations. We are not already committed to rationalism simply because we recognize that moral obligations entail moral reasons.

One might think that the only true or genuine reasons are reasons-without-qualification. This would mean that so-called 'moral reasons' are not *reasons* unless they are reasons-without- qualification. Of course, I have no objection to the policy of reserving the word 'reason' for reasons-without-qualification, but we ordinarily do not do this. A rational person responds appropriately to reasons of all kinds, taking their true measure from the point of view of reason; she is not necessarily motivated by reasons of every kind. An irrational person is a person who fails to respond to reasons in this appropriate way. So to establish that there is a reason of a certain kind to do something is not yet to establish that a rational person would be motivated to do the thing, or that it would be irrational to fail to be motivated to do it. It is not yet to establish that there is a reason-without-qualification to do it.

Christine Korsgaard has proposed an "internalism requirement" to the effect that reasons must be *capable* of motivating us insofar as we are rational.[62] But Korsgaard's proposal does not undercut my view. On my view, there is a moral reason to do something just in case a justified moral standard calls on us to do it. A rational person is capable of subscribing to such a standard, and if he subscribes, he is motivated to conform to the standard. Hence, moral reasons are capable of motivating us even if they are not Reasons.

It would obviously be beyond my capacity to consider every internalist argument against the kind of externalism I have proposed. I have merely attempted to show that the standard-based account of moral judgment and the associated account of moral conviction stand up well against Michael Smith's arguments. Moreover the accounts go some way toward explaining why many philosophers are convinced that internalism is correct, for they imply the truth of doctrines that are very similar to the internalist doctrines we have considered. They imply that moral propositions are intrinsically normative. They imply that moral considerations are sources of moral reasons. They account for the fact that good persons are not generally motivated by the desire-to-do-what-is-obligatory. And they imply that moral conviction is partially constituted by moral motivation. In all of these respects, my account is congenial to internalism even though, strictly speaking, it is externalist.

---

62 Korsgaard, "Skepticism about Practical Reason." In some places she speaks of "reason-claims" or of "rational considerations," rather than of reasons, and she speaks of their "success" in motivating us rather than of their being capable of motivating us. See pp. 11, 15, 23. For a superficially similar view, see Williams, "Internal and External Reasons."

CANADIAN JOURNAL OF PHILOSOPHY
Supplementary Volume 21

Attacking Morality:
A Metaethical Project

.ALLEN W. WOOD
Yale University

Metaethics is the philosophical study of what morality is. It differs from ethical theory, which attempts to systematize (and possibly ground) moral judgments, and also from practical or applied ethics, which reflects on particular moral issues or problems. As it has been done in this century, metaethics has usually involved three interrelated projects: a *metaphysical* investigation into the nature of moral facts and properties, a *semantic* inquiry into the meaning of moral assertions, and an *epistemological* account of the nature of moral knowledge. In all three areas, the questions raised by twentieth-century metaethics have apparently been radical, and the dominant position was even openly nihilistic. In metaphysics it was antirealist, maintaining that there are no moral facts, in epistemology noncognitivist, denying that there is moral knowledge, and in semantics emotivist or prescriptivist, holding that moral assertions aren't assertions at all, but are speech acts utterly devoid of truth conditions.[1]

---

1 This is the best way to put it, since 'disquotational' theories of truth allow emotivists to equate 'S is true' with 'S.' Even if the semantic function of 'S' is solely to express an emotional reaction, someone who sympathizes enough to be disposed to utter 'S' is saying something equivalent to 'S is true,' and someone who expresses antipathy can, correspondingly, say something equivalent to 'S is false.' Even utterances whose only function is to express emotions therefore can, in this minimal sense, be said to possess truth *values*. But of course there are no truth *conditions* for mere expressions of emotion.

Perhaps most nihilistic of all was the comparatively recent variant of this position put forward by J.L. Mackie. His position on moral language was semantically realist but metaphysically nihilistic (or as he put it, "skeptical"). It held that moral talk does assert the existence of distinctively 'prescriptive' properties, but that no such 'queer' properties exist, or even could exist. Moral language is thus to be accounted for only through an 'error theory' which explains why people systematically project their feelings and attitudes on the world.[2]

What is strange, however, is that this utterly nihilistic metaethical tradition has almost never seen itself as an attack on morality. On the contrary, it has usually treated with contempt (as an elementary misunderstanding) any suggestion that its views should be seen as undermining the moral point of view or questioning the high esteem in which people ostensibly hold moral values. Mackie, for example, insists that his view concerns only 'second-order' questions or issues of 'conceptual analysis' and not 'first-order' or 'factual' questions about morality itself.[3] (Imagine someone who insisted that theistic religion is a system of error, that all belief in divine beings is nothing but a tissue of lies and superstitions, and yet held it to be an elementary confusion to think that accepting this 'second-order' claim has any tendency to discredit the 'first-order' activities of religious people such as sacrificing or praying to deities.[4])

If the nihilistic metaethical views just mentioned are not meant as attacks on morality, this does not mean that such attacks have been absent from philosophy. On the contrary, in the continental tradition they have been quite prominent, associated with such names as Hegel, Stirner, Marx and Nietzsche. Recent critics of morality have included

---

2 John L. Mackie, *Ethics: Inventing Right and Wrong* (Harmondsworth, Middlesex: Penguin 1977)

3 Ibid., 22-4

4 We might consider such a person to be either contradicting himself or talking nonsense. But following Mackie, perhaps that accusation could in turn be treated as only a 'higher order' assertion which should not be interpreted as criticizing the philosopher's views on religion.

Bernard Williams, Susan Wolf, and John D. Caputo.[5] Of course not all the attacks on morality havé been equally radical. Some are less attacks on morality itself than on certain positions in moral theory, or else they are attacks on certain specific moral values or on 'morality' in a technical sense which is contrasted with 'ethics' (which is not regarded as vulnerable to the same objections).

I will be concerned here with certain ways of attacking morality which are both radical and distinctively metaethical in nature. These views are *radical* in that they attempt to some degree directly to undermine our commitment to all moral values or to the moral point of view generally, typically by showing that such commitment is based on illusions about morality, regarded as a psychological or social phenomenon. The distinctively *metaethical* character of such critiques of morality consists in the fact that they rest on claims about *what morality is* (and that commitment to the moral standpoint is based on errors or deceptions at this metaethical level).

Hence I will not be interested in Mackie's view, for instance. For although he apparently regards the moral point of view as involving metaethical error (since according to him it involves the 'projection' or 'objectification' of feelings and attitudes, after the pattern of the so-called 'pathetic fallacy'), he does not think that exposing such errors is going to undermine our commitment to morality itself. He seems to think that exposing the systematic errors of moral language will have no effect on our moral feelings and attitudes themselves or our commitment to them. Mackie's metaethical view could with some plausibility have been developed into the relevant sort of radical metaethical critique of morality, if Mackie had claimed that our commitment to moral attitudes as such is dependent on our understanding them as grounded in objective values, and inferred from this that when we recognize there are no such values, then that must tend to undermine a rational person's commitment to morality. The same could be done

---

5 Bernard Williams, *Ethics and the Limits of Philosophy* (Cambridge, MA: Harvard University Press 1985) ch. 10; Susan Wolf, "Moral Saints," *Journal of Philosophy* **79** (1982); John D. Caputo, *Against Ethics* (Bloomington: Indiana University Press 1993)

with other antirealist and noncognitivist positions, such as emotivism, if they were combined with the view that it would undermine our commitment to moral emotions to find out that moral statements are no more than expressions of emotion and make no claims having truth conditions. I have always thought, in fact, that these radical variants of metaethical nihilism are far more interesting and plausible than the tediously complacent and uncritically moralistic versions of metaethical antirealism common among Anglophone philosophers. But it will not be my purpose to pursue that point here.[6]

Instead, I will explore some specific examples of two general kinds of critique to which morality as a whole has been subjected. One sort I will call 'content critiques,' the other 'formal (or structural) critiques.' Content critiques of morality claim that moral norms, principles and ends have a certain unavoidable content, disguised from or misperceived by those who are committed to morality, whose recognition tends seriously to undermine that commitment. Formal or structural critiques deal with features of the psychology or sociology of morality which pertain to it irrespective of the content of moral norms. In this paper, for example, it will involve a theory about the psychology of two fundamental and indispensable moral feelings: indignation and guilt. The critique displays such feelings as irrational or pathological, thus undermining our commitment to all patterns of thinking and feeling in which these feelings are involved either actually or virtually (that is, all properly moral patterns of thinking). The modified form of Mackie's position described in the previous paragraph

---

6 *"There are no moral facts at all.* Moral judgments agree with religious judgments in believing in realities which are no realities. Morality is merely an interpretation of certain phenomena – more precisely, a misinterpretation" (Nietzsche, *Twilight of Idols*, "The Improvers of Humanity," § 1). When Nietzsche wrote this, he intended it as a radical attack on morality, as the foundation of his "demand upon the philosopher, that he should take his stand beyond good and evil" (ibid.). Yet English speaking metaethical antirealists usually regard Nietzsche's inference here with impatient condescension, as the sort of thing one might expect from a particularly naive and annoying undergraduate. On this point I have always sided with Nietzsche and the naive undergraduates.

would also fall under the heading of a 'formal (or structural) critique.' For it would say that our commitment to morality depends on the false belief that moral attitudes are grounded on objective moral facts, so that the discovery that there are no such facts tends to undermine that commitment, at least in a rational person.

1

One of the earliest content critiques of morality is the position of Thrasymachus, as presented in the first book of Plato's *Republic*. According to Thrasymachus, justice is the advantage of the stronger.[7] This theory is based on a piece of sociology or political theory: In societies, there are some who rule, while the rest are ruled. 'Justice' refers to a disposition on the part of the ruled to obey the laws made by the rulers (338c-339a). Those who rule seek their own advantage at the expense of the ruled, as shepherds carry on their activities for their own advantage rather than that of the sheep (343b). This means that to act justly is really to obey laws that are made in someone else's interest (343c), and hence that just conduct is always foolish, disadvantageous and deserving of contempt, while unjust conduct (whenever one can get away with it) is advantageous and therefore wise (343c-344a). Thrasymachus notes that justice is generally praised, but thinks that his theory shows this esteem to be based on deceptions. The praise of justice is due to bold cunning and self-serving bluster on the part of rulers, fear and high-minded foolishness on the part of the ruled (344c). Those who know what justice really is do not praise it, but rather despise it. They consider injustice to be good, intelligent and wise (348c-e).

In the terminology of twentieth-century metaethics, Thrasymachus' position is best understood as a form of realism (both metaphysically and semantically) and cognitivism (epistemologically). 'Justice' refers

---

7 Plato, *Republic*, tr. G.M.A. Grube (Indianapolis: Hackett 1974). Cited below by Stephanus number. Quotations and paraphrases follow Grube's translation, with some modifications.

to a real property of actions, namely, their conduciveness to the interests of the rulers and consequent disadvantageousness for the agent. For example, the assertion 'Paying taxes is just' means that paying taxes has the objective property of benefiting those who rule and harming the taxpayer. Of course Thrasymachus does not suppose that the description 'benefiting the rulers at my own expense' is associated in most people's minds with the term 'just' when they pride themselves on their justice. On the contrary, he maintains that people are systematically deceived about the real nature of justice, and would be quite incapable of identifying justice with the referent of this phrase (at least until they have been enlightened by his metaethical doctrines). But he does think that the property referred to by this phrase is, unbeknownst to them, the real referent of the term 'justice' and what governs their use of this term.

It has been noted before that views such as Thrasymachus's are very difficult to make sense of if one accepts an antirealist, noncognitivist and emotivist metaethics.[8] Emotivists hold that 'just' is used most basically to express praise or approval. But that would make a view like Thrasymachus's close to self-contradictory, since its fundamental claim is that justice is contemptible and that what is just receives praise or approval only from the foolish and ignorant. Since Thrasymachus's position, though unconventional and perhaps quite mistaken, is clearly intelligible and in no danger of contradicting itself; it poses serious problems for emotivism.[9]

---

8 See Philippa Foot, "Moral Beliefs," *Proceedings of the Aristotelian Society* **59** (1958-1959) 420-425; Nicholas Sturgeon, "What Difference Does It Make if Moral Realism is True?" *Southern Journal of Philosophy* **24** (1986) 126-7.

9 For similar reasons, the intelligibility of Thrasymachus's view casts serious doubt on any semantical form of 'internalism,' which takes it to be part of the *meaning* of words such as 'just' that people have some reason or motive for doing what is just. It presents no difficulty, however, for other forms of internalism, such as those which say merely that there necessarily is a reason or motive for doing what is just. Such views are, to be sure, committed to denying that Thrasymachus's account of justice is correct, but they can easily admit that it is intelligible and not self-contradictory. Their contention is rather that justice is a different property from the one identified by Thrasymachus and that of this property it is in fact true that there is necessarily a reason or motive for doing actions which have it.

Thrasymachus's definition of justice is like the claim that water is H_2O or that gold is the element with atomic number 79. People in earlier ages could not have had these descriptions in mind when they used the words 'water' or 'gold,' but their usage of 'water' may nevertheless have been governed by the property of being H_2O, and hence H_2O may have been the correct referent of the term. The semantics of the term 'water' need not defer to their mistaken theories about water (their belief, for instance, that it was an element rather than a compound). Likewise, Thrasymachus's theory about the term 'just' does not need to defer to what is associated with the term in people's minds, such as the idea that justice is what is impartially good and that justice is worthy of honor and respect. For these ideas according to Thrasymacus, are nothing but false popular beliefs about justice (in fact, they are the very illusions his theory means to expose).

Suppose there were an ignorant people who superstitiously believed that gold was possessed of magical properties, or mistakenly thought that ingesting it cures many sorts of illnesses. If their philosophers engaged in metaethical speculations, making the same mistakes that philosophers have made in our century, then they might come to regard being magical, or medicinal, or simply desirable, an indispensable part of the meaning of the word 'gold.' On a view like Thrasymachus's, the superstitions of this people would be analogous to our belief that justice is deserving of praise, and the errors of their philosophers would be like the error regarding praiseworthiness as essential to the very meaning of the word 'justice.'

A much later and more sophisticated version of Thrasymachus's view is articulated by Marx, when he defines the justice of transactions as their 'correspondence' or 'adequacy' to the prevailing mode of production.[10] Marx does not hold that justice is directly the property of benefiting those that rule, nor does he think of the relation between

---

10 *Marx-Engels Werke* (Berlin: Dietz Verlag 1966-) 25: 351-2; *Capital* vol. 3, translated by David Fernbach (New York: Random House 1981) 460-1

those who legislate politically and those legislated to as the fundamental power relation in society. But like Thrasymachus, Marx takes justice to be an objective property of transactions, whose content is determined by social facts. He thinks justice is a property usually unknown to people, even disguised from them, when they think and talk about justice, and that ideological illusions are typically involved in their motivation to perform just acts. And like Thrasymachus, Marx thinks that once we gain a clear view of what justice is, we will acquire more sober ideas about how praiseworthy or desirable it is.[11]

---

11 See Allen Wood, *Karl Marx* (London: Routledge 1981) ch. 9 and "Marx Against Morality," in P. Singer, ed. *A Companion to Ethics* (Oxford: Blackwell 1990) 511-24. Thus in Thrasymachus's view, someone who holds, for instance, that just laws are those made in the interest of the governed is making a fundamental mistake about what justice is. This is precisely the sort of mistake which benefits the rulers and makes the notion of justice so useful to them. Such a person may nevertheless believe correctly that the actually existing laws are just, and they may in fact be just. If a party came to realize that the existing laws benefit the rulers at the expense of the ruled, it might propose a new legal code which benefits the ruled, and argue for these new laws on the ground that they are more just than the present ones. In Thrasymachus's view, their argument would rest on the same confusion by which they had previously been hoodwinked; it would be based on the party's substitution of a vulgar and mystified conception of what justice is for a correct one. There is no sign that the Thrasymachus of Plato's dialogue would have shared the goals of this party, but if he had shared them, then he would still criticize the party for articulating its views in terms of an erroneous and mystified conception of what justice is. What this party wants, he ought to say, is not justice, but rather injustice – and he would add (if he agreed with the party's goals) that this injustice is precisely what would make the proposed laws desirable and worthy of adoption. This, in effect, was Marx's reason for condemning those in the working class movement who advocated socialist distribution on grounds of justice (see *Marx-Engels Werke* 19:8; *Marx Engels Selected Works* [New York: International Publishers 1967] 325). For what the socialists demand is not a distribution which corresponds to the prevailing (capitalist) mode of production, but rather one which contradicts it. What they demand may be quite all right, but their way of articulating the demand betrays a fundamental misconception about the nature of justice, resting on even more fundamental misconceptions about social reality.

2

The most tempting response to all such content critiques of morality is probably to claim that they are based on confusing morality itself with people's erroneous ideas about it. It might be conceded, for example, that Thrasymachus is right in saying that what serves the interest of the rulers is identical to what people (erroneously) call just. But, so the objection goes, the very fact that his definition, if accepted, would undermine our commitment to 'justice' (to what it defines as 'justice') is sufficient to show that Thrasymachus's definition fails to capture what we really consider justice itself to be.

This objection certainly coheres with emotivist metaethical theories which hold that the central function of terms like 'just' is merely to express approval, and whatever content they have beyond that is constrained by the requirement that what we regard as 'really' just has to be something toward which we have, all things considered, a 'pro'-attitude. But its reinterpretation of Thrasymachus does an extremely poor job of capturing his intentions, and in effect it accuses him of quite elementary confusions. From his point of view, however, the objection reveals the objectors' hopeless entanglement in the very errors his own theory is intended to expose.

Thrasymachus is clearly not saying merely that what people (perhaps erroneously) call just has the property of benefiting the rulers, any more than when we say that water is H_2O or gold is the element with atomic number 79 we are asserting merely that these properties belong to what people (perhaps erroneously) call by those names. Likewise, the notion that the referent of 'just' has to track our pro-attitudes is like saying that in a society which attributes magical powers or medicinal virtues to the ingestion of gold, 'gold' really refers to nothing at all (if nothing has these powers or virtues) or perhaps that 'gold' might turn out to refer to penicillin (if penicillin turns out to have some significant portion of the medicinal virtues they attribute to gold).

The whole point of content critiques of morality is to insist that a term such as 'just' has a referent whose proper content is fixed, or at least severely limited, by certain facts (in the case of Thrasymachus and Marx, social facts) – and limited in such a way as to undermine our commitment to justice once we understand the limitation. The objection just considered, on the other hand, is based on a prejudice which is widely held but seldom explicitly stated: namely, that the 'true' content of moral principles is whatever content we decide, in the end and all things considered, these principles should have. This prejudice tempts us to respond to every content critique of morality by reinterpreting it as a clumsy and needlessly paradoxical way of disagreeing with conventional moral beliefs, hence not as a critique of morality but merely a disagreement within morality. For example, if 'justice' has up to now usually referred to what is to the advantage of the rulers, and on reflection we favor the interest of the ruled, then we say that it is what is 'really just' is what favors the ruled. According to this view, justice itself should not be attacked, but pernicious ideas about it need to be reformed.

There are powerful reasons, rooted in the cultural fact of modern 'morality' and its history, why this prejudice, and the consequent interpreting-away of any content critique of morality, should be very tempting to us. The same history, however, equally reveals why we should not expect such attempts at reinterpretation always to succeed.

What we call 'morality' in modern liberal society is the outcome of a cultural process through which social norms and customs, most of them originally with a premodern (usually religious) basis and content, have been appropriated, modified and rationalized so as to accord with a culturally diverse society whose only workable common basis has proven to be universalistic and secular. Some writers, such as Alasdair MacIntyre, who mistrust the power of thinking with such a basis, have emphasized the moral fragmentation inevitably involved in such a process. Others, such as John Rawls, have more optimistically brought out the indispensable role which must be played in modern society by an 'overlapping consensus' with a liberal content.[12]

A strong argument for the pessimistic side of this controversy can be drawn from the value commitments of the social traditions out of which modern morality arose. They reflect a premodern society in which the division of society into unequal orders or estates was taken

---

12 MacIntyre, *After Virtue*, 2nd ed. (Notre Dame, IN: Notre Dame Press 1981, 2d. ed. 1984); Rawls, *Political Liberalism* (Cambridge, MA: Harvard University Press 1993)

for granted, in which social forms involving personal domination and dependence (slavery, serfdom and various forms of indentured servitude) were common, and in which women were routinely treated as sexual property or domestic labor, to be disposed of as their fathers and husbands saw fit.

Partly as a consequence of this last point and partly for other reasons, the norms of traditional morality were focused compulsively on the social regulation of the sexual conduct of individuals in ways that are plainly pathological, patriarchal and homophobic. Such morbid obsessions, which undeniably continue to belong to the principal connotations of the word 'moral,' can never be made intelligible on the assumption that the point of morality is the greatest happiness of the greatest number or the self-government of free and rational beings. It may still have been possible for Prussian Protestants (such as Kant) or English Victorians (such as Mill) to deny the obvious contradictions here, but it is no longer possible for us to do so. It may be the greatest lasting contribution of such twentieth-century thinkers as Freud and Foucault to have revealed the patterns of individual pathology and social oppression on which traditional sexual morality rests.

One way out of this dilemma – a way which betrays a deep commitment to 'the system morality' – is to say, as Bernard Williams does, that "there is no distinctively sexual morality," that 'sexual matters' engage moral principles only to the extent that they involve issues which are recognizably 'moral' (in a recognizably sane, modern, secularized sense) – issues of 'trust, betrayal, and so forth.' In response to such a view, David Carr is surely quite correct to insist that the virtue of sexual chastity itself constitutes an original and irreducible element of *morality*.[13] Williams is probably correct, of course, in thinking that it would be 'better,' all things considered, if people's sexual conduct were not culturally regulated according to such standards of chastity (insofar as these resist reduction to values which are more rational, healthy, autonomy-respecting, and felicific). But it does not follow that these

---

13   David Carr, "Chastity and Adultery," *American Philosophical Quarterly* **23** (1986) 363-71. Williams's quoted remarks, taken from a 1971 radio broadcast, are cited by Carr on p. 370.

standards can be either eliminated from the content of morality or reflectively reformed so as to make them acceptable to modern, enlightened sensibilities. Their ineliminability may be merely a reflection of
the fact that the content of morality in whatever form, contains
ineliminable elements of neurosis, patriarchy, homophobia and so on.

Yet there is equally little doubt that the content of what we call 'morality' is now decisively determined by the such modern, secular, rationalistic values as human rights, human dignity and human happiness.
Even those who crusade against 'secular humanism' have no choice
but to conduct their public relations campaigns so as to avoid open
conflict with these values (thus betraying the fundamental intellectual
and spiritual bankruptcy of their position). Whatever their differences,
both moral traditionalists and moral modernists are therefore deeply
committed to the project of reconciling morality's traditional form with
a content suited to a modern secular society oriented to the freedom,
welfare and fulfilment of individuals. 'Morality' (whatever its content)
is by now most fundamentally a name for just that project, and strug-
gles within morality are merely over the precise terms of the treaty of
reconciliation.

3

The two perennially favorite moral theories, utilitarianism and
Kantianism, are quite transparent attempts to adapt inherited social
and psychological materials to the needs of a modern, hence more reflective, individualistic, and rationalistic culture. Utilitarians accept
from the tradition the conceptual and psychological substructure of
morality, especially the notions of moral right, wrong and obligation,
and the supporting feelings and attitudes of praise, blame, guilt and
conscience, even sometimes the standards of individual rights and social
justice, but seek to reform their content according to the rational principle that conduct should be conductive to the collective welfare of all.
Whatever the original cultural or religious meaning of moral concepts,
feelings, and forms of reflection, the utilitarian wants to detach them
from the contingent and often irrational 'sympathies and antipathies'
they usually express. Conscience, as Mill says, is simply an artificial
association of a painful sanction with certain rules of conduct, through

which a society controls the behavior of its members.[14] The utilitarians' aim is to reform, re-educate and socially re-engineer these associations, directing and manipulating human conduct toward more rational, secular, universalistic ends.

Kant recognizes that morality has arisen historically out of social standards of 'decency' (*Sittsamkeit*), or 'propriety' (*Anständigkeit*), that is, forms of customary behavior through which individuals have sought to gain social status, or at least to avoid the contempt, of others by conforming their conduct to the expectations of social custom.[15] He emphasizes that both the basis and the content of many of these socially enforced norms were originally religious and hardly deserving of rational respect. They were, he points out, statutory observances superstitiously directed to winning the special favor of supernatural beings, and usually designed to maximize the tyrannical power which a class of priests wielded over people's thoughts, feelings and actions.[16] The decisive break with this traditional morality, in his view, occurs with enlightenment, "the human being's release from self-incurred minority," through which people begin for the first time to think for themselves.[17] This gives morality a new basis, not fear of social disapproval or divine displeasure, but the autonomy of reason, through which their own faculties give universal laws which accord with the dignity of their rational nature.[18] Thus for Kant the rational reform which brings us to a consciousness of true morality does not merely modify the content of traditional social norms, as utilitarianism proposes to do, but even revolutionizes their character as forms of social control, turning them instead into laws which realize the freedom of individuals as moral agents.

---

14 Mill, *Utilitarianism*, ed. G. Sher (Indianapolis: Hackett 1979) 28-30

15 See Kant, *Conjectural Beginning of Human History, Kants Schriften*, Berlin Academy ed. 8:113.

16 Kant, *Religion within the Bounds of Mere Reason*, Academy ed. 6:151-90

17 *Answer to the Question: What is Enlightenment?* Academy ed. 8:35

18 Kant, *Groundwork of the Metaphysics of Morals*, Academy ed. 4:431-41

Alasdair MacIntyre has claimed that modern morality is made up of leftover scraps of various social traditions, which Enlightenment universalist rationalism is impotent to unify or to provide with a common ground. He seems to me to underestimate both the power of reason and the distinctive and positive contribution the Enlightenment tradition plays in grounding and shaping the values of modern culture. Nevertheless, I am arguing that in the end something rather like his contentions turns out to be true. For both utilitarian and Kantian theories reveal a deep tension within morality, between its social basis and content and what modern reflection wants to make of it.

The culture of premodern society obviously did not rest on values such as the maximal tendency of individual pleasure over pain or the autonomy of the human will. Even modern society, insofar as its basic form is capitalism, though its ideologies are grounded on these values, is deeply hostile to them, so that the tension is not only between modern and premodern values, but also between modern values and modern practice. Since this is so, it should not be surprising that our moral consciousness should resist the radical transformation customary moral norms would have to undergo if modern values were fully accepted. It is therefore hard to be convinced by the optimism to which moralists (whether traditionalist or reformist) are irrevocably committed. We should not believe them when they say, for example, that moral principles have always achieved stability only through the unacknowledged influence of the utilitarian standard,[19] or that autonomy of the will suddenly solves the problem of grounding morality, which defeated all previous moral theories[20] – in other words, that traditional morality grounded on custom and religion was really modern morality all along, only it did not understand itself.

---

19 Mill, *Utilitarianism*, 3

20 Kant, *Groundwork* 4:441-45

4

The best-known radical critic of morality is, of course, Friedrich Nietzsche. Some of Nietzsche's attacks on morality can be interpreted as content critiques analogous to those of Thrasymachus and Marx. It is a familiar theme in Nietzsche, for instance, that morality's content is determined by its social function of asserting the dominance of society over the individual, hence of controlling or suppressing whatever is 'deviant' or creative in human beings, whatever stands outside or rises above the 'herd' and its perspective. His attack on Christian morality – and even more on its modern, humanist descendants – may also be viewed as a content critique of morality insofar as Nietzsche regards 'slave values' as having defeated 'master values' in the historical struggle, and thus as monopolizing the content of morality. And of course Nietzsche was one of the first philosophers to notice the destructive tensions and incompatibilities in modern morality, and to draw radically anti-moral consequences from them.

For just this reason, however, many of Nietzsche's attacks are not so much content critiques of morality itself as polemics against certain specific moral values – of the value ascribed to compassion, for instance, or of moral principles such as human equality and universal human dignity – which he himself views as competing with other values, such as strength or creativity, which might also be affirmed as part of a 'master morality.' It is significant in this respect that Nietzsche's earliest discussion of the opposition between 'slave morality' and 'master morality' concludes with the observation that "our current morality has grown on the soil of the *ruling* tribes and castes."[21]

For this reason as well as others, it may be more illuminating to consider aspects of Nietzsche's polemic against morality which constitute formal or structural critiques. Specifically, I will briefly discuss two themes in Nietzsche's chief work on the topic, *On the Genealogy of Morals*. The first is the theory of *ressentiment*, presented in the 'First

---

21 *Human, All-Too-Human*, § 45

Essay,' and the second is the theory of self-directed aggression and its rationalization, presented in the 'Second Essay.' We will regard these two theories as structural critiques of two basic moral attitudes, blame and guilt, which are fundamental formal or structural features of morality. Attitudes of blame and guilt, that is to say, are indispensable to any morality whatever its content, since they are directed toward what is perceived as morally evil, irrespective of what moral good and evil are taken to consist in. Hence, if Nietzsche can convincingly display the psychology of these attitudes in a way that discredits them, then he will thereby succeed in undermining our commitment to morality as such, irrespective of its content.

The fundamental psychological mechanism involved in *ressentiment* is quite simple. Someone does you an injury, trespasses on territory you hope to occupy, takes away something you wanted, or in some other way causes you pain or humiliation. The natural reaction is to strike out at the person who has done this to you, to assert yourself by perpetrating an even greater aggression, inflict an even greater pain or humiliation, visiting on your tormentor an even greater suffering than the one you have been forced to endure; and this pain you want to inflict is seen by you not as a means to your well-being but rather as desirable for its own sake, simply because it deprives the other of a happiness equal to or greater than that of which you have been deprived. Suppose, however, that you are aware that you cannot strike out in this way, that you are too weak, that you are impotent to do the other any harm, or that this other is so much your superior that if you dare to strike back you will be crushed by the overwhelming power of the one you hate. The fact that your reactive impulse does not find an outlet does not mean that this impulse disappears. On the contrary, Nietzsche theorizes, it merely accumulates, grows and festers. And if you are so aware of your own impotence that you are often offended by external powers and can seldom give expression to your reactive instinct, then the consciousness of your position may easily become psychologically untenable. Your rancor will then change its form, it will be transmuted, disguised. And if it does not dare to assail its real object directly, it will seek out another object, or manufacture an imaginary object on which it may mount an attack with impunity. Nietzsche's theory is that the concept of moral evil first arises as such an imaginary object, and the attitude of moral blame is the accumu-lated *ressentiment*, assuming a concentrated, purified form.[22]

When we confront evil, we get all worked up. We draw on a store of negative psychic energy which is sometimes surprising or even terri-fying in its strength and vehemence. Our opposition to evil is not driven by mere anger, still less by any offense to ourselves personally. To the extent that it is, our indignation is felt to be tainted, not purely moral in character. In moral blame, that is to say, we are driven by a force more sublime than any immediate impulse to retaliate against an injury, whether done to ourselves or to someone else in particular. The par-ticular object of our indignation is merely an example, and we may feel all the nobler if we feel no hatred of *it* (him, her or them) as an individual (we 'hate the sin, not the sinner'). The real object of our moral attitude, we tell ourselves, is simply *evil itself*, of which the mis-creant before us is simply an example. It is evil, we tell ourselves, that calls forth blame, as what it inherently deserves. Nietzsche's theory, however, explains this by reference to the vast reservoir of unconscious *ressentiment* which has built up in us through a long series of injuries to which our impotence has prevented us from reacting in a healthy and spontaneous way. We require an object on which to vent these feelings, an object distinct from any particular individual, but capable of taking up residence in individuals, when awareness of their vulnerability, or lack of our self-control, or some other contingent factor makes them seem fit objects toward which to direct our pent-up hostilities. This is, on Nietzsche's theory, the psychological meaning of *evil*, regarded specifi-cally as an object of feelings such as an indignation and blame.

On Nietzsche's theory, it would be hopelessly naive, from the stand-point of psychology, to ask whether 'evil,' in this sense, is a real prop-erty of actions or people in the world. We understand where the idea of evil comes from only if we understand the self-concealing mecha-nism of creative imagination which produces evil as a way of making our suppressed *ressentiment* psychologically tenable. We grasp the nature of evil, and of the blame it calls forth, only when we understand

---

22 Nietzsche, *On the Genealogy of Morals*, First Essay, especially §§ 10-11, 14-15

the sick and self-opaque psychological process through which our imagination was compelled to posit it. Moral evil, as the 'proper' object of blame, is not a moral 'reality' of any sort, which might rationally guide our conduct or figure in the explanation of what happens. It is only a symptom of a psychological process whose irrationality necessitates its being hidden from consciousness.

5

The 'Second Essay' in the *Genealogy* provides a similarly psychological (and deflationary) account of guilt feelings. For Nietzsche, as for Kant, the historical origin of morality is to be found in the social customs through which a culture forms and controls its members, a regimen to which Nietzsche gives the name 'the morality of mores' *Sittlichkeit der Sitte*).[23] The mores of the community frustrate many of the individual's instincts especially the aggressive ones, since their natural expression would threaten others and make a secure social life in general impossible for all.

Once again Nietzsche argues that powerful psychological needs do not go away merely because their direct satisfaction is inhibited. Instead, they once again assume a form which is acceptable – to the psyche of the individual, and also to society. Once the individual human animal has been caged up in civilization, its suppressed aggressive impulses – Nietzsche calls them the "instinct for freedom" – are left with only one acceptable object: the only thing on which it is permissible to inflict pain is *oneself*.[24]

As in the case of *ressentiment*, however, this redirection of a destructive instinct would be psychologically untenable if it were consciously recognized for what it is. Before the individual's consciousness it requires articulation in an acceptable form. Nietzsche argues that this

---

23 Nietzsche, *On the Genealogy of Morals*, Second Essay, § 2; cf. also *Human, All-Too-Human*, § 96; *Mixed Opinions and Maxims*, § 89; *The Wanderer and His Shadow*, § 48; *Daybreak*, §§ 9, 14, 16.

24 Nietzsche, *On the Genealogy of Morals*, Second Essay, §§ 17-18

form developed at a comparatively early stage of civilization, based on the then existing social relationship between creditors and debtors. At an earlier stage of culture, Nietzsche observes (he is thinking mainly of the relevant provisions of the Roman Twelve Tables, promulgated about 450 B.C.), when a debtor was unable to pay a creditor what was owed, the latter was permitted to amputate a part of the former's body commensurate with the size of the debt (we are bound to think of Shakespeare's Shylock in this connection). Nietzsche argues that we entirely misunderstand this practice if we see it as a *deterrent* to those who would voluntarily escape their obligations; voluntariness on the part of the debtor did not come into it at all. The point, rather, was simply to compensate the creditor for a pecuniary loss by permitting him to receive an acceptable substitute – "the pleasure of being allowed to vent his power freely upon one who is powerless, the voluptuous pleasure *de faire le mal pour le plaisir de le faire.*"[25]

This way of dealing with unpaid debt, Nietzsche maintains, also functioned in people's thinking about crime and punishment. Life in society, under the protection of its laws, was something individuals have been given, and for which they owe society a recompense, in the form of obedience to those laws. When I break the law, I am viewed as a debtor who has not paid my debt to society, and it therefore may inflict pain on me to compensate itself for my transgression.[26]

These institutions, Nietzsche hypothesizes, provided people with a way of dealing consciously with the psychological results of social prohibitions. We have a need to inflict pain on ourselves, but we do not understand why, and we have to explain this need in a way we find acceptable. But we understand that when we owe a debt we cannot pay, or have done something wrong, pain is rightly inflicted on us, in compensation to our creditor, or to the law or the authority we have offended. The sufferings we endure at our own hands, then, can be made intelligible if we see them as punishments or compensation for unpaid debts. All we need in order to make this explanation work is to

---

25   Ibid., §§ 5

26   Ibid., §§ 9, 12-13, 15

find (or invent) an unpaid debt or a crime we have committed, and a creditor who demands our pain as satisfaction.

Nietzsche points out that today we think of debt and crime in very different ways than they were thought of back when the concept of guilt and the feeling of bad conscience were invented. But he finds traces of their genealogy in the fact that the German word *Schuld* means both 'guilt' and 'debt.'[27] The moral attitudes of guilt and bad conscience, owing to the persistence of the social and psychical necessities which gave birth to them, long ago acquired a life of their own, though they are supported today by the same diseased psychology they had at the beginning.

As for our need to find debts and a creditor, crimes and someone to take satisfaction in our punishment, the human imagination makes quick work of these requirements. Ancestors and gods are easily viewed as benefactors, to whom we owe more than we can possibly repay.[28] Crimes are also easily found, all the more easily as we purify the demands of our morality, so that we make not only the deed but even the wish into a transgression. This device even does double service in our present predicament, since our need to be punished arises precisely from the fact that we have aggressive desires on which we may not act; there is admirable psychic economy exhibited in the fact that we are finally able to express these desires when we punish ourselves simply for having them.[29]

On Nietzsche's theory, there is also a profound symbolism in the Christian doctrine of original sin, the idea that our real guilt lies far deeper than any of our particular misdeeds, and they merely provide so many occasions for this guilt to manifest itself. For Nietzsche the truth in this is that the origin of our feelings of guilt does not lie in any

---

27 Ibid., § 6

28 Ibid., § 19

29 The maximal invention of this sort, Nietzsche thinks, is that of the forgiving God who had to sacrifice himself for our sins because these were too profound and heinous ever to be expiated by any punishment we might undergo: the infinite love and infinite beneficence of such a God, and the infinite debt we incur on its account, is sufficient to provide endless occasions for the most exquisite forms of self-torment (ibid., §§ 20-21).

transgression we have committed against the laws of society, but is due on the contrary to society's aggression against us, in checking and suppressing our instinct for freedom, which therefore seeks opportunities to vent itself on us by taking our acts as occasions for punishment.

If Nietzsche's theory is correct, then we should expect a somewhat paradoxical consequence: If guilt feelings are the results of aggression suppressed by social mores, then *ceteris paribus* those who are least outwardly aggressive should be most sensitive to them, while those who express their aggressiveness most freely should be least susceptible to the unhealthy psychology of guilt and hence should feel the least guilty about what they do. And this is what we do see; for it is saintly people like Augustine who still feel guilty over the pears they stole as children, while brutal conquerors seldom feel guilt about what they do (unless, Nietzsche thinks, their innocence has been corrupted by Christian moral sicknesses).[30] Morality, of course, has its own account of all this, telling us that this is because the former type of person, being especially 'good,' is also especially sensitive to his own flaws, while the latter type ignores them because he is 'evil.' But neurotic and ideological patterns of thinking always have resources for explaining away the obvious facts in a manner which keeps us within the circle of illusion. Nietzsche contemptuously rejects such 'moral explanations,' as part of the systematic web of myths, diseased imagining and outright lying which characterizes moral consciousness in general.[31]

6

Nietzsche writes as if his theories provided a complete account of the nature and psychological origin of morality, of feelings such as blame and guilt, as well as the value Christianity and its successors in modern secular morality place on such things as compassion and equality. This suggestion is admittedly pretty outrageous. To that extent, his

---

30 Nietzsche, *On the Genealogy of Morals*, First Essay, § 11

31 Ibid., § 14

genealogy of morals is fairly easy to dismiss. There are no doubt any number of saner and more humdrum theories of moral psychology which have greater plausibility without in the least discrediting moral concepts and feelings. But Nietzsche's theory cannot be altogether ignored, because it is not easy to discredit entirely the possibility that the psychological mechanism he describes have a significant influence on the expression of people's moral attitudes, even that they are partly constitutive of those attitudes themselves. It is this more moderate contention which I propose to take as a hypothesis, to see what its metaethical consequences might be for the kind of morality theorized by Kant and the utilitarians.

We should ask how far the ends and principles of morality, as the theorists portray them, may be plausibly served by a system of thoughts and feelings having such psychological origins, even if Nietzsche's theory of these origins is only part of the story. None of these feelings, to begin with, has anything felicific about it. None involve the pursuit of pleasure or happiness, even for the agent, much less for sentient creation as a whole. All of them aim chiefly at inflicting *pain*, even pain for its own sake, either on oneself or on someone else. From this point of view, it is at least initially implausible that moral feelings, to the extent that they have the origins Nietzsche ascribes to them, could serve utilitarian ends.

Utilitarians sometimes note that certain moral feelings have an origin in vengeful impulses, and then like to suggest that in their moral form these feelings, perhaps combined with sympathy, function to deter injury, hence to serve the general happiness.[32] Now to begin with this is just about as plausible as saying that sadistic impulses might be moral feelings in good standing, since they too, if properly manipulated and directed, might conceivably have a felicific tendency on the whole. But to the extent that Nietzsche's theory is correct, there are also psychological constraints on both blame and guilt as regards their object and as regards the occasions on which they're likely to be manifested. The manifestation of pent-up *ressentiment* will be selected in

---

32 Cf. Mill, *Utilitarianism*, 50-51.

part because they can be easily associated in imagination with the arche-type of 'evil' representing the perceived causes of our past frustrations and humiliations, partly because they are easy and safe targets, suit-able scapegoats on which to release all the hostilities we have been unable to vent naturally on their real objects. To the extent that Nietzsche's theory is correct, then, we might expect moral blame to be most commonly directed not at those whose actions pose the greatest threat to the general happiness, but rather at those whom it feels natu-ral to bring under convenient stereotypes associated with people's images of evil, and also at people in vulnerable positions, on whom one may inflict injury with least fear of retaliation.

We need only look at the social types at which it seems easiest for people to direct blame – people driven by poverty to desperate acts, unwed mothers living on public assistance, racial minorities, people whose lifestyle is readily perceived as 'other' and 'deviant' – to see that Nietzsche's theory has many confirming instances. If feelings with this psychological origin are then combined with a utilitarian morality, the result is that convenient social pariahs are then judged – without good evidence, perhaps, but nevertheless with perfect consistency – to be the cause of all manner of social ills. The frequency with which this happens should provide us with some basis for deciding how far the utilitarians are right when they say that morality puts vengeful feel-ings in the service of promoting the general happiness. When we con-sider this question, we may well ask pointedly what is being put in the service of what.

On the standard utilitarian account, guilt feelings would be useful when associated in people's minds with unfelicific acts, and as deter-rents to committing acts of the same kind in the future. To the extent that they originate in the way Nietzsche supposes, however, there is no reason to expect them to have such an effect. On the contrary, Nietzsche's theory tells us that feelings of guilt, other things being equal, are proportional to the extent to which we have repressed our impulses to harm others. Moreover, these feelings arise along with a need to attribute guilty acts to ourselves, or, if we find that too difficult, a need to commit crimes in order to bring our perception of ourselves into line with our guilt feelings, a phenomenon Freud noted in some of his patients.[33] In that case, far from serving to prevent unfelicific acts, guilt feelings should be expected to cause them.

To whatever extent we think a Nietzschean account of morality may explain attitudes such as blame and guilt, to that very same extent we make it more difficult to reconcile the psychology of moral attitudes with a utilitarian account of the purpose they are supposed to serve. But if such a reconciliation is *difficult* for a utilitarian theory of morality, it surely becomes utterly *impossible* in the case of a Kantian theory, which takes the autonomy of reason as morality's fundamental principle. For the minimum we could ask of a morality of autonomy is that agents who are influenced by moral feelings and attitudes should act with self-transparency, that their interpretation of their attitudes should be correct, and that they should be able to act on these attitudes as they understand them. To the extent that moral feelings arise in the way described by Nietzsche's theories, however, they are essentially self-opaque: one has them at all only insofar as aggressive or reactive impulses undergo repression, disguise and unconscious transformation. If Nietzsche's theories of blame and guilt are even partly correct, then those who take such attitudes toward themselves or others are always thereby involved to a degree in the subversion of their own rational autonomy. The same is obviously true of morality to the extent that Freud is correct in regarding the superego as an introjection of the father as a way of resolving Oedipal conflict.[34]

To many people it is so obvious that some such account is true of moral feelings and impulses that as soon as they see how far Kant's theory captures the spirit of ordinary moral consciousness, they immediately become unable to take seriously Kant's insistence that his moral theory is founded on the autonomy of reason. It is only on the basis of such a misunderstanding, for example, that Bernard Williams could suppose that Kantian morality might pose any threat to personal

---

33 Freud, "Some Character Types Met With in Psychoanalytic Work," *Standard Edition of the Complete Psychological Works* (New York: Macmillan 1964-) 19:53. Nietzsche anticipated this point: see *Thus Spake Zarathustra*, First Part, § 6: "The Pale Criminal."

34 Freud, *The Ego and the Id, Complete Psychological Works* 19:36, 48, 167

integrity.[35] The ease and commonness of such a misunderstanding, however, testifies to the deep tension which exists, on the purely formal or structural level, between morality as a social and psychological fact and Kant's attempt to produce a rational theory of it.

7

I have claimed that Nietzsche's formal critiques of morality are far more plausible if taken to express part of a complex metaethical truth than if taken to be complete reductive psychological analyses of blame and guilt. The same should surely be said regarding the content critiques we have examined. Thrasymachus's conception of justice, for example, is based on some extremely crude social analysis; even its more sophisticated Marxian variant is far more plausible if taken to capture only a partial truth. Appeals to justice generally stabilize the prevailing mode of production, but often enough they also destabilize it. Any view which sees justice as always on the side either of the oppressor or the oppressed has yet to arrive at a fully satisfactory theory of it.

Both Nietzsche and Marx were, I think, clearly aware of this point, even if their polemical intentions usually made them reluctant to admit it. Marx pretty clearly regards his reductive, historical materialist account of justice as only a rough approximation, the best that one can (or need) do with concepts in the purely ideological sphere, which admits of less scientific precision than the economic foundation on which it rests.[36] Nietzsche, on the other hand, was unconcerned with tidiness because he celebrated unsystematic thinking. Like some of his recent admirers, he did not much care that the overall import of his thoughts about morality is in many respects obscure and even self-contradictory.

---

35 Williams, *Ethics and the Limits of Philosophy*, 184-95

36 "A distinction must be made between the material transformation of the economic conditions of production, which can be determined with the precision of natural science, and the ... ideological forms in which human beings become conscious of this conflict" (*Selected Works*, 183).

The harder question is what conclusions *we* should draw from radical metaethical critiques of morality, granted that the theories which undermine our commitment to morality contain a measure of truth but give a partial rather than a total account of the moral phenomena they propose to explain. The most intensive investigations into this question are to be found in the writings of philosophers in the recent continentally inspired tradition. But they are unfortunately of little help. For although they are lucidly aware of its difficulty – and even the difficulty of formulating it properly – they usually content themselves with 'deconstructing' morality, in other words, reveling in confusion for its own sake, tracing out the multifaceted ambiguities and ramified mystifications it introduces into every aspect of the moral life, and show little or no concern with proceeding toward any clarity about the questions it raises, much less toward answers to them.[37]

Perhaps they are right, though, to think it is worthwhile merely to make us painfully aware of the mere presence and urgency of such questions. For as we have seen in the case of traditional Anglophone metaethics, there is a powerful resistance to admitting their existence at all. Arguments which purport to undermine our commitment to morality and even to discredit it are likely to elicit fear and revulsion, or if not that, then a detached attitude of idle intellectual amusement which is equally effective in preventing us from thinking seriously about what those arguments imply, if they are sound. Even those who do not consider moral principles to be categorical imperatives, even those who do not consider moral reasons to be overriding in all cases, are apt to be reluctant to admit that there could be shades of grey regarding moral principles and moral feelings considered simply in themselves.

We may be frightened that radical critiques of morality threaten to leave us defenseless against all the cruelties and injustices people do to one another, with no support for any of the decent impulses which make human life bearable. If this is our reaction, then we would do well to ask ourselves how much good we think mo-

---

37 This is obviously true of Caputo, *Against Ethics*; see also Charles C. Scott, *The Question of Ethics* (Bloomington: Indiana University Press 1990).

rality actually does in these respects, and how much faith we really place in moral motives to direct people's conduct as we think it should be directed. Moreover, the thrust of most radical metaethical critiques of morality is to insist that morality itself – meaning not the *que voulez-vous* of philosophical theories but the actual social and psychological phenomena to which a whole system of words and concepts like 'morality,' 'justice,' 'evil,' and 'guilt' are correctly applied – is responsible for no small proportion of cruelty, oppression, suffering, and degradation against which we hope 'morality' will protect us. These critiques show us that looking to morality for such protection is like an oppressed people looking to their tyrannical ruler for justice, or an abused wife looking to her husband for protection.[38]

The next thought is likely to be that morality is needed even to articulate our objections to the ugly practices with which radical critiques charge morality; hence to undermine our commitment to morality, as radical metaethical critiques seek to do, is simultaneously to undermine the values on the basis of which those same critiques are carried out, and therefore the radical critiques show themselves to be self-refuting or internally incoherent. There is clearly some force in this line of objection. I think something like it is quite telling against many so-called 'postmodernist' critiques of Enlightenment values (for example, those of Foucault) which make no sense except on the basis of precisely those same modern, Enlightenment values.

Yet here it is important to draw a distinction between radical critiques of morality that claim to provide a reductive and deflationary account of the whole phenomenon of morality, and more moderate forms of these critiques claiming only that critical accounts of morality tell a significant part of the story. The former are indeed self-defeating if they're carried out on the basis of values that themselves belong to

---

38 And not only *like* such things, but, as a matter of culture and institutions, actually entwined with them. Also, the point is not to deny that morality does sometimes protect us from cruelty and barbarism, just as tyrants sometimes do justice among their subjects and abusive husbands sometimes protect their wives.

morality. In order to avoid this self-defeat, these critiques must appeal solely to non-moral values, such as self-interest.[39] But this restriction would make them less compelling. The latter, more moderate versions of a radical critique of morality, however, are not rendered incoherent if they appeal to values that themselves belong to morality. Their gist is rather that morality itself is a complex and internally contradictory phenomenon, so that it makes perfectly good sense to be committed to one strand of the tangled fabric in mounting a criticism against other strands.

For example, it makes perfectly good sense to appeal to the modern Enlightenment values represented by utilitarian or Kantian morality (that is, to the value of human happiness or rational autonomy) in attacking those aspects of morality (whether contextual or structural) which are premodern, antirational and counter-Enlightenment in nature (that is, to the aspects of morality which derive from such things as psychological dysfunction, religious superstition, social oppression, or sexual repression).

'Postmodernists' usually do not make clear where they stand here. Their love of paradox for its own sake makes them reluctant to distinguish between coherent and incoherent forms of their own doctrines, even where this would make those doctrines more plausible. Moreover, they usually do appeal in practice to Enlightenment values, but they often confusedly identify the very values to which they in fact appeal with the enemy they mean to attack. I conclude that their way of criticizing morality will remain hopeless and undeserving of serious attention unless it places some value on rational coherence and consequently sorts out the (modern rationalist Enlightenment) values to which it is ultimately committed from the (anti-modern, anti-rationalist, counter-Enlightenment) features of modern culture which are the proper objects of its attacks. But of course in order to achieve this degree of self-clarity 'postmodernism' would have to abandon that

39 Thrasymachus's radical critique of morality, for example, avoids any threat of self-defeat in just this way. Marx's critique of morality is self-consistent only if the values on which his critique of capitalism rests are non-moral values. Most of the controversy over Marx's anti-moralism comes down to the question whether this is a possible interpretation of the basis of his social critique.

name, as well as most of the vain rhetorical posturings to which its adherents are so devoted.

Thus the sort of radical critique of morality I am advocating is one which remains deeply and even ruthlessly committed to the modernist values, such as rational autonomy and the greatest happiness of the greatest number, which ground modern moral theories. But it is nevertheless anti-moral to the extent that it recognizes (as these theories do not) that *morality* is a less than perfect vehicle for expressing these values, in some ways a vehicle which may be unsuitable or even dangerously self-subverting. It would acknowledge that human autonomy and happiness sometimes come into conflict with morality, that they are worth pursuing even when they do, and that the consequence of such an acknowledgment is not only that we must look at the content of morality as something in need of continuous rational criticism and reform, but that in the name of autonomy and happiness even the essential forms of morality (for example, the feelings which serve as its essential psychological vehicles) and its role in human life need constantly to be brought into question.

Thus even if Rawls's famous remark that justice is the most fundamental virtue of social institutions is seen as expressive of the moral point of view, that should not prevent us from doubting whether justice should be one of our first or fundamental concerns. Systems of concepts and impulses such as blame and guilt, desert and punishment, for example, may need to be kept under strict rational surveillance; and the fact that these are attitudes fundamental or even dispensable to morality should not be regarded as providing a sufficient defense of them.

What I have been saying in the last few paragraphs is, of course, only one of many possible options opened up by the recognition that radical metaethical critiques of morality are a viable sort of enterprise. This option would be easier to articulate, and more such options would be available for development, if metaethics had taken the radical critique of morality as one of its proper tasks. The present essay will have its intended effect if it stimulates metaethical inquiry to focus on these unresolved and even largely unexplored questions.

CANADIAN JOURNAL OF PHILOSOPHY
Supplementary Volume 21

Postmodern Argumentation and Post-Postmodern Liberalism, with Comments on Levinas, Habermas, and Rawls*

JEFFREY REIMAN
The American University,
Washington, D.C.

I. The Paradox of Postmodernism

Modernism is, roughly speaking, the Enlightenment belief in a single unified rational perspective, founded on some indubitable evidence given in human experience – either innate concepts *à la* Descartes and the rationalists, or sensations *à la* Locke and the empiricists – and elaborated according to reliable logical rules. This view was first attacked for its 'foundationalism.' Philosophers, such as Nietzsche, Dewey, Heidegger and the later Wittgenstein, denied that there is any indubitable given upon which truth can be founded. There is no experience, no testimony of the senses or of reason that blazons forth the undeniable truth. Rather the 'given' is, so to speak, constructed – which is to say, not given to us, but made by us. Some experience or other evidence is interpreted as this or that with this or that epistemological status, on the basis of beliefs that one already has about, say, space or mathematics or sense perception or the nature of what is ultimately real. Postmodernism is an intensification of this attack, with a distinctive political spin.

The intensification takes the following form. If there is no given, interpretation is 'fundamental' (not of course in the sense of a new

---

* I am indebted to Joseph Flay, emeritus professor of philosophy at Penn State, and Jonathan Loesberg, professor of literature at American University, for numerous helpful comments, many of which I have incorporated into this paper. The mistakes are mine.

foundational given, rather quite the reverse, in the sense of something beneath or behind which we cannot get, something that stands eternally between us and any foundational given). Interpretation is fundamental in the sense that it is the furthest down we can ever get.[1] If interpretation is as far as we can ever get, then every experience is part of a tapestry (textile, text) of beliefs against which it gets its interpretation. And the beliefs themselves are only what they are for us as a result of interpretation of their meaning in light of other beliefs, and other interpretations, and so on.

Accordingly there can never be just one interpretation of anything. This is sometimes exaggerated into the claim that there are unlimited valid interpretations of everything, a claim that would make it impossible to write a single sentence, since one would have no reason for choosing one string of words rather than another to express one's thoughts! The more modest claim is enough, however, to ground the distinctive postmodern strategy of *deconstruction*. Any supposedly canonical interpretation can be shown to have been purchased by the arbitrary exclusion of other possible ones. There can only be a canonical interpretation if some meaning in a text has been taken as if it were an unquestioned given from which the canonical interpretation then follows. The deconstructer finds the meaning that has been taken as if simply given, and shows that it is in fact only one interpretation among other possible ones in view of the 'textily' way in which it is woven

---

1   In *Speech and Phenomena*, Jacques Derrida gives an argument for the non-givenness of meaning and thus for the fundamentality of interpretation from within phenomenology itself. He does so by playing Husserl's *Phenomenology of Internal Time-Consciousness* off against Husserl's own theory of the intuitive givenness of linguistic meaning. The latter requires there to be an instantaneous grasp of the meaning of a term, while the former shows that there is nothing in consciousness that is instantaneous. Everything in consciousness is elapsing in time, and that implies that the appearance of an instantaneous grasp of meaning is really the product of a gathering-up of flowing elements of experience into some meaningful totality, which is to say, interpretation. Nor should the term 'elements,' here, be taken as implying yet other instantaneous givens, since that too is denied by the elapsing nature of consciousness. As far down as we go, all we get are interpretations. See Jacques Derrida, *Speech and Phenomena and Other Essays on Husserl's Theory of Signs* (Evanston, IL: Northwestern University Press 1973).

together with other beliefs. Then, taking a different interpretation of the given as her starting point, the deconstructer shows that other interpretations of the whole text can be spun. Such alternative interpretations must still meet the normal standards for successful interpretation, namely, plausibility, fit with the text, and so on. This is not the 'anything goes' that is sometimes associated with deconstructive technique. Rather, the canonical interpretation is deconstructed by means of showing its illicit appeal to sheer given meanings, and the way in which it has been promoted by excluding other possible plausible interpretations.

Related to this technique is the political dimension of postmodernism. Much as any canonical interpretation is necessarily based on excluding alternative possible interpretations, any universal vision is based on excluding what doesn't fit by defining it as 'other,' 'lesser,' 'lower,' 'bad,' 'crazy,' 'primitive,' etc. Consequently, Enlightenment universalism based on, say, the shared rationality of human beings, reflects (in various versions of the critique) the definition of rationality by exclusion of deviants, or women, or third-world people. Or, at the very least, the establishment of the universal standard becomes a tool or weapon by means of which some can be defined as second rate because they are held not to share the prevailing trait, or not to embody it completely, or the like. Thus, for example, Zygmunt Bauman, in his *Postmodern Ethics*, describes the moral universalism of the modern era "as but a thinly disguised declaration of intent to embark on *Gleichschaltung,* on an arduous campaign to smother the differences...."[2] With this, deconstruction becomes a political weapon in defense of the people who have been oppressed because their natures or ways have been excluded from the universal standard – as the means to define that very standard.

Here enters the paradox: The critique of universal standards because they exclude certain individuals or groups of individuals is a critique of those standards for not being universal enough! Consequently, rather than abandoning or opposing universalism, the critique is itself based on an implicit universal valuation, albeit one that aims to be more inclusive than the ones critiqued.

---

2 Zygmunt Bauman, *Postmodern Ethics* (Oxford: Blackwell 1993) 13

In short, what postmodernism needs, what virtually every postmodern writer writes as if he or she had, but in fact does not have, is a universal standard for valuing human beings which is compatible with the postmodern critique of universals. I will argue that such a universal can be found and can be defended while keeping to postmodernism's own critical requirements of argumentation.

II. The Requirements of Postmodern Argumentation

If postmodernism understands itself as (*a*) a form of antifoundationalism, and (*b*) a protest against the exclusion of certain human individuals and/or groups from the universal measure of full moral standing, then certain things follow about the way arguments must be made if they are to be acceptable to postmodernists. First of all, arguments must be explicitly based on assumptions actually held by those to whom they are addressed (rather than appealing to foundational givens). Second, arguments must be addressed to all human beings. Put together, arguments must start from assumptions that are shared by all human beings. Arguments must be *universal* in their aim, and *ad hominem* in their logical structure.

Actually, the second condition is already suggested by antifoundationalism. If there is no indubitable given, if all starting points are, so to speak, created by interpretation in light of other beliefs, then there is no Archimedean point from which all of a person's beliefs can be shown true or false. Consequently, all arguments must proceed from beliefs that people already hold, which is to say, they must be *ad hominem*.

Two examples from different contemporary philosophical directions will show the prevalence of *ad hominem* argumentation in present-day thought. Consider, for example, Rawls's political liberalism, which starts openly by appeal to beliefs held by participants in liberal democratic cultures, assumes explicitly that even within this framework there will be irreconcilable disagreement among reasonable people on fundamental metaphysical and moral beliefs, and proceeds to argue for its very modest liberalism from the hopefully actual overlapping consensus among those fundamental views which presumably permit allegiance to liberal ideals.[3] Consider, for a quite different example, the approach of Habermas's 'discourse ethics' which starts from the presuppositions of rational argument aimed at justifying moral norms. Since the implicit aim of such argument is rational persuasion, and since rational persuasion is uncoerced assent in the face of open argumentation and full information, those who engage in justification can be taken as implicitly committed to seeking uncoerced and fully informed assent to their proposals.[4] Accordingly, one can only justify moral norms to which all can freely and informedly consent – the result being not very far from contractarianism of the Rawlsian sort.

There can be postmodern universals if there are *ad hominem* arguments that can appeal to assumptions necessarily made by all human beings. However, the demand that arguments must appeal to assumptions that all human beings can be taken to share surely seems impossible in the condition of postmodernism, with its objections to universalism and its emphasis on irreducible differences. But the situation is more hopeful that it appears at first; for postmodernists do assume that human beings are rational insofar as they speak of and to them as users of language, interpreters of texts, bearers of culture, and so on – all of which are rational operations. I shall argue that the assumption that human beings are rational leads to other beliefs which form the basis for a universal moral principle.

Ironically, I shall find these beliefs in an unlikely place: Descartes's philosophy, which has been the target of considerable postmodernist criticism. What I am going to argue in the next section is that in Descartes's *Meditations* one finds a way of establishing a universal which does not violate the postmodern requirements for argumentation. That is to say, the very form of *ad hominem* I discussed above in connection with Rawls and Habermas is first hinted at in Descartes, and with more far-reaching implications. (Indeed, at the end of this paper, I shall suggest how what we find in Descartes provides what is missing from

---

3 John Rawls, *Political Liberalism* (New York: Columbia University Press 1993)

4 See Jürgen Habermas, "Discourse Ethics," in his *Moral Consciousness and Communicative Action* (Cambridge, MA: MIT Press, 1990) 43-115.

Rawls's and Habermas's ethical theories.) Postmodernists, unable to resolve their paradox on their own grounds, can do so if they turn back to a discovery of the very Enlightenment they have criticized.

III. The Authority of Rational Beings: Descartes's Discovery

Descartes made a discovery whose nature is very much the opposite of that for which he is mainly credited – and yet, I contend, that it is this very discovery which inspired his successors even when they were not able to put it into words.

Descartes, as hardly needs retelling, subjected all his beliefs to radical doubt, deduced his existence from the fact of his doubting, and then proceeded to restore enough of his beliefs to ground physics by arguing that God existed and that it was contrary to God's nature to allow His creatures to be irremediably deceived. The apparently circular nature of this argument – that Descartes had to believe in his proof of God in order to prove that he didn't have to doubt all his beliefs – was not lost on Descartes's readers. The charge of circularity crops up numerous times in the seven sets of objections that Descartes published along with his *Meditations on First Philosophy*. And, in the replies to those objections, Descartes tried gallantly to show that there is no circle. I think it is fair to say that none of Descartes's important philosophical successors thought he succeeded.

Indeed, it seems to me that, willy-nilly, Descartes taught his successors a different lesson than that God is the authority for the validity of our beliefs. What he taught them rather was that we, and we alone, can be, must be, and are the only authority for our beliefs. I make no claim about what Descartes's conscious intention was here. Nonetheless, I cannot help thinking that, in arguing, 'I think, therefore I am,' Descartes knew that he was taking for the thinking subject the Biblical name of God.

The important point is that when Descartes doubted, he always doubted for a reason: that he might be dreaming, or that there might be an evil demon bent on deceiving him. Thus, rather than undermining our confidence in our rational judgments, Descartes's doubt presupposes it. In a letter to Clerselier, Descartes gave his replies to Gassendi's replies to Descartes's original replies to Gassendi's objections, which were the fifth set of objections published along with the

Meditations. In this letter, Descartes pointed out that "before we can decide to doubt, we need some reason for doubting: and that is why in my First Meditation I put forward the principle reasons for doubt." And then, a few pages later in the letter, Descartes added:

> Even with respect to the truths of faith, we should perceive some reason which convinces us that they have been revealed by God, before deciding to believe them. Although ignorant people would do well to follow the judgment of the more competent on matters which are difficult to know, it is still necessary that it be their own perception which tells them they are ignorant; they must also perceive that those whose judgment they want to follow are not as ignorant as they are, or else they would be wrong to follow them and would be behaving more like automatons or beasts than men.[5]

What this means is that we must trust our own judgment in order to doubt, we must trust it in order to have religious faith, and even to appeal to authority because of our own ignorance! *A rational being cannot help but trust her judgments.* Even when she distrusts them, it is only by trusting some other judgment to the effect that this one is worthy of doubt. But this means that a rational being implicitly presupposes her authority to believe in her judgments, including the authority to believe her judgments about which of her judgments are not to be trusted.

And this is an 'authority,' precisely because judgments go beyond any general rules or any general competence. Even the generally competent judge may be wrong in any given case; his preceding correct judgments are never sufficient to assure correctness in the present case. But, he must judge the present case, and he must trust that judgment, for reasoning to proceed at all. Precisely because he may be wrong in his current judgment and yet rightly trusts it, we are dealing not with the rightness of his judgment but with his right to make and trust it. Moreover, this must be the subject's right, since it is a condition of reasoning and thus of the very possibility of obtaining knowledge at all.

Note here the emphasis on judgments, acts of reason, actual conclusions actually reached by particular reasoning beings at particular

---

5 René Descartes, *The Philosophical Writings of Descartes* (Cambridge: Cambridge University Press 1984) 2; 270 and 272-3.

moments. We are rational, not just in that we can entertain rational arguments, but here most importantly because we actually conclude arguments, actually judge this way or that. Focus on judging as the distinctive feature of rationality shifts attention away from rationality understood as capacity for the application of rules, logical or otherwise. Judging involves more than entertaining logical possibilities – it means actually plumping for one possibility over another. Judgment brings to the fore that we are dealing not with rationality as an abstract system, but with a rational being, a particular individual embodiment of rationality who doesn't just entertain possibilities but actually concludes, opts for particular thought products over other logically possible ones.

Indeed, judging implies a double individuation of rationality. First, it is individuated in the sense of being possessed by (instantiated by) a rational individual, traditionally, a *person*. (Early Christian thinkers gave this word its modern meaning as they struggled to make sense of the doctrine of the trinity. In the sixth century, Boethius defined 'person,' as "an individual substance of rational nature.")[6] Second, it is individuated in the sense of describing not a general capacity, but particular acts. Rational individuals engage in individual acts of reasoning – inferring, deducing, concluding, and the like – all of which take individual shape via judgments.

Judgment is the individual's individual act of applying the general rules to an individual case, which the general rules cannot do of themselves. Rather they must be judged appropriate to the case. Judgment reaches beyond the general rules in a way that can never be a mere product of general rules. (Wittgenstein obscured this in saying that it takes a rule to apply a rule. It takes a judge to apply a rule, and while his judgment may be formulated as a rule, that rule itself will still have to be applied by a judge and so be insufficient. But, if a judge is always both necessary and sufficient to apply a rule, then it adds little to say that it takes a rule to apply a rule. Better to say: *it takes a person to apply a rule*.) This reaching beyond to the individual case makes judgment

---

6 See Peter Singer, *Rethinking Life and Death* (New York: St. Martin's Press, 1995), 180; and A. Trendelenburg, "A Contribution to the History of the Word 'Person'," *Monist* **20** (1910) 336-63.

fallible, but at the same time it makes the rational capacity to judge a kind of authority rather than a mere general ability.

The effect of Descartes's emphasis on judgment and thus on individuated reason is also to be seen in the way that Descartes's argument necessarily occurs from within an individual reasoner, a subject. To grasp the crucial nature of judgment to the reasoner, we cannot take the external point of view. From the outside, a reasoner's judgment is itself a fact that can be judged, not only for its validity but for its other implications. From the inside, however, the reasoner's judgment can only be evaluated in light of other judgments that are not evaluated: the judgment that this judgment should be evaluated, the judgment that it passes or fails evaluation, and so on. In short, from the inside, there is always (at least) one judgment too many. This one (or several) must be trusted for the prior ones to be evaluated. In this way, the subject always presupposes an authority that reaches beyond his competence understood as a general capacity.

This necessary presupposition of authority to make and trust one's judgments doesn't imply or assume that one's judgments are infallible – it is a condition of their being judgments at all. If I 'make' a judgment but don't trust it, I am not really judging. Indeed, from within the subject, it is wrong to speak of an authority to make *and* to trust one's judgments as if these were two separate steps. The last judgment, the one that is one too many, is not first made *and then* trusted. That would introduce another judgment: that the earlier one is trustworthy. Rather, to make the judgment *is* to trust it. The subject doesn't confront her current judgment like a fact to be evaluated. She simply judges, makes and trusts and lives inside her judgment. Thus, the subject's assumption of authority to make and trust her judgments is simply the subject's assumption of authority to judge for herself, for the one she is. And, again, this assumption must be rightful, since it is the condition of reasoning and of knowledge.

Finally, that the subject lives inside his judgment is meant to be taken literally. We are rational beings, not merely in that we are beings with the capacity for rationality. We are rational beings in the deeper sense that our being lies in our enactment of rationality. Here too, I read Descartes's 'I think, therefore I am,' as containing more than meets the eye: *In the act(s) of thinking, I exist.* This idea is less strange than it might at first seem. It develops a notion hinted at in the *Nicomachean Ethics*, where Aristotle writes: "a man is said to have or not to have self-control according as his reason has or has not the control, on the assumption that this [his reason] is the man himself," and further, "reason more than anything else *is* man."[7] What this means is that there is no self over and above or under or behind the acts of thinking. The self and its thinking are one: You are what you think. Or, the self is just the inside of thinking: You are what thinks you. The self is, so to speak, at stake in its judgments – invested, ventured, even gambled, in its acts of thought. My judgments are not a set of lenses between me and the world, they are the very shape of my 'I.'

IV. Descartes's Discovery Meets the Postmodern Requirements of Argumentation

The subject's authority to judge is not presupposed, so to speak, once and for all. It is implicitly asserted anew with each judgment. It is asserted for the particular rational being that I am, which, Descartes notwithstanding, we can understand as the unitary conscious rational embodied being that I am. It is asserted in person, from the inside, inseparable from the judgments I make, which are inseparable from the self I am. Thus, there is a universal *ad hominem* argument for this claim: Whoever doubts it, accepts it because he presupposes his own authority to judge for himself that it is doubtful.

Moreover, such a person accepts that his rationality is necessary and sufficient ground for that authority. So, then, here is another universal *ad hominem* argument: Every reasoning person accepts that her rationality is a necessary and sufficient ground for her authority to make/ trust her judgments. Notice, in support of this, that it is just this authority that we deny to people we think are insane, when we treat their judgments as symptoms rather than as engagements. Indeed, we

---

7 Aristotle, *Nicomachean Ethics*, David Ross, trans. (Oxford: Oxford University Press 1980) bk. IX, sec. 8; bk. X, sec. 7. For interesting commentary on these passages, their translation and their significance in Aristotle's ethical theory, see Richard Kraut, *Aristotle on the Human Good* (Princeton, NJ: Princeton University Press 1989) 128, 183, 189.

acknowledge that the self is constituted by this authority, when we say of those we label insane that they are really not themselves.

Now, the assumption that rationality is a sufficient condition of one's authority to judge implies as well that whoever is regarded as rational must be regarded as having that authority. Much as a judgment is only a judgment for one who assumes his authority to judge, so can I argue in hope of changing the other's judgment only by assuming her authority to judge. Then, to argue with another, to aim to persuade her by reason, is implicitly to grant her authority to judge. Indeed, to regard her judgments as judgments and not just the output of some mechanical process is to grant her authority to judge for herself. *The assumption of the subject's authority to judge for herself is a necessary presupposition of any operation of rationality at all, and the mutual assumption of each other's authority to judge is the presupposition of any interpersonal rational argument.*

It follows that postmodernists must presuppose their own authority to judge, and that of their counterparts in argument, and ultimately that of all human beings. This puts a new face on the postmodern requirement of *ad hominem* argument. Where previously it appeared as a kind of *'faute de mieux'* strategy in light of the impossibility of reaching an indubitable given beyond interpretation, it now appears as part of recognition of the rationality of one's audience. Because, as rational, the audience has as much authority for its judgment as the speaker, the speaker must persuade in a way that grants that equal authority. That means that argument must appeal to the recipients' own judgments, and take the form of showing that a conclusion is in contradiction[8]

---

8 All *ad hominem* arguments appeal the logical law of noncontradiction, insofar as they aim to show that a given conclusion is either acceptable because compatible with the listener's judgments, or unacceptable because incompatible with them. It might seem, then, that the law of noncontradiction is an exception to the requirement of *ad hominem* argument, since it is presumably held valid independently of the listener's endorsement of it. But this misconceives the role of the law. The law of noncontradiction is not an arbitrary rule which a person can judge appropriate or not. It is the material condition of having a judgment of one's own at all. I simply cannot judge that P, if I also think that not-P. So did Aristotle use an *ad hominem* argument for the law itself, holding, in the *Metaphysics*,

with those judgments. And that postmodernists do argue this way suggests that they do recognize the authority claimed by their listeners: Otherwise, why bother to convince them by rational *ad hominem* argument, rather than using trickery or brainwashing or the like?

V. Postmodern Argumentation and Post-postmodern Liberalism

I think I have shown, strictly by *ad hominem* argument, that postmodernists must implicitly grant the authority to judge that all rational subjects necessarily claim. However, there is more that one can say about rationality from within the requirements of postmodern argumentation. The subject uses her reason not simply to reach judgments *period*; but to reach judgments about what to believe and about how to act. And this too is presupposed in the exercise of rationality: Whoever reasons must treat reasons *as reasons*, that is, as bestowing on facts a 'pro' or 'con' valence for whatever acts (theoretical or practical) of which the thinking subject is capable. For a reasoner, facts become reasons by becoming grounds for actions appropriate to the nature of those facts. And rational subjects must presuppose this for their exercising their reason to count as reasoning, rather than as just going through the motions. Then, there is an *ad hominem* argument that all reasoners must, as reasoners, presuppose that they are required to believe and to act in ways that are appropriate to the objects of their reasoning. This conclusion, taken together with what we have said so far about the necessity of recognizing the authority of the subject to judge for himself, brings us in sight of a universal moral principle established wholly within the requirements of postmodern argumentation.

---

that if one affirms that the same thing can at the same time both be and not be, then this affirmation affirms the truth of its own negation. To deny the law of noncontradiction is to deny that denial. To deny the law of noncontradiction, one must implicitly affirm that the truth of the denial of the law is incompatible with the truth of the affirmation of that same law, and that means that whoever would deny the law of noncontradiction must assume the law's truth to do so. See Aristotle, *Metaphysics*, bk. XI, sec. 5, in J. Barnes, ed., *The Complete Works of Aristotle* (Princeton, NJ: Princeton University Press 1991) 2; 1677-8.

That a postmodernist must grant that people have authority to judge for themselves what to believe is not in itself a moral principle, since it can be granted even while brainwashing or drugging or coercing the other into believing this or that. The coerced other will still only believe what he judges belief-worthy. However, if there is no logical contradiction between recognizing people's authority to judge for themselves and brainwashing them into believing this or that, there is at least a discordance. To recognize people's authority to judge for themselves in any more wholehearted way than paying mere lip-service requires that we not force judgments upon their minds. Rather we must allow them to form their own judgments. In this way, recognition of people's authority to judge for themselves provides moral undergirding for the postmodernist's requirement of universal *ad hominem* argument.

A similar argument applies to action. There is no logical contradiction between granting people the authority to judge what to believe and then acting toward them in terms of one's own judgments and contrary to theirs, leaving them still believing what they judge belief-worthy. But there is discordance. Since the authority of the subject extends to her judgments about what is of value to her and about how the unitary conscious rational embodied being that she is ought to act, that authority naturally points outward beyond her beliefs to her actions and the fate of her body. (This is 'natural' in view of the fact that the subject about which we are speaking is an animal, whose rational capacities have been selected in evolution to govern its body's actions.) Then, to recognize people's authority to judge for themselves in any more wholehearted way than paying mere lip-service requires that we not force our judgments upon their bodies. Rather, we must allow them to extend their authority along its natural course to their actions. And this requires not forcing people to act in ways that they do not themselves judge proper. In this way, recognition of people's authority to judge for themselves provides moral undergirding for the postmodern protest against the oppression of those wrongly excluded from full standing in the human community.

Wholehearted recognition is more than merely not contradicting the claim to authority but positively allowing it to operate in its natural, embodied, active way. It does no violence to usage to call such 'wholehearted recognition' *respect*, since, as Kant suggested, respect is a kind of stepping back from the other, making way for him.[9] If it can be shown that this wholehearted recognition or respect is the appropriate treatment of rational beings, we will have arrived at a postmodern moral universal: *In light of the nature of human subjects as reasoning beings who naturally claim authority for their own judgments, it is wrong to force our judgments on their minds or on their bodies.*

It might be thought that 'appropriateness' is too soft a notion to ground a moral universal. This will certainly seem to be so if appropriateness is understood in the tepid way in which we speak of the requirements of etiquette. However, the appropriateness that I have in mind is the logical relationship between facts and judgments about action[10] that I earlier argued must be presupposed by the very use of reason: Reasoners must presuppose that they are required to treat the objects of their reasoning (in this case: human subjects) in ways that are appropriate to their nature. If it can be shown that there is a form of treatment that is most appropriate to rational beings, then the exercise of reasoning itself presupposes the requirement that they be so treated.

Respect is most appropriate to rational subjects because (*a*) it recognizes wholeheartedly a kind of authority that rational subjects necessarily and rightly claim, (*b*) that authority is claimed by subjects who are embodied beings reasoning to form judgments about reality and about how to act in it, and (*c*) that authority is the only authority in the world that is naturally claimed. Reason (*a*) makes it appropriate to give the subject's claim to authority some normative weight, (*b*) makes it appropriate to extend that weight to the judgments and actions over which the subject makes its claim, (*c*) makes it inappropriate to give any other claim as great a weight as this one. Reasons (*a*), (*b*), and (*c*)

---

9 "[B]y the principle of respect which [people] owe one another they are directed to keep themselves at a distance" (Immanuel Kant, *The Metaphysical Principles of Virtue*, Part 2 of *The Metaphysics of Morals*, in *Ethical Philosophy* [Indianapolis, IN: Hackett Publishers, 1983], 113).

10 Given the logical gulf between facts and values, 'appropriateness' may be just the relationship that one should expect at the core of a moral doctrine – even one that is not argued within the requirements of postmodern argumentation.

together make it most appropriate, more appropriate than any other form of treatment, to refrain from imposing judgments on the minds and bodies of rational beings because it is their nature to assert authority to judge for themselves. I think that is the strongest kind of moral argument one can make – at least in the condition of postmodernism.

If it is wrong to impose judgments on the minds and bodies of rational human beings, on their thoughts and on their actions, then two principles must guide our treatment of them:

Principle 1: People must be treated according to judgments that they freely form and endorse.

Principle 2: People must be protected against violations of principle 1.

We should then treat people according to their own beliefs, and according to those principles necessary to make sure that everyone is treated only according to their own beliefs. The result is recognizably a form of liberalism, and one which not only meets, but, indeed arises out of, the requirements of postmodern argumentation. However, since it reinstates universal moral principles with the very tools that postmodernism has used to attack universal moral principles, I call it *post-postmodern liberalism.*

VI. Comments on Levinas, Habermas and Rawls

To strengthen the case for post-postmodern liberalism, I shall close by suggesting very briefly how it provides what is missing in the important ethical theories of Emmanuel Levinas, Jürgen Habermas and John Rawls. All three of these thinkers have been attacked by postmodernists. Nonetheless, I don't think it is inaccurate to call these thinkers 'postmodern liberals,' since they all try to steer clear of the bolts hurled by postmodernism against moral universalism: Levinas by seeking an ethical experience that eludes concepts, Habermas and Rawls by building *ad hominem* argumentation directly into their theories. And they all end up affirming the core notion of liberalism: Individuals are to be at least allowed, and to some degree helped, to live their own lives according to their own lights without violence or oppression from others.

Note that my argument in this section no longer claims to take place within the requirements of postmodern argumentation; in particular, I shall not try to establish my conclusions vis-à-vis Levinas, Habermas and Rawls, in an *ad hominem* fashion. Rather, I shall argue that the liberalism that has been established in this way supplies something that these three thinkers' doctrines need and lack.

In keeping with the critique of modern or Enlightenment universalism, Levinas maintains that any attempt to define the other individual by means of principles or concepts must deny his real otherness. "Modernity," writes Levinas, "will subsequently be distinguished by the attempt to develop from the identification and appropriation of being *by* knowledge toward the identification of being *and* knowledge.... Identical and non-identical are identified. The labor of thought wins out over the otherness of things and men."[11] Moreover, this elimination of all otherness by thought is of a piece with the "wip[ing] out [of] all otherness by murder."[12]

The real basis of the ethical lies, for Levinas, prior to principles or concepts, in the "proximity of the other," the encounter with the excess of the otherness of the other, that by which that otherness exceeds our attempts to tame it by capturing it in the net of our concepts. Levinas describes this encounter as "the irruption of the face into the phenomenological order of appearances.... The proximity of the other is the face's meaning...."[13] "The face ... is that whose *meaning* consists in saying 'thou shalt not kill'."[14] And with this comes a responsibility for the other older than concepts:

> The Other becomes my neighbor precisely through the way the face summons me, calls for me, begs for me, and in so doing recalls my responsibility.... A guiltless responsibility, whereby I am none the less open to the accusation of

---

11 Emmanuel Levinas, "Ethics as First Philosophy," in Sean Hand, ed., *The Levinas Reader* (Oxford: Blackwell 1989) 78

12 Ibid., 85

13 Ibid., 82

14 Emmanuel Levinas, *Ethics and Infinity: Conversations with Philippe Nemo* (Pittsburgh, PA: Duquesne University Press 1985) 87 Emphasis in the original.

> which no alibi, spatial or temporal, could clear me.... A responsibility for my
> neighbor, for the other man, for the stranger or sojourner, to which nothing in
> the rigorously ontological order binds me – nothing in the order of the thing, of
> the something, of number or causality.[15]

Says Levinas of his work, "I analyze the inter-human relationship as if, in the proximity with the Other – beyond the image I myself make of the other man – his face ... *ordains* me to serve him."[16] And elsewhere he writes, "To thematize this relation is already to lose it...."[17]

Now, it is one thing to say that we have a certain sense of the sheer otherness of other people, quite another thing to say that this sense is an experience prior to and thus unshaped by our conceptualizing or thematic thinking, and yet a third thing to say that this experience reveals not just the fact of the other's otherness but my real duty not to murder the other, my true moral responsibility for the other. The first of these is unobjectionable. There is certainly some sort of experience of the otherness of the other, and no doubt it is of moral relevance.

The second claim, however, appeals to exactly the sort of experience of the given – an undeniable intuition of the morally laden 'face' – that postmodernism and antifoundationalism reject. Bear in mind that Levinas is saying not merely that other people in travail do sometimes actually call out to us, appeal to us with their sobs or moans or words, and urge upon us a responsibility for them. He is saying that the other, as such and always, without acting or speaking in any way to appeal to us, simply in and via her otherness, calls us to responsibility for her. This is to read a content into the experience of the other which is, quite strictly, an intuition of meaning. Its authority lies in its being a sheer given, not something imposed or added by us. If there is no given, no undeniably true intuition, then the bottom falls out of Levinas's theory. The power of his vision lies in the notion of an experience of otherness

---

15 Levinas, "Ethics as First Philosophy," 83-4

16 Levinas, *Ethics and Infinity*, 97 Emphasis in the original.

17 Levinas, "Substitution," in *The Levinas Reader*, 110

and responsibility that eludes the net of our concepts, and this is just what postmodernism denies is possible.[18]

Moreover, Levinas's claim goes beyond the standard fare of phenomenological description insofar as it 'describes' not just what 'is,' but an 'ought.' The responsibility to which the face calls me is my true responsibility. I am, for Levinas, truly ethically bound to the other. Suppose we suspend the objections raised in the previous paragraphs and accept that we do intuit in the face of the other a call to our responsibility for the other, to our duty not to murder him. That would be a fact. That the other calls me to responsibility doesn't imply that I am responsible, however, anymore than that the other says I owe him money implies that I do. Even if the call of the other makes me feel responsible for him, there is still a distance between this feeling and being truly morally responsible for the other. No phenomenological description of facts could ever add up to a real moral duty. The result is that, while his assertion of the otherness of others is appealing, it and the supposed moral duty it evokes are supported by nothing more than Levinas's inescapably mystical pronouncements.

Post-postmodern liberalism can remedy these shortcomings while preserving what is appealing in Levinas's doctrine. We have already seen how post-postmodern liberalism provides a non-mystical route to a moral duty to respect the other. But it also gives us a non-mystical account of the irreducible otherness of the other. Precisely in the difference between the inescapable status of the other's judgment for her compared to this existence for me as a fact still to be judged, I confront the irreducible distance between separate subjects. To recognize the way the other makes/trusts her judgments from within is to see the other from within and yet, since I cannot make/trust her judgments as if they were my own, to fail ultimately to establish strict identity with the being of the other. Her being then is not absorbed into my knowledge, rather their nonidentity is known.

To recognize the other's authority over her judgments, all the while not identifying with them, is to hear the moral call of the other to my

---

18 Curiously, Bauman bases the positive doctrine of his *Postmodern Ethics* on Levinas's teaching without even considering its apparent violation of this key tenet of postmodernism. See note 2, above.

responsibility from across the unbridgeable distance between us. And given that accepting that responsibility is the most appropriate response to beings that make that moral call, that call does invoke my true moral responsibility. Herein, then, without mysticism, and without foundational intuitions, we get the morally laden otherness of the other out of recognition and respect for her as a reasoning subject.

Habermas maintains that anyone who engages in rational justification to others implicitly accepts rational argument's commitment to uncoerced and informed assent from its audience. On these grounds, Habermas contends that the arguer is committed to treating the other according to norms to which the other can uncoercedly and informedly assent. The problem, however, is that, even if the arguer presupposes commitment to persuasion by uncoerced consent, nothing requires him to shape his actions by the conditions of interpersonal argument. Put otherwise, even if there are morally laden commitments built into justification to others, these commitments do not require people to engage in justification in the first place, or to conform their actions to their justifications if they do so engage. These are separate substantive moral requirements, not provided for by the conditions of justification themselves. Thus Habermas's theory can have no moral claim on anyone who does not believe that he must justify his actions to others before acting, or that he must act only in ways that he can justify to others.

The needed substantive moral requirements are provided by post-postmodern liberalism in the notion that wholehearted recognition of people as rational authority-claiming subjects requires that we allow them to form their own judgments and that we refrain from treating them according to judgments they do not themselves make – except where necessary to assure that no one is so treated. Here, then, we get the obligation to conform to the conditions of argument, regarding both beliefs and actions, out of recognition and respect for the nature of human beings as rational subjects.

In *Political Liberalism*,[19] Rawls defends a version of liberalism which is political both in its subject and in its justification. Its subject is the

---

19 See note 3, above.

basic structure of society (the main political, economic and social institutions), thus leaving large areas of 'private' or 'civil' life subject to citizens' personally held ideals. As for justification, it is put forth as a 'freestanding view.'[20] By this Rawls means that it is not based on a comprehensive philosophical, religious or moral doctrine that aims to determine all or most of what is valuable in life. Thus it is unlike Mill's liberalism, which was founded on the comprehensive doctrine of utilitarianism, and unlike Kant's which was founded on his comprehensive doctrine of pure reason. To establish his liberalism as a freestanding view, Rawls hopes to avoid taking a position on any metaphysical issues by starting instead from an idea he finds embedded in our democratic culture: the idea "of society as a fair system of social cooperation between free and equal persons."[21] This way, Rawls's political liberalism is meant to appeal to the holders of a wide range of irreconcilable though reasonable comprehensive doctrines – religious, philosophical, and moral – as long as they can find within their particular doctrines some reasons to join an "overlapping consensus" on the ideas distinctive to liberal democratic culture. As he has recently summarized it in replying to Habermas,

> The central idea is that political liberalism moves within the category of the political and leaves philosophy as it is. It leaves untouched all kinds of doctrines, religious, metaphysical, and moral, with their long traditions of development and interpretation. Political philosophy proceeds apart from all such doctrines, and presents itself in its own terms as freestanding. Hence, it cannot argue its case by invoking any comprehensive doctrines, or by criticizing or rejecting them, so long of course as those doctrines are reasonable, politically speaking. When attributed to persons, the two basic elements of the conception of the reasonable are, first, a willingness to propose fair terms of social cooperation that others as free and equal also might endorse, and to act on these terms, provided others do, even contrary to one's own interest; and, second, a recognition of the burdens of judgment [grounds for expecting that reasonable people will differ irreconcilably in their comprehensive doctrines] and accepting their consequences for one's attitude (including toleration) toward other comprehensive doctrines.[22]

---

20 Ibid., 12-13, inter alia.

21 Ibid., 9, inter alia.

22 John Rawls, "Reply to Habermas," *Journal of Philosophy* **92** (March 1995) 134; I have omitted Rawls's references.

As for the notion of "citizens as reasonable," it is drawn "from the public political culture of a democratic society."[23]

The problem here is that if the concept of the reasonable only holds for those who share a democratic culture, then those who do not share that culture – though they live within its midst, say, as Ku Klux Klanners or other extremists – cannot be said to be unreasonable, only different. Then, the upholders of democratic liberal politics cannot say that the dissenters are wrong, only other. And that means that the relation between the democratic liberal state and the dissenters, particularly when the state uses force to repress the dissenters' 'principled' violence, is strictly a power relation rather than a moral one. The dissenters cannot be said to have failed in an obligation owed to the democratic liberal citizens, since the claim for that obligation goes no further than the shared beliefs of those citizens.

Put more generally, a liberal political theory that aims to be "political not metaphysical"[24] cannot generate a moral obligation for those who do not share its liberal political culture. Indeed, even those who do share that political culture only *believe* they are obligated. They are only *truly* obligated if, either liberal political values are truly worthy of allegiance independent of any comprehensive doctrine and/or if the comprehensive doctrines that teach them that liberal values are worthy are true. However, as a political doctrine, Rawls's theory eschews appeal to, or even judgment about, its own truth (Rawls will only call it reasonable)[25] or the truth of the comprehensive doctrines held by its citizens. Thus, political liberalism cannot generate a moral obligation to its own liberal values. It must rest content with the hope that the citizens will fill this in for themselves.

The needed moral obligation is provided by post-postmodern liberalism in the notion that it is most appropriate to the nature of rational

---

23 Ibid., 135

24 Rawls, *Political Liberalism*, 10. See also "Justice as Fairness: Political Not Metaphysical," *Philosophy and Public Affairs* **14** (summer 1985) 223-51.

25 "[P]olitical liberalism, rather than referring to its political conception of justice as true, refers to it as reasonable instead" (Rawls, *Political Liberalism*, xx).

beings to treat them only according to the judgments they are prepared to make. Then, it is wrong not to be reasonable in just the way that Rawls and democratic culture have defined it. And there is a moral obligation to be reasonable that goes beyond subscribing to reasonable comprehensive doctrines supportive of reasonable liberal political values. It is an obligation on all rational beings, including the extremists in but not of "the public political culture of a democratic society." Of course, this would make Rawls's theory not just political, but ever so slightly metaphysical.[26]

---

26 Actually, I think that would vastly improve Rawls's theory, and that it is in any event necessary at other points in the theory as well. Consider the fact that the abortion controversy needs a solution within the non-metaphysical framework of political liberalism. Rawls is quite sure this is possible, as he points out in a lengthy footnote: "As an illustration, consider the troubled question of abortion. Suppose ... that we consider the question in terms of three important political values: the due respect for human life, the ordered reproduction of political society over time, including the family in some form, and finally the equality of women as equal citizens. (There are, of course, other important political values besides these.) Now I believe *any reasonable balance of these three political values will give a woman a duly qualified right to decide whether or not to end her pregnancy during the first trimester*. The reason for this is that at this early stage of pregnancy the political value of the equality of women is overriding, and this right is required to give it substance and force ..." (*Political Liberalism*, 243 n.32; emphasis mine).

But note right away that Rawls's conclusion about abortion only follows on the assumption that a first-trimester fetus is not among those equal persons who are to be protected by the laws of a liberal state (otherwise the political value of women's equality would not be overriding). This is clearly a metaphysical, not merely political, claim.

CANADIAN JOURNAL OF PHILOSOPHY
Supplementary Volume 21

Afterword:
Whither Moral Philosophy?

JOCELYNE COUTURE
Université du Québec à Montréal
and
KAI NIELSEN
University of Calgary and Concordia University

I

Most of the essays collected here are essays *in* metaethics seeking in exacting and interesting ways to resolve problems raised by the familiar options in metaethics we outlined in our Introduction. Richard Brandt, for example, forcefully argues, going much against the at least modestly holistic grain of our time, for a foundationalism (noncognitivist though it be) which would be foundational in both metaethics and normative ethics. R.M. Hare makes a brief but systematic defense, which is both spirited and clear, of his prescriptivism (a species of what we, following tradition, have called 'noncognitivism,' but which he argues should instead be called 'nondescriptivism'). His arguments here for his position – call it nondescriptivism or noncognitivism – are directed forcefully against ethical naturalism (descriptivism) and specifically against the naturalism of Philippa Foot. Nicholas Sturgeon and David Copp contribute elaborate and rigorously argued defenses of ethical naturalism, or, as they might prefer to call it, 'moral realism.'[1] Copp agues that we can have all the advantages of

---

1 As David O. Brink points out, ethical naturalism and moral realism should not be taken to be identical. Moral realism is, he has it, a metaethical view committed "to the objectivity of ethics." Moral realists believe that there are "moral facts and moral properties whose existence and nature are independent of people's beliefs and attitudes about what is right and wrong." While moral realism is

ethical naturalism's externalism while still retaining, in what is none-theless a strictly externalist framework, the insights of internalism. Sturgeon indirectly defends ethical naturalism through a critique of both J.L. Mackie's 'error theory' and Simon Blackburn's revisions of it, arguing that, besides its internal difficulties, error theory revised or unrevised fits badly with both Mackie's handling of the problem of evil and that of rational revisions of such a treatment, where evil is taken as a reality to be squared with God's ways to human beings. Allen Wood, for whom Mackie is again an object of critique, as he is as well in Jean Hampton's contribution, argues that a really thorough-going and powerful error theory would provide a metaethical critique of the very institution of morality and its practices. Mackie himself pulls back from the deep iconoclasm of such a critique insisting instead that he is providing a *second-order* critique of objectivism and objectivizing ontologies of value – the familiar claims of moral and religious intuitionists and ethical naturalists – while treating morality itself and its various *first-order* practices as something that is generally intact, though admitting of some internal tinkering by good normative ethicists. But no claim is in sight that *morality as such* stands massively in error. His moral skepticism, in short, is not a skepticism about morality itself, or holus bolus, concerning its practices and *first-order* moral beliefs, but about *philosophical* accounts of morality, including the ill articulated accounts of common sense. It is a *second-order* matter directed against what Mackie would call 'objectivist ontologies' and what we would call 'objectivist theories' (intuitionism and moral realism) in metaethics. Wood, like Gilbert Harman, regards this as a tepid kind of moral skepticism hardly deserving the iconoclastic tag – 'moral nihilism' – with which Sturgeon tags it. Wood argues that to see the articulation of a non-tepid form of error theory, we should turn instead to Marx and Nietzsche, most particularly to Nietzsche. In their writings we will find a profound theoretical challenge to our very morality and

---

compatible with objectivist forms of ethical naturalism (forms that have the above views about moral facts and moral values), it can, and has, taken intuitionist forms as well, as it did with G.E. Moore, W.D. Ross and. A.C. Ewing. However, the typically held forms of *present day* moral realism are objectivist forms of ethical naturalism (Brink 1995, 511-12).

moral practices and ways of being: the genuine *first-order* stuff that constitutes our moral lives.

Wood seeks to isolate within Marx's and Nietzsche's writings a rational kernel of at least a putatively sound critique of morality that, he argues, our complacent Anglo-American and Scandinavian metaethical accounts seem at least not to even recognize exists. Mackie spoke in an early essay, "The Refutation of Morals," of the error of *believing in morals* (Mackie 1946, 77-90). What his own critique comes to, as distinct from Nietzsche's and Marx's more radical critiques, is that of a claimed error in *objectivist moral theory*. The challenge of Marx and Nietzsche, Wood has it, is to *morality itself:* to the very idea that morality is something to which a rational and clear-sighted person must be, or even should be, committed. This is a far more radical critique than Mackie's, though the dangling, tell-tale little words 'must' and 'should' leave us, of course, with questions here. Such a radical critique, put just like that, may be incoherent. The interesting question is whether it can be coherently demythologized.

We will now shift gears. What is largely ignored in this volume, Francis Sparshott's contribution apart, is any discussion of the dissatisfaction with metaethics that has arisen since the 1970s. Many moral philosophers, even those who do systematic ethical theory, who, for the most part, just stick self-consciously to doing substantive ethics, do not characterize even a part of their work in these terms. They just do not utilize the metaethics / normative ethics distinction. John Rawls, Thomas Scanlon, Kurt Baier, Onora O'Neill, Thomas Nagel, Charles Taylor, Alasdair MacIntyre and Martha C. Nussbaum stand out as prominent examples. Moreover, none of them are skeptical about the philosophical enterprise itself and in this way are anti-theorists (anti-theory *theorists*, if you will), or even just anti-theorists in ethics or even philosophers not committed to doing systematic ethical theory (Williams 1985 and Nielsen 1989). Rather they just do not make the distinction at all, let alone take the doing of metaethics as the *principia* of moral philosophy, though it might in turn be countered (perhaps with some force) that they in effect make metaethical arguments and, in effect, though not in name, adopt metaethical positions.

The revolt, particularly against Golden Age metaethics (roughly 1930–60), goes even deeper. Perceptive philosophers such as Alasdair MacIntyre, Annette C. Baier, Martha C. Nussbaum, Cora Diamond and

Hilary Putnam have argued that the dichotomy metaethics/normative ethics, if not forcefully jettisoned, should at least be benignly neglected. It isn't that philosophers should stop doing metaethics and turn to doing normative ethics instead, but that philosophers should have no truck and trade with either. We should no more do philosophy, after the fashion of Henry Sidgwick, Hastings Rashdall or W.D. Ross than we should do it after the fashion of Axel Hägerström, A.J. Ayer or Charles Stevenson. Normative ethics and metaethics take in each other's dirty linen. We should break with those traditions and conceive of moral philosophy quite differently, more in line with, as, say, for Martha Nussbaum, a certain understanding of how a naturalized Aristotle (liberated from the dead weight of the Thomistic-Aristotelian tradition) proceeded or, as for Annette Baier, with how Hume – building on Aristotle, but more thoroughly eschewing rationalistic elements – proceeded (Nussbaum 1990; Baier 1985, 207-91). If we do either of these things, the claim goes, we will get a moral philosophy that looks very different from either metaethics (even the new metaethics) or normative ethics. Moreover, it will not only look very different, it will yield, it is said, a much better understanding of what is involved in the moral life of our attempts to ascertain how we should live and what is the good for human beings and indeed what the correct answers to these questions are. And, after all, this is what we most want out of moral philosophy. It is, that is, what we should most want to come to know in reflecting about morality. Said just like that, the proffered alternative is cryptic and has something in it of a cluster of dark sayings, engendering, understandably, skepticism. We will, as we set it out, in contrast with metaethics and normative ethics, in Sections III and IV, make what is involved clear.

However, things do not end here with metaethics and its discontents. There are also questions about scope. Martha Nussbaum, for example, wants to do systematic ethical theory in a naturalized Aristotelian way and where philosophy and literature get integrally linked. Annette Baier, with her Humean model, is less clearly committed to systematizing and pragmatist philosophers still less. Bernard Williams and Susan Wolf are also philosophers who remain wary of grand scale ethical theorizing. And Richard Rorty and Kai Nielsen, in a thoroughly pragmatist manner, reconceptualizing philosophers into being critical intellectuals, take it as a task of such philosophers to try to see a little better, and in a non-hedgehogish way, how things hang together (Rorty l982 and Nielsen 1991). But in doing so, they see moral critique (critique of ideologies, moral practices, conceptions of life) as the central thing and they set aside both metaethical theory and systematic ethical theory, though they are not above making in a Wittgensteinian manner what in effect are metaethical remarks when that would be useful in dispelling some moral-cum-conceptual confusion. This is often called 'anti-theory *theory*' in ethics. But in a way this is a misleading description, as if a Deweyan concentration, which theirs resembles, *not* on the problems of philosophy, but on the problems of life was anti-theoretical or anti-intellectual Ludditism raising its ugly head. But we will let the phrase 'anti-theory theory' stand for it does suggest an important contrast with much else that is done in moral philosophy.

What these various things add up to is to the fact that the challenges to metaethics, old and new, and its model(s) for proceeding in investigations concerning ethics, are both deep and varied. Moreover, much of it comes from inside analytical philosophy itself and not from phenomenologists, existentialists, Heideggerians, deconstructionists, the Thomistic tradition, or anything of the kind. Cora Diamond, at the end of her wonderfully insightful "Having Rough Story about What Moral Philosophy Is," puts our situation well when she remarks that the attempt by some philosophers (she has in mind Nussbaum but it would apply widely)

> to take as a starting point a widely agreed and inclusive notion of the aim of moral philosophy is pretty much doomed. No one knows what the subject is; most widely agreed accounts of it depend on suppositions that are not obvious and that reflect particular evaluations and views of the world, of human nature, and of what it is to speak, think, write or read about the world. The more inclusive an account is, the more likely it will include what many philosophers would not dream of counting as part of their subject (Diamond 1991, 380).

We will return to these issues in Sections III and IV. We will there examine the conceptions of moral philosophy articulated by Annette Baier and Martha Nussbaum in contrast both with avowedly metaethical conceptions and traditional normative ethical theories. In doing that we will try to ferret out something of what is most deeply at issue and try to see if we can get a sense of how we should proceed when we try to do moral philosophy. Theories like those of Annette

Baier and Martha Nussbaum seem at least, in contrast with metaethical theories (even the new metaethics), more anchored in life. Vis-à-vis metaethics we shall be asking Francis Sparshott's question, "What is the function of such an ethic in the course of life?"

II

Before we turn to that, we want to examine a cluster of issues arising from two of the essays we have collected here: Peter Railton's "Made in the Shade: Moral Compatibilism and the Aims of Moral Theory" and Jean Hampton's "Naturalism and Moral Reasons." Railton's essay is wide ranging and insightful, articulating a naturalistic account of both substantive naturalism (ethical naturalism and, as well, cosmological or worldview naturalism) and methodological naturalism.[2] He shows how

---

2 Methodological naturalism is a conception we did not deploy in our Introduction when we sorted out some types of naturalism. However, both Hampton and Railton use it. Methodological naturalism is, as Hampton puts it, "the view that philosophy, and indeed, any other intellectual discipline must pursue knowledge via empirical methods exemplified by the sciences and not by a priori or non-empirical methods." Peter Railton characterizes it, as involving "a commitment to employing the norms and methods of inquiry characteristic of the developed empirical sciences." Railton's characterization is a weaker one, and, just for that reason, may be preferable, for it leaves a less controversial place for mathematical reasoning, which is surely, in many of its deployments, a part of scientific reasoning. As Hampton characterizes methodological naturalism, a methodological naturalist would have to rule out "logic and mathematics," and the characteristic modes of reasoning that go with them, unless they can be shown to be "empirical enterprises after all." But that, to state it conservatively, is a very problematic claim. The Railton conception of methodological naturalism seems at least more plausible for, *if* our understanding of mathematical and logical reasoning, as it forms a part of science, requires an understanding of them as a priori forms of reasoning, we can still accommodate them, so construed, as "methods of inquiry characteristic of the developed empirical sciences." This, though less 'metaphysically satisfying,' gives far fewer hostages to fortune. It should further be noted that one can be a cosmological naturalist and an ethical naturalist without being a methodological naturalist and vice versa. Moreover, noncognitivists can without any strain at all be methodological naturalists. A

they interrelate, argues that both cosmological and methodological naturalism comport well with factualism (descriptivism) and argues that this combination yields the best funding conception of ethics available to us and that it provides the best grounding and rationale for moral critique and for constructing a critical normative ethic. Railton, in a fair-minded way, as well as with subtlety and rigor, articulates a comprehensive project. His account arguably does much to move things along in moral philosophy. In a similarly subtle, rigorous and programmatically articulated essay, Jean Hampton argues that we do not have a clear conception of what an adequate naturalism would look like. The conceptions in hand, she argues, are rather plainly inadequate and particularly so for the purposes of ethical and social theory. Ethical naturalism, noncognitivism and error theory alike are all methodologically and cosmologically naturalist, but we have, she claims, no even nearly adequate understanding of what naturalism is. We have, she argues, no notion of 'natural' that has been precisely defined and we have "no commonly accepted statement of what makes a theory scientifically acceptable or unacceptable." Yet Hampton, argues for – or at least seems to argue for – a form of ethical naturalism that is, as she puts it, a form of 'moral objectivism' and a 'moral realism.' (She clearly argues for a moral objectivism and moral realism. It is less clear that she is an ethical naturalist. See our third note.) She powerfully argues that a "naturalism hostile to morality" – an error theory, a moral nihilism, and noncognitivist theories in their extreme forms – does not make out its case and it operates with an inadequately specified conception of naturalism: the so-called scientific worldview with which our thinking about morality must, such naturalists have it, be in accordance.

She, however, makes too much out of not being able to get *conclusive* or *decisive* arguments here. We have very good reasons to believe

---

methodological naturalist need be neither a cosmological nor an ethical naturalist, though cosmological naturalism and methodological naturalism *usually* go together. They are, as the compatiblist Railton might put it, nicely compatible. They fit together, though without there being any mutual entailments. The quotations from Hampton and Railton are from this volume.

we will never get that for any interesting issue in philosophy. An account cannot reasonably be defeated, unless it itself foolishly claims conclusiveness, by showing it is not conclusively established. All we are going to get – indeed the very best we can get – are plausible arguments that are always less than conclusive. The aim should be not conclusiveness or decisiveness but greater plausibility (Smart 1966, 377-90). But that notwithstanding, her criticisms of J.L. Mackie, Gilbert Harman and Bernard Williams – in effect, good plausibility arguments on her part – are very much to the point. Moral skepticism has not made out its case for opting for a form of naturalism which claims that moral beliefs are not vindicable because they do not, or, more strongly still, cannot, pass scientific muster and as a result stand in conflict with a properly naturalistic scientific worldview. These bold iconoclastic claims, she argues, have not been made out. Neither do we have in hand, she argues, an account which has clearly and usefully specified what naturalism is, nor has it been clearly specified what a 'scientific worldview' is or what is 'scientifically acceptable and unacceptable.' These notions have not been articulated in sufficiently clear and untendentious ways so as to clear the extant views on these matters of dogmatism, arbitrariness and vagueness. Neither the moral skeptic nor anyone else has done anything to show that the funding theories of an objectivist naturalism or moral realism are scientifically problematic.

She and Railton *appear* at least to be allies in the articulation and defense of an objectivist naturalistic project. Yet Hampton's probing critique at least seems, like a dog biting his tail, to cut back on that very naturalistic project. It appears, after all, if Hampton's arguments are sound, that no one has a sufficiently clear conception of naturalism such that it can provide the kind of funding theory that she and Railton, along with many others, want.[3] It is not only error-theorist, projectivist,

---

3 That Hampton is arguing for an objectivist form of ethical naturalism seems reasonably evident in her essay and that is how we have read her. But some remarks in her final footnote cast some doubt on that reading. Moral objectivism and moral realism are staunchly affirmed. But, bucking trends, she *may*, surprisingly enough, be returning (some would say reverting) to some form of the older intuitionist (nonnaturalist cognitivist) form of moral realism. She remarks in that footnote that in her forthcoming *A Theory of Reasons* she will

and subjectivist-naturalist accounts that come acropper, but – or so it seems at least – objectivist-naturalist accounts, too. If things are as bad for naturalism, as she believes, being a naturalist of any kind comes to just taking a dogmatic stance and an unclear one to boot. It is, if Hampton's account is on the mark, to do little more than to uncritically accept the folklore of our *scientistic* culture. It seems reasonably clear that Hampton does not want that result. She wants to be a good moral objectivist-naturalist: a good, soundly thinking, robust moral realist. (But again, see our note 3.) Still, such difficulties may be an unintended and untoward consequence of her own perceptive critical account.

We shall argue that naturalism is not nearly as badly off as she believes, and that a sound conception of a non-scientistic naturalism is available to us, that, tied with Railton's generalized compatibilism, makes naturalism a very attractive conception on which to fund morality, if we are to be in the funding business at all. Assuming for the nonce we are in that business, we should attempt, in Railton's words, to give "a fairly general, coherent account of what sort of thing morality is, what it presupposes or entails, how it stands in relation to the rest of human activity and inquiry, and what it would need to be in good order." More than that, a naturalistic account such as his own or Richard Miller's goes some way toward showing that some of our moral beliefs actually are in good order by showing that we have some empirically confirmed moral knowledge: knowledge of, among other things, natural properties on which moral properties asymmetrically *supervene*. In that very broad and non-scientistic sense, we can speak, as John Dewey did, of having a scientific ethic (Dewey 1946, 211-49. This article was actually written in 1903, the same year as *Principia Ethica*.).

---

argue, as a *moral objectivist*, that "objectivist moral theories contain occult, nonnatural elements, but go on to show that the same occult, nonnatural elements occur and *must* occur in scientific theories" (italics ours). This sounds like, and perhaps is, a complete, root-and-branch, rejection of naturalism. A defense of the necessity of appealing in both science and morality to occult elements, as no doubt Hampton recognizes, is to defend a very paradoxical claim that would take very powerful arguments to make even plausible. But no such strong claims are made in her essay in this volume, though her arguments against some forms of naturalism may prefigure them.

A plausible form of substantive naturalism will not be scientistic (Bernstein 1995, 57-76 and Nielsen 1996). It will not claim that all our knowledge is scientific knowledge or derivable from scientific knowledge. It will only claim that what is known must not be incompatible with what is, or at least can be, known by the best scientific theories and thus, that is, be compatible with a naturalistic framework. But Hampton well sees that there is a problem with speaking of 'a naturalistic framework' and with the 'that is,' for we do not know very exactly what naturalism is and the 'that is' begs the question. We have no precisely defined notion of 'natural' or of 'natural properties' or 'natural characteristics' or 'natural facts.' We will run into difficulties, if we try to go operational and use what she calls (using scare quotes) 'the science-based definition' in effect making "current theories of science the ultimate arbiters of what counts as natural...." If we so proceed, we "do not define science in terms of the natural, but the natural in terms of science. Naturalism is just what current science is and what is compatible with current science. The empirical world contains just what a true complete physical science would say it contains." Why, Hampton queries, should we give to physics or anything else the authority to define or be the arbiter of what is real? Without a prior conception of what is real why should we make physics or biology such an arbiter? As she puts it:

> The metaphysical authority of physics is puzzling if the natural is defined in terms of it rather than vice versa. If it is true that the world is made up of all and only the sorts of entities that physics studies, then what physics tells us about the world should be authoritative for our beliefs. But if we don't have any way for knowing, or even characterizing, what is real independent of any particular theory, then for any of our favorite theories (take your pick) we have no particular reason to believe that (only) this theory depicts the real or the natural.

We have, she stresses, no justification for believing that all that exists or is real is what science at any given time posits. As Hampton puts it, that "ontological faith is undefended, and difficult to know how to defend." It is one thing to claim that we have good reason to believe that the statements of physicists or biologists in their particular domains are the most reliable claims in those domains that we can have during the period when they are being made. It is another thing again to say that what they say is determinative of the real. If you want to know what is the most reasonable thing to believe at a given time about DNA or AIDS, consult the relevant scientists. It is reasonable there to accept their authority. Over such matters should we, by contrast, each make our own investigations and be our own authorities? That is plainly absurd. But it does not follow that, if we have no science about what is humorous or what is right, there can be no sound truth claims about humorousness or rightness.

Some naturalists of a very *scientistic* sort say that it is physics, and physics alone, which tells us what the ultimate constituents of the world are. However, even if we try to take this at face value, the notion of these particles being natural is itself bizarre. But, more importantly, as Quine (a charter member *scientistic* naturalist) argues, and here Hampton is one with him, all this talk of the *ultimate* components of the universe is foolishness at best. Such a conception could not be a proper part of science. *Such* ontological speculation is at best idle. (Perhaps *all* ontological speculation is idle, but that is another matter.)

Suppose, instead, we attempt a substantive definition of 'natural.' 'Natural,' so conceived, denotes the kind of object or property which is the opposite of nonnatural. So conceived, what is natural is, as Hampton puts it, "conceptually prior to our understanding of science, and (at least in part) determinative of the subject matter of science." But that distinction (putative distinction) is not very helpful for we do not understand the supposedly contrastive term 'nonnatural.' As discussion of G.E. Moore's gesturing at a use brought out, we do not know what a nonnatural property is or, in the relevant sense, what a 'nonnatural object' is. We are caught with something like a *via negativa* here; we do not know, with that mystery term 'nonnatural,' what the relevant contrast with 'natural' is. 'natural object' and even 'natural property' can seem pleonastic. Of course, 'natural' answers to a number of reasonably (in many contexts) unproblematic distinctions: natural/artificial, natural/conventional, natural/contrived, natural/social, or perhaps even, as in old-fashioned natural moral law discussions, natural/unnatural. But, for what is at issue in the naturalism discussion, none of the above contrasts and the distinctions that go with them are relevant. For naturalism, an artificial object is just as natural as a natural object. For what we are trying to capture with the conception of naturalism both rocks and cars are natural objects. But then it starts to look like 'natural object' really is pleonastic. What we are trying to capture in speaking of naturalism, is the distinction (putative distinction) between natural/

supernatural where 'supernatural' refers to theism, deism, idealism and the like. A naturalist is someone who rejects such beliefs. She *may* even reject the conceptions that go with them, regarding them as somehow incoherent. Still, it is not clear how to be more complete about 'the like' and 'such' here. We seem just to have some examples.

It would, we believe, be helpful in trying to make sense of 'naturalism' to turn away from thinking of physics and the so-called basic stuff or basic structure of the universe and to think instead of Darwin and biology and of human beings in Darwinian terms. We should, as Dewey did, and after him as Daniel Dennett, Richard Rorty, and Donald Davidson do, look at human beings as complicated language-using animals whose minds should be thought of as a very large network of intentional states: states attributed to an organism with a behavior that is very complex. These intentional states are elements in a causal interaction of this organism with its environment. We are animals – albeit intelligent and reflective animals – that in certain respects are like and in certain respects different from the other animals. We differ, as Hume stressed, in being language-using animals, capable of reflection and of forming and acting on moral conceptions. All of this is shown in how our behavior is in certain respects distinctive from that of the other animals and how this behavior, instantiating these concepts, is shown likewise to be useful for animals like ourselves in coping with our environment. In such a way we are complicated objects (macro-objects) from the point of view of physics. To so view human beings is to be the kind of non-reductive physicalist that Dennett, Rorty and Davidson are (Rorty 1991, 113-25). And it is the kind of naturalist that Dewey was, as he Darwinized Hegelian conceptions, and that David Hume was still earlier. It is a thoroughly secularist way of viewing things eschewing *recherché* objects and transcendental conceptions. While Kant postulated a *noumenal* realm – something that is plainly nonnaturalistic – to square free agency with conceptions of science (something that many present-day Kantians find difficult to swallow), contemporary naturalists, as Hobbes, Spinoza, and Hume did before them, will adopt some form of compatibilism. And unlike nonnaturalists such as Kant, Thomas Reid, or Richard Price, they will take acting from duty to be realizable by, and explainable of, as Peter Railton put it, "a being who is (among other things) a causal being situated in a causal world."

The distinction between naturalism and nonnaturalism, between natural objects, properties and conceptions and nonnatural ones, comes out in the above contrasts. Naturalism takes human beings to be complicated animals (and thus objects) in causal interaction with other physical objects, and it will not postulate entities acceptable to, and in some instances required by, nonnaturalism, to wit, *noumenal* beings, God, gods, bodiless minds, minds as some private physically indescribable something mysteriously interacting with bodies or as remaining somehow distinct from but still parallel to bodies. So, after all, we do get, where the human animal and other animals are concerned, a natural/nonnatural contrast. Moreover, as can be seen from the above, it is a contrast which is nonvacuous, at least if we do not push too hard about the coherency of the nonnatural notions, e.g., *noumena*, God, spirits and the like. It is not the case (*pace* Hampton) that we cannot specify what the nonnatural is as distinct from the natural. And, though we appealed to Darwinian notions rather vaguely and generally, the specification of natural here is conceptually prior to our scientific understanding. Hume, whom Darwin read, put it, much as we have put it, commonsensically, but in a way which comports well with Darwinianism.

In speaking of a substantive conception of what is natural, Hampton rightly observes,

> in the seventeenth century naturalists called themselves 'materialists,' insofar as they thought of the world as made up of 'solid, inert, impenetrable and conserved' matter that interacts deterministically and through contact.

Unfortunately for naturalists, she remarks, physics itself came to undermine in our century this "popular and seemingly sensible conception of the natural...." Twentieth-century physics "posited entities, and interactions between these entities, that do not fit the materialist characterization of the real." But we do not need to consider microphysics when we are talking about macro-particles (middle-sized objects like us). Whatever an ant, toad, or a human being 'ultimately' is made up of, they are observationally identifiable and, their movements are quite deterministically predictable. Something roughly like Newtonian mechanics works there. And a biologically and socially oriented naturalism centrally concerned with human and other animal behavior is concerned with middle-sized objects, and there is no good reason to think that materialism and physicalism of a non-reductive sort are not quite in place here. Moreover, it is the complex behavior of just such objects – including their social behavior – in its interaction with their environment that is relevant to morals, and this does not require the specification of anything that cannot be specified in naturalistic terms. 'Freedom ('counter-causal freedom') among the electrons,' if indeed there is any, is quite irrelevant.

It may be responded that this is not a conception of a *complete* naturalism. A naturalism that is complete would be a specification of the entire world, showing what the world – all of it – is made up of, its micro-particles as well as its macroparticles. The above Deweyan-Dennettian-Darwinian account does not show how everything in the universe, including microentities, can be specified in naturalistic (physicalistic) terms.

Why, it can be replied, should we find it important for our naturalism to be complete, particularly when the very idea of a complete specification of the entire world is not a very lucid idea? What is important is to be able to talk of human beings and the environment in which they interact in naturalistic terms. And that we have done. Moreover, talk about the *nature* of microparticles is a slippery business. And if we think that is the way to get at 'ultimate reality,' then we should, in turn, respond to this with Quine's ridicule, shared by Hampton, concerning talk of the ultimate constituents of the universe. To this we should add here, following J.L. Austin, how it is nonsense to speak, as Hampton does, of 'the materialist characterization of *the real*' or of 'the idealist characterization of *the real*' or 'the theistic characterization of *the real*.' No sense has been given to 'the real' here, and it is unclear that any non-tendentious sense can be given to it. It is as bad as talk of being or being as such or of the ground of being. We have something sensible when we talk of 'real beer' as distinct from 'beer without alcohol,' or 'real butter' as distinct from margarine, or 'real philosophy' as distinct from the philosophy of sport, or a 'real hike' as distinct from a stroll. *Persuasive* definitions of 'real' are, of course, at work here, but still we do have a genuine contrast and, not infrequently, a contrast with a point, a contrast that is clearly not arbitrary. Stevenson, who, along with I.A. Richards, showed us so deftly how *persuasive* definitions work, was also concerned to stress that they were not *all* arbitrary and without a reasonable point. But when we just, *sans contexte,* speak of an investigation of, or reflection on, *the real*, there is no contrast with the unreal. What is the difference between a materialist characterization of the real and a materialist characterization of the unreal, unless the characterization we have in mind is to speak of trees, seas, lemurs and human beings in contrast with gods, *noumena*, pure spirits, bodiless intellects, entelechies, the *élan vital* and the like? (Note again the trouble with completing 'the like.') But the latter cluster of terms in the comparison are of doubtful coherence. It is not at all like comparing 'real cream' and 'nondairy creamer.' But, if this is so, we are back with the familiar Deweyan-Dennettian-Darwinian contrast which was not thought to be a general-enough specification of 'natural' to identify it with the real. But the point is that there is no sensible talk of 'the real' except in a *determinate context* (Hägerström 1964, 41-74 and 313). But the kind of naturalism relevant to a social understanding of *our* world is much more contextualist than such a vast speculative endeavor as a putative investigation of the real *sans phrase* (Nielsen 1996). There is no context-free identification or discovery of 'the real,' or defining of 'the real.' Put otherwise, *contra* scientistic forms of naturalism, a non-anthropomorphic naturalism is both unwelcome and unnecessary. To try to go for it reflects the metaphysical compulsions of philosophers and some scientists (usually physicists or mathematicians) running out of control. Again language has gone on a holiday.

Hampton, as a self-proclaimed moral objectivist and moral realist, is in search of "the only true description of the world" but such a quest is unintelligible. There is, of course, a deep and persistent metaphysical temptation to try to speak of the way the world is just in itself or of how things just are anyway. But it is incoherent to speak of how the world is or of how things are independently of any choice of a vocabulary, independently, that is, of how they can be described, or of how a vocabulary we have, or can come to adopt, characterizes them or will come to characterize them, as if nature has something like 'her own language.' Nature, so to speak, speaks to us. But in cold sobriety we need to recognize that it makes no sense to try to discover the way the world is apart from any linguistic description of it (Putnam 1990 and 1994). Hampton cannot have her one true description of the world. There can be no such thing. Rather, descriptions are products of human needs, interests, and purposes, the problems and resulting perspectives that people come to have. There is no intelligible 'point of view from nowhere' or 'absolute conception of the world,' that is, a point of view or a conception that is interest-free, perspective-free, and could yield the one true description of the world, so that, free of some determinate human interests, scientific or otherwise, we could just say – describe how – the way the world is *anyway* quite apart from any human interests and resultant ways of describing and conceptualizing things, so that we could intelligibly say that the world really is mereological sums of space-time parts or *whatever*. There is (*pace* Hampton) *no just finding out about reality so that we could discover whether, after all, it is really naturalistic or otherwise.*

Hampton takes Bernard Williams's conception of an absolute perspective to be relatively unproblematic and claims that he has just arbitrarily excluded moral properties and objects from being a part of the absolute perspective. But this misses the problem, pressed by both Putnam and Rorty, concerning whether such a conception makes any sense at all, so that a coherent debate could be carried on between her and Williams over 'moral realism.'

We have found unpersuasive some of the things Hampton says about difficulties in deciding what passes muster scientifically and what doesn't and about 'the natural' in naturalism; and we have found, or thought we have found, alternative naturalistic accounts that are not vulnerable to her acute criticisms of some forms of naturalism. But all that notwithstanding, it should be stressed that her tightly organized, and carefully reasoned, series of arguments are formidable and deserve careful scrutiny, including skeptical sober second thoughts concerning the soundness of the above criticisms of her account. She has, at a minimum, put forms of *naturalism hostile to morality* (to adopt her not untendentious way of putting things) very much on the defensive. But all of that is on her *nay*-saying side, the side that she is principally concerned with in her essay in this volume. But, along the way, she also makes positive claims and utilizes distinctive conceptions which are at least as vulnerable as the naturalistic claims and conceptions she finds problematic. She announces on the first page of her essay that she is a moral objectivist, as if, with that, we have anything even reasonably clear or unproblematic. Someone (Rawls, for example) not tempted by moral skepticism or subjectivism might still well want to say that the notion of objectivity, particularly in such domains, is elusive. Perhaps to speak of objectivity in such a context is only to speak of some form of rather full intersubjectivity or of what would be affirmed in *wide* and *general* reflective equilibrium? (Rawls 1995, 140-1) Yet some philosophers have wanted something more, but what that is, or whether they can have it, is anything but clear. There has, in the history of our subject, been metaphysical cravings for all kinds of things, cravings that have, again and again, turned out to be incoherent. What it is to be a moral objectivist does not wear its meaning on its sleeve. The same thing is true of moral realism, which Hampton also unselfconsciously avows. Even if Mackie's and Harman's arguments do not go through, the very idea of moral realism remains thoroughly problematic. It seems to have all the difficulties of metaphysical realism plus the additional ones connected with normativity as well (Couture and Nielsen 1993, 365-87). Even noncognitivists can correctly say, and account for, the claim that moral utterances are either true or false, if they stick, as well they might, with a minimalist or deflationist account of truth (Smith 1994). If the moral realist claims a stronger substantive correspondence theory of truth, all the standard difficulties arise concerning whether we can make sense, in any domain (even the-cat-is-on-the-mat domain) of correspondence, beyond Tarski's correspondence-platitudes, platitudes accepted by both minimalists and deflationists. We have Donald Davidson's point that the very "notion of fitting the facts, or of being true to the facts adds nothing intelligible to the simple concept of being true" (Davidson 1984, 193-4). Realism, moral or otherwise, has arguably an incoherent, or at least an unnecessary, conception of truth: more metaphysical baggage standing in the way of gaining a good understanding of morality.

However, we need not, and indeed should not, flee to anti-realism or to irrealism either, and adopt some form of noncognitivism. We can perfectly well, not going beyond minimalism, say that moral utterances can be true, and, if they are, then there are moral facts again in the perfectly minimalist and uncontroversial sense that a fact – moral, mathematical, empirical or whatever – is just what a true statement states. But that platitude (true all the same) does not take us to moral realism or metaphysical realism, where there is a claim that truth is correspondence to facts, where, as Peter Strawson puts it ironically, facts are taken to be non-linguistic sentence-shaped objects: kinds of replicas of *that*-clauses – very queer kinds of objects indeed – somehow just there in the universe. But this is an obvious reification which neither nature nor the *noumenal* realm (if such there be) dictates by already containing in the natural world or in the *noumenal* world sentence-shaped objects, like *that*-clauses, simply, in a quasi-language, depicting the way the world is, including the way the moral world is, that we can somehow just access in a passive way and, if our language is to get things right, it must simply so record what we so passively access. But this is pure mystification. Yet Hampton quite unblushingly speaks of moral objects (a particularly fishy-sounding notion) and of moral facts to which we somehow have direct access.

We would hope that Hampton's account could be demythologized into an ethical naturalism something like Peter Railton's, which is a naturalism, including an ethical naturalism, that *needs* make no commitment either to moral realism or to moral anti-realism or to a moral objectivism that involves anything other than wide and general reflective equilibrium (Daniels 1996 and Nielsen 1996). (We can have objectivity without objectivism, to wit, a thoroughgoing and general intersubjectivity.) The funding theory Railton articulates squares with a scientific worldview – the Darwinian view we gestured at – unless we unrealistically mean by 'scientific worldview' a view that would not in its account contain anything evaluative or normative, insisting on a normatively neutral vocabulary, again assuming, given the infusion of the normative into our language, that anything like that even could obtain, i.e., be a coherent possibility.[4] But Railton does not believe that a scientific worldview should, or perhaps even could, be so sparsely Galilean. His is "a funding theory of morality that would enable us to see the compatibility of our moral categories and assumptions with going empirical theory."

In coming to understand the strength of ethical naturalism, it is important to consider *supervenience* and specifically the supervenience of the normative on the factual. Railton says important and on the whole convincing things here. But it is well to start with a leaner remark of

---

4 In note 5 of his essay in this volume, Peter Railton makes it clear that what he calls 'a funding theory' could also be called 'a metaethical theory' as 'metaethics' is construed by the *new* metaethics. What it is incompatible with is the restrictions of analytic metaethics.

Allan Gibbard's made in his "Reply to Railton" (Gibbard 1993, 52-9). "Norms," Gibbard remarks, "apply to types of possible circumstances. If they apply, then, to two possible circumstances differently, that must be because the circumstances are of different types. *No normative differ-ence without a factual difference*: if what to do differs in two possible cir-cumstances, the facts differ" (ibid., 55; italics ours). This notion is obviously naturalist-friendly, but nonnaturalistic cognitivists (if there still are any) and noncognitivists also can acknowledge it, as indeed they would have to if it really is, as Gibbard takes it to be, an a priori and necessary truth (in whatever sense we are going to make of that notion in these post-Quinian times) (ibid., 55-6). We say it is naturalist-friendly for, as Railton put it, without any identification (even *de facto* identification) of the moral with the natural or moral properties with natural properties, "the supervenience of moral properties upon natu-ral properties brought an inevitable commitment to seeing morality as such that the natural world could support it." That this is so, and how it is so, if it is so, Gibbard's remark makes plain. Railton comments that some take supervenience to be a metaphysical or a normative claim. But these are confusions, if Gibbard's claim is so, for then the super-venience of the moral on the natural is a conceptual, in a broad sense a logical, claim rooted in our use of normative, including moral, lan-guage. It is, if Gibbard is right, a feature of what in the bad old days would have been called 'the logic of moral discourse.' But seen in this 'clean' way, as Railton stresses, it "carries no presupposition of the ex-istence of moral properties." One is only constrained to believe, if one cares about consistency and intelligibility, that if two situations differ morally they must also be different in their (non-indexical) natural prop-erties. 'No moral difference without a factual difference' is not a moral or even meta-moral imperative, but has the same status as 'No bach-elorhood without unmarriedness.' We would not even understand moral talk, or other normative talk, unless we had at least an implicit recognition of supervenience. (It might with many, indeed most, just be a knowing how rather than as well a knowing that.)

Two situations, to see rather more concretely what is involved here, cannot differ *solely* in their moral character. Sven and Erik are two adults similar in all relevant respects and relevantly similarly situated. We cannot intelligibly say that it was vile the way Sven was slashed, beaten, and strangled and go on to say that it was perfectly all right the way that Erik was slashed, beaten, and strangled when that way was the same and there are no relevant differences between Erik and Sven or in their circumstances (Nielsen 1985, 91-101). We are not here just making moral judgments from which someone might coherently dissent, but we are in effect reminding ourselves of how the moral language game is played. Calling it 'vile' is no doubt a strong moral response expressive of our moral emotions and tending to evoke similar emotions in others, but it is rooted in our seeing what happened to Sven and in knowing that, if the same thing happens to Erik and there is no relevant difference between Sven and Erik or in their circumstances, we must – to be consistent, must – whether we feel the same emotion or not, believe the same thing about what happened to Erik. We can, of course, say that consistency is simply a hang-up of pedantic minds, but then we convict ourselves of irrationality. If, in turn, we respond 'So what!', then it is not clear what more is to be said. But it is understandable that people will quickly lose interest in the discussion, if that is what it is to be called, if it takes that turn. We are held to a certain kind of consistency patterned upon the sameness of the facts in the case (the natural facts, if that is not pleonastic) (Stevenson 1983, 13-37).

Whenever something is good, right, just, fitting, suitable to the situation, and the like, it is so because of certain non-ethical, factual characteristics. The noncognitivists may be right that to say that something is good, right, fitting, and the like is not to report or describe some natural state of affairs (let alone some 'non-natural' state of affairs), but to express a pro-attitude toward such states of affairs or to prescribe that such states of affairs obtain. Nonetheless, as Railton puts it, such moral judgments "have an intimate relation to such states of affairs – moral qualities are constituted by or grounded in natural qualities." Moreover, this is a strong connection. It is not the claim that moral judgments merely correlate with or harmonize with such statements of fact. Rather, the naturalist claims, again in Railton's words, that if "moral judgment is ever in place, it is in place because the world (apart from moral opinion) is such as to make it so." But then questions about the way the world is (under some description, of course), questions about what explains what, about what might constitute what – "in short, questions raised by the development of empirical inquiry – can reach to the heart of morality." Moreover, the supervenience of the moral on the factual is not a reciprocal supervenience, but an asymmetrical one:

the factual must constitute or at least produce the moral, but surely not the other way around. We see here what Railton calls "a core truism of the moral realm – the dependence of the moral upon the natural." (*If* Hampton's account is on the mark, considerable havoc would have been played with that claim.) Moreover, if Gibbard is right, this 'No normative difference without a factual difference,' as distinct from 'No factual difference without a normative difference' is a proposition that is "a priori and necessary: it holds independently of experience, and applies to all possible situations" (Gibbard 1993, 55-6). This core truism, if it really is that, if it could be successfully linked with compatibilism, would strongly underwrite ethical naturalism. Moreover, it would be a non-reductive, non-definitional naturalism that need not be troubled by the *open-question argument*: the open question could remain *open* and still this naturalism could remain firmly in place. Moreover, it could, and indeed should, accept the expressiveness and prescriptivity stressed by noncognitivists as well as the essential action-guidingness, and, in that sense, the practicality of moral judgments also stressed by noncognitivists. Moral utterances could, in their very nature (if there is such a thing), be expressive-evocative and action-guiding and still asymmetric supervenience would obtain: with the factual producing the moral such that if someone claims that something is good, right, just, fitting, suitable to the situation and the like, it must (*a*) be because of certain natural facts about it and (*b*) that, as well, when the same situation obtains, or a relevantly similar situation obtains, including the sort of people involved being the same or relevantly similar, the same moral judgment must, in consistency, be made.

We only have *lebensraum* for normative argument here over whether the situation is relevantly similar (Nielsen 1985, 91-101). Moreover, as Railton also stresses, this non-reductive ethical naturalism is compatible with the acceptance of an 'is'/'ought' gap. Natural facts can produce or even constitute values while it remains true that there is "a logical gap between any alleged fact and any conclusion expressed in moral terms." We can begin to see that and how this is so, if we consider the fact that supervenience is compatible with Mackian-Blackburnian moral skepticism: "the possibility that our moral thought is massively in error." If Hampton's and Sturgeon's arguments are on the mark, such an error theory is very problematical. But neither would claim, nor could they reasonably claim, to have decisively or conclusively disproved it. It still seems to be at least a logical possibility that our moral thought is massively in error. So the truth, indeed the logical truth, of the asymmetric supervenience of the moral on the factual does not guarantee that fixing the natural properties of the actual world a priori guarantees the presence of *any* moral properties. If an error theory is right, then there are no real oughts, not even *ought nots*. Facts produce or constitute oughts, *if there are any oughts*, so we cannot have a moral difference without a factual difference. If there is something we ought to do, it is, Railton argues, because of something in the world that makes it so. But perhaps there is nothing at all that we either ought to do or ought not to do, because the very idea of 'ought or ought not to doness' is illusory: there being no genuine ought, neither oughts nor ought nots. *If* there is something we ought to do, the facts will show it, but *if* there is nothing that we ought or ought not to do, the facts will show that too. But an appeal to the facts is not sufficient to *logically* guarantee which situation actually obtains, which situation is the case. This should hardly be surprising. It was a notion that Hume and Kant very early were onto as later Henri Poincaré and Max Weber were as well, and it was expressed forcefully by Moore and by the non-cognitivists. The acceptance of asymmetric supervenience does not affect that. There still remains, even with the acceptance of such an ethical naturalism, something of the 'is'/'ought' gap.

However, Railton argues, rightly it seems to us, that, though an ethical naturalist can and should accept that much of the autonomy of ethics (the 'is'/'ought' gap), she also should be a good fallibilist – perhaps even a pragmatist-fallibilist – and, accepting the logical autonomy of ethics, deploy the method of wide and general reflective equilibrium, a method, as Railton puts it, that "knows of connections that are more than logical." It will want to display the most plausible fit between our various moral judgments and our actual beliefs, including the (for us now) best established "substantive and methodological elements of empirical science." Moreover, wide and general reflective equilibrium will seek to show how we can have a cluster of moral beliefs that avoids "intolerable strains with the substantive and methodological elements of empirical science." Suppose that Sturgeon and Hampton are right against Harman. Central moral notions (virtue, duty, and agency) play not only a *justificatory* role, but also an *explanatory* role, explaining in particular situations not only what we do, but what we believe we ought to do in those situations. Note, however, that to explain what we *believe* we ought to do is not *eo ipso* to explain what we ought to do. Still, if people are not worked up, not bombarded with ideology and have good and accurate information concerning the situation in question, then, if they believe they ought to do something in that situation, then we have a very good reason to believe they ought to do it. There is, of course, no entailment, but people who work with reflective equilibrium routinely use connections that are weaker than entailments. It is reasonable for us to want to be compatibilists about this, if we can: we will want these explanatory roles we attribute to moral notions to square with whatever we know or reasonably believe about how the world operates. We are not, to repeat, looking for entailments, but to see how these notions can be compatible. How, for example, we can be free even if the universe, for macroscopic objects at least, is deterministic. "Showing compatibility is a way of promoting the autonomy of moral reasoning for it would show that we are not running afoul of our own convictions about the relation of the moral to the natural" (105). Given what we know, or at least plausibly think we know, about the world, including its continuing, though with ups and downs, demystification, we do not wish to postulate Kantian *noumenal* agency, *contra*-causal freedom, a space of reasons holding independently of what has empirical warrant, systematic error to all moral thought, complete lack of human freedom, and the like. We will eschew such notions, if we reasonably can. We will try to get a wide and general reflective equilibrium without such notions, a wide and general reflective equilibrium within an utterly naturalistic framework (no transcendental notions, no *élan vital*, no *noumena*).

We want, and reasonably so, to be able to see, and to perspicuously represent, how things hang together in a way that makes sense of our moral convictions and, as well, of our scientific and commonsense knowledge of the world (commonsense knowledge that has good empirical backing). Error theory is something we would reasonably accept only if all such attempts at wide reflective-equilibrium rationalization fail and fail after repeated and careful attempts.

So reasonability dictates a compatibilist strategy (a generalization from its original home in the freedom-determinism controversy), though it does not a priori, or in any other way, guarantee its truth. But that is no defect, for it is foolish to look for such guarantees. To quest for certainty is always a mistake. Reflective equilibrium sets us, instead, to the articulating of a naturalistic funding theory (in the broad latter-day sense, a metaethical theory) rooted in our very ordinary reflective thinking about ethics, which will also be a theory that will ground our moral thought and practice in the natural world and, though some moral beliefs will be revised and some abandoned, it will fund as well many of our most centrally embedded moral convictions, showing there can be a moral life that has a rationale and a point without our succumbing to illusions or to blinding ourselves to how our world is (Daniels 1996 and Nielsen 1996). Here, as we have seen, asymmetric supervenience is a crucial conception. Reflections on it and on the plausibility of a general compatibilist strategy make the case for a nonreductive, nondefinitional ethical naturalism (what we called in our Introduction a 'synthetic ethical naturalism') very attractive. It is an ethical naturalism that leaves the open question *open*, and the 'is'/ 'ought' gap in place. But note the sea change here. In the history of metaethics it has often been taken to be a definitional truth that to be an ethical naturalist one must deny that there is an 'is'/'ought' gap. But this is a very tendentious history, for it would turn John Dewey into someone who was not an ethical naturalist.

III

In the previous section we argued, for the most part, from within metaethics, and, in doing so, we argued that, both building on and criticizing Hampton's and Railton's accounts, (*a*) that there is a strong case for ethical naturalism rooted in general naturalism and (*b*) that a strong case has also been made for setting aide those naturalisms, such as error theories, that support moral skepticism. We now, doing a bit of a *volte face*, want to turn to a discussion of those conceptions of moral philosophy mentioned in Section I which, on the one hand, reject metaethical conceptions (old and new) of doing moral philosophy, as well as the tradition of normative ethics, and, on the other, not content with just *nay*-saying, set out an alternative substantive conception of moral philosophy. We will spell out a bit what is involved here and contrast such accounts with metaethical conceptions, particularly with a new metaethics which utilizes the method of wide and general reflective equilibrium. In doing this, we will try to ascertain whether we can come to see a little better how we should proceed in engaging in moral philosophy.

Annette C. Baier, Cora Diamond, and Martha C. Nussbaum are much more skeptical than we are over whether, with such metaethical funding theories, we have a good conception of what we should be about in doing moral philosophy. They, Diamond most deeply, are skeptical of what goes on in both the metaethics and the normative ethics business. We have already quoted Diamond to that effect; Baier is not that deeply skeptical, but she certainly is skeptical of what she takes to be the rationalist ways of going on that are typical of most ethical theorizing (both metaethical and normative ethical). Yet, after expressing her skepticism concerning "system lovers who want to construct moral theories," Baier still goes on to speak of wanting and seeking to articulate a more adequate moral theory constructed on different lines (Baier 1994, 15-16). And it is indeed something she sets out to do. But, given what ethical theory has been, there must be for her a *nay*-saying prolegomena. We must break the rationalism that has so obsessed moral philosophers, both rationalist and empiricist. Still, like Diamond, she is perplexed by, and skeptical about, how to proceed, remarking: "I think we still need to learn how best to reflect on morality" (Baier 1985, 220).

Systematizing, after the fashion of Kant, Sidgwick, or W.D. Ross, Baier takes to be at best pointless. But she is also unwilling to say that "we should live by our inherited fuzzy moral intuitions and do no moral philosophy at all" (ibid., 224). We should, she has it, only acquiesce in our untutored intuitions "if there is no way to think about our morality except by attempting to contemplate a better world with its perfect moral system": a world with precise moral principles and rules, with definite decision procedures and perfect compliance (ibid., 223-4). *If* this is the only way of doing systematic moral philosophy on offer, then it is more reasonable to be against theory. But we have alternatives other than those which – going back to analytic metaethics – just consist in analyzing and explicating moral concepts. Moreover, and for her more importantly, we can try instead to reflect on the actual phenomenon of morality, to see what it is, how it is transmitted, and what difference it makes in our lives. We may, as a result of the emerging reflective consciousness of what morality is, think "we can make some improvements in it ..." (ibid., 224). But this, she adds, "will not come from surveying abstract possibilities but from seeing how, given the way it is, it can, by some move we can now make, improve itself, work better, correct its faults" (ibid.). But philosophers should not run off like Don Quixotes' taking the high a priori road, for only "when we think we know what [morality] is, how it is now working, what it is doing will we be in any position to see how it might really change, let alone know if that change would be for the better" (ibid.). In this endeavor, if we are going to get anything with real substance, philosophers, anthropologists sociologists, historians, political economists, sociobiologists, psychologists must work together, "to find out what an actual morality is ..." (ibid.). We must not assume that just by sitting in our studies and taking thought, even careful thought, that we will come to have a good understanding of this. We need, as well, to study history to find out how morality has changed and, making a point also stressed by Diamond and Nussbaum, Baier adds, "we need to read novels to see how it might change again" (ibid.).

Having said all this, things we take to be perfectly unexceptional, she then goes on to say, rightly, but, as we shall see, also perplexingly, that to have any proper confidence that "a really possible change, a takeable step from here, is an improvement," we have to have some sense of the direction it is taking. We need, as she puts it, "some sort of moral compass" to "guide us, not only in our individual actions but in our institutional and educational reforms and innovations" (ibid.). But, after all, 'moral compass' is a metaphor, and it may be no better than another much used metaphor, 'Archimedian point,' and this may be to damn it with faint praise. How do we cash in the metaphor 'moral compass'? A metaphor that can have no literal paraphrase is no metaphor at all. After all, conceptually speaking, it is always in order to ask of a metaphor, or putative metaphor, what it is a metaphor of. Well, in trying to cash our moral compass metaphor in, we may say that we are speaking here of a norm that guides us, that tells us, or suggests to us, what direction we should take: what we should do now along with an explanation of why. But then what kind of norm is it? Is it some principle specifying some end that we should strive to attain? But, assuming it is, how do we, or how can we, come to know that this end is desirable or even reliable, that it is the end, or even an end, that we reflective moral agents should strive to realize? What kind of knowledge or sensible hunches could we have here? Traditional metaethical questions galore come trippingly on the tongue.

Baier, we think, is plainly right, against the whole tradition of rationalist philosophers from Plato to Alan Gewirth, in claiming that such a guide is "not something we are likely to think up in an armchair, but something that will evolve by the testing of generations" (ibid.). But what reason do we have to think anything in the domain of morals or of ethics *evolves* rather than just changes, going from *Sittlichkeit* to *Sittlichkeit*? What criteria do we have here for evolution or development? We can be as Darwinian as we like and still feel stumped here.

It is fair enough to say with a kind of proper caution that the most we philosophers can do is "to see ways of tinkering with existing moral compasses, not ways of inventing them *ex nihilo*" (ibid.). But how are we to ascertain, or how are others, say generations of people, to ascertain when our tinkering has been an improvement: whether we have constructed or discovered a better cluster of norms? It is not exactly like building a better mousetrap. What is testing and 'seeing' here, and what role in this process do novels, dramas, history, and the social sciences play, or do they only show what morality is, how it can change, and in what direction it might change (a not inconsiderable set of achievements), while the philosopher supposedly retains his grand specialist's position of showing how it *should* change? We are confident that Baier, Humean anti-rationalist that she is, would not have such a purist or specialist, philosopher-king conception of philosophy and of how philosophers should proceed; yet, good intentions notwithstanding, these rather traditional problems remain to trouble Baier's conception. We do not say that they cannot be surmounted, and adequately so, but simply that they do not appear to have been or to have been justifiably set aside and that they need somehow to be responded to. This is a pressing matter before we conclude that we actually have with Baier's conception a new departure in moral philosophy from business as usual.

Baier rejects and deplores, as we have noted, what she takes to be the contemporary rationalist trend in moral philosophy, Kantian in spirit, whether utilitarian or pluralistic, deontologist or perfectionist. It is a conception of moral philosophy which does not even see that there still could be such a thing as moral philosophy, if there is no such thing as 'the moral law' or 'moral principles' or 'moral rules.' She tells us that she does not think that such a conception can, its pretensions to the contrary notwithstanding, provide the moral compass we need. Philosophers as diverse as Richard Brandt, Alan Gewirth and David

Gauthier, Baier argues, though in different ways, have theories which in essentials suffer from the rationalism of an essentially Kantian conception of moral theory, a conception which Alan Donagan puts more straightforwardly than they do when he says that "the Theory of Morality is a theory of a system of laws or precepts binding upon rational creatures as such, the content of which is ascertainable by human reason" (ibid., quoted from Donagan 1978, 7). She thinks that this is little more than a Kantian prejudice, for which no justification has been given. We have no reason to believe that morality stands so grounded in rationality. All attempts to establish such grounding have failed, and there have been many, some of them impressive, in the long history of moral philosophy. It is not here where we can reasonably look for a moral compass.

By contrast, Hume, Baier believes, gives us a distinct, distinctive and viable nonrationalist, but not irrationalist, alternative to the prevailing rationalist morality. It has the kind of concreteness previously described, where we start, using history – remember that Hume was also a historian – and the human sciences, and careful everyday observation and reflection on our common life, to see what our actual moralities, including centrally our moral practices, are like and how this *mélange* functions and indeed how mélangeish it actually is. As she sees it, Hume's account is not a normative theory, and it is not a metaethics either, though in passing Hume sometimes makes what some of us would call metaethical remarks. Contrasting Hume's approach to ethics "with the post-Kantian and post-Benthamite moral philosophy that went in for theory construction," Baier remarks that "Hume's way involves no normative theory ..." (ibid., 236). It does, however, involve "a psychological theory ... and it involves a political-economic theory, about the actual workings of human right-determining institutions" (ibid.). The psychological theory gives us an empirically testable account of the human emotions and how they can be self-regulating. His political theory, rooted in his psychological theory and historical research, again is an empirical activity. Working within this empirical framework, Hume gives us a thoroughly empirical account of human nature and, in relation to it, an account of the workings of institutions and of how they affect the lives of people and of how human beings sometimes change these institutions and why.

Baier goes on to remark that given "this factual base, the moral philosopher's special interest will be in the workings of all the reflective sentiments, those sentiments reacting to other sentiments and in particular those that claim to be moral reflections, that is reflections from a steady and general viewpoint" (ibid., 237). This is moral philosophy, to use Hume's own phrase, as *mental geography:* a "descriptive moral and social philosophy, understanding the modes of individual and moral reflection as they actually exist now ..." (ibid.). It is, as we have already said, thoroughly empirical and naturalistic, eschewing transcendental arguments and availing itself neither of "Kantian noumena nor any of those full compliance human utopias favoured by normative theorists" (ibid.). This mental geography does not seek to set out 'the logic of moral discourse' (not trying to do analytic metaethics), but rather seeks, doing an interpretative and descriptive job, to provide an accurate map of the actual moral terrain, but not of the abstract possibilities of what morality might be in various possible worlds. This mental geography must rely on historical studies and the human sciences. But in doing this, this mental geography cannot, like metaethics, old and new, be a purely armchair activity. However, to return to our earlier problem with Baier's account, *a map is not a compass*: It perspicuously displays the terrain, if it is a good map, but it still does not tell us where to go or even predict where we are going. However, if, other than rather blindly, we are going anywhere, we will need it. Still, the cashing in of her moral compass metaphor in a Humean nonrationalist, empirically oriented moral philosophy is a task yet to be accomplished.

What follows might take us part of the way. Philosophy, if carefully cultivated by a reasonable number of people, and by being "gradually diffused ... throughout the whole society," will, Hume has it, "bestow a ... correctness on every act and calling" (ibid.). The fact aside that it is rather utopian to think that anything like this is going to happen, how is it (to raise a conceptual problem) that this interpretative-descriptive map – this mental geography – bestows a *correctness*, tells us not only what we *do* and *why*, but, as well, what we *should* do? How can a description, even a very clear description, provide a moral compass? Hume, so understood, has a moral philosophy that is a mental geography. It gives us, let us suppose, an account of procedures and practices of our common life and, in that sense, *methodizes* it. But, to repeat, how is it, and on what basis is it, in the very doing of this, sometimes as well a way of *correcting* these procedures and practices: a pointing out how they went wrong and of how they should be altered? How does *methodizing* them do this? How do we get moral criticism and assessment from even the most accurate moral description? How, that is, are we to get a critical moral theory out of such descriptive-interpretative theory?

Perhaps we can get a sense of how this can be done by keeping in mind that Hume's mental geography was, centrally a "geography of our powers of reflection and our reflective practices" (ibid., 238). Hume, in his thoroughly nonrationalist way of proceeding, argues that, as Baier put it, "the correction of motives, sentiments, and habits catering to them can be done by sentiment and custom, and is not the prerogative of a purely intellectual 'reason'" (ibid.). We can see well enough how the type moral reflection Hume advocated and practised can be empirically informed, rooted, as it is, in psychological, sociological, and historical knowledge or at least in careful speculation. But how it can be practical (action-guiding), beyond being informed, and critically reflective, is less clear. Perhaps just to be those things is to be action-guiding? And perhaps this is a sufficient response? Baier rightly sees Hume as launching a "bold antirationalist moral philosophy" yielding "a better way of being a moral philosopher, a way avoiding unworldly intellectualism." Moreover, it is to be a moral philosophy "as willing to correct its own methods as to criticize the customs of others" (ibid.). It is, again in Baier's words, "a call for a self-critical nonintellectualist and socially responsible moral philosophy" (ibid.). These are attractive notions, yet it remains unclear what they come to when looked at with a critically skeptical eye. Just how in such an account does careful observation, and arrangement of observations, lead to, or constitute, a *reflectiveness* that becomes *critical*? Reflectiveness, taken by itself, not infrequently is utterly undisciplined and free-spinning, not clearly distinct from dreamily ruminating. Presumably it is the careful observation and arrangement of observation that does the work. But these things can and do go on without reflectiveness and without criticalness. What we are trying to understand is how reflectiveness in such circumstances, or any circumstances, yields criticalness. It seems to be a necessary condition for it, but not a sufficient condition. But perhaps it is a mistake to look for necessary and sufficient conditions here or indeed in any substantive domain?

Moral sentiment, in continuing and in expanding the self-correction of our natural responses to the situations in which we find ourselves, is a *sentiment-correcting sentiment*, a *second-order* reflective sentiment to be sure, but a *sentiment* all the same. It supposedly is not our reason – our intelligence – correcting our sentiments. That is the rationalism that Hume, Baier, and Nussbaum as well want to over-throw, and it is not – or so they have it – just that our sentiments change with a fuller knowledge of the facts. Rather the claim is that our reflec-tive sentiments do the critical corrective work. We are, that is, being guided by our emotions. "Moral attitudes," Baier remarks, "are cor-rections of spontaneous human responses of trust and love, fear and hostility, corrections encouraging some responses, altering others" (ibid., 224). Being "such an inherently responsive thing, a response to natural responses," morality has "inbuilt into it a potential for self-correction" (ibid., 224-5). We have, that is, reflective responses turning on our more spontaneous responses. If we attend seriously to our emotions we will find they guide us, and sometimes reasonably so, in our lives. That they *sometimes* lead us astray, as they led Jacques, Flore, and Roubaud wildly and disastrously astray in Zola's *La Bête Humaine,* is no more reason for not trusting them than it is a reason not to trust our thinking because *sometimes* it leads us down the garden path, as it did Mary Baker Eddy, Berkeley and Schelling. Let us not compound a Cartesian error.

In this way, with such reflective responses to our responses, with due consideration (due reflective response), the sentiment of moral approval and disapproval is supposed to give us a moral compass. Or more exactly, that is what our moral compass consists in: reflective moral approval and disapproval in response to our more spontaneous re-sponses. In this way, reflective moral development is a bootstrapping operation. Again to quote Baier: "Morality is throughout responsive to already given responses, and its norms are reflective versions of natu-ral responses to the risks and opportunities interdependence involves" (ibid., 223). Seeing it in this way is supposed to preserve the critical element in morality – its critical normativeness – that normative theo-rists of the rationalistic tradition wanted to stress. But on Hume's ac-count, it is naturalized and freed of rationalistic residues. A proper moral philosophy should not only be an explainer and explicator of our norms, but be a *criticizer* of our norms and our beliefs about our norms as well, and that essentially so. Criticism is seen naturalistically as a reflective response emerging from morality's "more primitive role as corrector of natural responses" (ibid.). Little Johnny gobbles up all the cookies and little Sue has none. Mom or Dad corrects little Johnny's response by responding with disapproval, telling him 'That's not fair.' They enlarge, or try to enlarge, Johnny's repertoire of concepts with those responses – he now learns something about fairness – and in doing so Mom or Dad express disapproval of his unfairness, though the very norm fairness, on such a Humean account, is itself nothing more than a particular reflective response. (And there, it is reasonable to say, we see revealed an implicit metaethical theory of a noncognitivist sort.) But, the moral skeptic will ask, where is the *correction* there? Johnny may get changed – socialized as they say – one response overpowering another response, stressed as it is by powerful figures upon whom Johnny is totally dependent. But how does this count as a *correction* where that is not just a change as a response to another response? Well, though Mom's or Dad's responses are automatic, a result, as well, of their previous conditioning, somewhere along the line the expressive norm fairness – a response to a response – was, the account has it, a reflective response: a response, we might say, on due consideration and after taking the matter to heart.

However, if 'due consideration' means considering the causes of such a response and the consequences of so responding, we still have an intellectual something: something more than some vague mulling it over, something that Dewey might have called the use of intelligence in morals. But Hume-Baier (and Nussbaum as well) want more, they want *the criticalness to be in the very sentiment itself* and not just in our knowledge of the causes of the sentiment and of the effects on ourselves and others of having it and acting on it. The very sentiment in being reflective supposedly becomes critical. It does not just *goad* us, but it, as well, *guides* our lives. But, like the repressed, our question returns: how does it become critical and what does the distinction between goading and guiding come to here? What are we talking about here? How is it anything more than, or other than, a sentiment that we would approve of after reflection, a sentiment that would not be extinguished on reflection, a sentiment that we would continue to have with full information vividly present to us? Can we reasonably content ourselves with responding that, under such conditions our sentiment would *eo ipso* therefore count as critical? But that seems – though appearances *may* be deceptive here – a bit reductive and unjustifiably so, a bit like stipulating a result. How sentiments *qua* sentiments can be critical remains elusive on the

Hume-Baier account. How Humean interpretative-descriptive naturalism – a naturalism eschewing normative theory or even normative engagement – can become critical remains opaque.

I think here Hume, and Baier, as she follows him, in effect, rely, in a way Nussbaum does not, on a sharp dualism or dichotomy of reason/ sentiment, thought/desire, belief/attitude, thinking/feeling. What should be said instead is that these states are also not sharply separable. That is perhaps most easily seen with belief/attitude if we think back to the debates of the 1950s about 'independent emotive meaning' and whether there can be pure disagreements in attitude not rooted in disagreements in belief. The upshot of these discussions was the recognition that you cannot just have an attitude without having a belief and a belief that is suffused into the very attitude in question (the suffusion being reciprocal). To have an attitude of resignation, for example, is to have a somewhat distinctive range of beliefs – though that is not all it is – and the same is so with the other attitudes. So there is no dichotomy belief/attitude, though there are some beliefs, which are attitude-sparse (propositional attitudes apart) and other beliefs which are attitude-suffused. If a person has a certain sentiment – suppose she feels bitter, angered as she is, over the exploitation of children – that carries with it inevitably a certain range of beliefs. Moreover, they are beliefs which can be reasoned beliefs and can be affected by reasoning. Her sentiment is not a 'flashing thing,' an occurrence within her, like a sensation, say a shooting pain. Sentiments are not like that at all. Rather her sentiment is reason-structured, if not always reason-governed. And, conversely, what we take to be a reason, a rational ground, a rationale, or what we take to be reasonable and the like, is typically sentiment-suffused. We cannot sharply split those faculties (capacities) apart.

The same thing holds for thought and feeling. If a person feels like resigning from some position she holds, this cannot occur without having certain thoughts, and to think that one should vote is not just an intellectual operation, but carries with it certain feelings. Similarly with thought/desire. Someone cannot just desire apple pie or just want to be more conscientious without having certain thoughts, and these matters are not just contingently connected (except in the Quinean sense in which *everything* is contingently connected). These affective states cannot obtain without certain belief states (Nussbaum 1990, 41-3).

So Baier's setting reason and sentiment apart and trying to make reflective sentiments correct other sentiments makes a mystery where there isn't one. Or are we mistakenly foisting that dichotomizing on her where it actually isn't intended? Either way, the vital substantive point is to recognize that our sentiments, both reflective and unreflective, involve, and necessarily so, reason; and, with reflective sentiments, there is a big dose of reasoning. We (sometimes) take to heart what we feel, but such taking to heart involves thinking about it and turning it over; and, duly considering, even more plainly so (Falk 1986, 198-232 and 248-62). We feel strongly about, say, Québec secession, but that, and necessarily so, is both a matter of thought and feeling inextricably mixed. There is no possibility of sorting out the two components. To think that we can is to be held captive to the mythical picture of 'a pure norm.' In reasoning about it – thinking about, if you will – certain feelings get reinforced, altered, diminished, or sometimes even extinguished and with them certain beliefs. And the reasoning itself comes with certain feelings. We have emotion-guided thought and thought-guided emotion. Criticalness comes in this mix. It is not, as rationalist myth would have it, some pure taking thought. There has been too much talk of reason in the history of philosophy.

One can, as the last remark hints at, reject such a dualism while still accepting Baier's Humean critique of rationalism in ethics. Her proper object of critique, as was Hume's, is rationalistic normative ethics: abstract, hierarchically organized, ethical theory, with one or more first principles taken to be synthetic a priori truths, clear to the light of reason, from which, with the aid of 'purely factual' minor premises, all the conclusions of ethics, or at least most of them, could be derived and thereby justified. Such a picture, with its 'tyranny of principles' and deductive model of justification (as distinct from reflective equilibrium), as Baier well argues and as many others have as well, is deeply mistaken for a variety of reasons. But it should also be noted that such a rationalism is not an important contender among normative theories today. John Rawls's, Brian Barry's, G.A. Cohen's, Norman Daniels's, Thomas Nagel's, Thomas Scanlon's, Stuart Hampshire's, Richard Miller's or Peter Railton's accounts, different as they are, are not such rationalisms. They make none of the rationalistic assumptions mentioned above, assumptions that, Baier rightly argues, are out to lunch.

Baier has also failed to show how her appropriation of ethical theory as a Humean mental geography yields a new way of proceeding in moral philosophy, setting itself in contrast with the main currents of what is now being done. Hers is admittedly not a systematic, or for that matter an unsystematic, normative ethical theory, and it is plainly not an analytical metaethics of the Golden Age (as in the work of A.J. Ayer, Paul Edwards, P.H. Nowell-Smith, and the early R.M. Hare) which limited itself to the analysis or elucidation of moral concepts and to an examination of 'the logic of moral discourse.' But it is metaethical in the sense in which the work of Peter Railton, Allan Gibbard, Simon Blackburn and Richard Miller is metaethical, where to do metaethics is neither to try to proceed a priori, nor to limit oneself to an analysis of language, but to proceed instead empirically, utilizing elements of the relevant sciences, and not to claim normative neutrality. The difference between Baier's conception of how to proceed in moral philosophy and the conceptions of how to proceed utilized by Peter Railton, David Copp and Nicholas Sturgeon is not fundamental. They all proceed holistically, do not utilize in any pervasive way a deductive model of justification, seek to adumbrate a critical moral stance as something that emerges from their empirically oriented metaethics, or, as Railton prefers to call it, funding theory. The differences between them – differences in detail aside – are differences of *scope* and in the level of abstraction deemed to be suitable, on the one hand, and in the sciences they take as most relevant to moral theorizing, on the other. Semantic theory, decision theory, cognitive science, Darwinian theory, and rational-choice theory are important for ethical naturalists such as Railton and Copp, and as well for noncognitivists such as Gibbard and Blackburn, while Baier takes such concrete, nitty-gritty studies as anthropology, history, and political economy to be more useful and more enlightening for moral philosophy than decision theory, cognitive science, or evolutionary theory. But these are disputes, vitally important as they are, within metaethics (funding theory) and not deep disputes about radically different conceptions of what moral philosophy should be. Baier, her self-understanding to the contrary notwithstanding, is actually doing metaethics in the sense of the new metaethics, and so arguably was, at least sometimes, Hume, though in a less abstract way than Gibbard or Railton. Indeed the two somewhat different ways, it is not unreasonable to believe, or at least hope, complement each other. Baier's Humean way ties moral philosophy more clearly to our common life, while an account like Railton's or Gibbard's concentrates on more abstract matters. *Perhaps* their way yeilds a better understanding of criticalness and normativity than Baier's. At least these were places where Baier's account seemed at least not to be very satisfactory. Here we can rightly say, without succumbing to eclecticism, let many flowers bloom. Which flowers turn out to be the more frost-resistant may shake itself out with continued, sustained, careful and non-*parti pris* writing and discussion.

IV

We want now to characterize and consider the views of Martha C. Nussbaum on how moral philosophy and ethical theory are to be conceived of and practised, including her views on what we call, rather pedantically, ethical methodology. They are views which are becoming influential and which stand in both stark and interesting contrast to the dominant views in contemporary ethical theory, including the views represented in this volume. But there is a fresh wind ablowing and views like Nussbaum's may in the next decade become the dominant views. Moreover, if we go back a bit in time, we will see that she has very distinguished ancestors. Looked at from the perspective of the long view of history, metaethics (particularly analytical metaethics) is the maverick position. Nussbaum's return in moral theory to a kind of naturalized Aristotelianism in method, aim and structure, without the obscure blather of a Leo Strauss or Alan Bloom, and extensively sensitive to the latest developments in analytical philosophy, affords a new window on the world of moral philosophy. It is imperative that we consider it in relation to the development of metaethical theory and to the larger question of how we should conceive of and pursue moral philosophy.

Nussbaum's views in certain respects are similar to Baier's, but, unlike Baier's, they could never be mistaken for attacks on theory in ethics (as Gibbard and Scanlon mistook Baier's account to be; Gibbard 1995 and Scanlon 1995a). But, as we shall see, they also are in certain important respects, particularly with what we are centrally concerned with here, different than Baier's.

Nussbaum's views, like Baier's, are rich and subtle, informed not only by analytical philosophy but also by a close study of the classical authors. Moreover, her central working repertoire is not only Plato and Aristotle, the Hellenistic philosophers, the Greek tragedians and historians, but also the novel which she does not take (as it is often taken by moral philosophers) either as a casebook for ethical theory or as a kind of adornment to moral theory, but as central and distinctive to our moral understanding and (more surprisingly) to the working out of an adequate ethical theory. (On this see Diamond 1991, 367-81.)

Her conception of moral philosophy and its import and her working out of an ethical theory stand at a polar opposite to analytical metaethics as it was done in its heyday (say in the work of A.J. Ayer, Charles Stevenson, Paul Edwards, and R.M. Hare). She breaks, and not unintentionally, the restrictions they sought to impose. Indeed, most of what she does *for them* would not even count as philosophy. But how she conceives of her subject and how she proceeds will resonate with many philosophers and other reflective persons, though for some, including us, that resonating will be ambivalent. Her conception of the aim of moral philosophy speaks to what deep down, well below methodological hang-ups, many of us would wish to do, if we thought it could be done. It is something that brought many of us to the subject in the first place. Is it, we ask genuinely skeptically, merely a residual positivist prejudice to have reservations about the very idea of it? Be that as it may, it should be quite clear that to go Nussbaum's way involves breaking with the metaethical tradition both old and new.

However, we must first say what Nussbaum's way is. "Philosophical inquiry in ethics," Nussbaum remarks, is to be seen "as ways of pursing a single and general question: how human beings should live" (Nussbaum 1990, 15). We want to know what is a human life and how we should live it, if we are to flourish and be fully human (ibid., *'fully* human' here plainly functions normatively). And here, *pace* Richard Rorty, we do not regard 'a human life' *merely* as a biological category. The study of ethical matters classically has been and, Nussbaum believes, should continue to be, "practical and not *just* a theoretical enterprise" (ibid., 16 italics ours). This, of course, is not how the logical positivists saw it or linguistic philosophers or nonnaturalists such as Moore, Pritchard, and Ross. But this is how classically moral philosophy was understood.[5] "From Socrates and Plato," Nussbaum remarks, "straight through to the Hellenistic schools there was deep agreement that the point of philosophical inquiry and discourse in the area of ethics was to improve, in some manner, the pupil's soul, to move the pupil closer to the leading of the good life" (ibid.). Improving 'his soul,' or 'our souls,' presumably comes to making us better or more adequate persons, persons of greater sensitivity, reflectivity, decency, fairness, understanding, having more nuanced passions, having a better sense of life and, as well, to enable us to act with greater integrity, intelligence, and with fine attunement. Such a *practice-oriented* conception of moral philosophy requires, of course, a "good deal of reflection and understanding." This being so, producing understanding is an important part of moral philosophy. Still its underlying *aim* is not understanding but *practice*: to enable us, in our inescapable interdependence with others, to live better lives. It was to come to recognize truth in and concerning ethics and with that coming to have an enhanced sense of life, as she puts it, and with this enhanced sense of life to live more adequately. Moral philosophy must be such that it helps us to become the kind of people who could recognize truths about the good life and

---

5 However, one of the Golden Age metaethicists, P.H. Nowell-Smith, writing (1954) when analytic metaethics was the fashion, saw it exactly that way. Here, among analytic philosophers of his time, he stands alone. He thought in doing *metaethics* he should practice normatively neutral conceptual analysis. There he went with what at the time was the fashion in analytical circles. But he did not identify moral philosophy with metaethics and he thought that moral philosophers should do moral philosophy in much the terms Nussbaum describes, but he also left room, though as parasitic on moral philosophy as traditionally conceived, for the *second-order* task of conceptual clarification that just was, in his view, metaethics. It is what later came to be called analytic metaethics. And it is what he did, and impressively so, in his book, while all the while (and quite consistently) defending the idea that the goal of moral philosophy was *practice*. But metaethics, if properly done, was strictly *meta*. But unlike Ayer, for example, he did not see that to be *the* task, let alone the *sole* task, of a moral philosopher. *Au contraire*, for Nowell-Smith, "moral philosophy is a practical science; its aim is to answer questions in the form "What shall I do? ..."" (P.H. Nowell-Smith 1954, 319. See also 11-47.) For commentary, broadly in sympathy with, and explicatory of, Nowell-Smith here, see Nielsen 1967, 117-19 and Diamond 1991, 367-76.

to act in accordance with them. Moral philosophy tries to ascertain, Nussbaum has it, the most important truths of a really human life.

Having, though perhaps only through a glass darkly, seen something of this – something that always will be revisable – we should go on "to construct discourses whose form would suit the ethical task, enlivening those elements in our ethical sensibilities that seem to be the best sources of progress" and forming in us "desires in accordance with a correct conception of what matters, confronting them with an accurate picture of what has importance" (ibid., 16). The goal of moral philosophy is the good human life and not just to understand what 'good' means or what 'the good human life' means or what kind of ethical theory would utilize such conceptions. These matters are, of course, important too, but their *primary* value is instrumental to the living of a good human life.

To this, not unsurprisingly, analytical metaethicists, and not only them, will respond that to so characterize what moral philosophy is is to give it a task it cannot meet and, as well, to beg a lot of central questions about ethics or morality and about what philosophy can achieve. Nussbaum's account, they will argue, could not be *the proper starting point* in moral philosophy, for only if certain questions she begs have certain sorts of answers could anything like what she urges be achieved or even approximated. Conceiving of things as she does, just takes sides in the dispute between cognitivism and noncognitivism and, moreover, takes sides without ever either even entering into the argument or conceptually dissolving that dispute by showing that it rests on conceptual confusion. It just assumes moral utterances can be either true or false and *in some more than minimalist way*. It just assumes that we have some way of ascertaining which ones are known to be true, or at least have some reasonable warrant for some of them, such that we can justifiably accept them and guide our lives in accordance with them. It just begs the question by ignoring the alternatives that Edward Westermarck, Axel Hägerström, J.L. Mackie, and Simon Blackburn argue for, namely that there is such massive and pervasive error in our ethical thought that we cannot reasonably believe that any of our moral beliefs are justified. It just begs the question over the force, or indeed over even the existence, of the kind of metaethical attacks on the very institution of morals with its associated practices that Allen Wood ascribes to Marx and Nietzsche and that could plausibly be ascribed to

Michel Foucault and Jean Baudrillard as well. Moreover, even if (*pace* error theorists) we think that judgments about what is 'good' and 'bad' or 'right' and 'wrong' are sometimes in place, we may still doubt that the vaguer and more portentous notion of 'the good human life' is in place or that we have some reasonably firm sense of what we are talking about when we speak of such a thing or when we speak of 'good ethical development' or of 'general human flourishing.' It is not evident that it is unreasonable to doubt that any sound sense can be made of these notions. Having such doubts is not mere analytical fastidiousness, the nit-picking to which some analytical philosophers are addicted. Perhaps such Nussbaumian phrases lack any firm descriptive content and primarily function emotively, relying on implicit and unrecognized arbitrary *persuasive* definitions?

Nussbaum simply assumes that philosophy – the reflective activity that it is – could, and should so proceed. It should, that is, try to answer such desperately obscure questions. She simply assumes that we can come to have some non-ideological and coherent consensus concerning such matters. She assumes that there is some reasonable prospect of a non-ideological and coherent, and, if coherent, beyond that knowledgeable, consensus concerning what really matters in the good life for human beings or even a consensus over what it would be like to even gain 'an accurate picture of what has importance' in such domains. Not only postmodernists think that we have no coherent idea of what 'an accurate picture of the good life for human beings' could be. It isn't just that, in our diverse and pluralistic cultures, people, if they give 'answers' to such matters at all, often give different answers, but that neither we philosophers nor anyone else has a grip on what it would be like to answer such questions correctly. We do not know – it is possible reasonably to believe – exactly, or, worse still, even inexactly, what we are talking about or asking for here. We do not understand under what circumstances we would have come to have a correct conception of what really matters in the good life for human beings. It is not indifference to morals or even cynicism that triggers such reactions, but bafflement about what is going on and about what it would be like to find our sea legs here. Nussbaum just conceives of moral philosophy in such a way that, in the very doing of moral philosophy, we must just accept a cognitivist position in metaethics and indeed a strong form of cognitivism at that. Only if we *assume* that Gibbard,

Mackie, Harman, and Blackburn are fundamentally in error and *assume* that the right way to construe metaethical matters is either, on the one hand, some more Aristotelian version of a Railton-Miller-Sturgeon-Copp-type naturalistic cognitivism or, on the other, some rather Aristotelian nonnaturalist cognitivism, can we be justified in accepting Nussbaum's conception of moral philosophy and ethical theory. And even that would only be a necessary condition, for, remember, her cognitivism is also *practice-oriented*. We need a theory that not only informs the mind but as well galvanizes us differently so that we will become better persons and all from some 'philosophically justified vantage point.' But that is a very perplexing notion indeed. It is not at all unreasonable – or is this to be held captive to what are in effect positivist dogmas? – to be skeptical about that and to think Nussbaum is trying to give philosophy a task that it cannot coherently meet. In all these matters, Nussbaum just begs central issues concerning the new metaethics and concerning philosophy more generally, about which, as Cora Diamond put it, there is no consensus. Moreover, these issues were central during the Golden Age as well and have echoes in moral philosophy going at least back to the emergence of the Enlightenment. If we wish to be reasonable, we will not set things up such that philosophers in the skeptical tradition cannot even be doing moral philosophy, such that such reflections, however mistaken they *may* be, are not even a bit of moral philosophy.

Yet it is possible to feel – perhaps ambivalently feel – that such criticisms, natural and reasonable as they are, are still somehow blinkered or at least without the kind of charity that would aid perceptiveness about morality and about what we would reflectively want moral philosophy to do. Nussbaum's conception of the moral philosopher's task, vague and question-begging as it is, remains attractive. When we think – concretely and non-evasively think – about our own moral lives, the conflicts within ourselves, our interpersonal conflicts and tensions, as well as our aspirations for lives together, Nussbaum's conception strikes home. It also does so when we think of the deep and pervasive socio-economic and political problems in our societies and in our world seen globally. We very much, faced as we are with such matters, want moral philosophy to be something like what Nussbaum describes. We would like to know, if there is such a thing, what the good life for a human being is, what human flourishing is, what a truly human life would be like and the like. We would like to know, if such an understanding can be had, how we should live. Perhaps the existentialist's and prescriptivist's stark response that in the end you must just decide is all that can coherently be said. But we would have to have very compelling reasons to accept such a bleak picture. Moreover, the argument in our Introduction should be recalled here concerning the intelligibility of talking about 'in the end' or 'in the final analysis.' Such skepticism may be generated by an incoherent philosophical picture. Such skepticism, common as it is, may in reality be unmotivated.

We would very much like, as Nussbaum puts it, "an account of ethical inquiry that will capture what we actually do when we ask ourselves the most pressing ethical questions" (ibid., 24). We would like *that* even when we suspect (even strongly suspect) – heirs of a skeptical tradition that we are – that there can be no such inquiry, that these notions, e.g., 'the good life for humans,' are *short on sense*. Yet, after all, we do not know – skepticism about skepticism purring again – that they actually are so short on sense that we can make nothing of them. Moreover, these 'big questions' are close to our hearts. Only positivist or ordinary-language-philosophy self-deceptiveness can obscure this from us, can make us turn away from such questions with Carnapian scorn or Austinian irony. Moral philosophers who are philosophical foxes are likely also, and, of course, ambivalently, to have something of the hedgehog buried in their hearts. We would very much like to know if there is some reasonable form of inquiry into such hedgehogish questions, or (less intellectualistically) some kind of honest, nonevasive way to get a grip on such questions. We want to continue to ask, and to try coherently to answer, the question: 'How should we, as a society, as a global community, as individuals, live?' Traditionally moral philosophers, novelists, dramatists, religious thinkers, historians, even sometimes social scientists (Weberian scruples notwithstanding) have tried, as many plain people have tried, to answer, or at last get a grip on, these questions. There are books, engaged in this project, or linked with it, including skeptical ones, that we want to study attentively. We, as Nussbaum well put it, read for life. And, though with fear and trembling, if we are at all sensitive, we want to make such deliberations ourselves. Reading for life, we also, with that as a part integrated into the very web of who we are, want to think with integrity for ourselves, trying to get some grip on these questions, though with a sense of

Weber's warring gods in the background to keep us from sliding into Straussian obscurantism. Before we would abandon such a quest the arguments would have to be very strong and very conclusive indeed for abandoning all such deliberations as being in irremediable error: our gibbering together over questions which turn out to be incoherent questions, questions, their emotive wallop aside, that in reality are pseudo-questions. The skeptical argument would have to be sufficiently strong such that we would have conclusive, or close to conclusive, reasons for believing that no coherent positive answers to such questions are possible and that all we can intelligibly say is that they are so short on sense that nothing can be made of them. But (*pace* positivists, Max Weber and some ordinary language philosophers) such a case has not been made out. So in this way Nussbaum's attractive project stands.

However, it is also true that at least three other projects for how to proceed in doing moral philosophy so stand as well. (1) Can we (*sans* foundationalism) articulate an ethical naturalism as a funding theory (a metaethics), such as, say Peter Railton's or Richard Miller's, which might provide a more scientific support than we find in Nussbaum for doing things roughly in the way Nussbaum urges? Or is this *scientism* raising its ugly head again? (2) Can we and, if we can, should we, keeping its essential spirit, redescribe (partially reconceptualize) Nussbaum's project so that it is compatible with, without loosing any of its force, a sophisticated noncognitivism such as Gibbard's or Blackburn's? It is not clear to us that this could not be done or that the doing of it would be pointless or in any other way unhappy. *If* noncognitivism is indeed, as not a few believe, the best metaethics going, so combining it with Nussbaum's theory, if it could be done, would only strengthen her account. After all, their enterprise is resolutely *second-order*, while hers is, for the most part, directly normative and *first-order*. (1) and (2) – most particularly (1) – can generate a third project: (3) Jettison – this third project's central claim goes – all such metaethical or funding theories, 'theories hardly conducive to salvation,' and just engage directly in ethical inquiry (moral philosophy in a broad sense) as an inquiry into trying, quite directly, to ascertain how a human being should live or what the, or at least a, good life for human beings is. Don't worry about, or concern yourselves with, the assumptions with which we earlier said we should concern ourselves! (We refer here to the assumptions we noted that Nussbaum makes, at least seemingly unconsciously.) Just make, brusquely brushing these issues aside, an investigation which is both theoretical and practical: *with the underlying point of it being essentially practical*. We want to know what the good is so that we can live well. We know, this third project proposes, that we beg certain metaethical or funding questions in so proceeding. So we beg them then in order to get at, without endless, probably irresolvable, prolegomena, what we human beings really want to know, if we can, in our attempts to make sense of our lives and to find the best way to live together. We may – nay, no doubt will – repeatedly fail. And we will never get anything more than partial and incomplete answers, always in some ways unsatisfactory. Still, that is not nothing. We should not set ourselves on the quest for certainty and finality. Moreover, in this resolute fallibilism, we *may*, after all, not be so far from Nussbaum, for nothing that Nussbaum says or suggests should lead us to believe that she is on such a quest. She is not a *traditional* Aristotelian and certainly not a Thomistic-Aristotelian (Nussbaum 1992, 9-11).

Perhaps, however, things may even be worse than they are sketched above. Some form of *strong* noncognitivism may be true and, if that is so, then even the above modest project, i.e., (3), cannot, or so it would seem, succeed. But we cannot justifiably claim that the historical record establishes, or even makes probable, that pessimistic conclusion – recall Hampton on Mackie on disagreement in ethics. Gradualistic progress is compatible in ethics, as it is in science, with persistent disagreement: disagreement which is never total (indeed, we do not even understand what it would be like for it to be total) and, if Charles Peirce and Donald Davidson are near to the mark, must always presuppose a massive unproblematic background agreement.

We do not know whether we can in moral philosophy successfully do the sort of thing that Nussbaum both describes and tries to practice. But we do not know that we cannot, either. Fallibilism is inescapable. But something like the Nussbaum thing is something we want, and humanly and reasonably so, so why not, as so many of our ancestors have, continue such a quest? Perhaps we are knocking our heads against a brick wall, but then again perhaps we are not. We only need despair if we take ourselves, in making such an inquiry, to be on the quest for certainty. But we, by now, having *at most* something of a wistful nostalgia for the Absolute, have – or should have – been cured of the urge to go on such questing, having firmly learned the lessons of the fallibilism that is common to, and uncontroversially so, both modernity and postmodernity.

This third project is a pragmatic (in a broad sense) and practical way of defending giving a central place to Nussbaum's project for moral philosophy, though not exactly on her terms. There is, as well, and compatible with the above pragmatic approach, a more 'theoretical' Wittgensteinian defense of the core of Nussbaum's project that might find favor with Cora Diamond. However, Nussbaum might not, at least on first consideration, go for it, for it runs against her defense of a sturdy metaphysics (something she shares with Hampton), her refusal to join Williams and Rorty "in dismissive assaults on systematic ethical theory" and her conception of philosophy as "just the pursuit of truth" (Nussbaum 1990, 27, 29; and Nussbaum 1994b, 59-63). But if a Wittgensteinian conception of philosophy is on the mark, these metaethical disputes, as well as foundational claims in normative ethics, will be seen as houses of cards and not as articulations of accounts which need to be decided on – the correct or most plausible account established – before we are justified in doing Nussbaum's broadly, and naturalistically, Aristotelian thing. Nussbaum, that is, could adopt a Wittgensteinian metaphilosophy to chase away the wolves bent on attacking her modestly Aristotelian conception of moral philosophy without giving up anything in her practical philosophy except perhaps some high-soaring metaphors. Her Aristotelianism, after all, is deeply demythologized.

However, what is involved here needs some spelling out. Paul Horwich has put Wittgenstein's therapeutic conception of philosophy (metaphilosophy, if you will, though that is not the way Wittgenstein himself would talk) succinctly and accurately. Horwich remarks:

> I take the heart of Wittgenstein's philosophy to be his idea that philosophical questions derive from confusion rather than ignorance, that this confusion typically comes from being mislead by superficial aspects of language, that the questions cannot be answered but must be dissolved by exposing the mistakes on which they are based, and that the result will be no new knowledge but merely the absence of confusion. This view ought to be regarded, it seems to me, as an empirical generalization, justifiable to the extent that philosophical problems turn out to be susceptible to Wittgenstein's analysis. Nothing about meaning is presupposed. In particular it need not be assumed that philosophical questions and answers are all meaningless (though some may be). Their defect is rather that, engendered in confusion, mismotivated and uncalled-for, one has no reason to take them seriously (Horwich 1993, 155-6).

Wittgenstein said very little about ethics, though it has been said by some that his underlying intent was ethical or ethico-religious. But we can set that contestable claim aside and focus instead on Horwich's characterization. Stanley Cavell, James Conant and Hilary Putnam would argue that Horwich's Wittgenstein is too positivist. We think *au contraire* that such a reading of Wittgenstein makes the best and least obscurantist sense of what he was up to. But, too positivist or not, we will, for the point we wish to make here, let Horwich's characterization stand. After all, if we accepted the Cavell-Conant-Putnam claim, all that would be set aside concerning Horwich's remarks about Wittgenstein's view on what philosophical problems are like is Horwich's claim that it should be taken to have the status of an empirical generalization, and nothing in that would touch our appropriation of Horwich's understanding of Wittgenstein's metaphilosophy. What, that is, he says about philosophical questions deriving from confusions and being up for dissolution could stand. Only the claim that that claim is itself an empirical generalization would be dropped.

Taking, then, Horwich's understanding of Wittgenstein as it stands, we should note that Wittgenstein's principal cases on which he practised his conceptual therapy were on philosophical discussions of language, mind, mathematics, and knowledge. But the metaethical discussions going on in this volume and elsewhere, and in most traditional normative ethical theory as well, also raise typically philosophical (here conceptual) problems, problems – really confusions, if Wittgenstein is right – that arguably seem at least to be up for Wittgensteinian therapeutic dissolution. Take, for example, the issues which often divide noncognitivists and cognitivists: internalism/externalism, whether moral utterances are truth-apt, whether there is an is/ought divide, whether moral utterances are essentially expressive, whether descriptive meaning or emotive meaning is primary, the relation between thick and thin concepts, whether the descriptive and expressive elements of moral talk can be isolated, whether there are any 'pure norms' or 'pure normative components' which are just expressive-evocative, whether there is, or even can be, moral knowledge, whether, if there is, it is just a *knowing how* rather than sometimes, as well, a *knowing that*. These matters *may* very well be up for Wittgensteinian dissolution as resting on confusions rather than on ignorance and thus, if that is so, they are not things that need to be investigated. They are not objects of legitimate inquiry but puzzles to be dissolved. Entanglement with these problems may derive from confusions, confusions where our language has led us astray, where we are, that is, dominated by a mistaken, and, in some instances, even a delusive, picture of our language, a picture which obsesses us when we try to do philosophy and, in turn, continues to drive us to do philosophy. We neither say that Wittgenstein says that *all* pictures of language must be mistaken – after all he sometimes speaks of perspicuous representations – nor, Wittgenstein aside, that that is in fact so. Here we side with Putnam and Conant (Putnam 1994). But what is needed in circumstances where we are dominated by such a 'false picture' is not inquiry or investigation, but conceptual therapy (the providing of a sufficiently clear description of the troubling stretch of our language so as to free us from the obsessional hold a certain picture of our language has on us).

However, if this Wittgensteinian therapy applies to these metaethical 'theses,' why not just as much to Nussbaum's philosophical conceptions? How can this help Nussbaum rather than take her from the frying pan into the fire? Why would not this therapy apply just as well to Nussbaum's own pet philosophical conceptions: her conception of moral philosophy and her conception of philosophy *simpliciter*? Whether talk of the good for human beings, a truly human life, or talk of philosophy, as she does, as "just the pursuit of truth" have much sense beyond their visceral emotive appeal is not at all clear. As attractive as such notions may be to us, as attached as we may become to them, they may still be short on sense. Suppose close analysis of the truth predicate takes us, *via* Tarskian disquotationalism, to a deflationary conception of truth. Are we then going to, in cold sobriety, think that truth is the aim or end or goal of inquiry or of moral reflection? (Rorty 1995, 281-300). We would, if deflationism or even minimalism is so, have to do some fancy footworking demythologization of her talk of philosophy as the search for truth, and it is possible to think that similar things might obtain for talk of the good life or for any *general* account of what it is to live well. Yet, *à la* Wittgenstein, questions about these very questions about Nussbaum's notions can be turned back on themselves seemingly endlessly. Still, whatever way we go, it leaves us with wheels spinning in the mud. It leaves us both with wanting to ask certain questions, to carry out certain pursuits, *and* with the feeling that such questions and such pursuits may, after all, rest on confusions which need to be dispelled. So perhaps the way to go is the way Rorty, Williams, and Foucault go, and to jettison, while retaining moral and political seriousness, ethical *theorizing*: Nussbaum's naturalized Aristotelianism, Baier's Humeanism, as well as the grand tradition of systematic normative ethics and metaethical theory. Nussbaum would surely not wish to go this way, but, going this way, would continue to allow close attention, as we see in the work of Foucault, to the particularity and to the concrete detail of the moral life that she finds in novels and that can be found, as well, in historical interpretative description, anthropological description, good journalism and the like, unencumbered by philosophical theories often rooted in metaphysical conceptions that defy critical inspection. It is possible that to be serious about morality, politics and our lives, is to be *unserious* about ethical theories, metaethical or otherwise. This is anti-theory *theory* all the way down.

We are neither giving to understand that we endorse nor that we reject such anti-theory. Our Afterword is not very much in either the endorsing or rejecting business, as if that was a task of philosophy, but seeks instead to raise issues, seeks to locate tensions and to set out possibilities – sometimes neglected possibilities – for ethical theory, including anti-theory theory and for reflection *sans* theory about morality. It tries to depict some of the salient possibilities of how, with or without theory, to go, in thinking about ethics with honesty, integrity, and to some point, in trying to decide how we should live our lives. However, endorsement aside, we do not try for the impossible, namely, ethical neutrality or neutrality about how to do moral philosophy. We depict possibilities, but in doing so, we, not infrequently, make judgment calls about what is the most plausible and reasonable thing to believe or to argue for. We express views, as everyone else does who is not utterly bland, about what we think are the more plausible conceptions, while providing dissenting views with the strongest voice we can muster for them. In other words, we engage in dialectic. We engage, that is, in the unending task of this engagement – this attempt at honest reflection – that is also wide ranging, trying to cover, never very successfully, all the plausible bases. In doing this, at least one of us is *sometimes* strongly inclined to think that a thoughtful anti-theory theory response *may* be the best response in the unending task of trying to be truthful, clear-visioned, and serious in thinking about morality – in thinking about how to live in our inescapably, and not at all to be regretted, interdependency, and in thinking relatedly about how our societies should be shaped (Nielsen 1991 and Nielsen 1995). But again it may not. Perhaps philosophy need not be so chastened and *perhaps* a Wittgensteinian therapeutic approach may not be as applicable to Nussbaum's approach or to Baier's as it at least seems to be to grand normative ethical theories and metaethical theories. Nussbaum's and Baier's accounts are less plainly *conceptual*, than traditional accounts, either metaethical or normative ethical. Instead, they are broadly speaking empirical-cum-normative, putting the *ethical* back into ethical theory, something so many philosophers have failed to do, even in the doing of normative ethical theory.

We will illustrate our point about 'being less conceptual.' A metaethicist might say 'Moral utterances can neither be true nor false in any substantial sense.' That is a plainly *second-order*, and plainly a conceptual, remark, very possibly ripe for Wittgensteinian treatment. By contrast Nussbaum would have us as moral philosophers "search for ways of living together in a community, country, or planet" (Nussbaum 1990, 24). This is surely no easy thing. Part of what is said here is no doubt baffling and no doubt many of the things said have conceptual outcroppings. But the bafflement here is at least characteristically unlike the plainly conceptual perplexities Wittgenstein was so obsessed to free us from. Moreover, Nussbaum's searching for ways to live together, as daunting and demanding as it is, does not appear to reflect conceptual perplexity or at least not principally so. And, even to the extent that it is a conceptual perplexity, it does not appear to be, or at least not primarily, something deriving from confusion rather than from ignorance or a lack of deep and persistent sympathetic reflection. Nussbaum's search, vague as our and her understanding of it is, is still a *first-order* ethical-cum-empirical matter, not a conceptual puzzle, like whether there could be a private language or whether we could ever really know the mind of another or whether self-deception is possible. There are important differences between Nussbaum's question and these plainly conceptual puzzles. For these conceptual puzzles, we know that the answer that is blindingly obvious (e.g., 'Of course, self-deception is possible for people deceive themselves over and over again.') is not what is at issue. And it is also the case that we are not infrequently lost as to what is at issue. For Nussbaum's question, it does not seem amiss to try to answer it or at least to try to get some reasonable and reflective grip on it.

It is not like a puzzle up for dissolution. To be gripped by Nussbaum's question does not seem to place us in anything very like the situation of Wittgenstein's philosophers caught up in their obsessions which they may not even recognize to be conceptual. They are obsessionally in the grip of a false picture of how language works. But that seems at least to ring false for people trying to gain some purchase on Nussbaum's question. The self-deception puzzle, by contrast, is very much like the Achilles-and-the-tortoise puzzle. We know that self-deception is common, but when we think about self-deception we do not see how it could even be *possible*. Other-deception yes, but self-deception no! But Nussbaum's question does not look like that at all – though appearances here *may* be deceiving. It does not appear to be one of those conceptual puzzles up for Wittgensteinian dissolution. Perhaps appearances are misleading here, but certainly not plainly so.

There is – to shift gears again – a sense of both urgency and exuberance in Nussbaum's writing, and perhaps neither are misplaced. There is, in all kinds of complicated ways, and often, as well, in rather straightforward ways, much that is amiss in our lives and in our societies, and with some of these ways of being amiss we have the sense that time is running out on us. They, of course, are typically not ills that just getting a better grip on the sense of the question 'How are we to live?' will resolve or even do much to push forward toward a resolution. But they also typically are *in part* ethical, and perhaps really honest and thoughtful ethical investigations will help in their resolution, particularly when the people doing the investigating are factually well informed as well. Suppose, for example, we believe that our societies should be transformed into more egalitarian societies than the ones we are in. But, if this is what we believe, we must, if we are really in earnest, develop a reasonably feasible picture of how we might go from where we are now to a more egalitarian state of affairs. We must be able to give at least a rough sketch of some plausibly possible routes. Moral reflection here is not enough. But, that notwithstanding, both moral reflection *and* conceptual clarity are also vital. (We hope by now it is clear that they do not come to the same thing.) There has been in our world an extensive jolting-up of our thinking and feeling (of our very ethical *sensibilities*). Postmodernism isn't all bad, though there is *déjà vu* here. After all, this demystifying and resistance to re-enchantment has been going on since the beginning of the Enlightenment.

As a result of this jolting, we are faced with a bewildering array of options personal, and, on a national and global scale, political and socio-economic, and there is an imperative need in all sorts of contexts to answer Lenin's question 'What is to be done?' Hence the sense of urgency. But Nussbaum also has a sense of exuberance, in the face of all that, that many may not share. She tells us that "this is a rich and wonderful time in moral philosophy," unlike in the bad old dull days of analytical metaethics. Even by the time she was a graduate student at Harvard in 1969, these bad old days, she tells us, were becoming a thing of the past. She remarks "By this time, the positivist-metaethical movement in ethics that had for a long time discouraged the philosophical study of substantive ethical theories and practical ethical issues, confining ethics to the analysis of ethical language, was dying" (Nussebaum 1990, 13 and 169).

Nussbaum's exuberance needs to be counterbalanced by Diamond's skepticism, their partially shared outlook notwithstanding. Recall Diamond's remark, previously quoted by us, from her "Having a Rough Story about What Moral Philosophy Is," that

> No one knows what the subject [of moral philosophy] is; most widely agreed on accounts of it depend on suppositions that are not obvious and that reflect particular evaluations and views of the world, of human nature, and of what it is to speak, think, write or read about the world. The more inclusive an account is, the more likely it will include what many philosophers would not dream of counting as part of their subject. (Diamond 1991, 380)

Still, exuberance aside, it is perhaps not unreasonable to hope that something like the way Nussbaum recommends that we proceed could fruitfully be carried on, largely displacing anti-theory, traditional normative ethics and metaethical theory. Isn't this the way we should go in doing moral philosophy?

Let us run with this a little more. Nussbaum takes her starting point and procedure to be essentially that of Aristotle, whose procedure and starting point should be clearly distinguished, as she stresses, from his "own ethical conception which is just one of the conceptions it [his procedure] considers" (Nussbaum 1990, 25). This procedure or method is also a procedure or method followed by philosophers as different as Sidgwick, Hegel, and Rawls (ibid.). The method is dialectical and comparative. But we start, before we get on the dialectical see-saw, with "a very broad and inclusive question: How should a human being live?" (ibid.).

This question presupposes no creeping Kantianism, that is, no specific demarcation of moral and non-moral domains, but includes initially, a very wide conception of how we might live and what our distinctive goods are. Moreover, "his inquiry is both empirical and practical: empirical, in that it is concerned with, takes its 'evidence' from, the experience of life; practical, in that it aims to find a conception by which human beings can live, and live together" (ibid.). As is Sidgwick's and Rawls's as well, Aristotle's procedure, a procedure that Nussbaum adopts as her own, is *comparative*. It requires "a deep and sympathetic investigation of all the major ethical alternatives and the comparison of each with our active sense of life" (ibid., 27). We set out – attempt perspicuously to display – the different moral theories, Aristotle's own, religious ethical theories, perfectionist theories, Kantian theories, utilitarian theories, pluralistic deontological theories, and anti-theory theories. Each theory is worked through – both sympathetically and critically – held before our gaze in the clearest light we can muster, and compared with the other theories and also against our beliefs and feelings, our active sense of life (ibid., 26). Consistency, coherence, clarity of articulation are, of course, also sought. But that is not all. Perceptiveness, a vivid sense of life, a fine attunement, are sought as well.

What is looked for is what will provide "the best overall fit between a view and what is deepest in human lives" (ibid.). What is sought is "coherence and fit in the web of judgment, feeling, perception, and principle, taken as a whole" (ibid.). With Aristotle, Sidgwick and Rawls, it is only ethical theories or ethical and political theories that are so compared. What is distinctive, and significantly so, about Nussbaum's extension of this account, an extension fully in keeping with its dialectical structure, is that novels and dramatic works should enter into the comparison as well. They enter in, as something which in both *form* and *content*, yields a distinctive ethical understanding and attunement. Moreover, they should not enter as junior partners. Her prime examples are the novels of Henry James and Marcel Proust and the works of Greek tragedians, but many other literary works could and should be added as well, as should historians such as Thucydides, Gibbon, and Hume and profound essayists (if that is the right word for them) such as Montaigne, Pascal, and Newman. (Call them instead philosophers, if you will. 'Philosophy' does not name a natural kind.) They enter in, to, among other things, counter the rationalist bias that Hume, William James, and

Annette Baier find in most moral theory, enabling us to gain a richer and more inclusive sense of our opening question: how should a human being live? Without these texts, along with the standard philosophical texts as well, we will not be able even to approximate gaining "all that our sense of life urges us to consider" (ibid.). Without them, we will not get a full comparison of the ways of thinking morally and thinking about morality and about conceptions of ways of living and responding. The idea is not at all that we *substitute* the study of literary texts for that of philosophical treatises – including demanding philosophical treatises – on ethics. Rather the "proposal is that we should add the study of certain novels to the study of these works on the grounds that without them we will not have a fully adequate ethical conception, one that we ought to investigate" (ibid., 27). Novels, particularly James's and Proust's novels, are vital in this comparison because, against generalizing theories, with their tendency to overstress principles, they will teach us, in the overall procedure of ethical deliberation, the value of "attention to particulars, a respect for the emotions, and a tentative and non-dogmatic attitude to the bewildering multiplicities of life ..." (ibid.). They teach us the value, including the ethical value, of a passionate love of particulars, "the role of love and other emotions in the good human life"; they teach us the "epistemological value of emotion" and, relatedly, the importance of "commitment to cognitive guidance by the emotions" and they help us to realize that in certain circumstances relying on our emotions can be more reliable than what can be ground out by abstract reasoning (ibid., 186). In the very way she depicts how our understanding of life is enhanced by how the Jamesian and Proustian stress gives a particular spin on things, we also very much need, as a counterbalance to them, the different spin that the dramas of Brecht and the plays and novels by Sartre provide. In both cases there is a love of particulars and a fine attunement, but James and Proust, on the one hand, and Brecht and Sartre on the other, have very different views on the particularities of life and of what is most significant. It is important that we have such differences vividly before us.

This dialectical method which she describes as seeking a *perceptive equilibrium* has many features of Rawls's reflective equilibrium, but avoids what she thinks is its residual Kantian and rationalist biases. What is distinctive about perceptive equilibrium – it has also been called 'extended reflective equilibrium' – is what it *adds* to reflective equilibrium as conceived by Rawls. Indeed, as we see it, though we are inclined to think that these very notions are already at least implicit in Rawls's conception, the elements it 'adds' certainly ought to be part of any wide and general reflective equilibrium. And certainly Nussbaum has, and rightly, given these notions a stress that they have not generally received from philosophers using the method of reflective equilibrium.

What we need to do, is to intelligently, sympathetically, and impartially, with attentive attunement to detail and nuance, though not without a critical eye for their lacunae, attempt to see how these accounts of ethical life square with ascertainable fact, our considered convictions, what we deeply, but sometimes rather inarticulately, feel, including our emotional sensibilities and a sense of the details of life. We should also consider how, if at all, these different ethical conceptions (here taking a page from Hegel) are embodied in institutions and social practices and consider as well our felt reactions to these institutions and practices. Knowing that we will never get anything even within the ballpark of an algorithm here, in the inescapable *messiness* of the enterprise of perceptive equilibrium, we try to answer the question of how we are to live, to get, considering all these things, the most coherent conception we can get of how to live together and, of course, how to live as individuals as well, though our interdependence makes it the case that we are always in one way or another together (Baier 1987, 41-56; Code 1987, 357-82; and Nielsen 1987, 383-418). We seek to get a picture that will match best with what we know – or at least reliably think we know – and, as well, with our most deeply and persistently felt sensibilities and considered convictions.

For Nussbaum, no more than for Aristotle, Hume, Sidgwick, Hegel, or Rawls, is there a possibility of standing free from such sensibilities and convictions. We cannot, as David Gauthier thinks he can, set aside these sensibilities and convictions and, *trusting instead to theory*, go on with our ethical inquiries and deliberations (Gauthier 1986, 268-9).[6] It is also an open-ended process with nothing even remotely like final

---

6 For criticism of Gauthier here, see Nielsen 1994, 57-62.

closure. There is no Archimedian point or all-purpose moral compass. Life is not like that and theory will not be either, if it is any good. We need to avoid Cartesianism in morals as we need to avoid Cartesianism elsewhere. But we need also to recognize, what moral philosophers are almost professionally incapable of recognizing, that the *goal* of moral philosophy is not theory but *practice*; and that the intellect is not the only part of the reader worth addressing (Nussbaum 1990, 186). Nussbaum remarks in a passage that should be quoted in full:

> Throughout this open-ended inquiry, we will need to maintain as much self-consciousness as possible about our own method and our implicit ends, asking what evaluative content they themselves express. Perceptive equilibrium is not the same end as reflective equilibrium; it does not use the same judgments or the same faculties. This does not mean that there can be no objectivity in ethical inquiry; it does not mean that all choices of method are subjective. But it does mean that procedures themselves are value-laden, and thus part and parcel of the holistic enterprise they organize; replaceable, like any other part, to the end of a deeper and more inclusive attunement. So we must examine them at each stage, asking whether they are capable of doing full justice to everything that our sense of life wants to include. (ibid.)

This commitment to extending wide and general reflective equilibrium into an extended reflective equilibrium, including an equilibrium of the emotions, seems to us a very attractive way to go in moral philosophy. It can be combined with a metaethics of the new dispensation. Peter Railton, for example, in his nuanced, naturalistic account, uses the method of wide reflective equilibrium, and sensibility theories, such as those developed by John McDowell and David Wiggins, are thoroughly non-scientistic, non-moral realist (but also not irrealist) versions of ethical naturalism. Both of these accounts combine well with Nussbaum's account. Though at a more abstract metaethical level than Nussbaum's account, and designed for metaethical work, they are attuned to and account for the ethical phenomena with which Nussbaum is concerned. The sensibility theories in particular square well with Nussbaum's Henry Jamesian conception of moral perception. (But note Isaac Levi's criticism of McDowell on such matters in this volume.) So, as we move away from the old analytical metaethics and from rationalistic, and *sometimes* scientistic, conceptions of metaethics, such as we find moral realists committed to, conceptions which go hand and glove with metaphysical realism, there is with such a travelling no conflict in underlying structural conception between Nussbaum, on the one hand, and metaethical philosophers such as Miller, Railton, McDowell, and Wiggins, on the other, though there is a difference in emphasis (e.g., from explanation to practice), a difference concerning what is most worth doing in moral philosophy and a difference concerning where to place our priorities. (The underlying structural alignment to the contrary notwithstanding, it is tempting to respond that these are the really important differences and that they are considerable.) There is, as Nussbaum remarks herself, a considerable difficulty in "discovering a nonprejudiced description of ethical inquiry" (ibid.).

If we look at two much admired books in the recent tradition of metaethics, David Gauthier's *Morals by Agreement* and Allan Gibbard's *Wise Choices Apt Feelings*, and compare them with two also much admired books – and *sometimes* much admired by the same people – Martha C. Nussbaum's *Love's Knowledge* and Annette C. Baier's *Moral Prejudices*, we get the jarring impression of two very different *genres*, reflecting deep differences about what is important, how to proceed, how to read one's predecessors (compare, for example, Baier and Gauthier on Hume), and over what is most crucial to utilize from outside moral philosophy in doing moral philosophy. For Gauthier and Gibbard (though sometimes variously), rational choice theory, decision theory, cognitive psychology, Darwinian theory, microeconomics (for the most part, very abstract theories) is where it is at; by contrast, for Nussbaum and Baier (though again sometimes variously), social anthropology, history, sociology, political economy, clinical psychology and literature (all very concrete matters and, where theoretical, concretely theoretical) is where it is at. The resulting accounts of Gauthier and Gibbard are abstract, sometimes formidably abstract; the accounts of Baier and Nussbaum, by contrast, are concrete with fine attention to detail and context. The very aims of the contrasting types of theory *seem* at least to be at odds, or at least very different, so different that it is possible to wonder if they are in the same ballpark or if they are playing the same language-game or have much in the way of common underlying aims. Yet all four of these philosophers are very able and have a finely nuanced understanding of what they are about and a good understanding of at least some of the alternatives to their ways of doing things. Moreover, all of these philosophers are roughly contemporaries with a similar analytical training. Yet it is – or so it *seems* at least – difficult to think that there is much point in doing things the Gauthier-Gibbard way if we are taken by the Baier-Nussbaum way and vice-versa. (We are not suggesting that for either Gauthier-Gibbard, on the one hand, or for Baier-Nussbaum, on the other, their ways are identical. They certainly are not, but each member of the contrasting pairs stands in much the same tradition to the other in the same paired group, while, when the pairs taken together are contrasted, it is evident that they are 'worlds apart.')[7]

So in thinking for ourselves about how to proceed in doing moral philosophy which way should we go? Or should we try somehow to combine them? Or should we say 'A plague on both your houses' and go in some still different way? But, if so, what way and how shall we characterize it? Surely the above ways are not the only alternatives. Yet both of these alternatives are in their own ways attractive. They are two roads that "diverged in a yellow wood and sorry we cannot travel them both and be one traveller." But then which, if either, road should be taken? In trying to see how to proceed in moral philosophy, this remains a deep unsettled issue concerning which it is difficult not to fall into – in choosing or even in ambivalently swinging back and forth between them – a partisan stance (Daniels 1996 and Nielsen 1996).

V

We will in closing raise a still different issue about metaethics and the doing of moral philosophy. During the Golden Age of metaethics, even where metaethics was not taken to be all that was philosophically viable in moral philosophy, it was still taken to be its *principia*. We would, so it was thought, never have any plausible normative theories or reasonable practice-driven theories of the moral life or even secure reasonable moral practices, if we did not get to first things first, and to get to first things was to conceptually clarify our fundamental moral con-

---

7 For a paradigmatic articulation of such differences, see Annette Baier's critical notice of *Morals by Agreement* and Gauthier's response (Baier, 1988, 315-30; and Gauthier 1988, 385-418).

cepts, to gain an adequate analysis of moral terms and more generally of our moral language. The deepest and most fundamental reflection in or concerning morals consists in conceptual clarification – or so went the tacit assumption – an assumption that we think is a philosopher's conceit. In a characteristic drum roll for analytic metaethics made during its heyday, Henry Aiken remarked in his *Reason and Conduct* that "the task of clarifying such golden words as 'liberty,' 'justice,' 'democracy,' 'person' and 'love' is ... essential to the well being of any people whose way of life is expressed in terms of them. For if they are unclear or confused or inconsistent then the way of life is also" (Aiken 1962, 30). William Frankena, making similar remarks, believes that this task of metaethical clarification is essential in our age of cultural crisis (Frankena 1964, 452-4). Otherwise, he in effect has it, we will stagger from one irrationality to another defenseless before the siren songs of postmodernism.

Such remarks seem to us incredible; they attribute magical healing powers to conceptual clarification, but, more interesting theoretically, they have, as John Rawls argues in good Quinian spirit, things backwards. It is only when we have done good and reasonably systematic *substantive* work, made a careful broadly empirical study of our substantive moral conceptions, done what Hume calls our mental geography and done it well, will a useful analysis of moral terms and concepts be possible and then, in that circumstance, it may very well not be necessary or even of much value.

We will run a bit with Rawls's way of putting the matter in his "Some Remarks About Moral Theory" in his *A Theory of Justice* (Rawls 1971, 46-53). Rawls remarks, "I wish to stress that a theory of justice is precisely that, namely theory. It is a theory of the moral sentiments ... setting out the principles governing our moral powers, or more specifically our sense of justice" (ibid., 50-1). He goes on to remark,

> A theory of justice is subject to the same rules of method as other theories. Definitions and analysis of meaning do not have a special place: definition is but one device used in setting up the general structure of theory. Once the whole framework is worked out, definitions have no distinct status and stand or fall with the theory itself. (ibid., 51)

Rawls goes on to add that in "any case it is obviously impossible to develop a substantive theory of justice founded solely on truths of logic and definition. The analysis of moral concepts and the a priori, however traditionally understood, is too slender a basis. Moral philosophy must be free to use contingent assumptions and general facts as it pleases" (ibid.). Then, in a remark that is strikingly pertinent to the metaethics/substantive ethics distinction, to traditional claims for the former's priority and centrality and to claims, *à la* Aiken, Frankena, and a host of others, for the great clarifying powers of conceptual analysis, Rawls remarks:

> ... if we can find an accurate account of our moral conceptions, then questions of meaning and justification may prove much easier to answer. Indeed some of them may no longer be real questions at all. Note, for example, the extraordinary deepening of our understanding of the meaning and justification of statements in logic and mathematics made possible by developments since Frege and Cantor. A knowledge of the fundamental structures of logic and set theory and their relation to mathematics has transformed the philosophy of these subjects in a way that conceptual analysis and linguist investigations never could. One has only to observe the effect of the division of theories into those which are decidable and complete, undecidable yet complete, and neither complete nor decidable. The problem of meaning and truth in logic and mathematics is profoundly altered by the discovery of logical systems illustrating these concepts. Once the substantive content of moral conceptions is better understood, a similar transformation may occur. It is possible that convincing answers to questions of the meaning and justification of moral judgment can be found in no other way. (ibid., 51-2)

This fits very well with the development of analytic philosophy in a more holistic, contextually oriented and pragmatist manner with the work of Quine, Davidson, Rorty and Putnam (Rorty 1985, 89-121). Rawls, always a person of understatement, does not say anything so strong, but his remarks give a large part of the rationale of why metaethics, taken as a distinct enterprise, can be, and indeed should be, quietly laid to rest. It is a testimony to the good sense of philosophers that something like this is quietly happening. And, for the most part, those philosophers who still think of their work as metaethical, or in part metaethical, have so transformed the very idea of metaethics, that it no longer makes a significant contrast with substantive ethics. Our task is to do, and to work out good ways of doing, substantive ethics. Shall we go anti-theory all the way down like Richard Rorty and Michel Foucault, or shall we develop substantive theories after the fashion of John Rawls, Norman Daniels, Kurt Baier, Thomas Scanlon, or Brian Barry, or shall we take the 'less rationalistic ways' of

Annette Baier and Martha Nussbaum, or should we continue with something of a metaethics linked with substantive ethics after the fashion of Peter Railton or Richard Miller? All these options remain open and no one of them is clearly the most reasonable way of going about things. Moreover, it should be noted in this context, that the distance between Scanlon and Rawls, on the one hand, and Railton and Miller, on the other, is not that great. Still, across this whole spectrum there are important differences, perhaps even vitally important differences. Foucault and Railton – to fasten on the extremes – are up to rather different things, have very different priorities and agendas. So which way to go? There are a number of roads in the yellow wood with no agreement about which one we should take. But that need not be a matter for regret, and to speak of despair here is absurdly histrionic. Something rich and sound *may* emerge from this extensive, but sometimes also very self-conscious, dissensus? Still, a good dose of skepticism concerning this seems to us healthy. Perhaps, after all, Nussbaum is right and this is "a rich and wonderful time in moral philosophy" (Nussbaum 1990, 169).

Bibliography

Aiken, Henry (1962). *Reason and Conduct*. New York: Knopf

Baier, Annette (1985). *Postures of the Mind: Essays on Mind and Morals*. Minneapolis: University of Minnesota Press

Baier, Annette (1987). "The Need for More than Justice." In Marsha Hanen and Kai Nielsen, eds., *Science, Morality and Feminist Theory*. Calgary: University of Calgary Press. 41-58

Baier, Annette (1988). "Pilgrims Progress." *Canadian Journal of Philosophy* **18**, no. 2. 315-30

Baier, Annette (1991). *A Progress of Sentiments Reflections on Hume's Treatise*. Cambridge, MA: Harvard University Press

Baier, Annette (1992). "Hume." In Laurence C. Becker, ed., *Encyclopedia of Ethics*. New York: Garland. 565-77

Baier, Annette (1994). *Moral Prejudices: Essays on Ethics*. Cambridge, MA: Harvard University Press

Bernstein, Richard (1995). "Whatever Happened to Naturalism?" *Proceedings and Addresses of the American Philosophical Association*. 57-76

Blackburn, Simon (1984). *Spreading the Word*. Oxford: Oxford University Press

Blackburn, Simon (1992). "Through Thick and Thin." *The Aristotelian Society Proceedings Supplementary* vol. **66**. 285-99

Blackburn, Simon (1993a). *Essays in Quasi-Realism*. New York: Oxford University Press

Blackburn, Simon (1993b). "Can Philosophy Exist?" In Jocelyne Couture and Kai Nielsen, eds., *Méta-philosophie; Reconstructing Philosophy?* Calgary: University of Calgary Press. 83-106

Brink, David O. (1995). "Moral Realism." In Robert Audi, ed., *The Cambridge Dictionary of Philosophy*. Cambridge: Cambridge University Press. 511-12

Code, Lorraine (1987). "Second Persons." In Marsha Hanen and Kai Nielsen, eds., *Science, Morality and Feminist Theory*. Calgary: University of Calgary Press. 357-82

Couture, Jocelyne (1989). "Méta-éthique." In *L'Encyclopédie Philosophique Universelle. Vol. I: L'Univers philosophique*. Paris: Presses Universitaires de France. 165-71

Couture, Jocelyne and Nielsen, Kai (1993). "Après-propos/S'entendre pour ne pas s'entendre." In Jocelyne Couture and Kai Nielsen, eds., *Métaphilosophie; Reconstructing Philosophy?* Calgary: University of Calgary Press. 365-87

Daniels, Norman (1996). *Justice and Justification: Reflective Equilibrium in Theory and Practice*. Cambridge: Cambridge University Press

Davidson, Donald (1984). *Inquiries Into Truth and Interpretation*. Oxford: Clarendon Press

Dewey, John (1946). *Problems of Men*. New York: Philosophical Library

Diamond, Cora (1991). *The Realistic Spirit: Wittgenstein, Philosophy and the Mind*. Cambridge, MA: MIT Press

Donagan, Alan (1978). *The Theory of Morality*. Chicago: University of Chicago Press

Falk, W.D. (1986). *Ought, Reasons and Morality*. Ithaca, NY: Cornell University Press

Frankena, W.K. (1964). "Ethical Theory." In Roderick M. Chisholm et al., eds., *Philosophy*. Englewood Cliffs, NJ: Prentice Hall. 347-461

Foot, Philippa (1995). "Does Moral Subjectivism Rest on a Mistake?" *Oxford Journal of Legal Studies* **1**. 1-21

Gauthier, David (1986). *Morals by Agreement*. Oxford: Oxford University Press

Gauthier, David (1988). "Moral Artifice." *Canadian Journal of Philosophy* **18**, no. 2. 385-418

Gibbard, Allan (1990). *Wise Choices Apt Feelings*. Cambridge, MA: Harvard University Press

Gibbard Allan (1992). "Thick Concepts and Warrant for Feelings." *The Aristotelian Society Proceedings* Supplementary vol. **66**. 267-283

Gibbard, Allan (1993). "Reply to Railton." In Enrique Villanueva, ed. *Naturalism and Normativity*. Atascadero, CA: Ridgeview. 52-9

Gibbard Allan (1995). "Why Theorize How to Live with Each Other?" *Philosophy and Phenomenological Research* **55**, no. 2. 220-31

Hägerström, Axel (1964). *Philosophy and Religion*. Trans. Robert Sandin. London: George Allen & Unwin.

Horwich, Paul (1993). "Meaning and Metaphilosophy." In Enrique Villanueva, ed. *Naturalism and Normativity*. Atascadero, CA: Ridgeview. 153-8

Jackson, Frank (1994). "Realism, Truth and Truth Aptness." *Philosophical Books* **35**, no. 3. 162-9. With a response by Crispin Wright, 169-75

Levi, Isaac (1992). "Conflict and Inquiry." *Ethics* **102**. 814-34

Little, Margaret (1994a). "Moral Realism I: Naturalism." *Philosophical Books* **35**, no. 3. 145-53

Little, Margaret (1994b). "Moral Realism II: Non Naturalism." *Philosophical Books* **35**, no. 4. 225-33

Mackie, J.L. (1946). "A Refutation of Morals." *The Australasian Journal of Psychology and Philosophy* **64**. 77-90

Mackie, J.L. (1977). *Ethics: Inventing Right and Wrong*. Harmondsworth, Middlesex: Penguin

Miller, Richard (1992). *Moral Difference: Truth, Justice and Conscience in a World of Conflict*. Princeton, NJ: Princeton University Press

Nielsen, Kai (1967). "Problems of Ethics." In Paul Edwards, ed., *The Encyclopedia of Philosophy*. New York: Macmillan and The Free Press. 3: 116-34

Nielsen, Kai (1985). "Universalisability and the Commitment to Impartiality." In Nelson Potter and Mark Timmons, eds., *Morality and Universality*. Dordrecht: D. Reidel. 91-101

Nielsen, Kai (1987). "Afterword: Feminist Theory Some Twistings and Turnings." In Marsha Hanen and Kai Nielsen, eds., *Science, Morality and Feminist Theory*. Calgary: University of Calgary Press. 383-418

Nielsen, Kai (1989). *Why be Moral?* Amherst, NY: Prometheus

Nielsen, Kai (1991). *After the Demise of the Tradition. Rorty, Critical Theory and the Fate of Philosophy*. Boulder, CO: Westview

Nielsen, Kai (1994). "Methods of Ethics: Wide Reflective Equilibrium and a Kind of Consequentialism." *Journal of Social Philosophy*. 57-72

Nielsen, Kai (1995). *On Transforming Philosophy: A Metaphilosophical Inquiry*. Boulder, CO: Westview

Nielsen, Kai (1996). *Naturalism without Foundations*. Amherst, NY: Prometheus

Nowell-Smith, P.H. (1954). *Ethics*. Harmondsworth, Middlesex: Penguin

Nussbaum, Martha C. (1986). *The Fragility of Goodness*. Cambridge: Cambridge University Press

Nussbaum, Martha C. (1988). "Nature, Function and Capability: Aristotle on Political Distribution." *Oxford Studies in Ancient Philosophy*, suppl. vol. 145-84

Nussbaum, Martha C. (1990). *Love's Knowledge*. Oxford: Oxford University Press

Nussbaum, Martha C. (1992). "Virtue Revised: Habit, Passion, Reflection in the Aristotelian Tradition." *Times Literary Supplement* (July 3, 1992). 9-12

Nussbaum, Martha C. (1993). "Non-Relative Virtues: An Aristotelian Approach." In Martha Nussbaum and Amartya Sen, eds., *The Quality of Life*. Oxford: Clarendon Press. 242-69

Nussbaum, Martha C. (1994a). *The Therapy of Desire Theory and Practice in Hellenistic Ethics*. Princeton, NJ: Princeton University Press

Nussbaum, Martha C.(1994b). "Feminists & Philosophy." *The New York Review of Books* (October, 20, 1994). 59-63

Nussbaum, Martha C. (1995). "Aristotle on Human Nature and the Foundations of Ethics." In J.E.G. Altman and R. Harrison, eds. *World, Mind and Ethics*. Cambridge: Cambridge University Press

Putnam, Hilary (1990). *Realism with a Human Face*. Cambridge, MA: Harvard University Press

Putnam, Hilary (1994). *Words and Life*. Cambridge, MA: Harvard University Press

Putnam, Hilary (1995). *Pragmatism: an Open Question*. Oxford: Blackwell

Railton, Peter (1993). "What the Non-Cognitivist Helps us to See the Naturalist Must Help us to Explain." In John Haldane and Crispin Wright, eds., *Reality, Representation and Projection*. New York: Oxford University Press. 279-300

Railton, Peter (1995). "Subjective and Objective." *Ratio* 7, no. 3. 259-76

Rawls, John (1971). *A Theory of Justice*. Cambridge, MA: Harvard University Press

Rawls, John (1995). "Reply to Habermas." *The Journal of Philosophy* 92, no. 3. 132-80

Rorty, Richard (1982). *Consequences of Pragmatism*. Minneapolis: University of Minnesota Press

Rorty, Richard (1985). "Epistemological Behaviorism and the De-transcendentalization of Analytic Philosophy." In Robert Hollinger, ed., *Hermeneutics and Praxis* Notre Dame, IN: University of Notre Dame Press. 89-121

Rorty, Richard (1992).*Objectivity Relativism and Truth*. Cambridge: Cambridge University Press

Rorty, Richard (1995). "Is Truth a Goal of Inquiry? Davidson vs Wright." *The Philosophical Quarterly* 45, no. 180. 281-300

Scanlon, T.M. (1992). "The Aims and Authority of Moral Theory." *Oxford Journal of Legal Studies* 12, no. 1. 1-23

Scanlon, T.M. (1995a). "Moral Theory: Understanding and Disagreement." *Philosophy and Phenomenological Research* 55, no. 2. 232-43

Scanlon, T.M. (1995b). "Fear of Relativism." In Rosalind Hursthouse et al., eds., *Virtues and Reasons. Philippa Foot and Moral Theory*. Oxford Clarendon Press. 219-45

Scheffler, Samuel (1987). "Morality, Through Thick and Thin: A Critical Notice of Ethics and the Limits of Philosophy." *The Philosophical Review* 96. 411-21

Schneewind, J.B. (1991). "Natural Law, Scepticism and Methods of Ethics." *Journal of the History of Ideas*, 52. 289-308

Seymour, Michel (1995). "Critical Notice of Crispin Wright Truth and Objectivity." *Canadian Journal of Philosophy* 25, no. 4. 637-50

Smart, J.J.C. (1966). "Philosophy and Scientific Plausibility." In Paul K. Feyerabend and Grover Maxwell, eds., *Mind, Matter and Method*. Minneapolis: University of Minnesota Press. 377-90

Smith, Michael (1986). "Should we Believe in Emotivism?" In Graham Macdonald and Crispin Wright, eds., *Facts, Science and Morality*. Oxford: Basil Blackwell. 289-310

Smith, Michael (1993). "Objectivity and Moral Realism: On the Significance of the Phenomenology of Moral Experience." In John Haldane and Crispin Wright, eds., *Reality, Representation and Projection*. New York: Oxford University Press. 235-56

Smith, Michael (1994). "Why Expressivists about Value should Love Minimalism about Truth." *Analysis* **54**, no. 1. 1-11

Stevenson, Charles (1963). *Facts and Values*. New Haven: Yale University Press

Stevenson, Charles (1983). "Value-Judgments: Their Implicit Generality." In Norman E. Bowie, ed., *Ethical Theory*. Indianapolis, IN: Hackett. 13-37

Wiggins, David (1993). "Cognitivism, Naturalism and Nonnaturalism: Reply to Peter Railton." In John Haldane and Crispin Wright, eds., *Reality, Representation and Projection*. New York: Oxford University Press. 301-13

Wiggins, David (1995). "Objective and Subjective in Ethics with Two Postscripts about Truth." *Ratio* **8**, no. 3. 243-25

Williams, Bernard (1985). *Ethics and the Limits of Philosophy*. Cambridge, MA: Harvard University Press

Williams, Bernard (1995). "Truth in Ethics." *Ratio* **8**, no. 3. 227-42

Wolf, Susan (1982). "Moral Saints." *Journal of Philosophy* **79**. 419-39

Wright, Crispin (1992). *Truth and Objectivity* . Cambridge, MA: Harvard University Press

Wright, Crispin (1995). "Truth in Ethics." *Ratio* **8**, no. 3. 209-26

Index